DRIFTING DRAGONS

Taku Kuwabara

1

DRIFTING DRAGONS

Table of Contents

Flight **2**

Bounty &
Dragonet
alla
Diavolo

67

Flight **1**

The
Quin Zaza

5

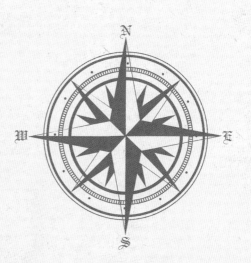

Flight
5

Sky
Pirates &
Pastrami

175

Flight
4

The
Shining
Dragon &
Smoked Salo

143

Flight
3

Reasons
for Flying
& Dragon
Terrine

101

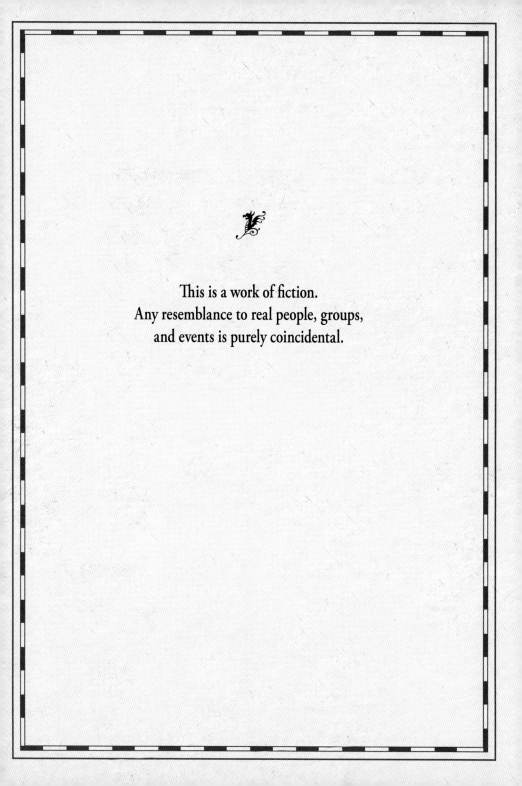

This is a work of fiction.
Any resemblance to real people, groups,
and events is purely coincidental.

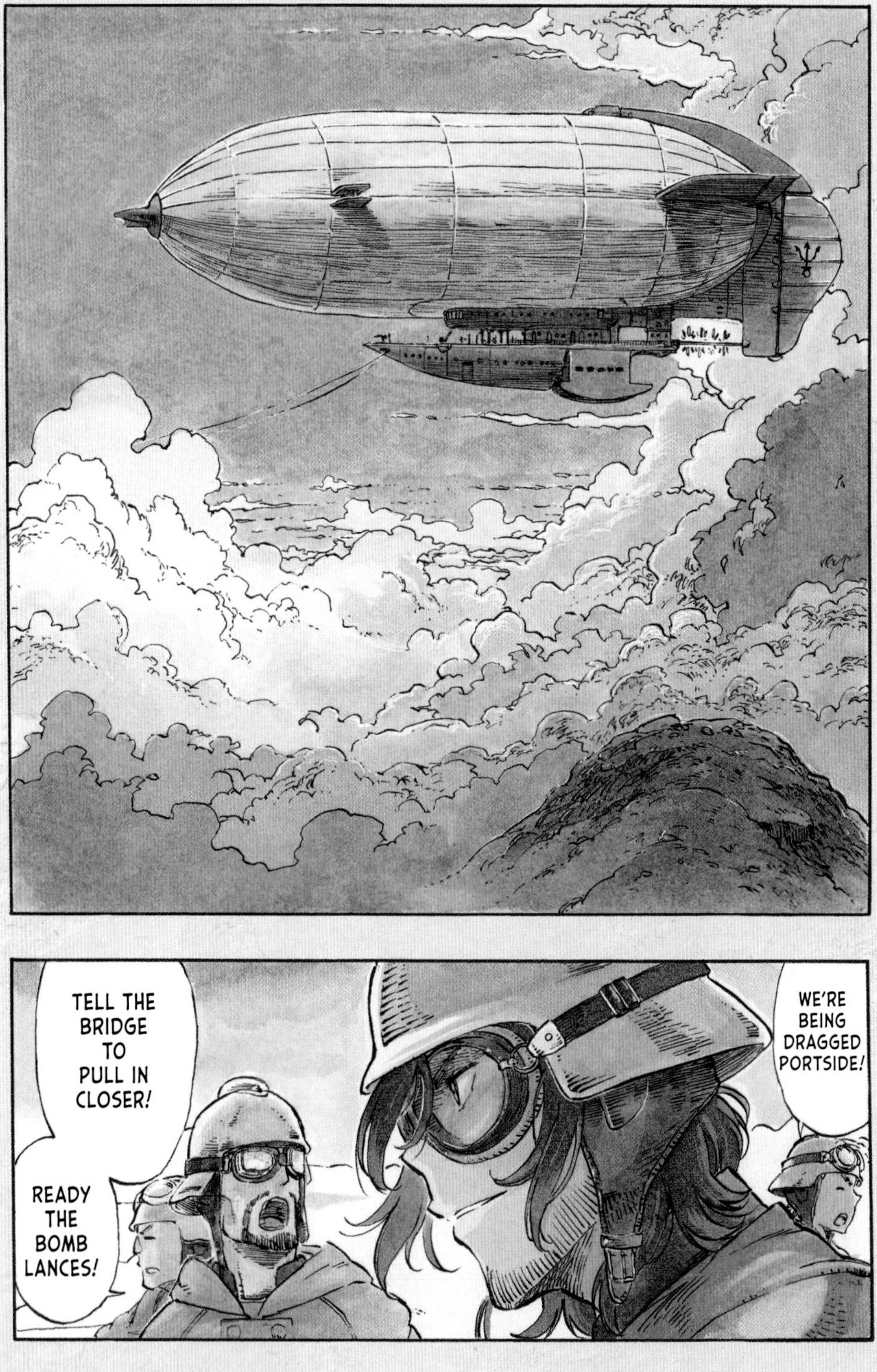
WE'RE BEING DRAGGED PORTSIDE!
TELL THE BRIDGE TO PULL IN CLOSER!
READY THE BOMB LANCES!

Flight 1 The *Quin Zaza*

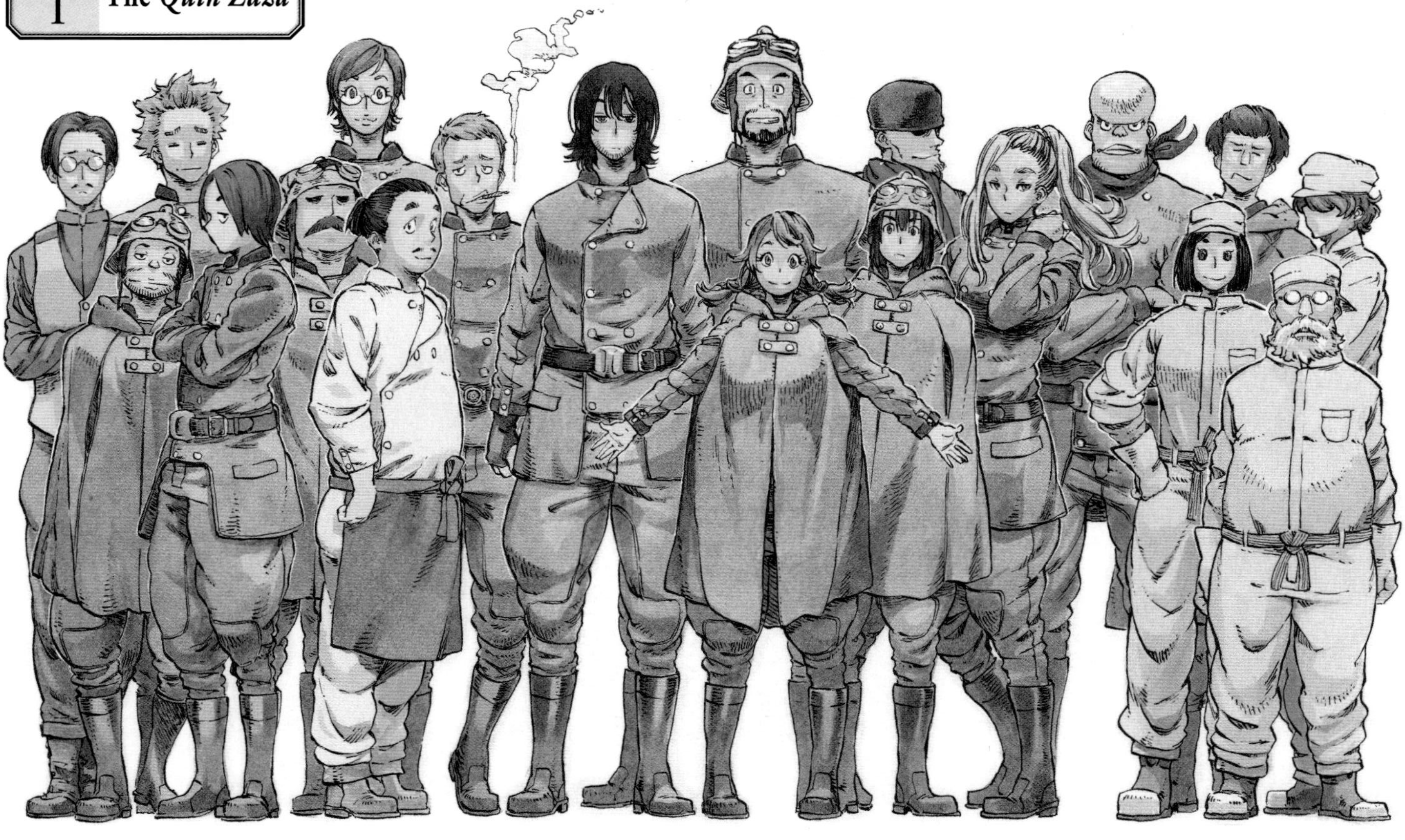

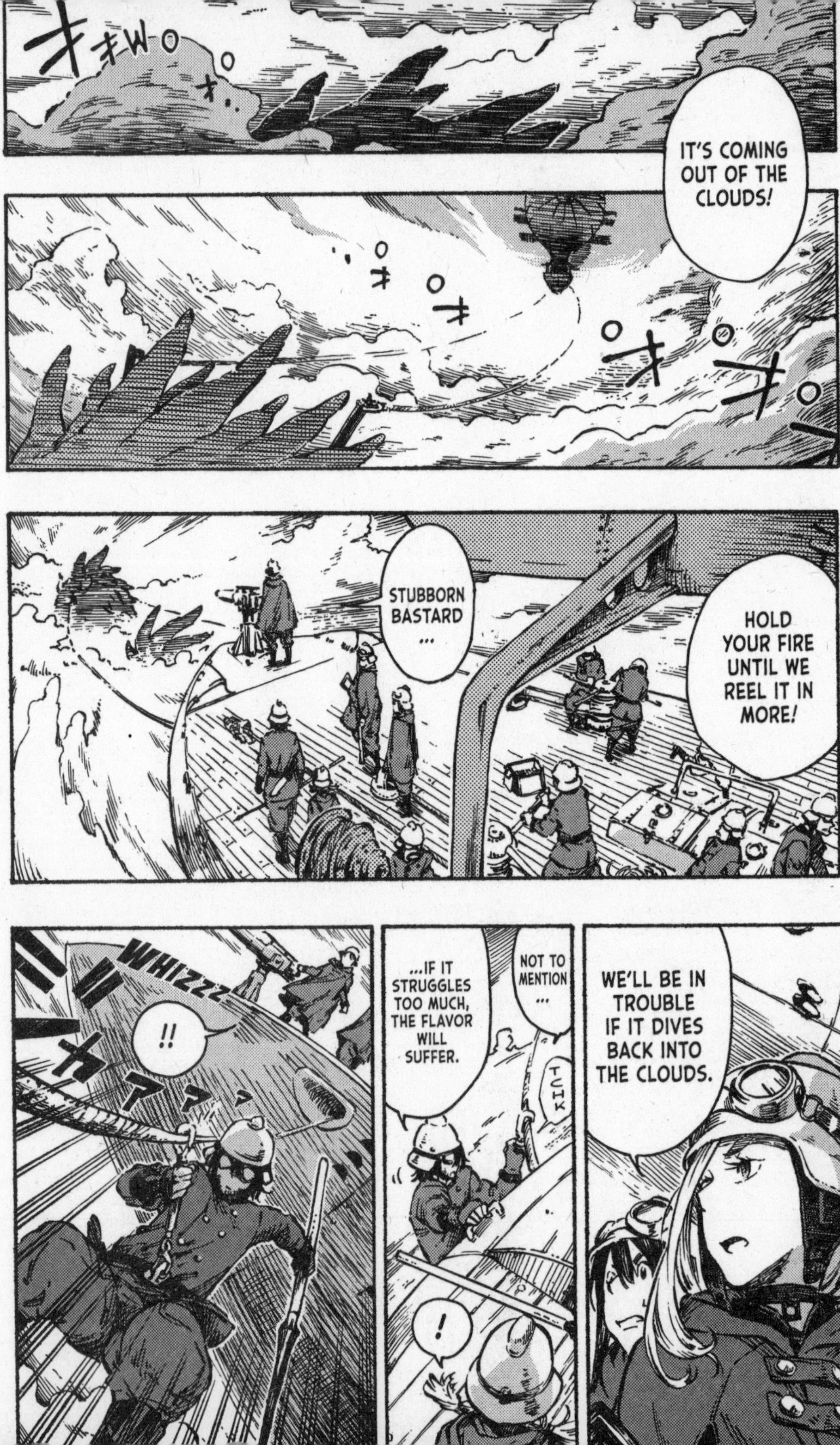
IT'S COMING OUT OF THE CLOUDS!
HOLD YOUR FIRE UNTIL WE REEL IT IN MORE!
STUBBORN BASTARD ...
WE'LL BE IN TROUBLE IF IT DIVES BACK INTO THE CLOUDS.
NOT TO MENTION ...
...IF IT STRUGGLES TOO MUCH, THE FLAVOR WILL SUFFER.
TCHK
!
WHIZZZ
!!

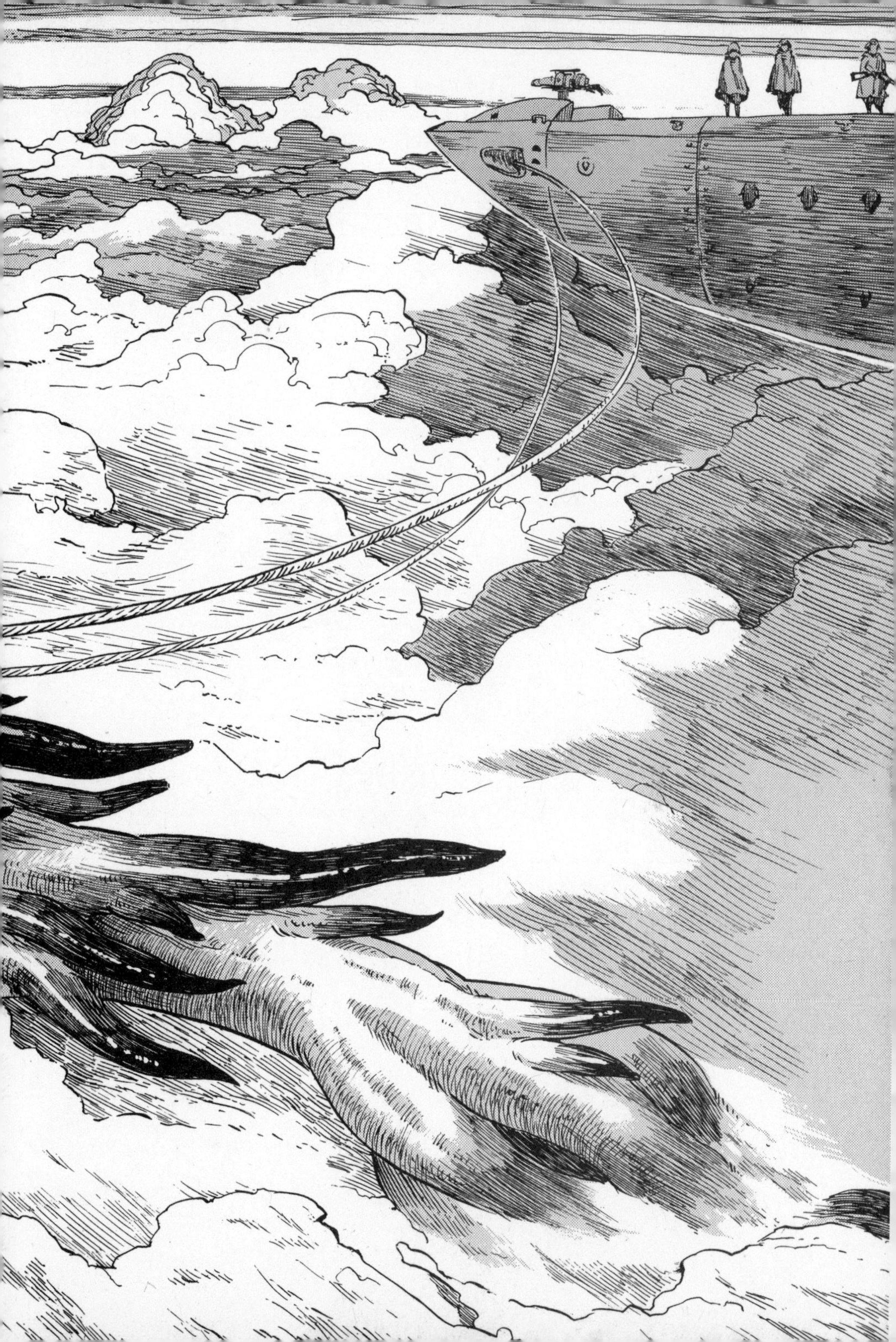

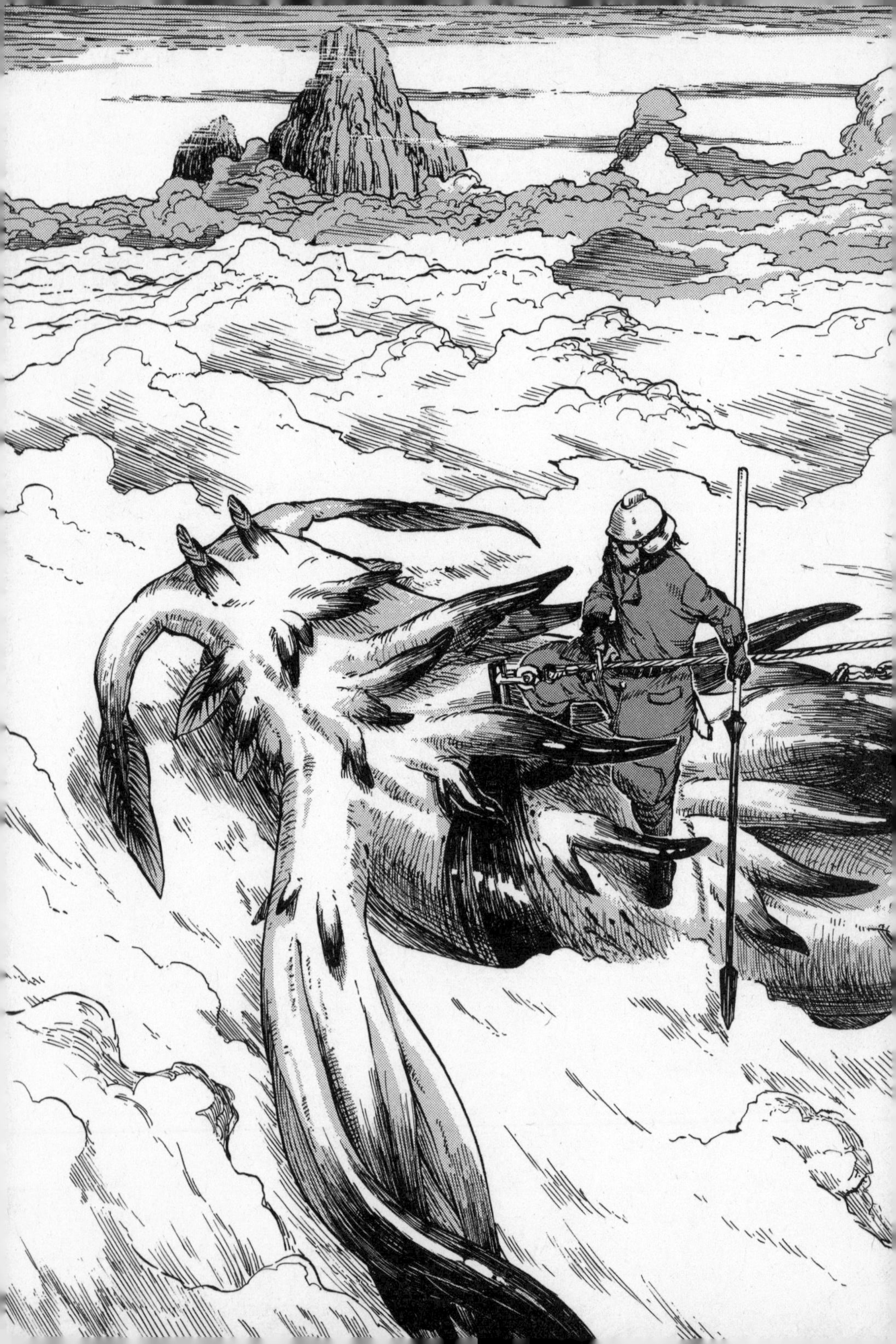

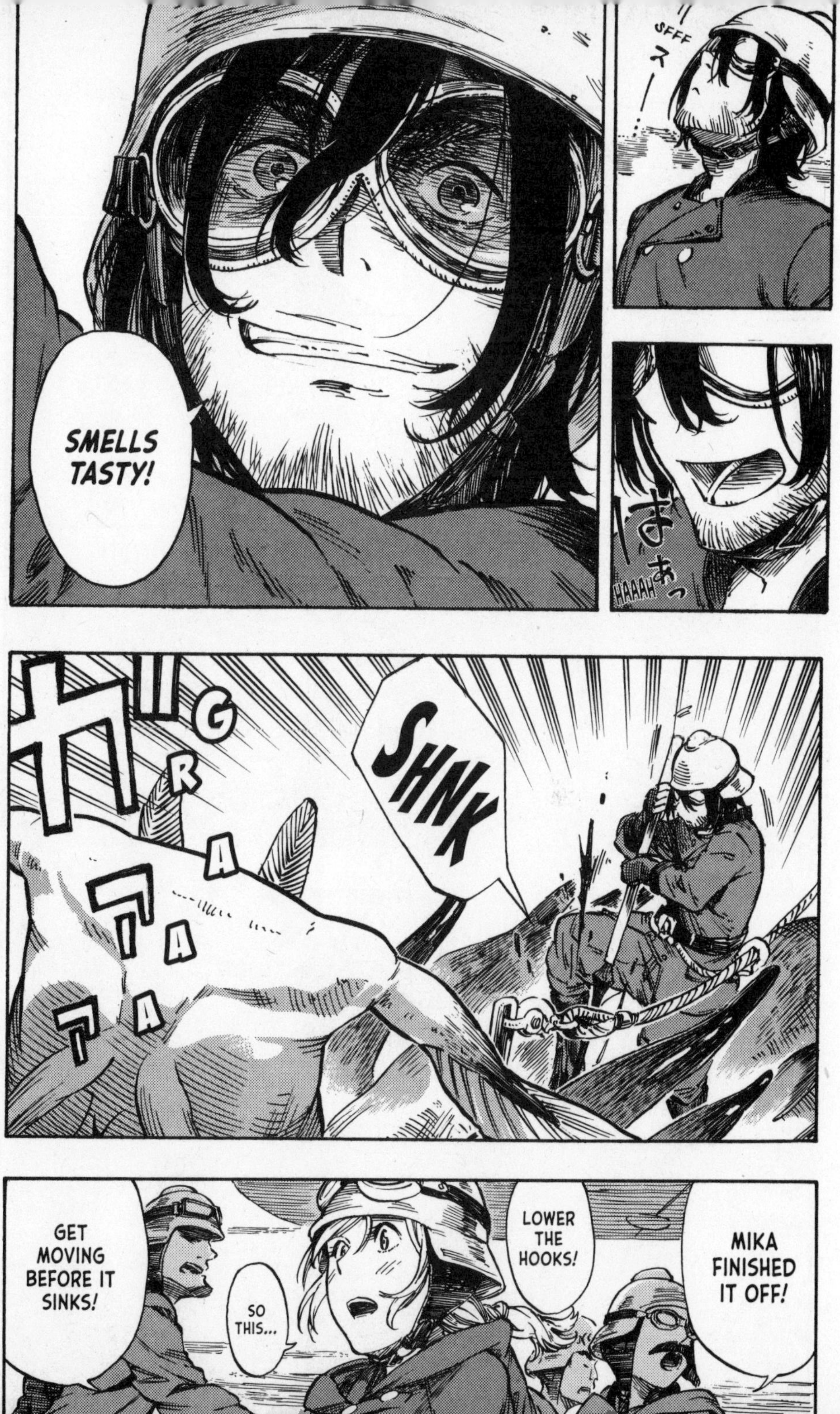

SFFF
HAAAH
SMELLS TASTY!
SHNK
GRAAA
MIKA FINISHED IT OFF!
LOWER THE HOOKS!
SO THIS...
GET MOVING BEFORE IT SINKS!

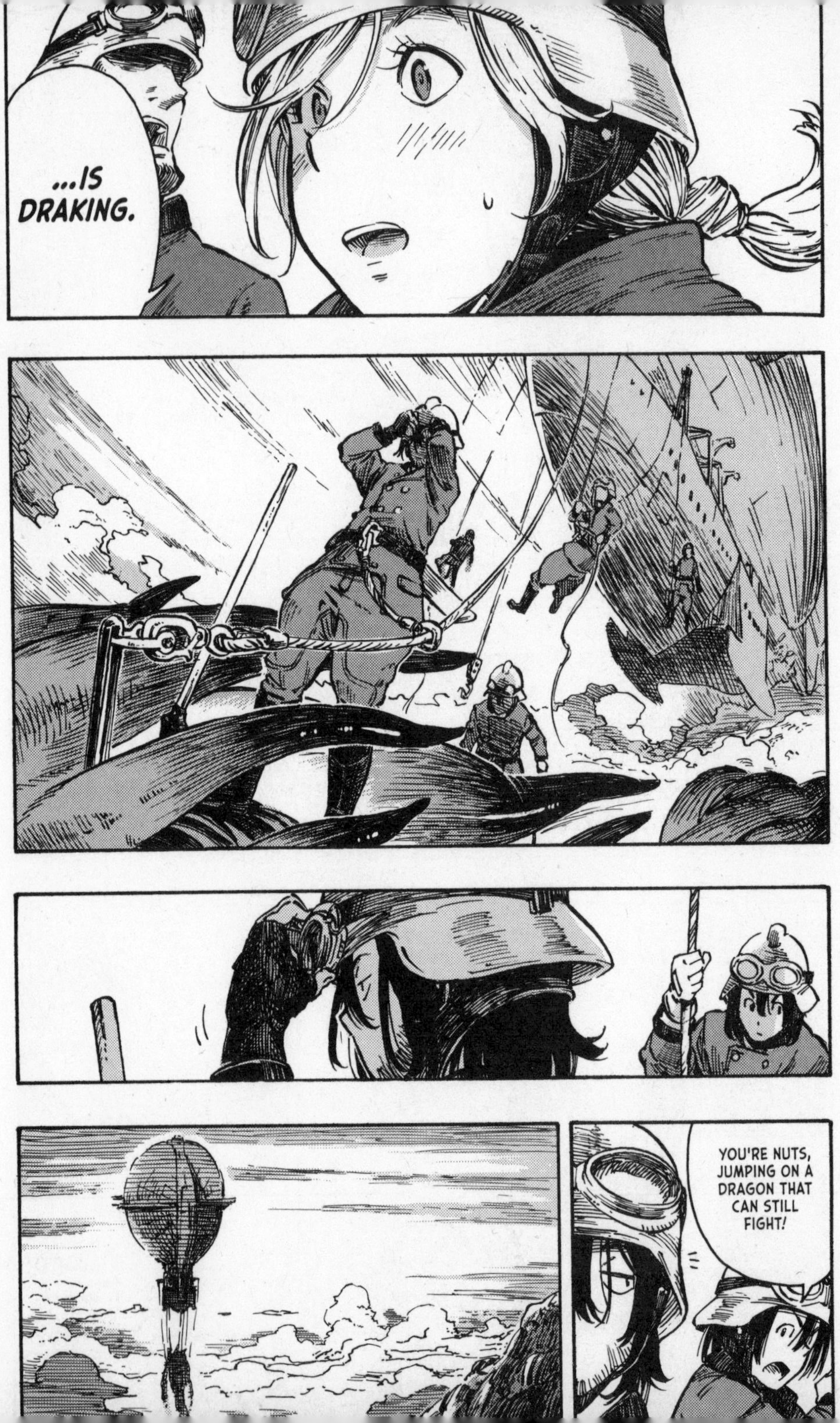
...IS DRAKING.
YOU'RE NUTS, JUMPING ON A DRAGON THAT CAN STILL FIGHT!

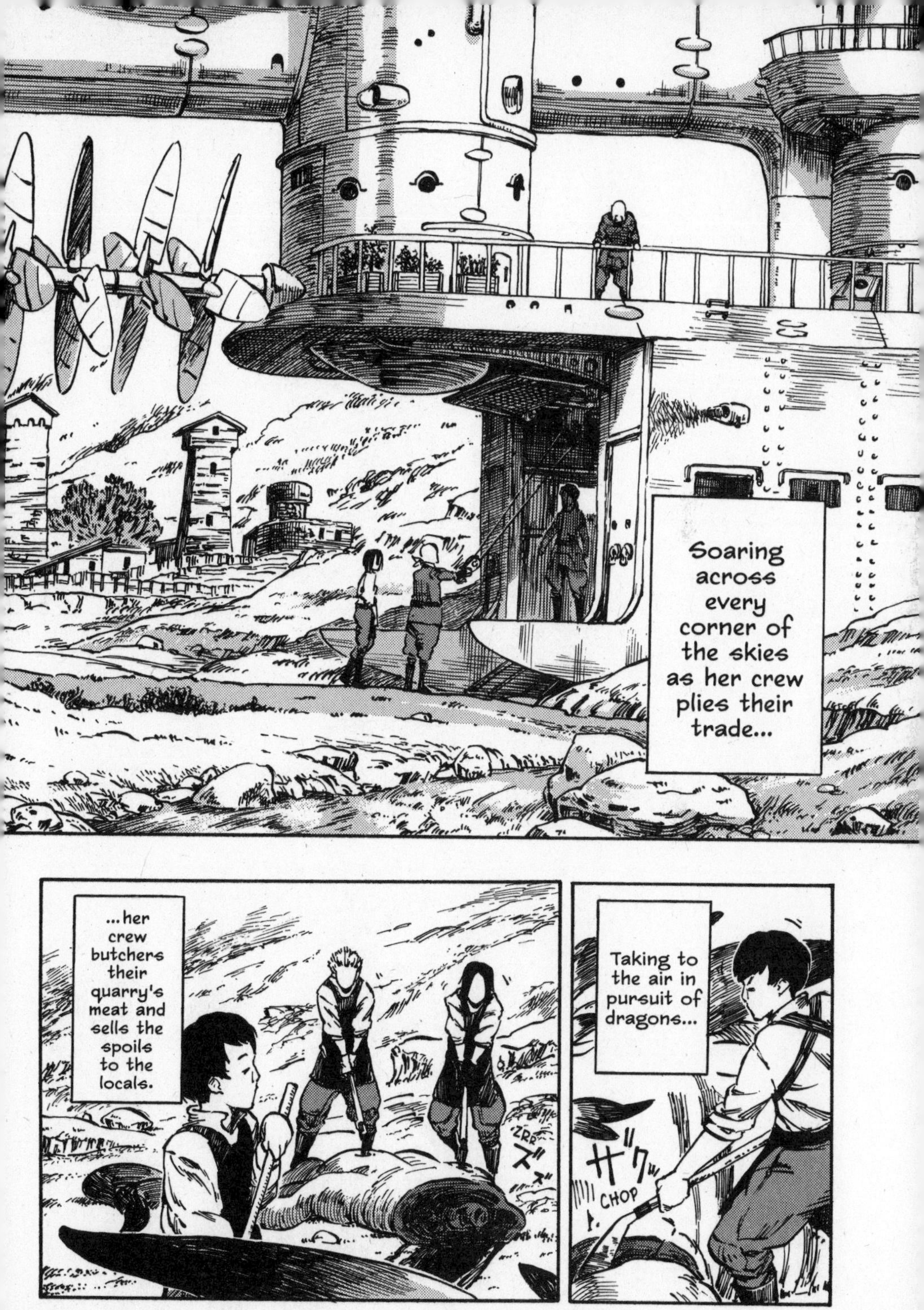
Soaring across every corner of the skies as her crew plies their trade...
Taking to the air in pursuit of dragons...
CHOP
...her crew butchers their quarry's meat and sells the spoils to the locals.
ZRR

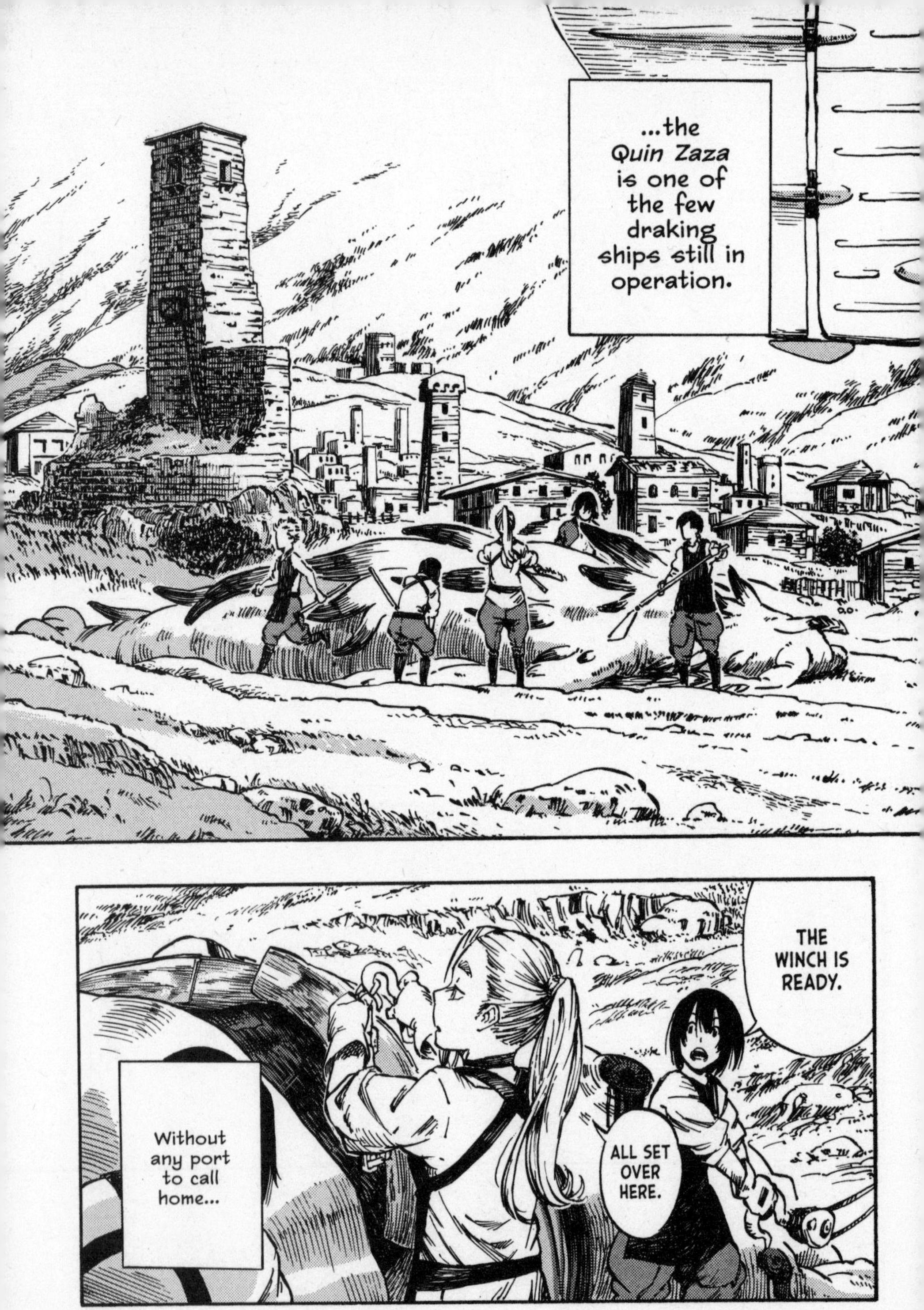
...the Quin Zaza is one of the few draking ships still in operation.
THE WINCH IS READY.
ALL SET OVER HERE.
Without any port to call home...

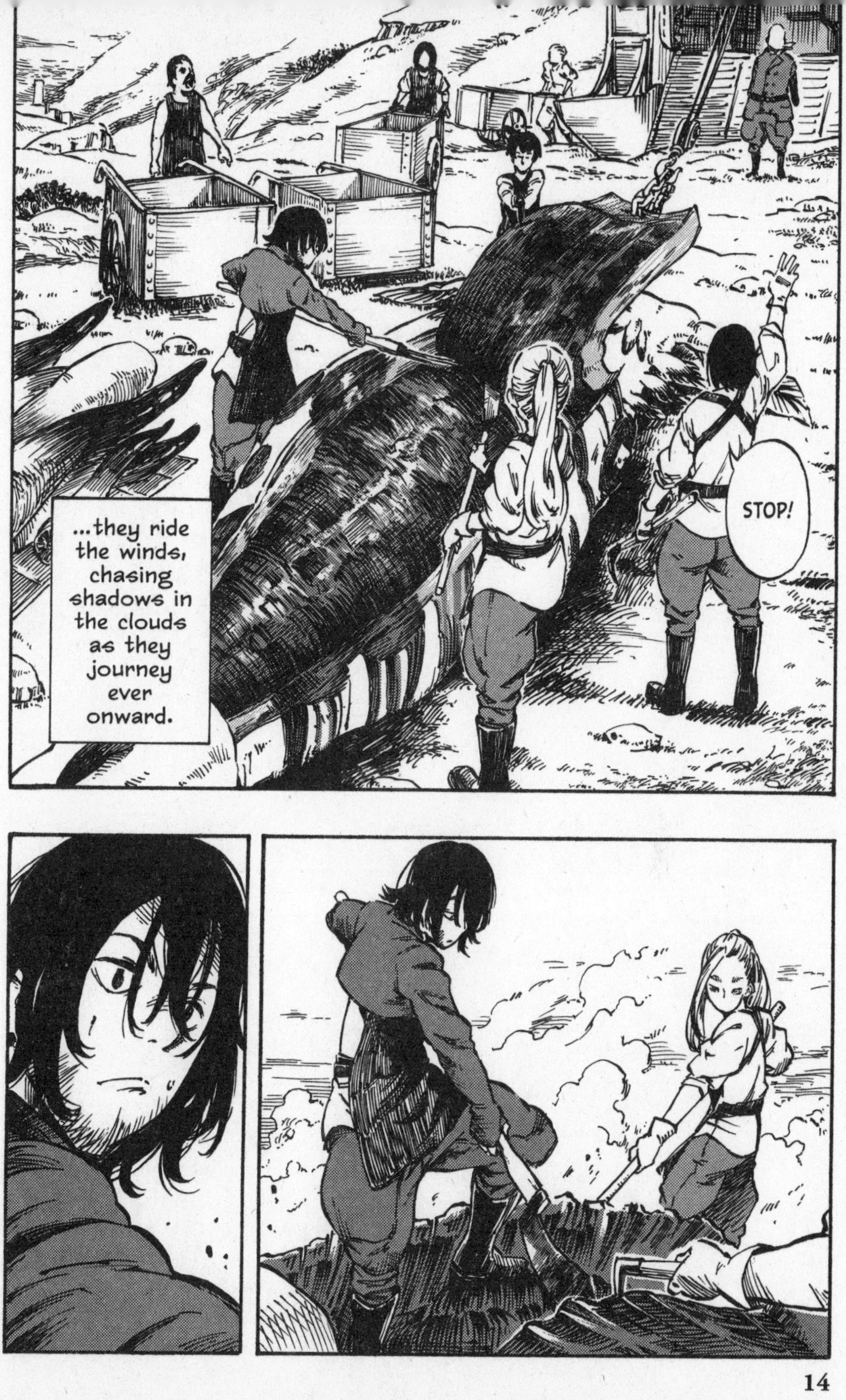
STOP!
...they ride the winds, chasing shadows in the clouds as they journey ever onward.

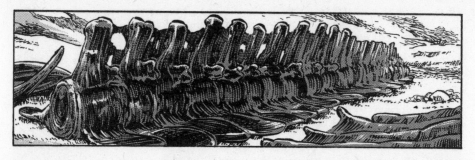

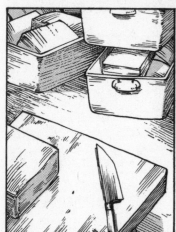

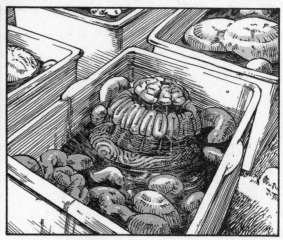

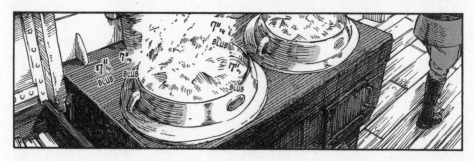

BLUB BLUB BLUB BLUB

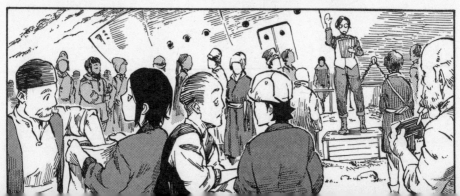

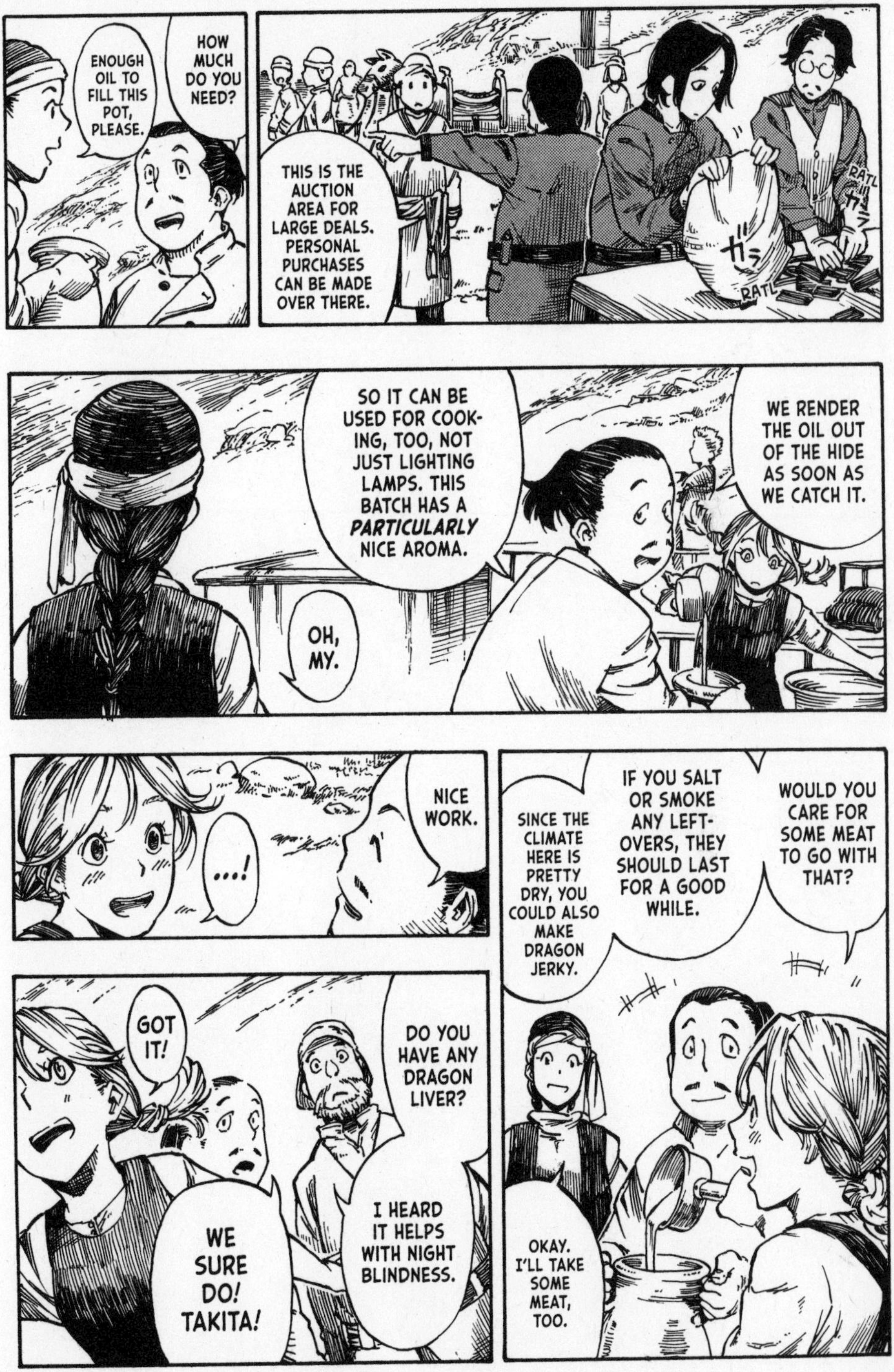
THIS IS THE AUCTION AREA FOR LARGE DEALS. PERSONAL PURCHASES CAN BE MADE OVER THERE.
RATL
RATL
HOW MUCH DO YOU NEED?
ENOUGH OIL TO FILL THIS POT, PLEASE.
WE RENDER THE OIL OUT OF THE HIDE AS SOON AS WE CATCH IT.
SO IT CAN BE USED FOR COOKING, TOO, NOT JUST LIGHTING LAMPS. THIS BATCH HAS A *PARTICULARLY* NICE AROMA.
OH, MY.
WOULD YOU CARE FOR SOME MEAT TO GO WITH THAT?
IF YOU SALT OR SMOKE ANY LEFTOVERS, THEY SHOULD LAST FOR A GOOD WHILE.
SINCE THE CLIMATE HERE IS PRETTY DRY, YOU COULD ALSO MAKE DRAGON JERKY.
OKAY. I'LL TAKE SOME MEAT, TOO.
NICE WORK.
...!
DO YOU HAVE ANY DRAGON LIVER?
I HEARD IT HELPS WITH NIGHT BLINDNESS.
GOT IT!
WE SURE DO! TAKITA!

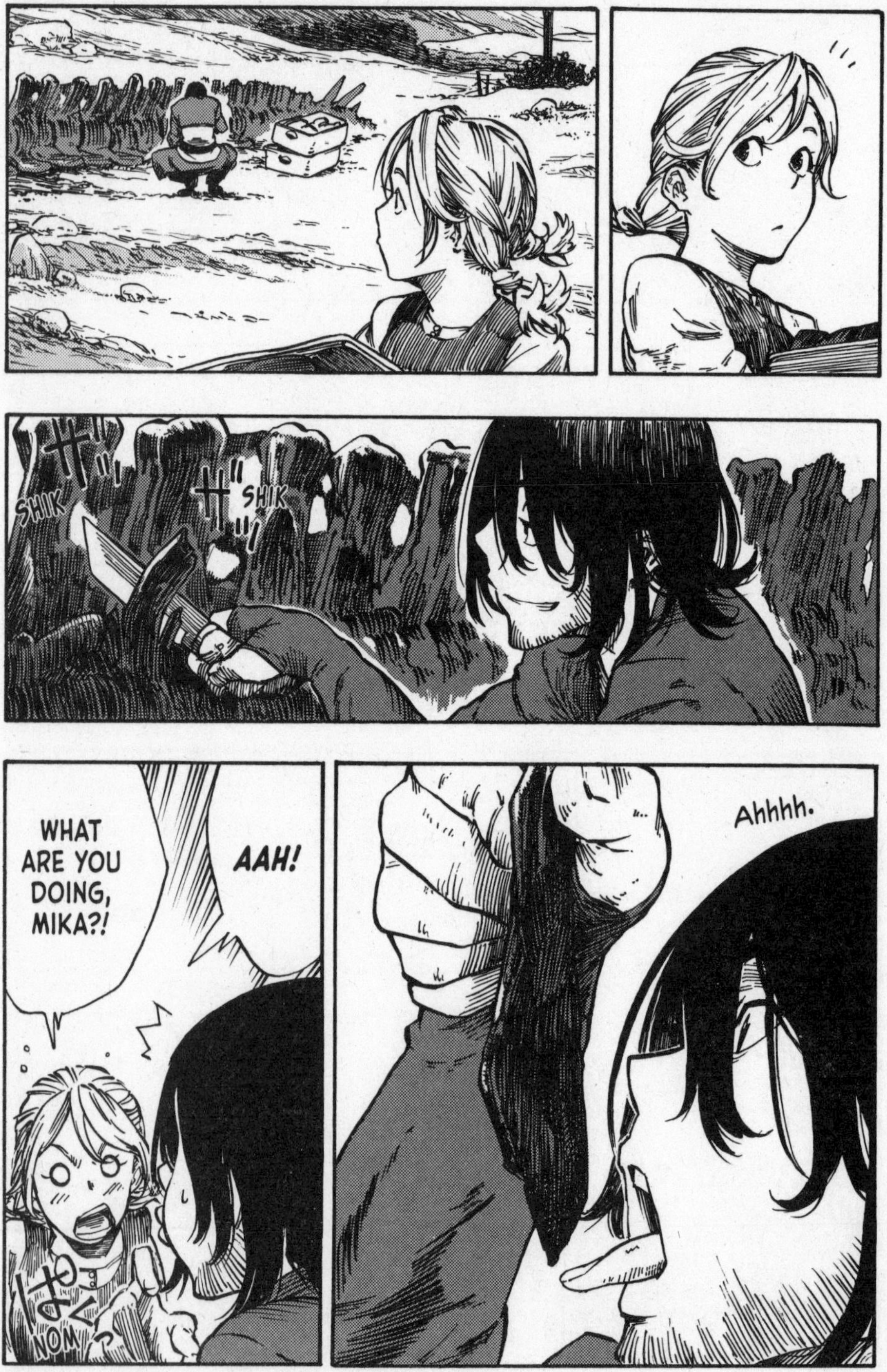
SHIK
SHIK
Ahhhh.
AAH!
WHAT ARE YOU DOING, MIKA?!
はぐっ
NOM

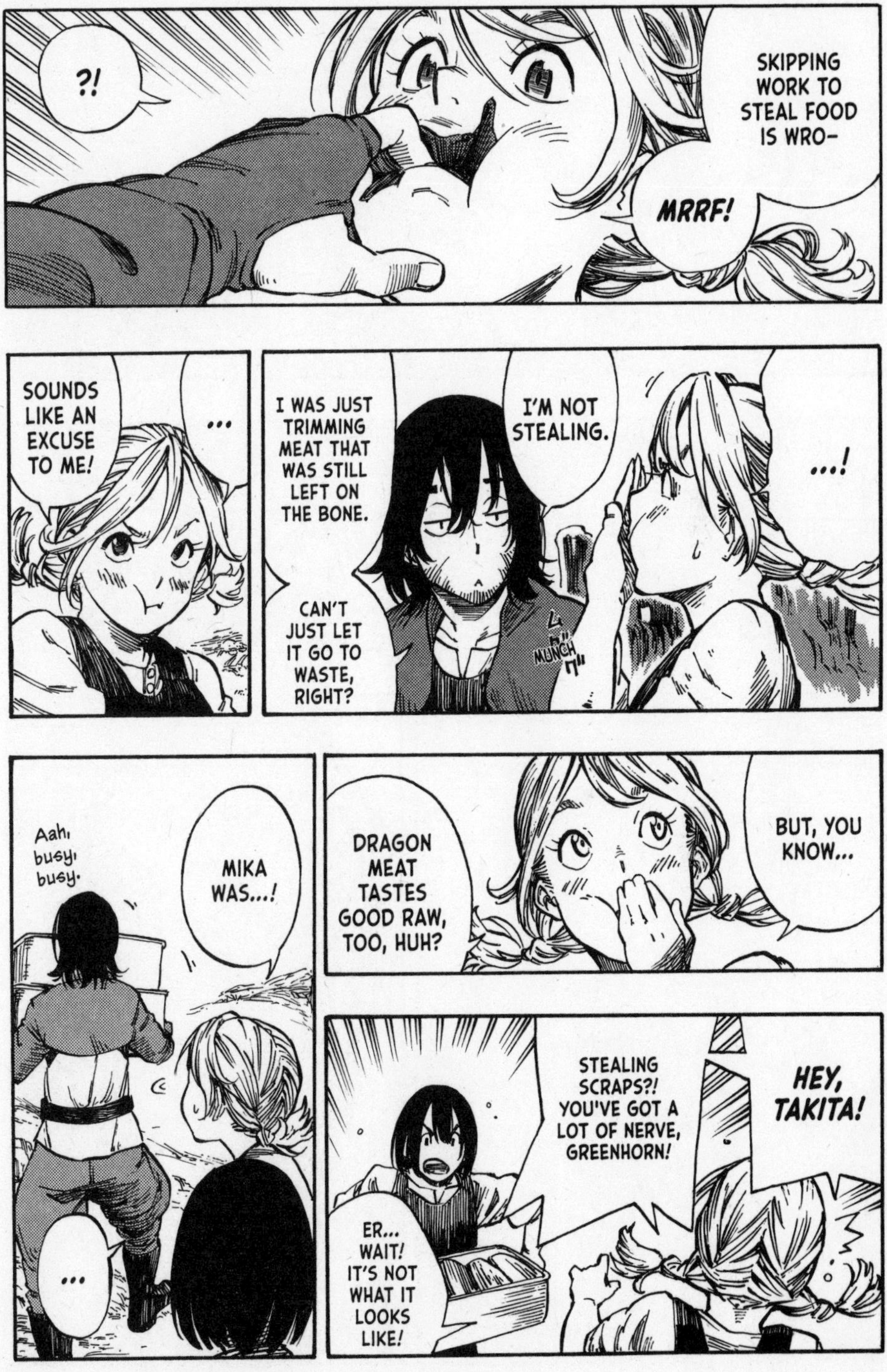
SKIPPING WORK TO STEAL FOOD IS WRO–
MRRF!
?!
...!
I'M NOT STEALING.
I WAS JUST TRIMMING MEAT THAT WAS STILL LEFT ON THE BONE.
CAN'T JUST LET IT GO TO WASTE, RIGHT?
MUNCH
...
SOUNDS LIKE AN EXCUSE TO ME!
BUT, YOU KNOW...
DRAGON MEAT TASTES GOOD RAW, TOO, HUH?
HEY, TAKITA!
STEALING SCRAPS?! YOU'VE GOT A LOT OF NERVE, GREENHORN!
ER... WAIT! IT'S NOT WHAT IT LOOKS LIKE!
MIKA WAS...!
Aah, busy, busy.
...

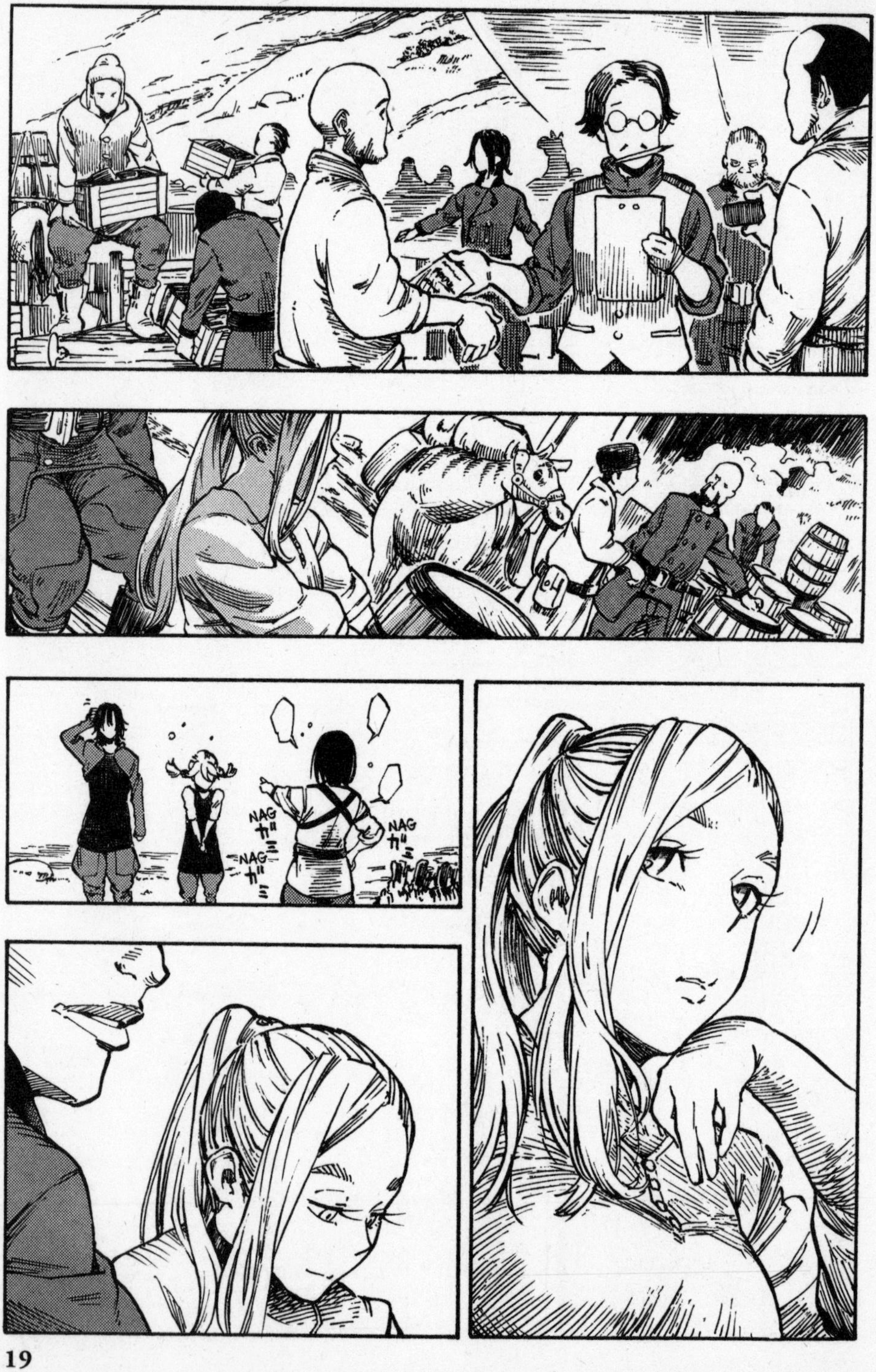
NAG ガミ
NAG ガミ
NAG ガミ

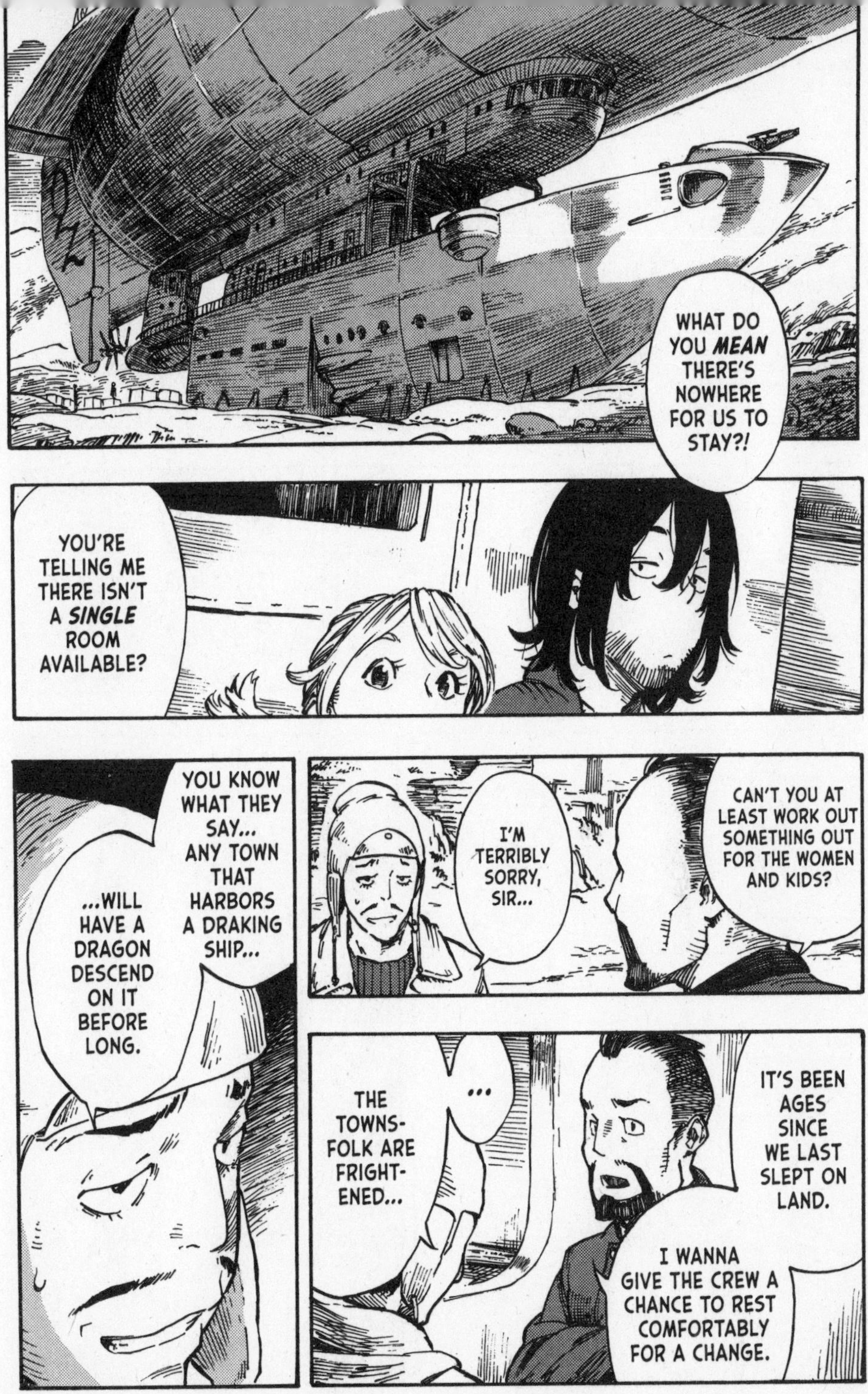
WHAT DO YOU *MEAN* THERE'S NOWHERE FOR US TO STAY?!
YOU'RE TELLING ME THERE ISN'T A *SINGLE* ROOM AVAILABLE?
CAN'T YOU AT LEAST WORK OUT SOMETHING OUT FOR THE WOMEN AND KIDS?
I'M TERRIBLY SORRY, SIR...
IT'S BEEN AGES SINCE WE LAST SLEPT ON LAND.
I WANNA GIVE THE CREW A CHANCE TO REST COMFORTABLY FOR A CHANGE.
...
THE TOWNS-FOLK ARE FRIGHT-ENED...
YOU KNOW WHAT THEY SAY... ANY TOWN THAT HARBORS A DRAKING SHIP...
...WILL HAVE A DRAGON DESCEND ON IT BEFORE LONG.

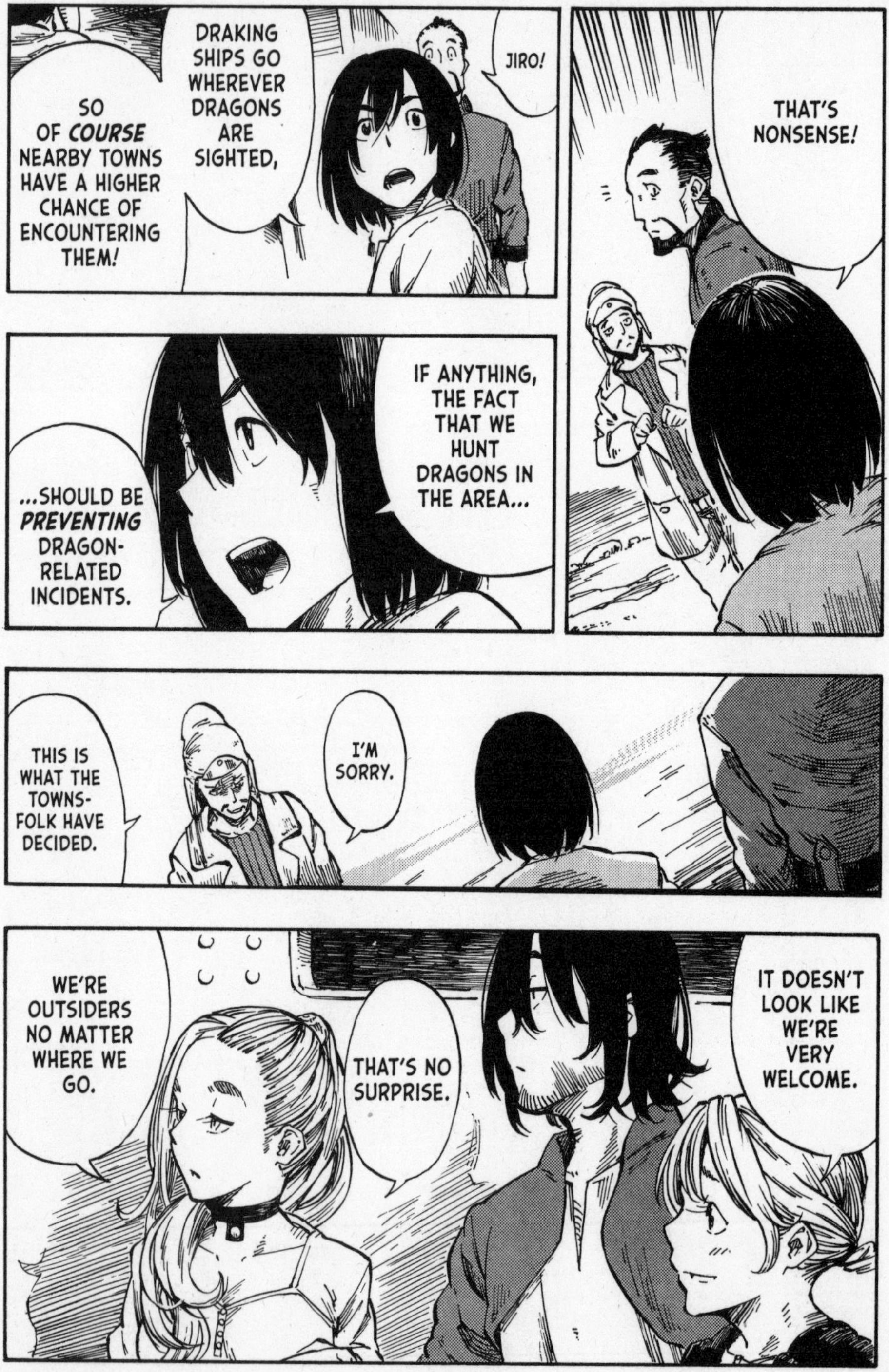
THAT'S NONSENSE!
JIRO!
DRAKING SHIPS GO WHEREVER DRAGONS ARE SIGHTED,
SO OF *COURSE* NEARBY TOWNS HAVE A HIGHER CHANCE OF ENCOUNTERING THEM!
IF ANYTHING, THE FACT THAT WE HUNT DRAGONS IN THE AREA...
...SHOULD BE *PREVENTING* DRAGON-RELATED INCIDENTS.
I'M SORRY.
THIS IS WHAT THE TOWNS-FOLK HAVE DECIDED.
IT DOESN'T LOOK LIKE WE'RE VERY WELCOME.
THAT'S NO SURPRISE.
WE'RE OUTSIDERS NO MATTER WHERE WE GO.

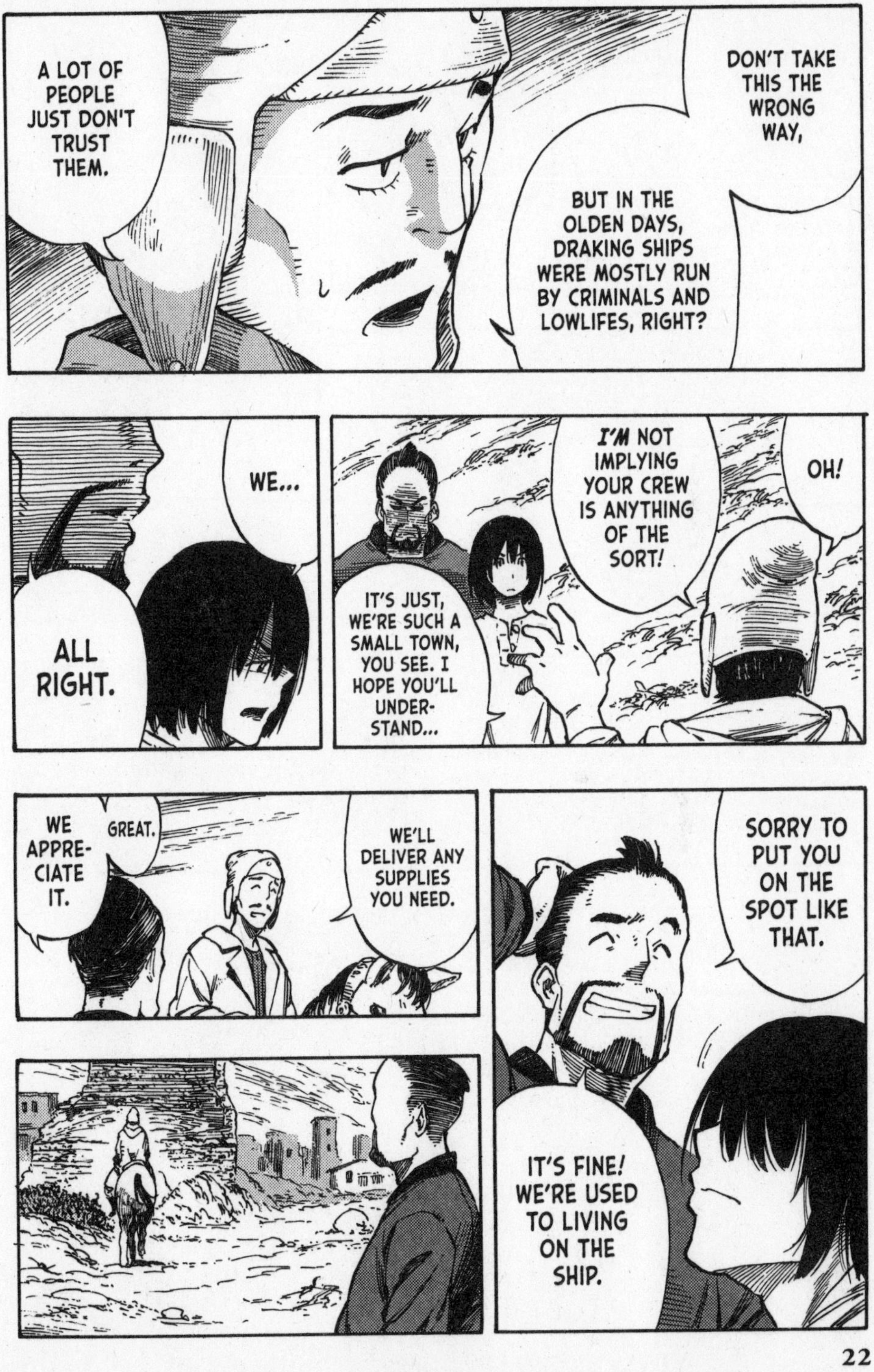
DON'T TAKE THIS THE WRONG WAY,
BUT IN THE OLDEN DAYS, DRAKING SHIPS WERE MOSTLY RUN BY CRIMINALS AND LOWLIFES, RIGHT?
A LOT OF PEOPLE JUST DON'T TRUST THEM.
OH!
I'M NOT IMPLYING YOUR CREW IS ANYTHING OF THE SORT!
IT'S JUST, WE'RE SUCH A SMALL TOWN, YOU SEE. I HOPE YOU'LL UNDER-STAND...
WE...
ALL RIGHT.
SORRY TO PUT YOU ON THE SPOT LIKE THAT.
IT'S FINE! WE'RE USED TO LIVING ON THE SHIP.
WE'LL DELIVER ANY SUPPLIES YOU NEED.
GREAT.
WE APPRE-CIATE IT.

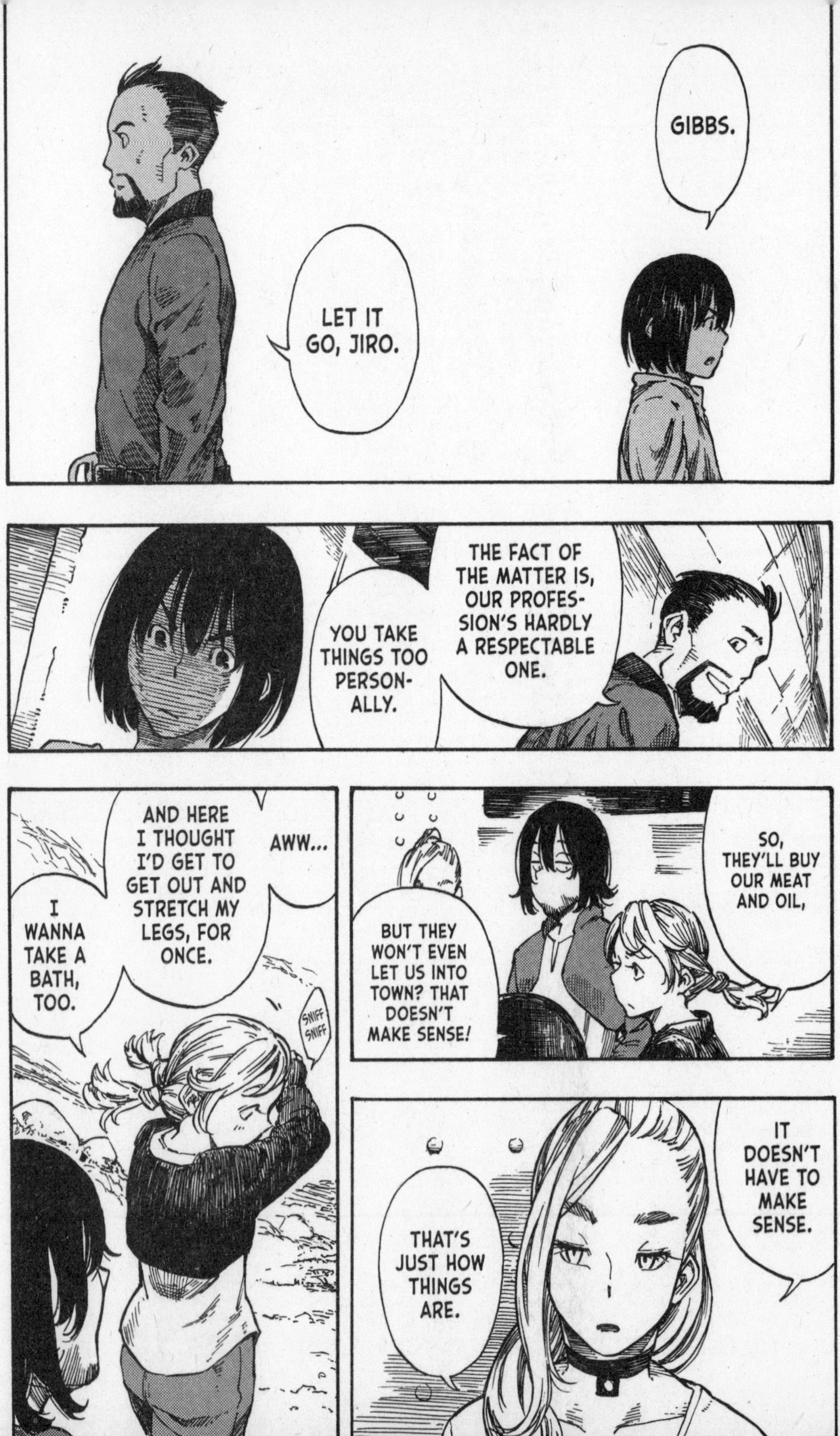
GIBBS.
LET IT GO, JIRO.
THE FACT OF THE MATTER IS, OUR PROFESSION'S HARDLY A RESPECTABLE ONE.
YOU TAKE THINGS TOO PERSONALLY.
SO, THEY'LL BUY OUR MEAT AND OIL,
BUT THEY WON'T EVEN LET US INTO TOWN? THAT DOESN'T MAKE SENSE!
IT DOESN'T HAVE TO MAKE SENSE.
THAT'S JUST HOW THINGS ARE.
AWW...
AND HERE I THOUGHT I'D GET TO GET OUT AND STRETCH MY LEGS, FOR ONCE.
I WANNA TAKE A BATH, TOO.
SNIFF SNIFF

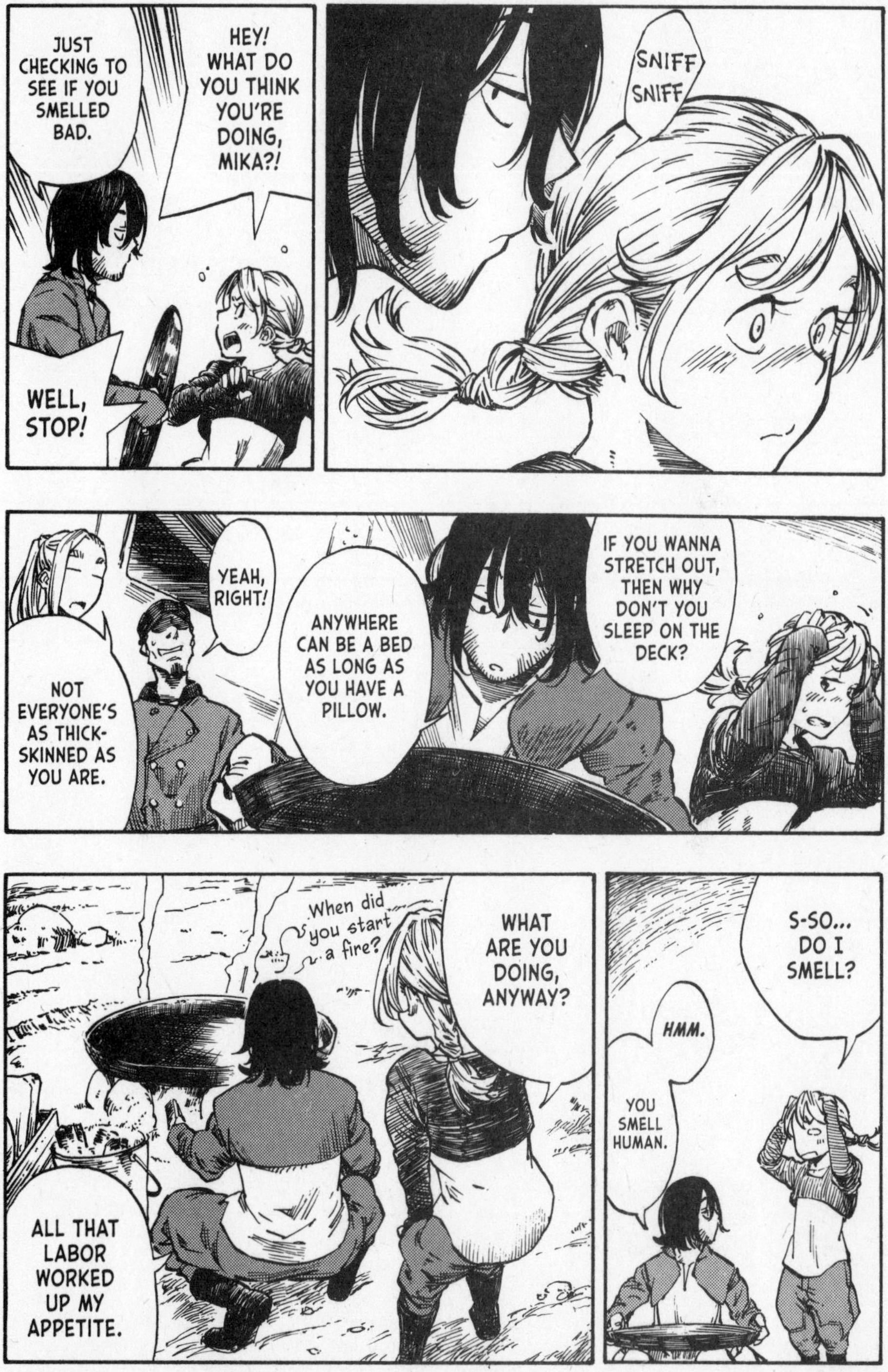
SNIFF SNIFF
HEY! WHAT DO YOU THINK YOU'RE DOING, MIKA?!
JUST CHECKING TO SEE IF YOU SMELLED BAD.
WELL, STOP!
IF YOU WANNA STRETCH OUT, THEN WHY DON'T YOU SLEEP ON THE DECK?
ANYWHERE CAN BE A BED AS LONG AS YOU HAVE A PILLOW.
YEAH, RIGHT!
NOT EVERYONE'S AS THICK-SKINNED AS YOU ARE.
S-SO... DO I SMELL?
HMM.
YOU SMELL HUMAN.
WHAT ARE YOU DOING, ANYWAY?
When did you start a fire?
ALL THAT LABOR WORKED UP MY APPETITE.

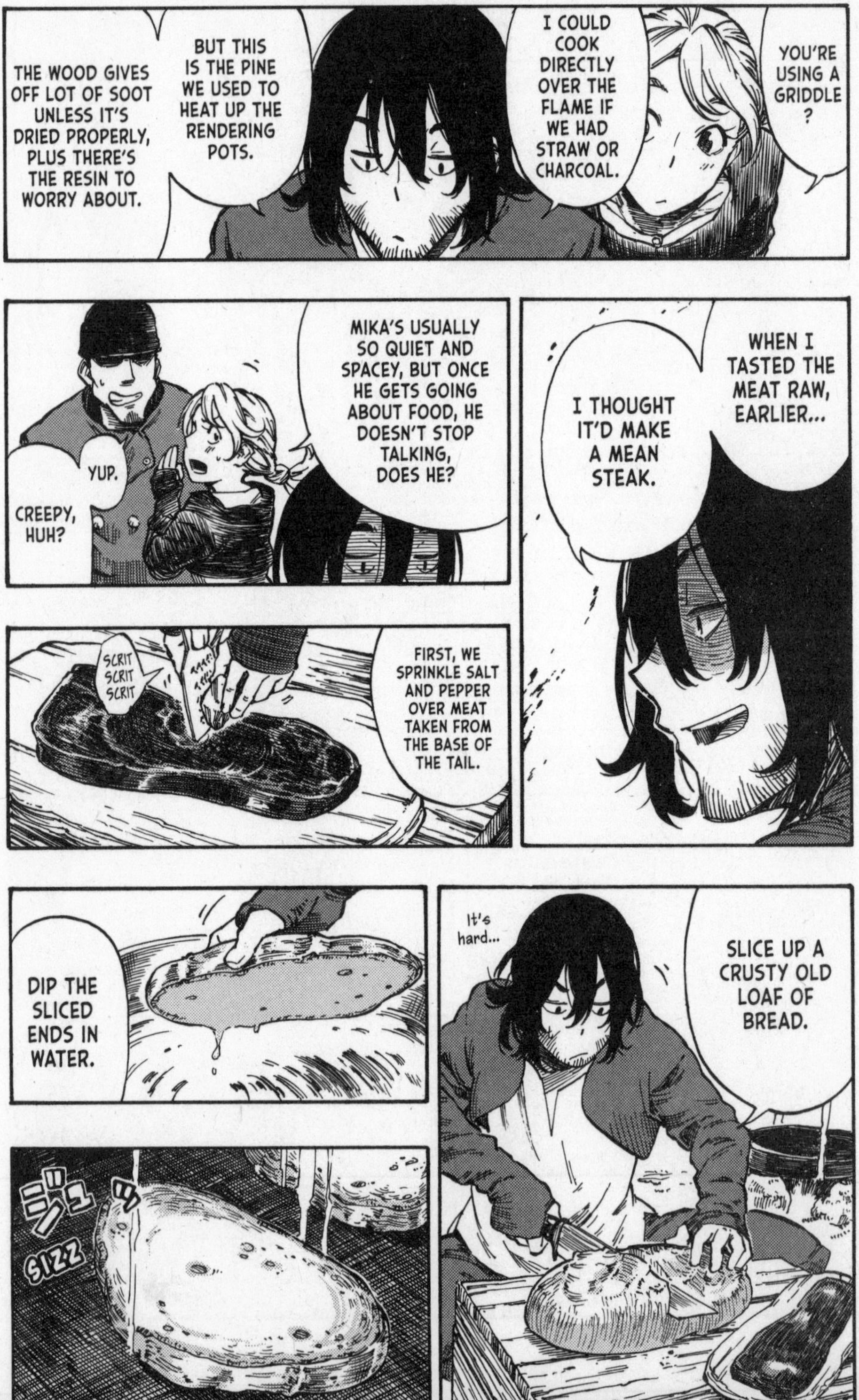
YOU'RE USING A GRIDDLE?
I COULD COOK DIRECTLY OVER THE FLAME IF WE HAD STRAW OR CHARCOAL.
BUT THIS IS THE PINE WE USED TO HEAT UP THE RENDERING POTS.
THE WOOD GIVES OFF LOT OF SOOT UNLESS IT'S DRIED PROPERLY, PLUS THERE'S THE RESIN TO WORRY ABOUT.
WHEN I TASTED THE MEAT RAW, EARLIER...
I THOUGHT IT'D MAKE A MEAN STEAK.
MIKA'S USUALLY SO QUIET AND SPACEY, BUT ONCE HE GETS GOING ABOUT FOOD, HE DOESN'T STOP TALKING, DOES HE?
YUP.
CREEPY, HUH?
FIRST, WE SPRINKLE SALT AND PEPPER OVER MEAT TAKEN FROM THE BASE OF THE TAIL.
SCRIT SCRIT SCRIT
SLICE UP A CRUSTY OLD LOAF OF BREAD.
It's hard...
DIP THE SLICED ENDS IN WATER.
ジュッ
SIZZ

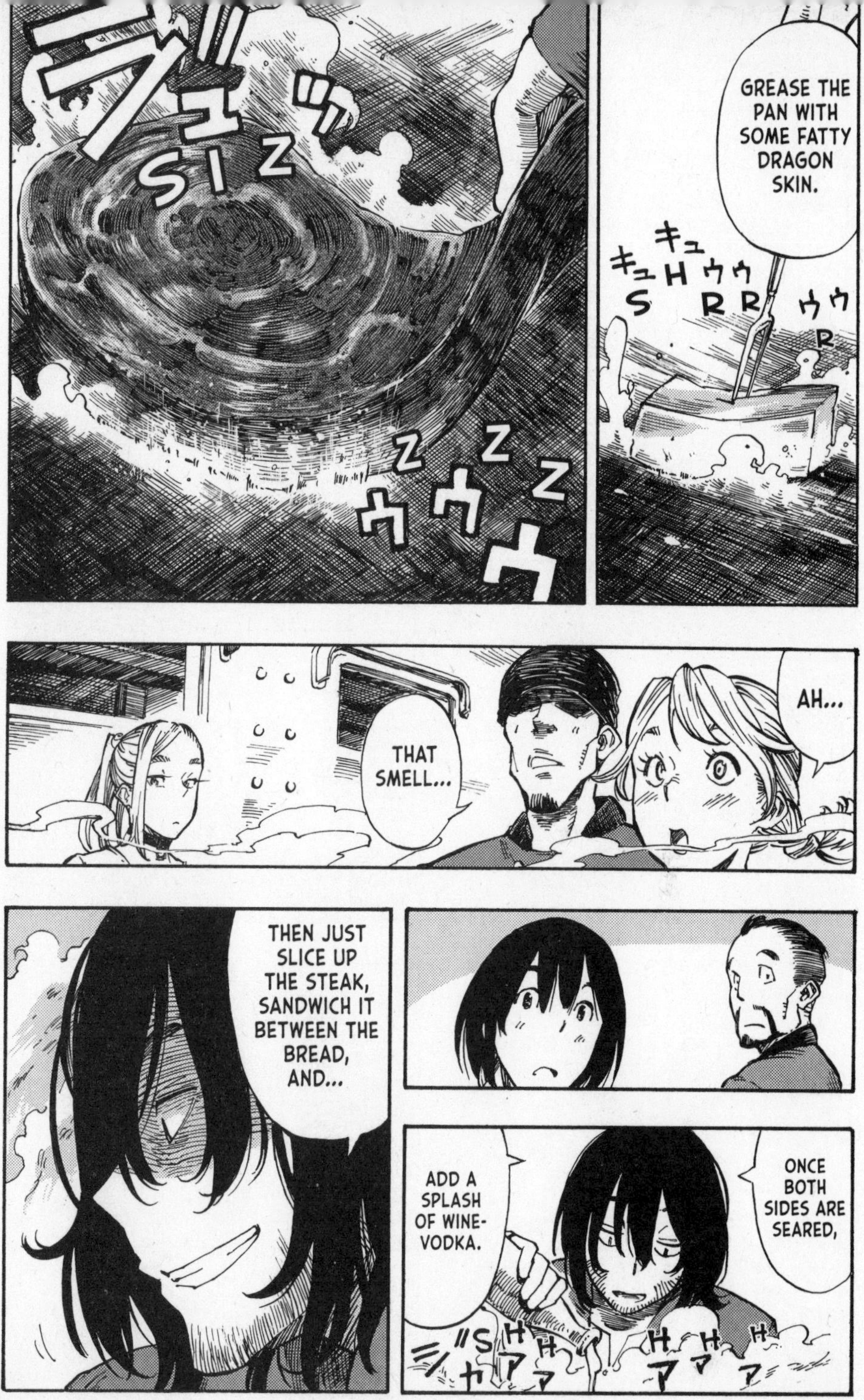
GREASE THE PAN WITH SOME FATTY DRAGON SKIN.
キュキュウウウウ
SHRRR
ジュッ
SIZZ
ZZZ
ウウウ
AH...
THAT SMELL...
ONCE BOTH SIDES ARE SEARED,
ADD A SPLASH OF WINE-VODKA.
ジャッ
SH
ハァハァハァ
HHHHH
THEN JUST SLICE UP THE STEAK, SANDWICH IT BETWEEN THE BREAD, AND...

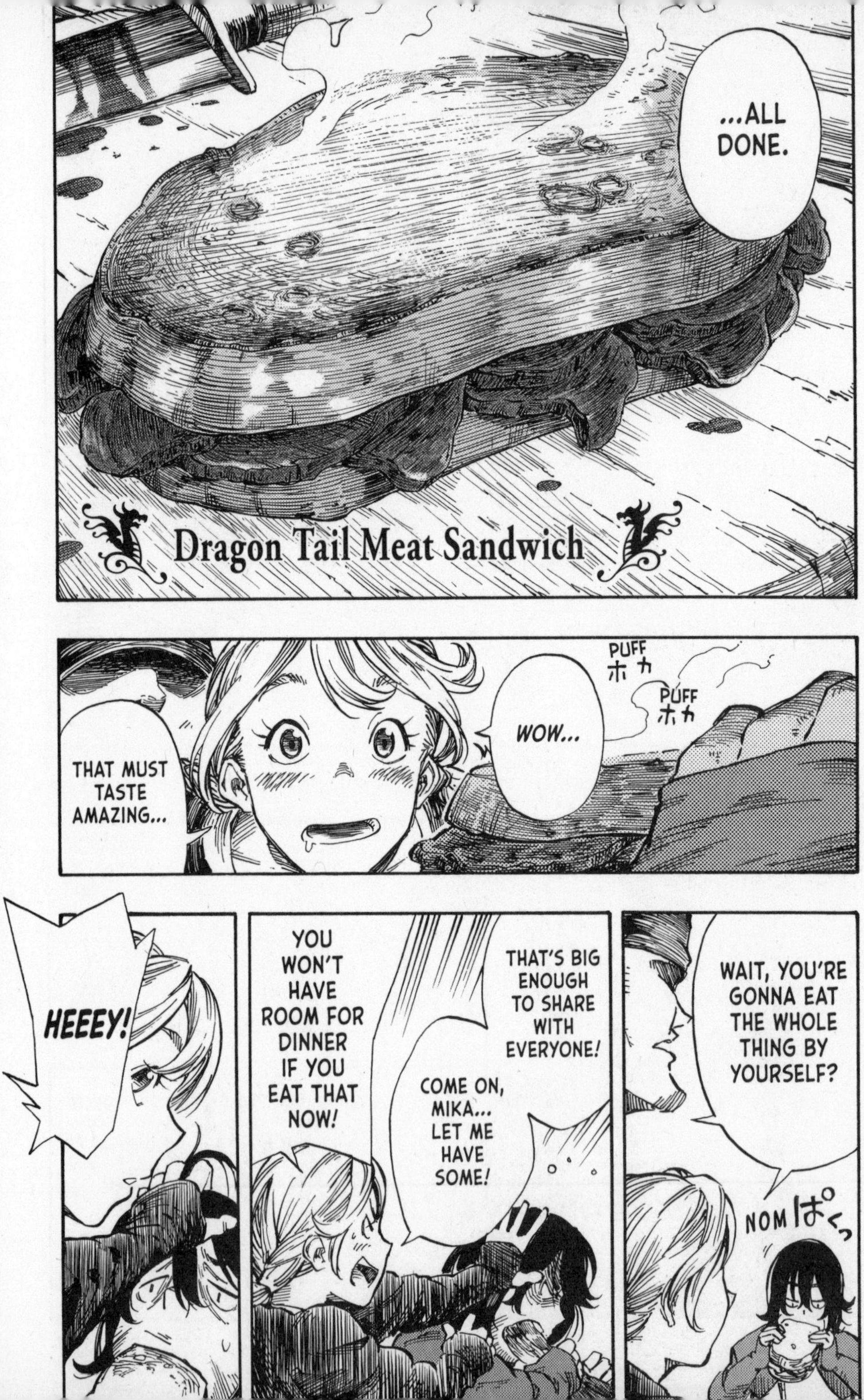
...ALL DONE.
Dragon Tail Meat Sandwich
PUFF ホカ
PUFF ホカ
WOW...
THAT MUST TASTE AMAZING...
WAIT, YOU'RE GONNA EAT THE WHOLE THING BY YOURSELF?
NOM ぱくっ
THAT'S BIG ENOUGH TO SHARE WITH EVERYONE!
COME ON, MIKA... LET ME HAVE SOME!
YOU WON'T HAVE ROOM FOR DINNER IF YOU EAT THAT NOW!
HEEEY!

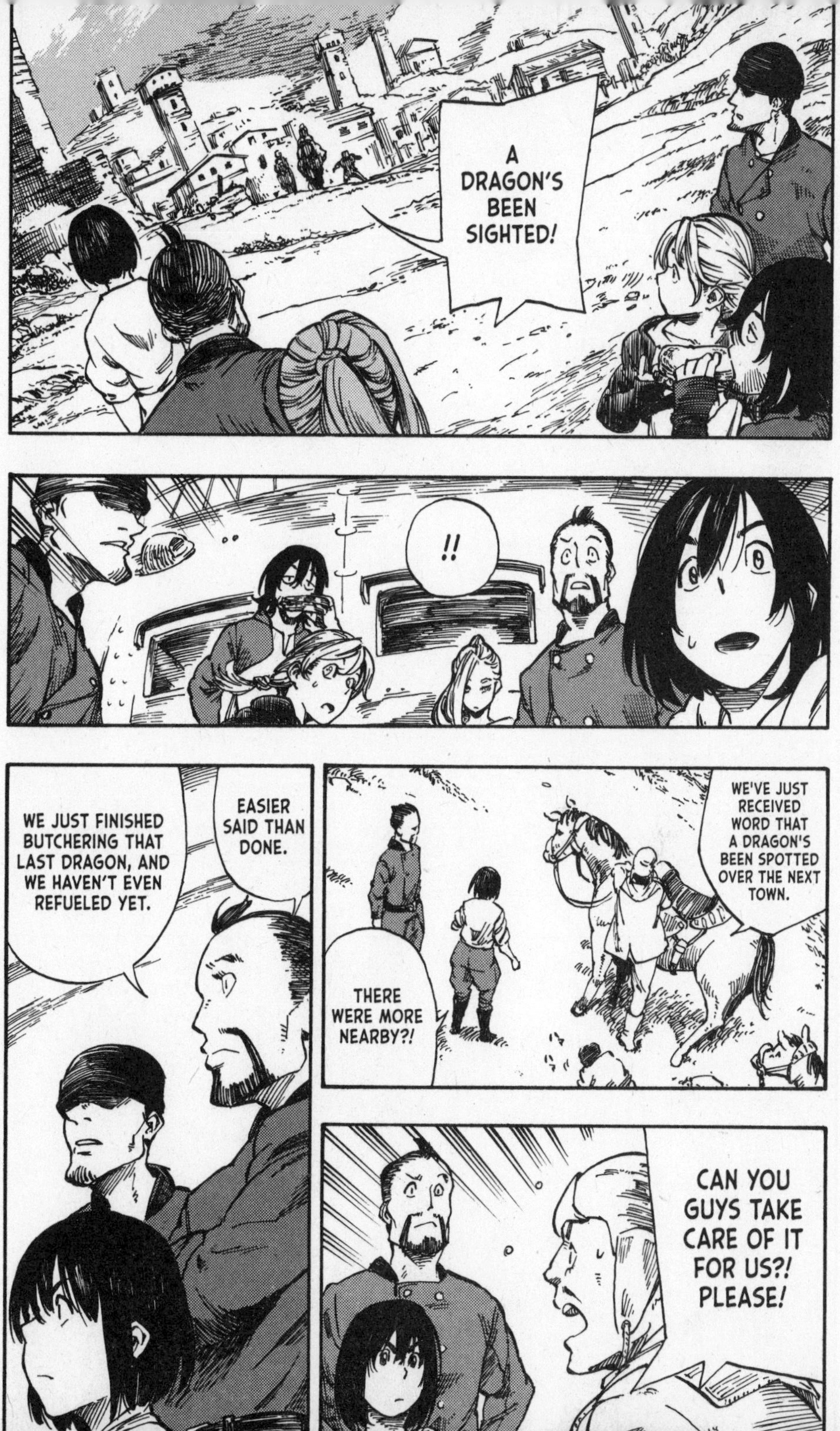
A DRAGON'S BEEN SIGHTED!
!!
WE'VE JUST RECEIVED WORD THAT A DRAGON'S BEEN SPOTTED OVER THE NEXT TOWN.
THERE WERE MORE NEARBY?!
CAN YOU GUYS TAKE CARE OF IT FOR US?! PLEASE!
EASIER SAID THAN DONE.
WE JUST FINISHED BUTCHERING THAT LAST DRAGON, AND WE HAVEN'T EVEN REFUELED YET.

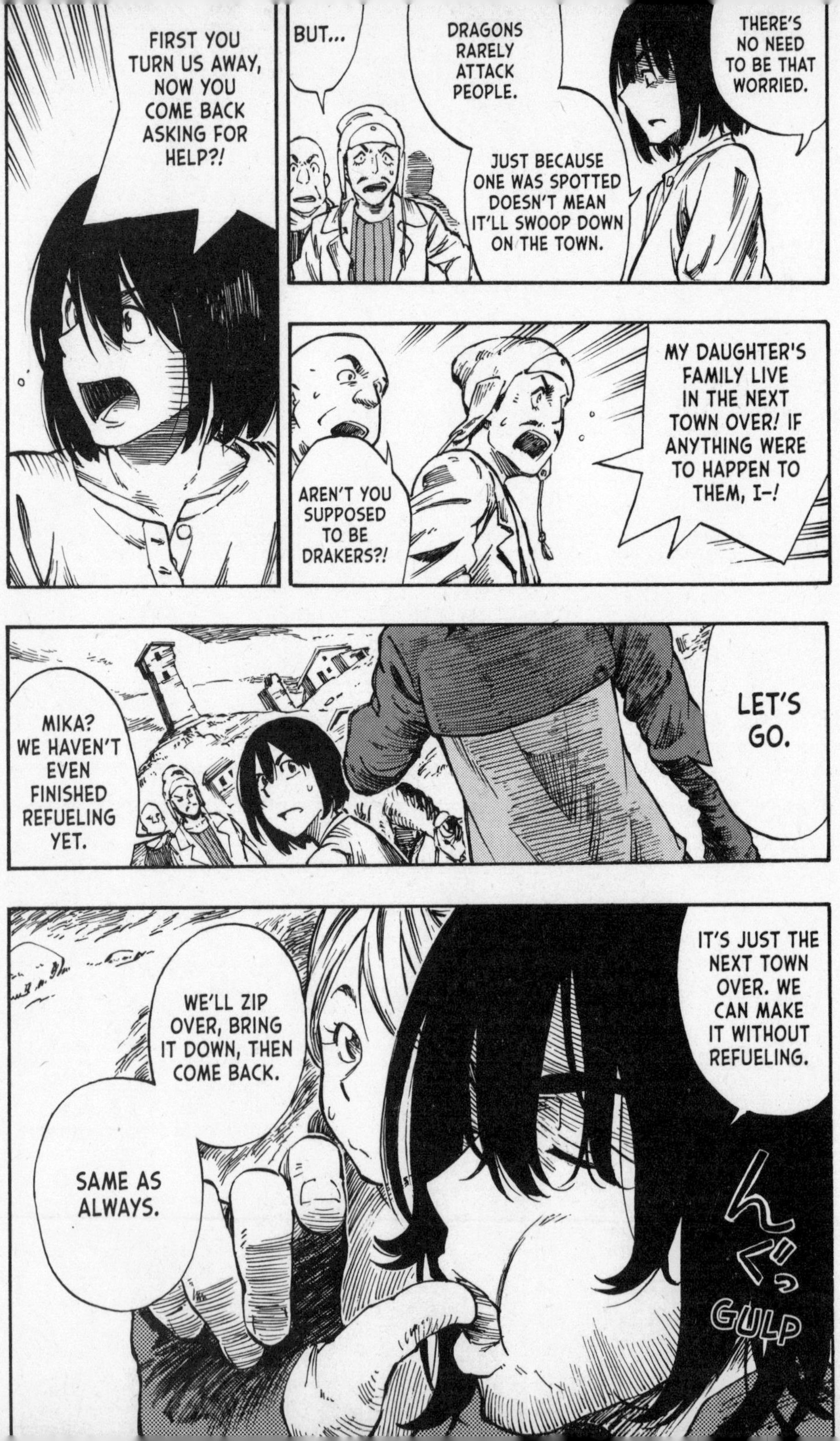
THERE'S NO NEED TO BE THAT WORRIED.
DRAGONS RARELY ATTACK PEOPLE.
JUST BECAUSE ONE WAS SPOTTED DOESN'T MEAN IT'LL SWOOP DOWN ON THE TOWN.
BUT...
MY DAUGHTER'S FAMILY LIVE IN THE NEXT TOWN OVER! IF ANYTHING WERE TO HAPPEN TO THEM, I-!
AREN'T YOU SUPPOSED TO BE DRAKERS?!
FIRST YOU TURN US AWAY, NOW YOU COME BACK ASKING FOR HELP?!
LET'S GO.
MIKA? WE HAVEN'T EVEN FINISHED REFUELING YET.
IT'S JUST THE NEXT TOWN OVER. WE CAN MAKE IT WITHOUT REFUELING.
んぐっ
GULP
WE'LL ZIP OVER, BRING IT DOWN, THEN COME BACK.
SAME AS ALWAYS.

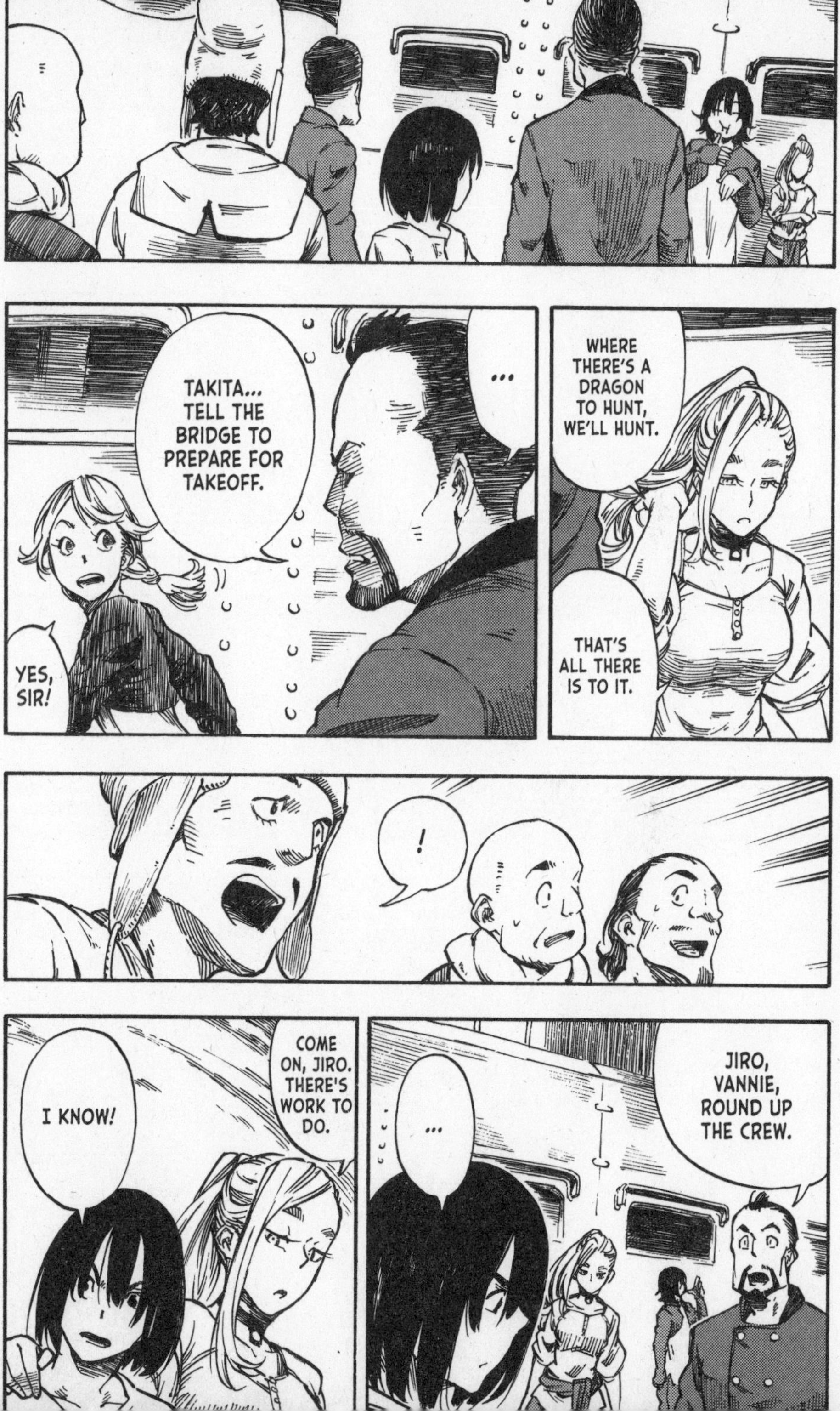
WHERE THERE'S A DRAGON TO HUNT, WE'LL HUNT.
THAT'S ALL THERE IS TO IT.
...
TAKITA... TELL THE BRIDGE TO PREPARE FOR TAKEOFF.
YES, SIR!
!
JIRO, VANNIE, ROUND UP THE CREW.
...
COME ON, JIRO. THERE'S WORK TO DO.
I KNOW!

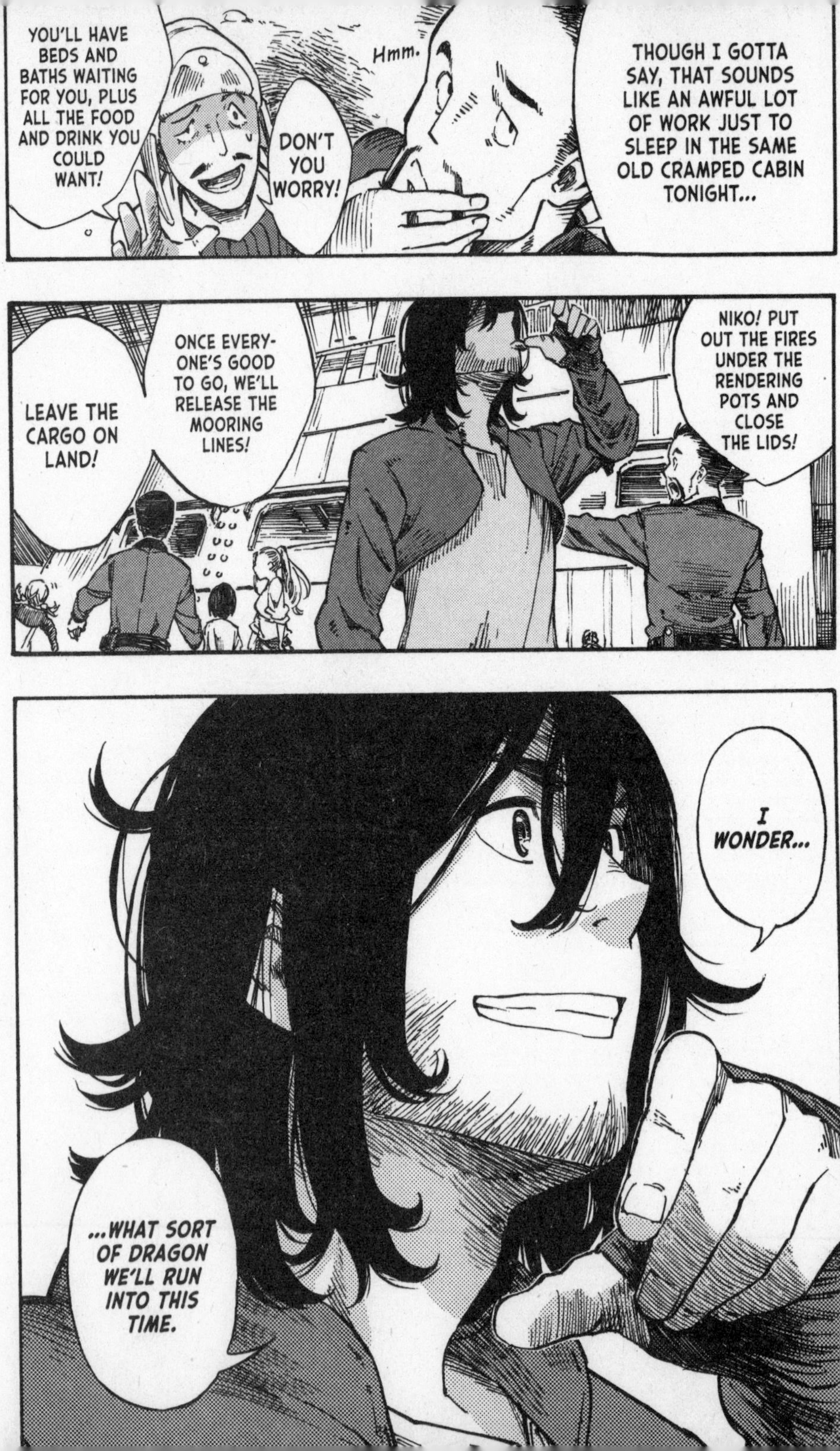
THOUGH I GOTTA SAY, THAT SOUNDS LIKE AN AWFUL LOT OF WORK JUST TO SLEEP IN THE SAME OLD CRAMPED CABIN TONIGHT...
Hmm.
DON'T YOU WORRY!
YOU'LL HAVE BEDS AND BATHS WAITING FOR YOU, PLUS ALL THE FOOD AND DRINK YOU COULD WANT!
NIKO! PUT OUT THE FIRES UNDER THE RENDERING POTS AND CLOSE THE LIDS!
ONCE EVERY-ONE'S GOOD TO GO, WE'LL RELEASE THE MOORING LINES!
LEAVE THE CARGO ON LAND!
I WONDER...
...WHAT SORT OF DRAGON WE'LL RUN INTO THIS TIME.

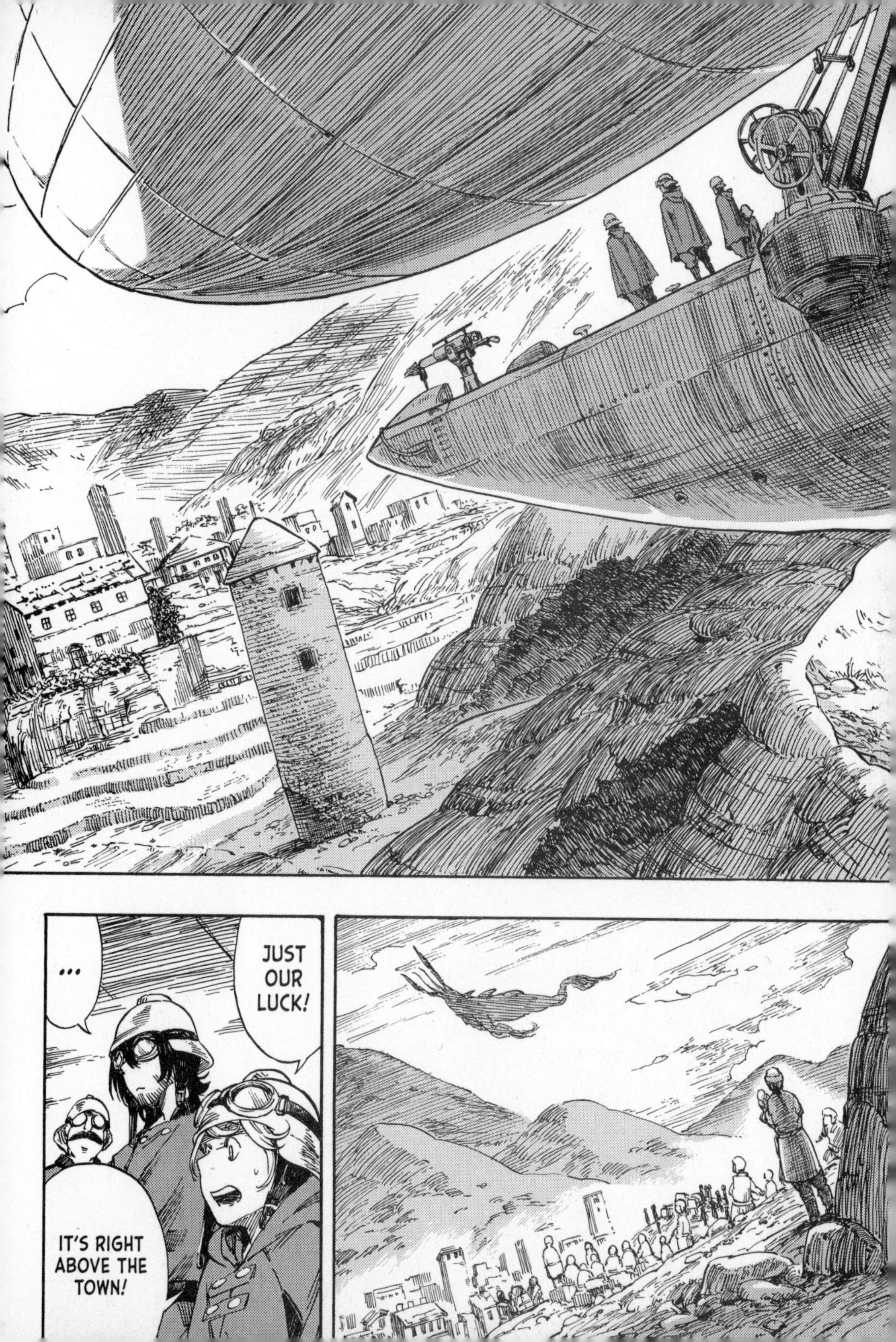
JUST OUR LUCK!
...
IT'S RIGHT ABOVE THE TOWN!

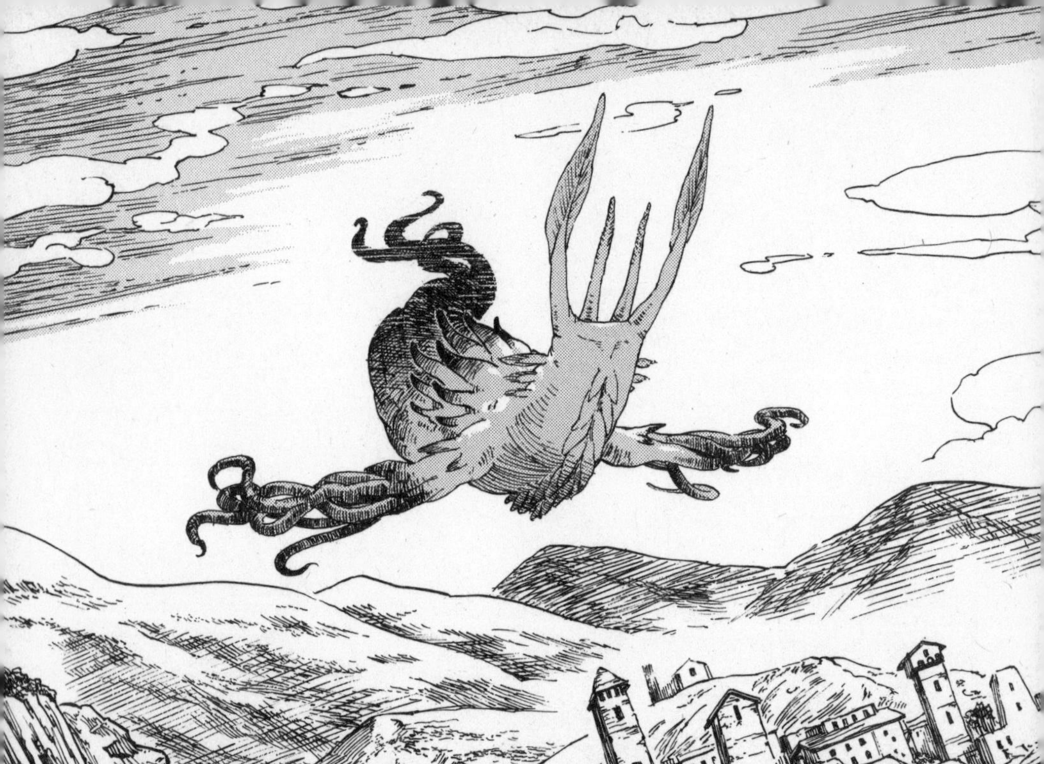

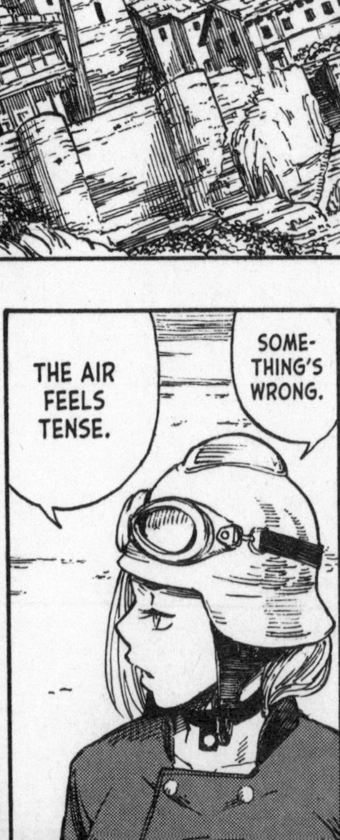
SOMETHING'S WRONG.
THE AIR FEELS TENSE.

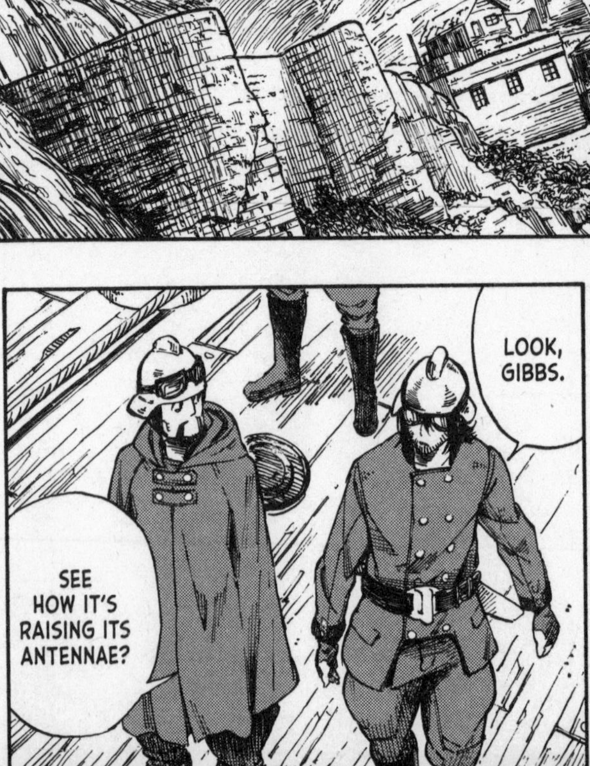
LOOK, GIBBS.
SEE HOW IT'S RAISING ITS ANTENNAE?

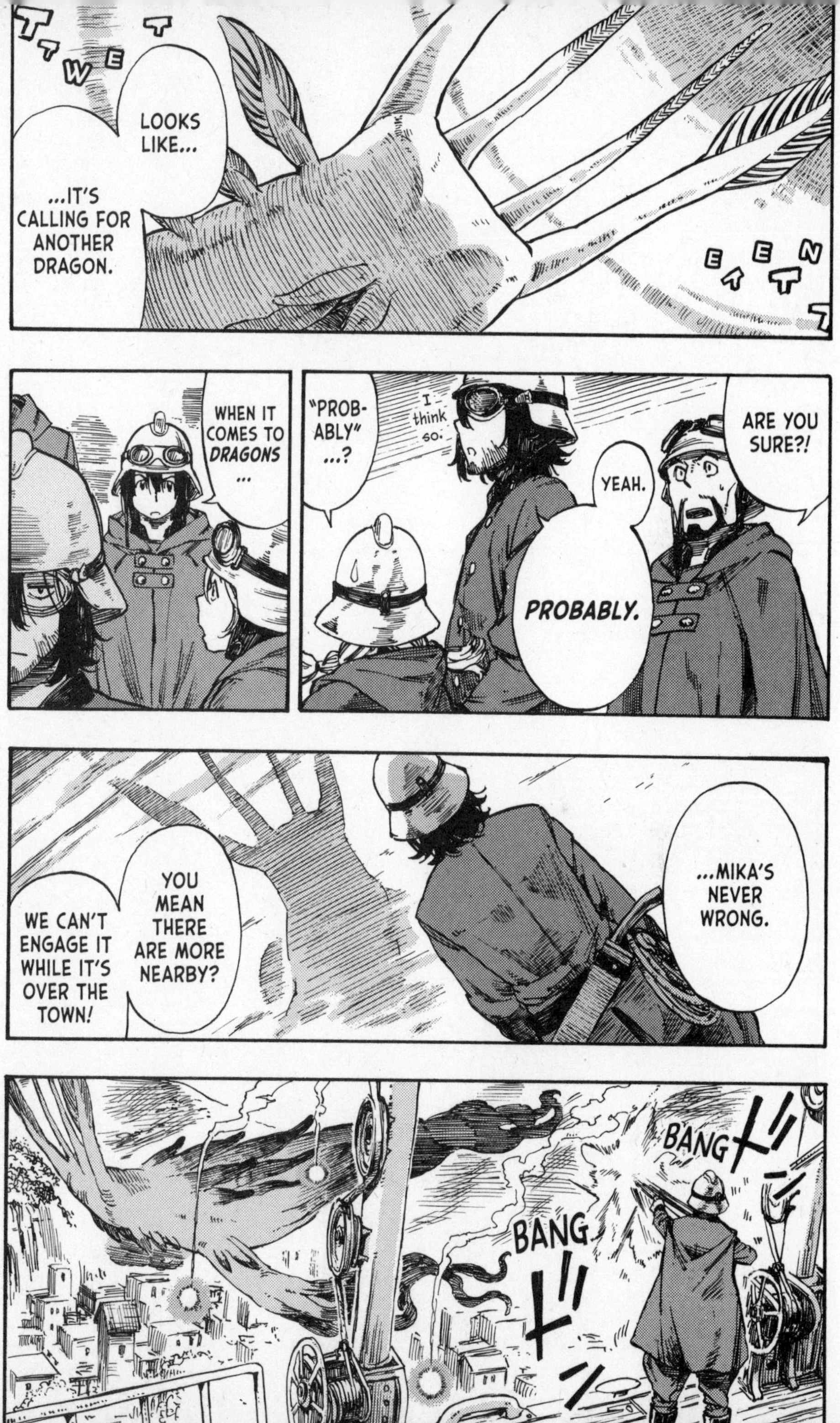
LOOKS LIKE...
...IT'S CALLING FOR ANOTHER DRAGON.
ARE YOU SURE?!
YEAH.
PROBABLY.
I think so.
"PROBABLY" ...?
WHEN IT COMES TO DRAGONS ...
...MIKA'S NEVER WRONG.
YOU MEAN THERE ARE MORE NEARBY?
WE CAN'T ENGAGE IT WHILE IT'S OVER THE TOWN!
BANG
BANG

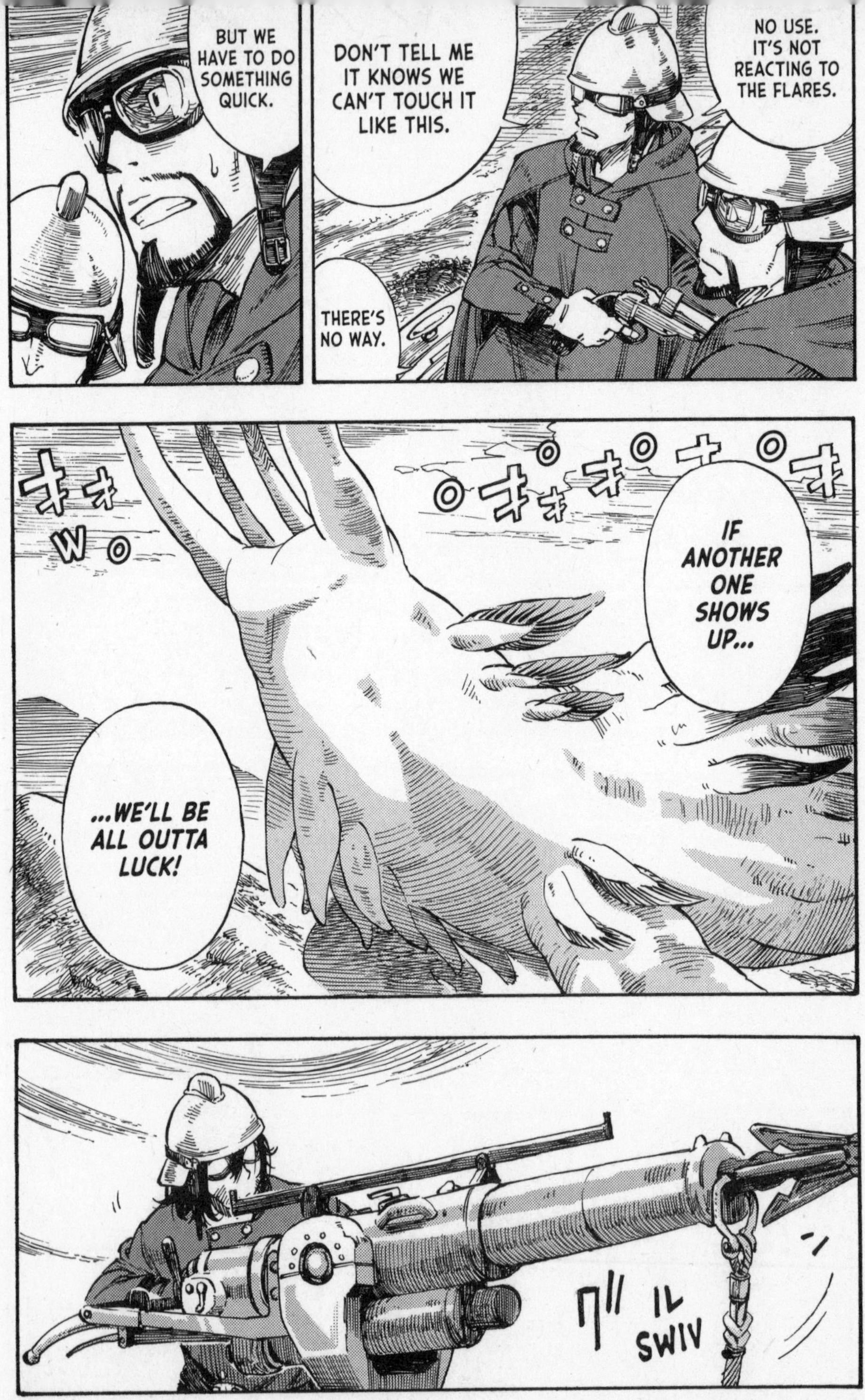
NO USE. IT'S NOT REACTING TO THE FLARES.
DON'T TELL ME IT KNOWS WE CAN'T TOUCH IT LIKE THIS.
THERE'S NO WAY.
BUT WE HAVE TO DO SOMETHING QUICK.
WO
IF ANOTHER ONE SHOWS UP...
...WE'LL BE ALL OUTTA LUCK!
SWIV

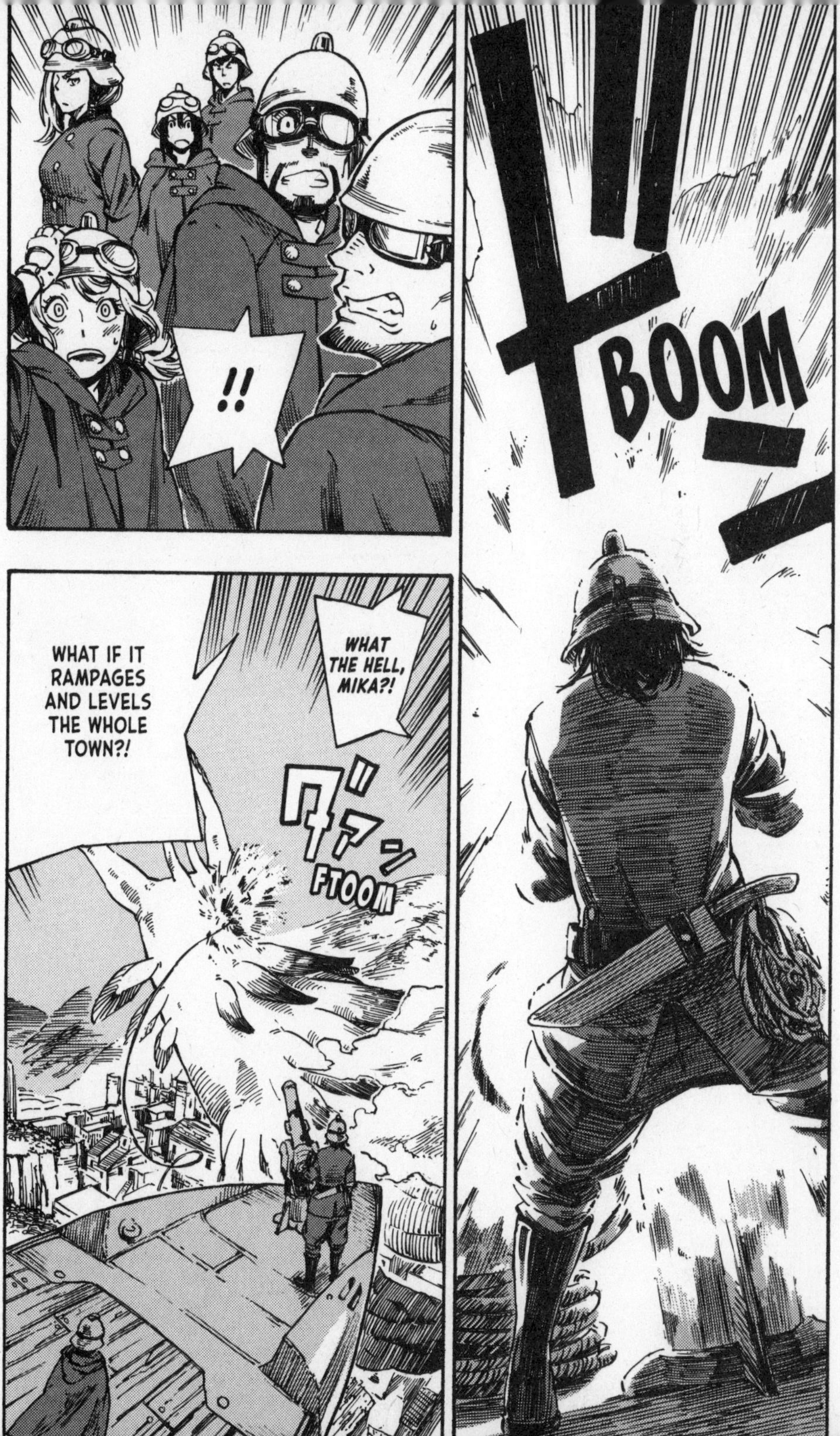
BOOM
!!
WHAT THE HELL, MIKA?!
WHAT IF IT RAMPAGES AND LEVELS THE WHOLE TOWN?!
FTOOM

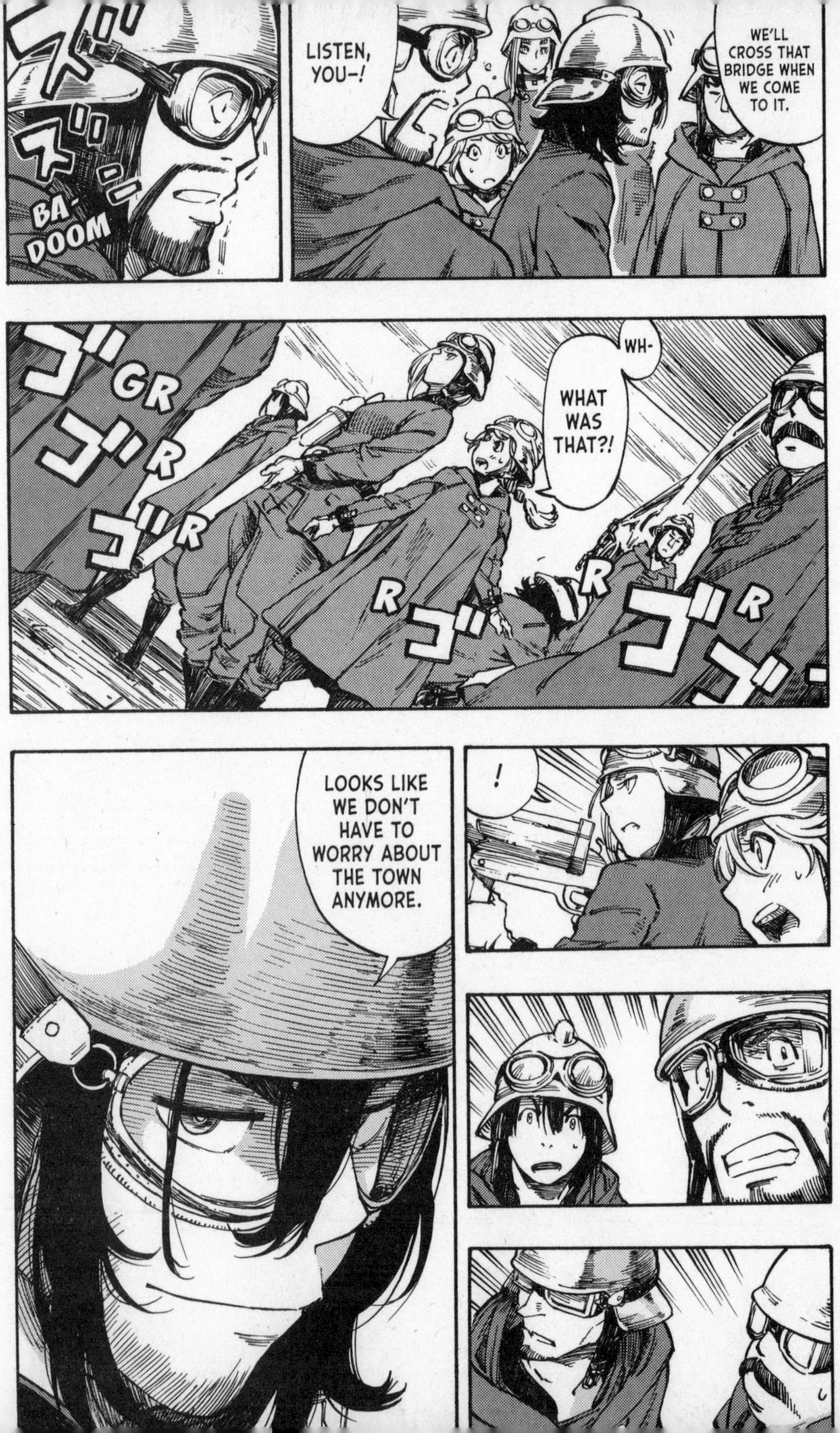
WE'LL CROSS THAT BRIDGE WHEN WE COME TO IT.
LISTEN, YOU–!
BA-DOOM
WH-
WHAT WAS THAT?!
GR
R
R
R
R
R
!
LOOKS LIKE WE DON'T HAVE TO WORRY ABOUT THE TOWN ANYMORE.

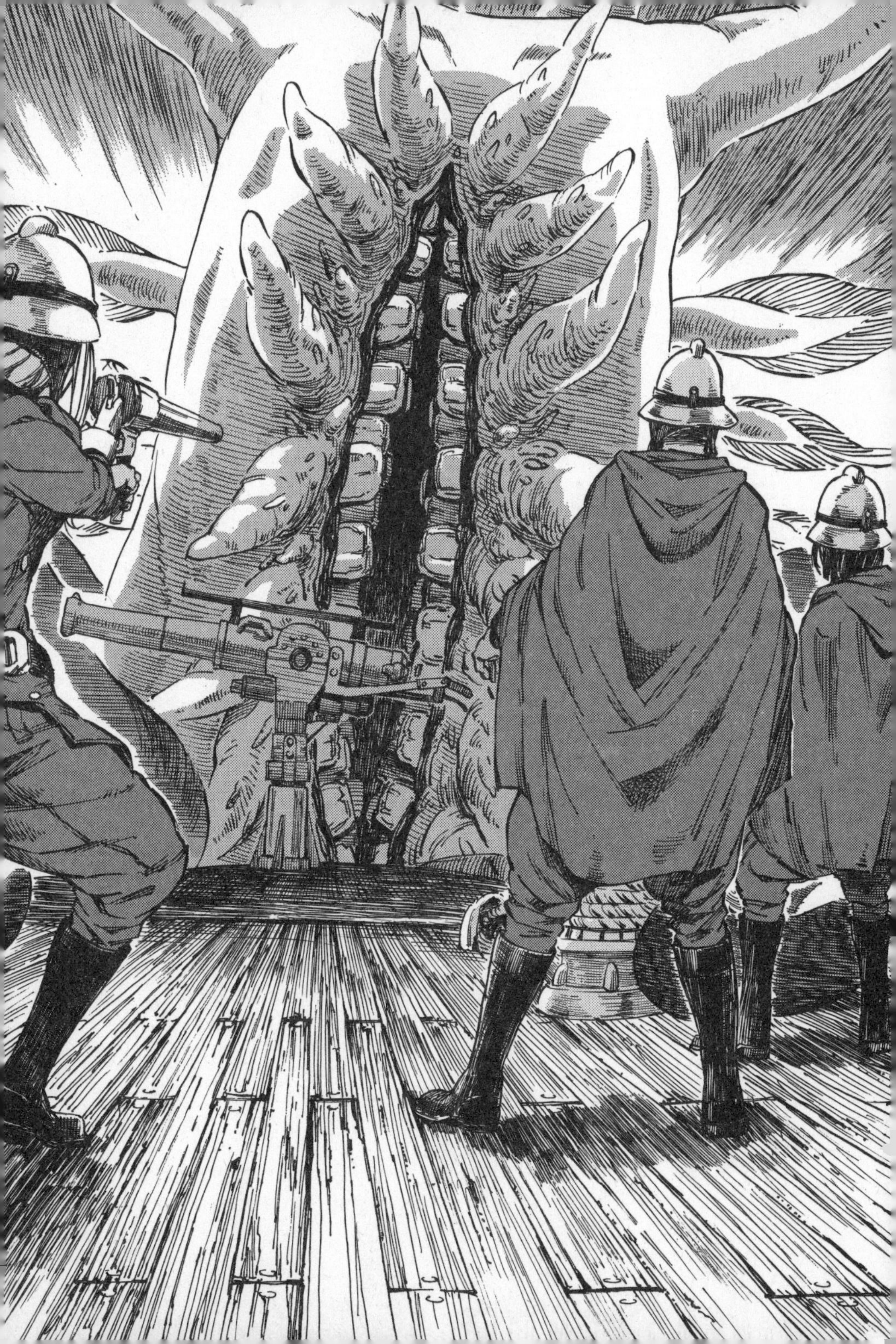

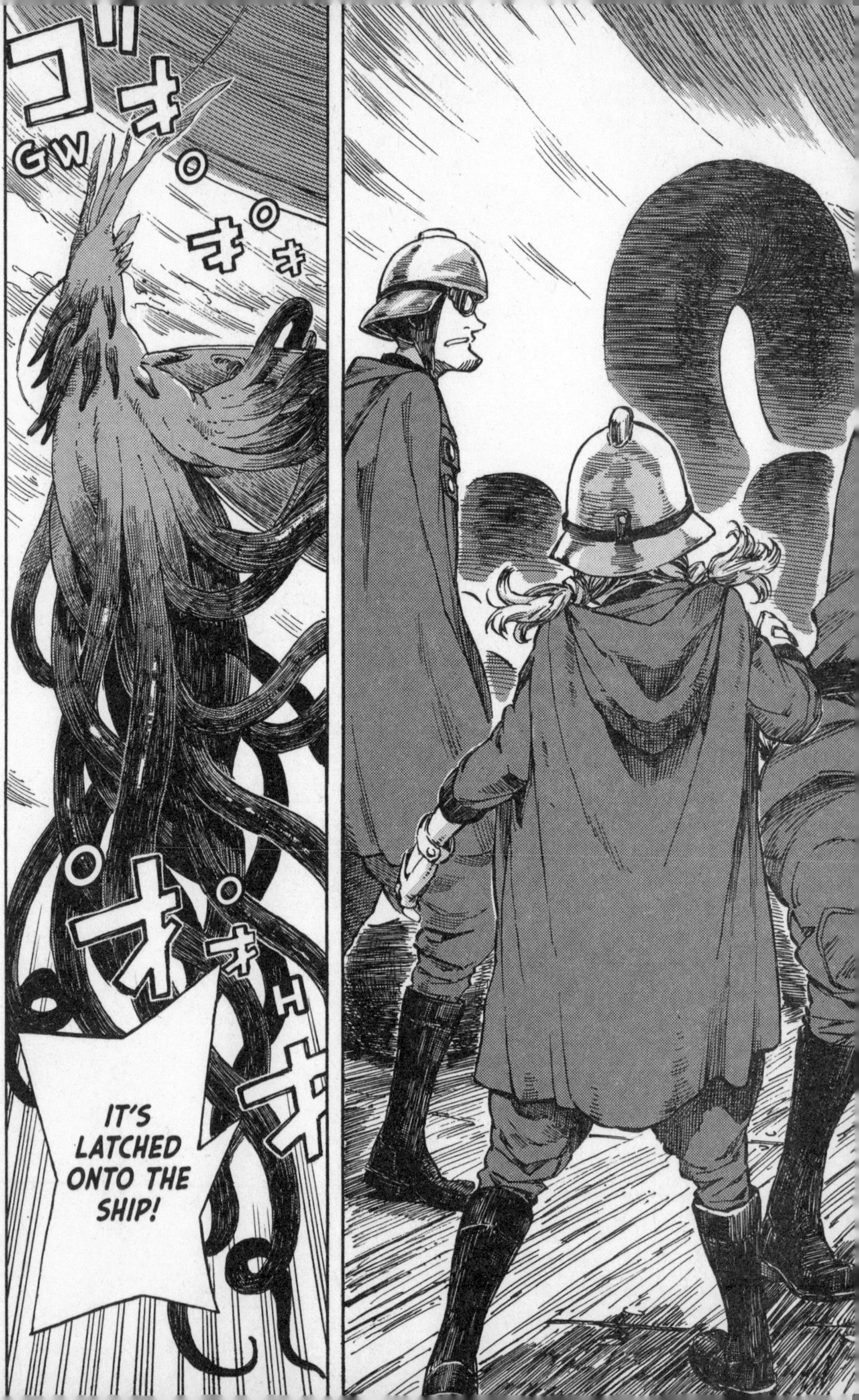
GW
H
IT'S LATCHED ONTO THE SHIP!

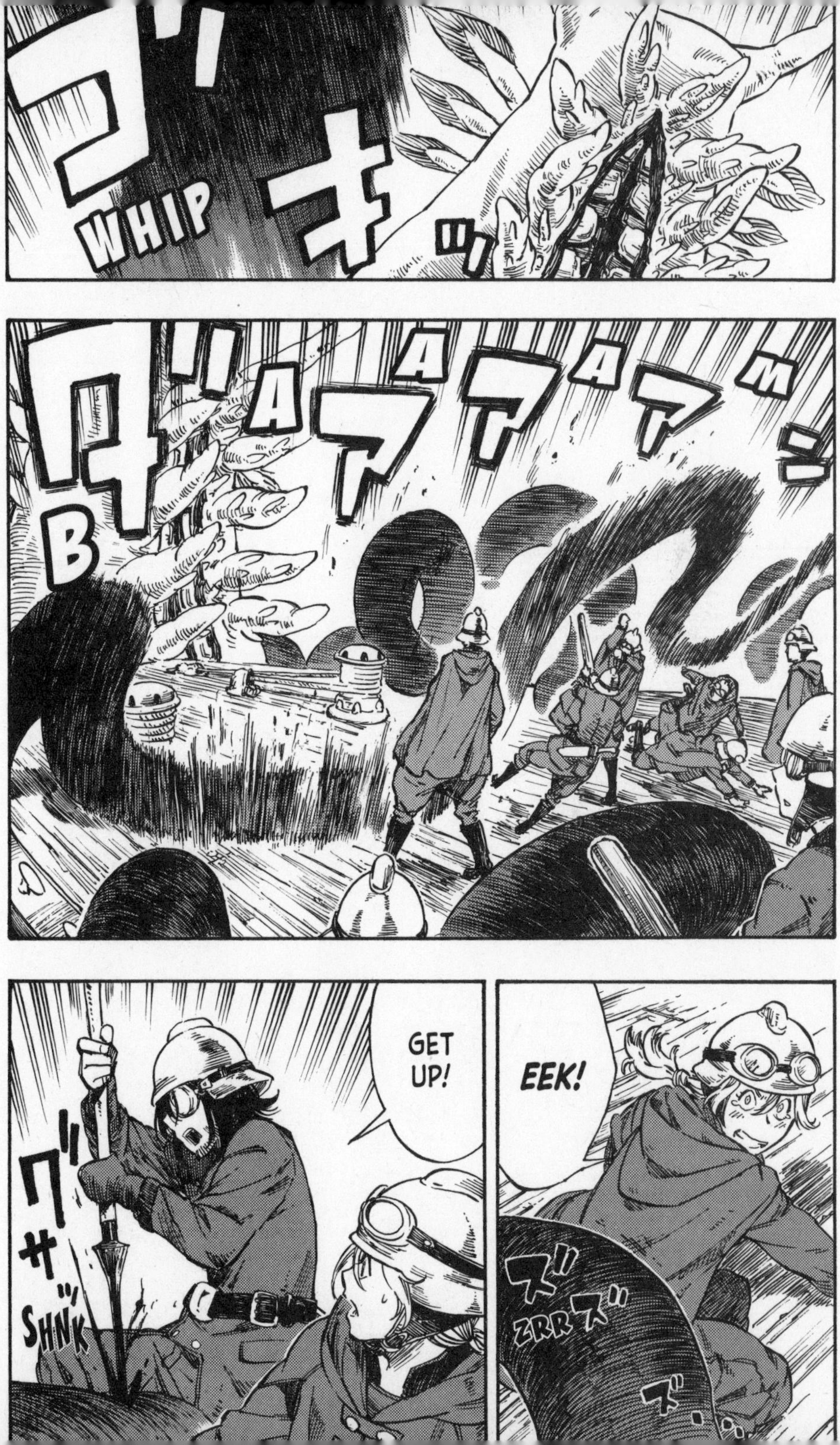
WHIP
BAAAM
EEK!
ZRR
GET UP!
SHNK

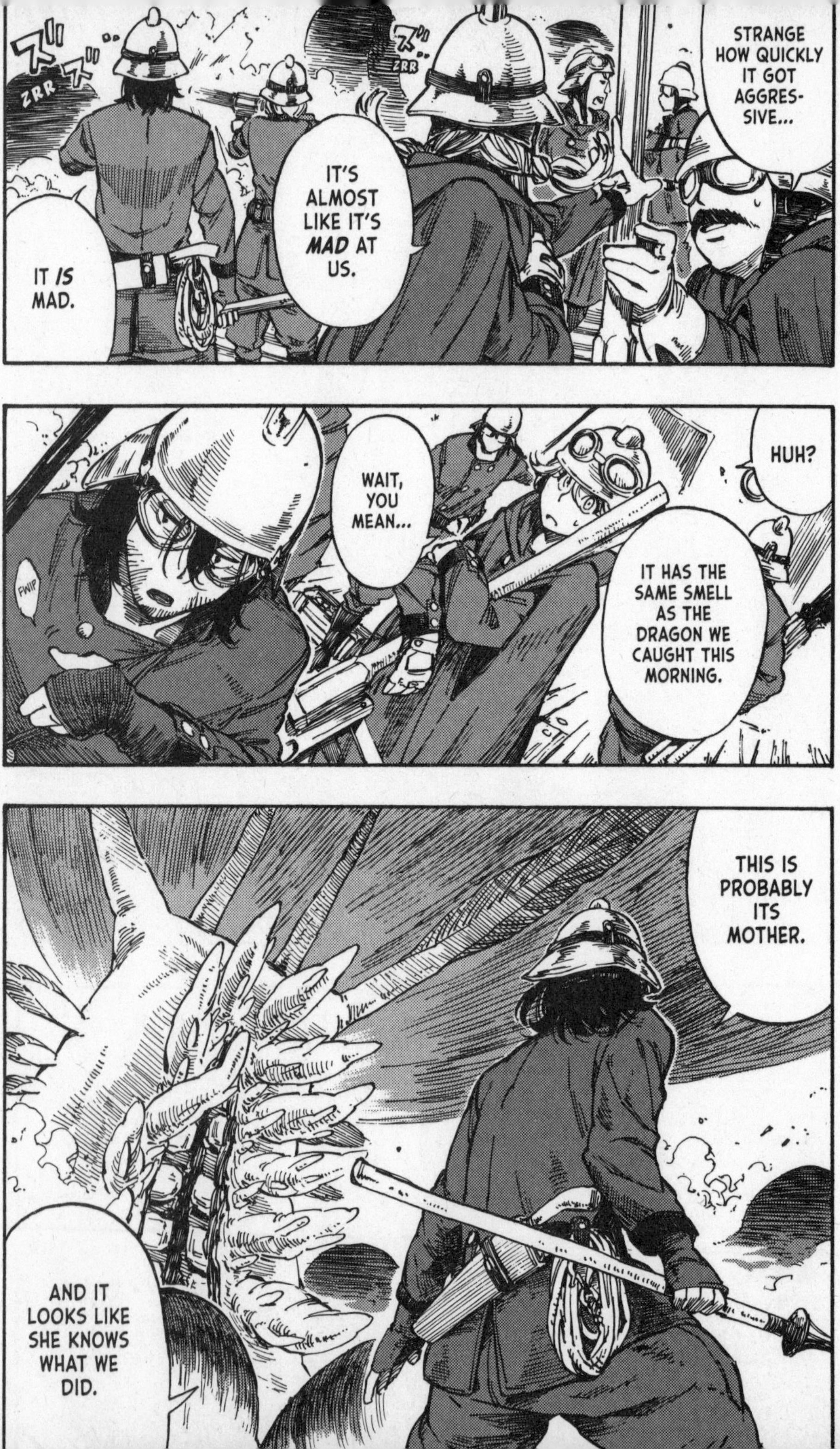
STRANGE HOW QUICKLY IT GOT AGGRES-SIVE...
ZRR
IT'S ALMOST LIKE IT'S *MAD* AT US.
ZRR
IT *IS* MAD.
HUH?
IT HAS THE SAME SMELL AS THE DRAGON WE CAUGHT THIS MORNING.
WAIT, YOU MEAN...
FWIP
THIS IS PROBABLY ITS MOTHER.
AND IT LOOKS LIKE SHE KNOWS WHAT WE DID.

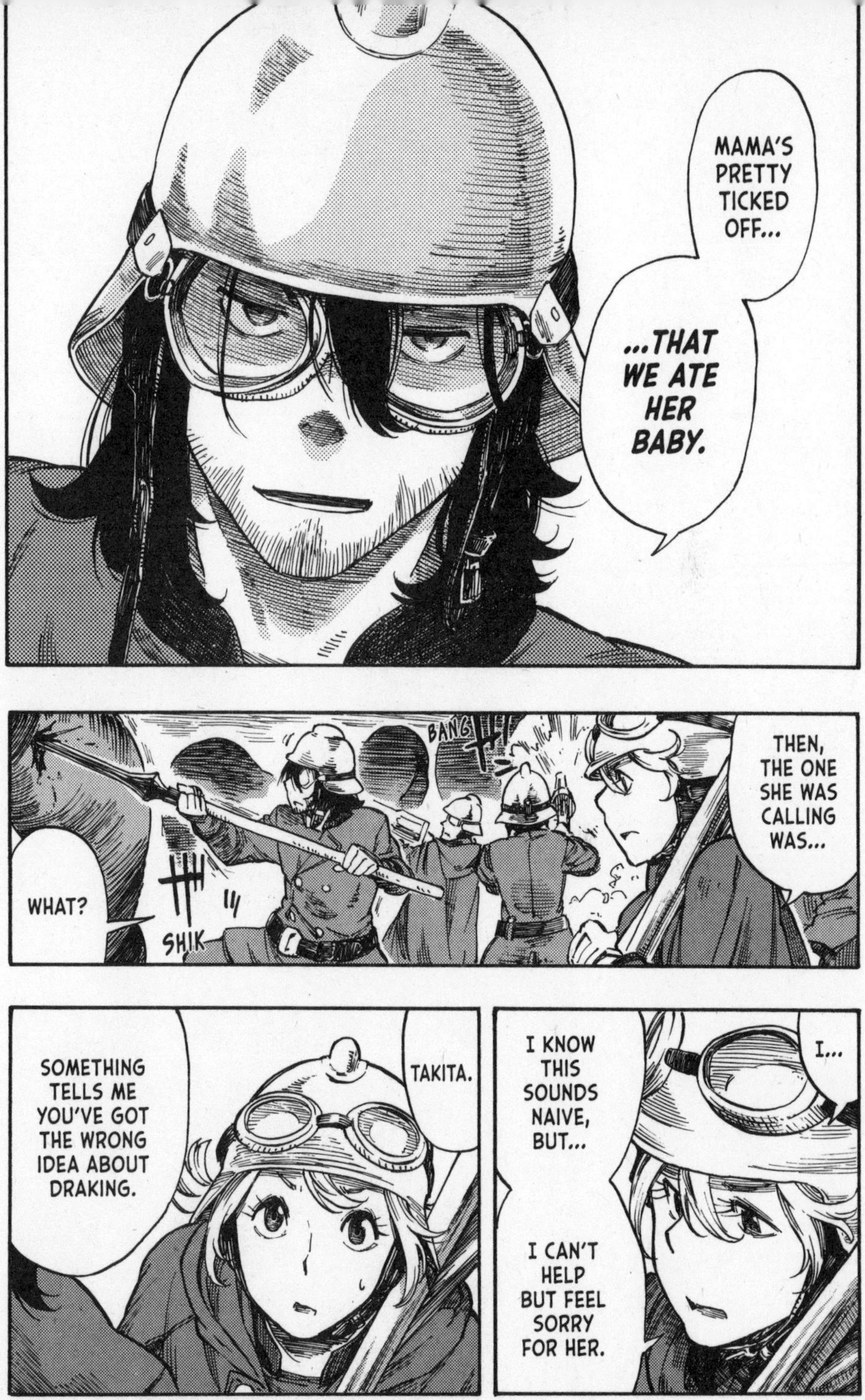
MAMA'S PRETTY TICKED OFF...
...THAT WE ATE HER BABY.
THEN, THE ONE SHE WAS CALLING WAS...
BANG
SHIK
WHAT?
I...
I KNOW THIS SOUNDS NAIVE, BUT...
I CAN'T HELP BUT FEEL SORRY FOR HER.
TAKITA.
SOMETHING TELLS ME YOU'VE GOT THE WRONG IDEA ABOUT DRAKING.

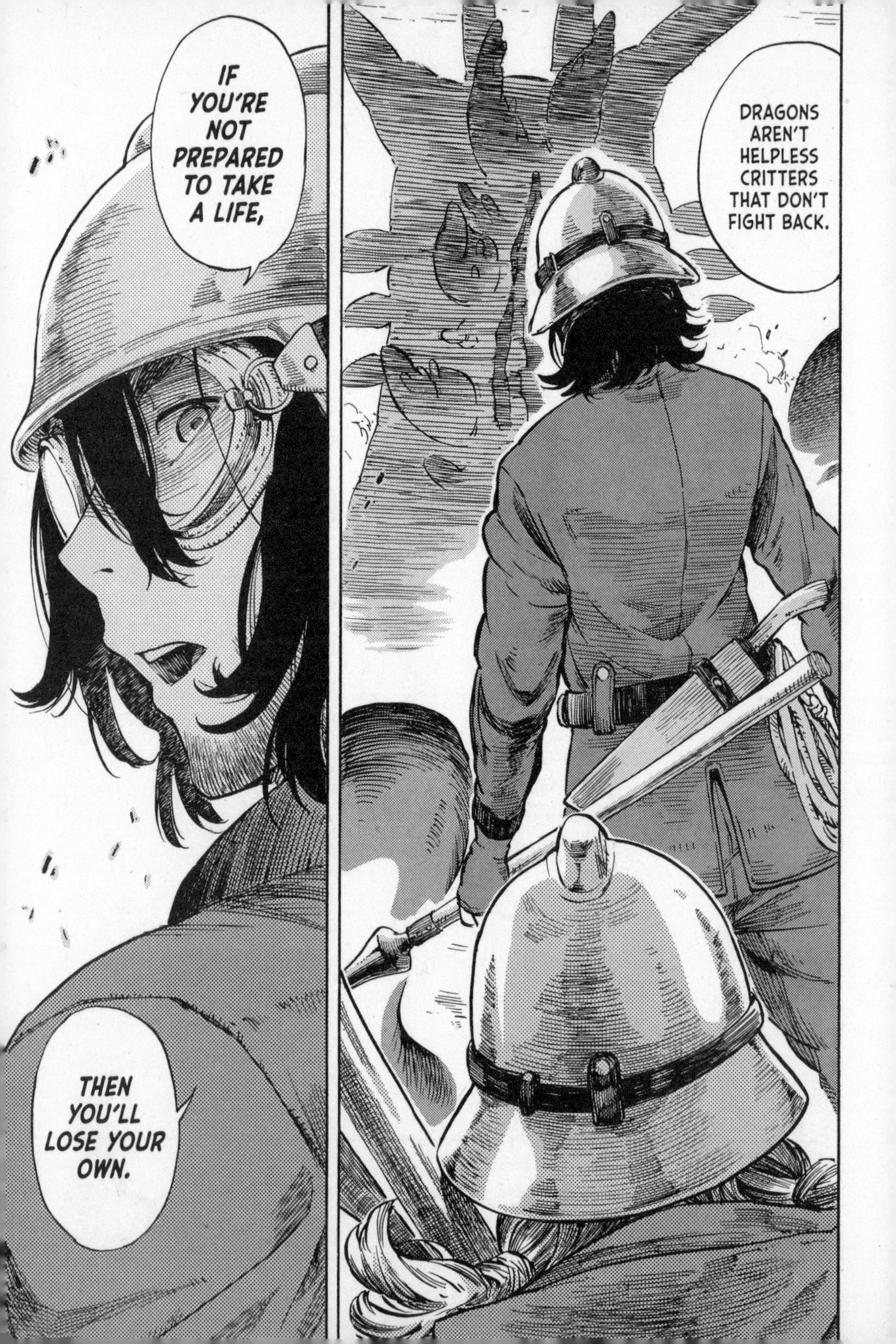
DRAGONS AREN'T HELPLESS CRITTERS THAT DON'T FIGHT BACK.
IF YOU'RE NOT PREPARED TO TAKE A LIFE,
THEN YOU'LL LOSE YOUR OWN.

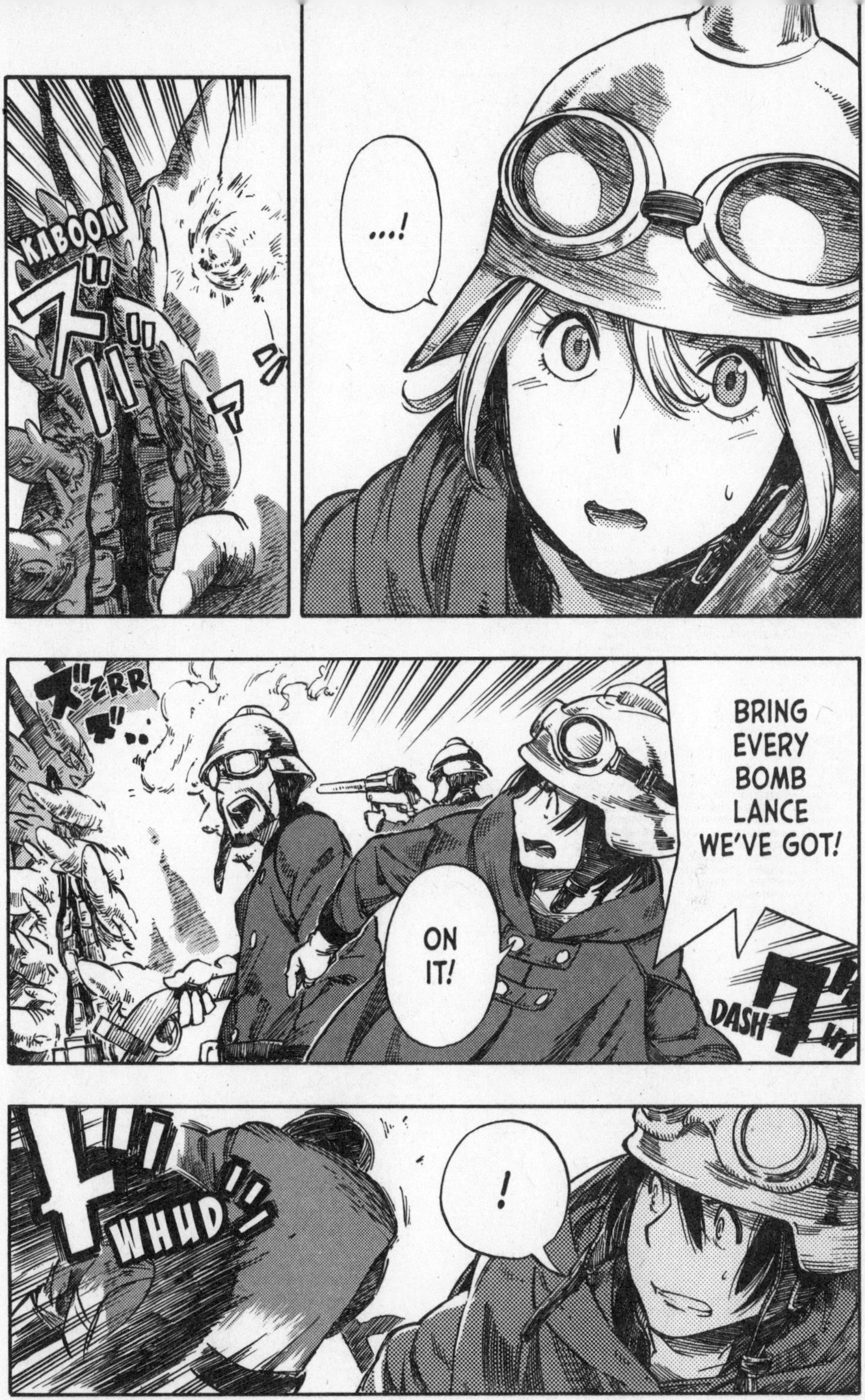
...!
KABOOM
BRING EVERY BOMB LANCE WE'VE GOT!
DASH
ON IT!
ZRR
!
WHUD

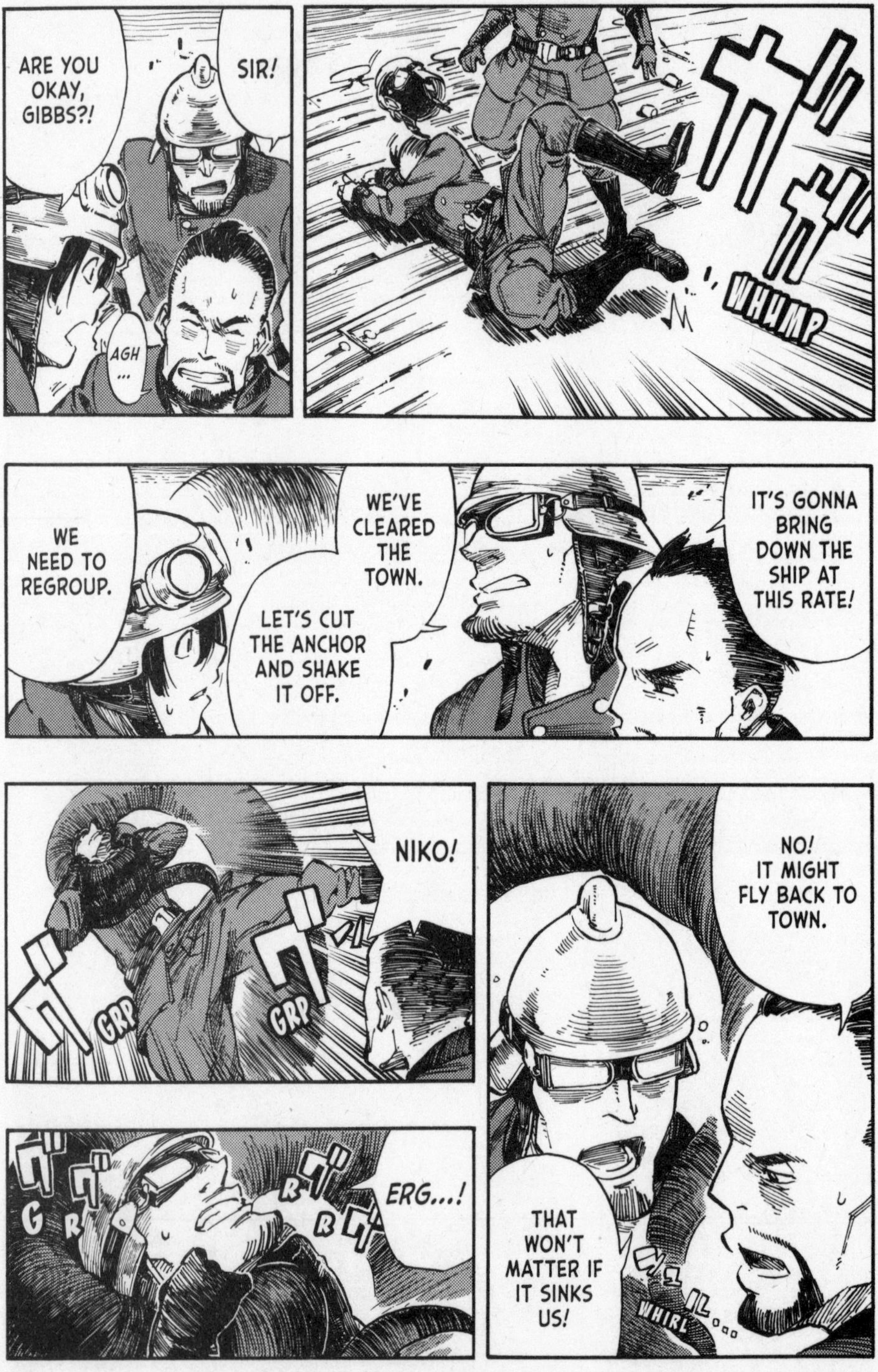
WHUMP
SIR!
ARE YOU OKAY, GIBBS?!
AGH ...
IT'S GONNA BRING DOWN THE SHIP AT THIS RATE!
WE'VE CLEARED THE TOWN.
LET'S CUT THE ANCHOR AND SHAKE IT OFF.
WE NEED TO REGROUP.
NO! IT MIGHT FLY BACK TO TOWN.
THAT WON'T MATTER IF IT SINKS US!
WHIRL...
NIKO!
GRP
GRP
ERG...!
G R R R R

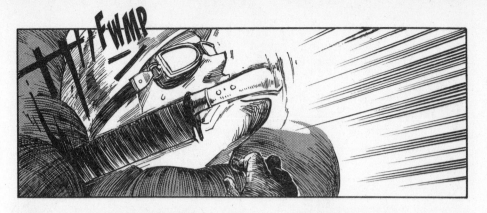

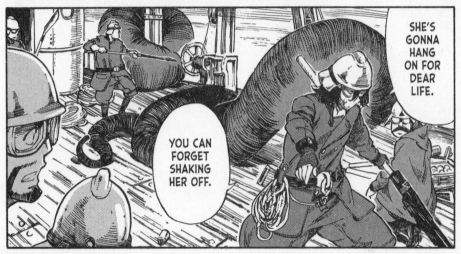

FWMP
SHE'S GONNA HANG ON FOR DEAR LIFE.
YOU CAN FORGET SHAKING HER OFF.
WE HAVE TO TAKE HER DOWN HERE AND NOW.
COULD YOU BE A LITTLE MORE GENTLE NEXT TIME?!
THUD

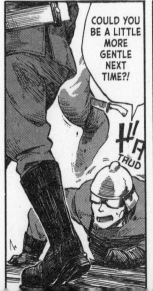

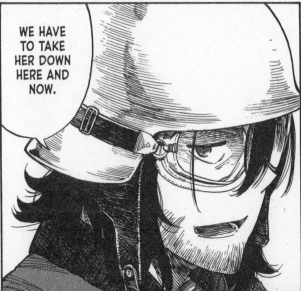

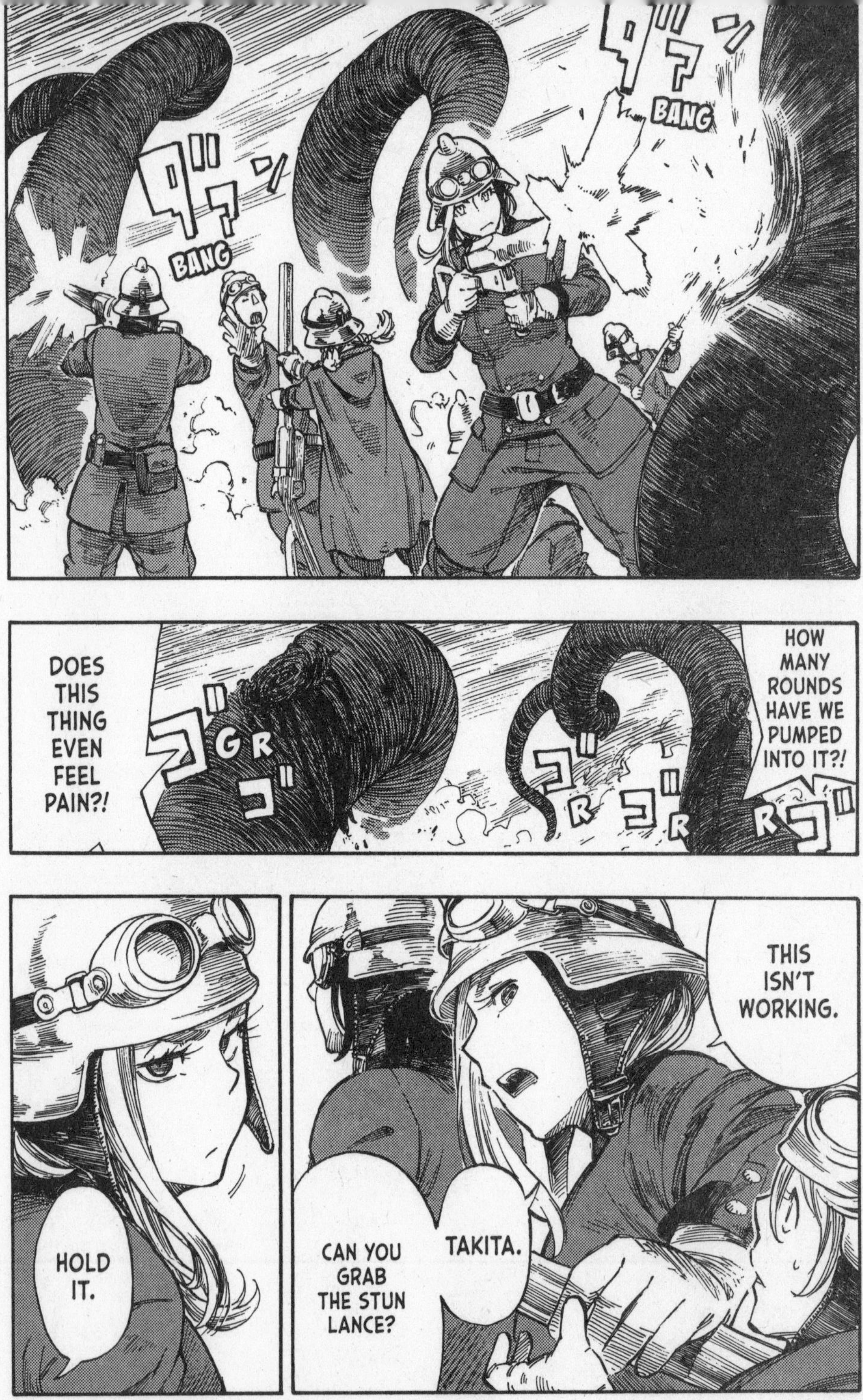
BANG
BANG
HOW MANY ROUNDS HAVE WE PUMPED INTO IT?!
R
R
R
GR
DOES THIS THING EVEN FEEL PAIN?!
THIS ISN'T WORKING.
TAKITA.
CAN YOU GRAB THE STUN LANCE?
HOLD IT.

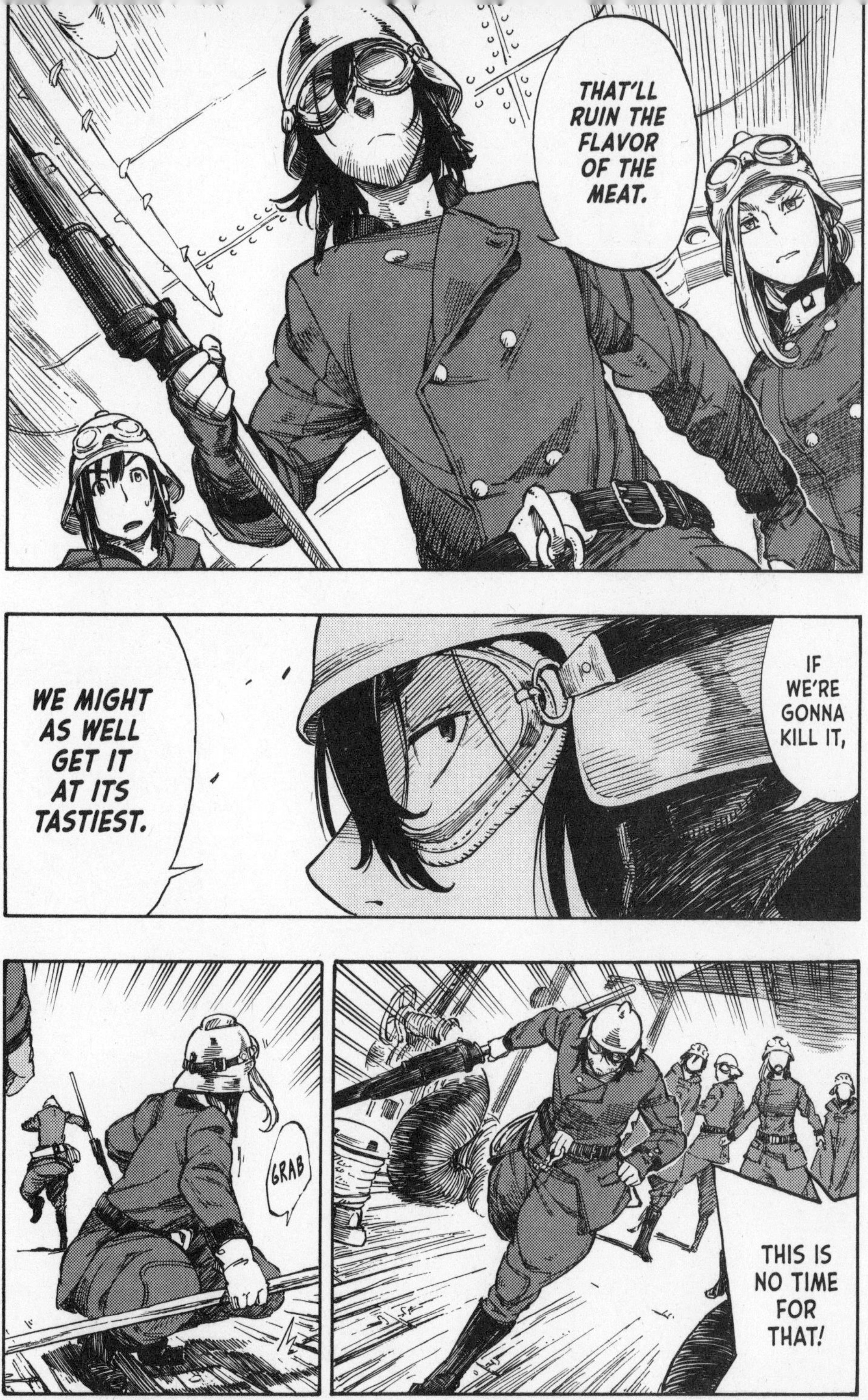
THAT'LL RUIN THE FLAVOR OF THE MEAT.
IF WE'RE GONNA KILL IT,
WE MIGHT AS WELL GET IT AT ITS TASTIEST.
THIS IS NO TIME FOR THAT!
GRAB

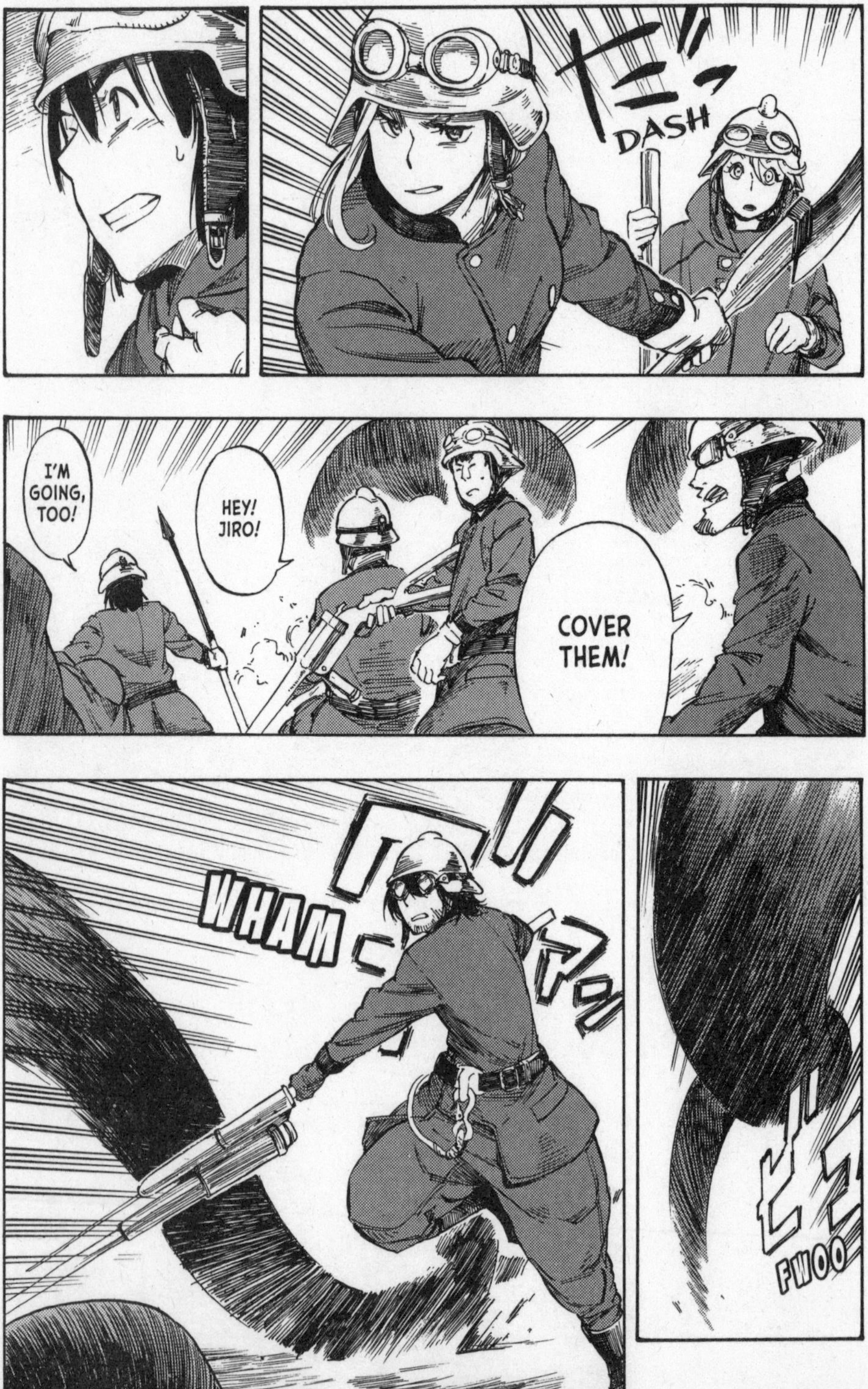
DASH
COVER THEM!
HEY! JIRO!
I'M GOING, TOO!
FWOO
WHAM

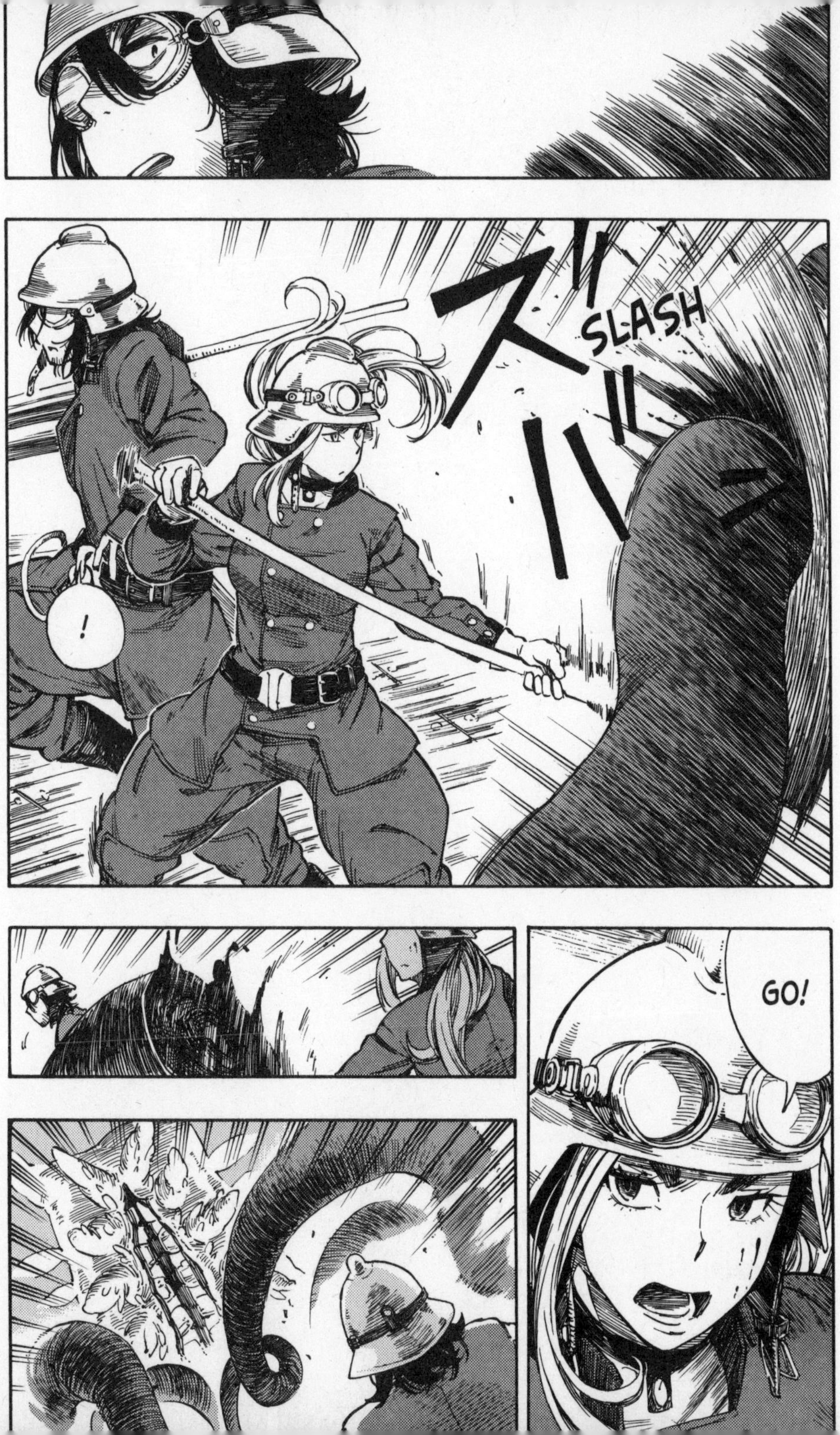
SLASH
!
GO!

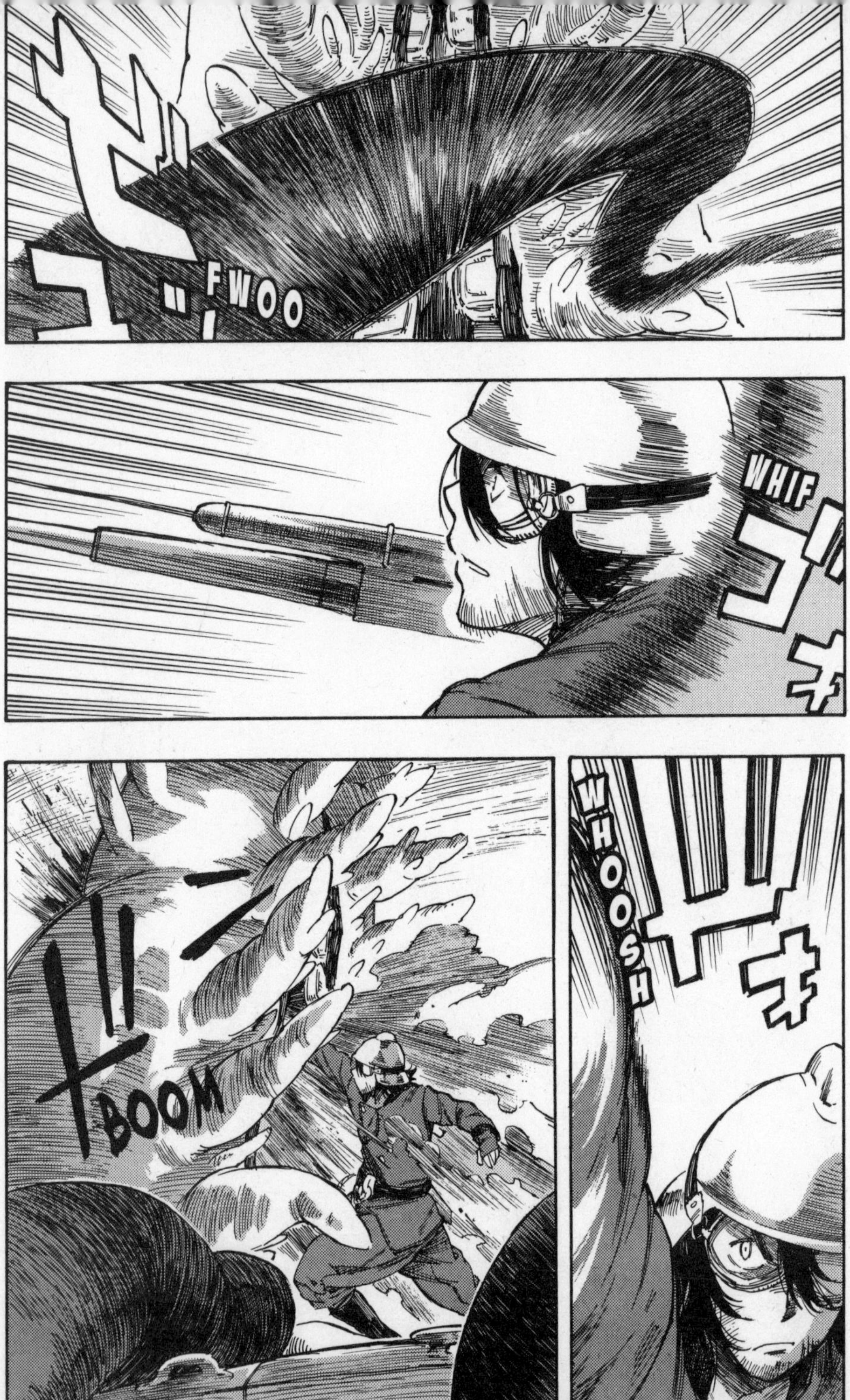
FWOO
WHIF
WHOOSH
BOOM

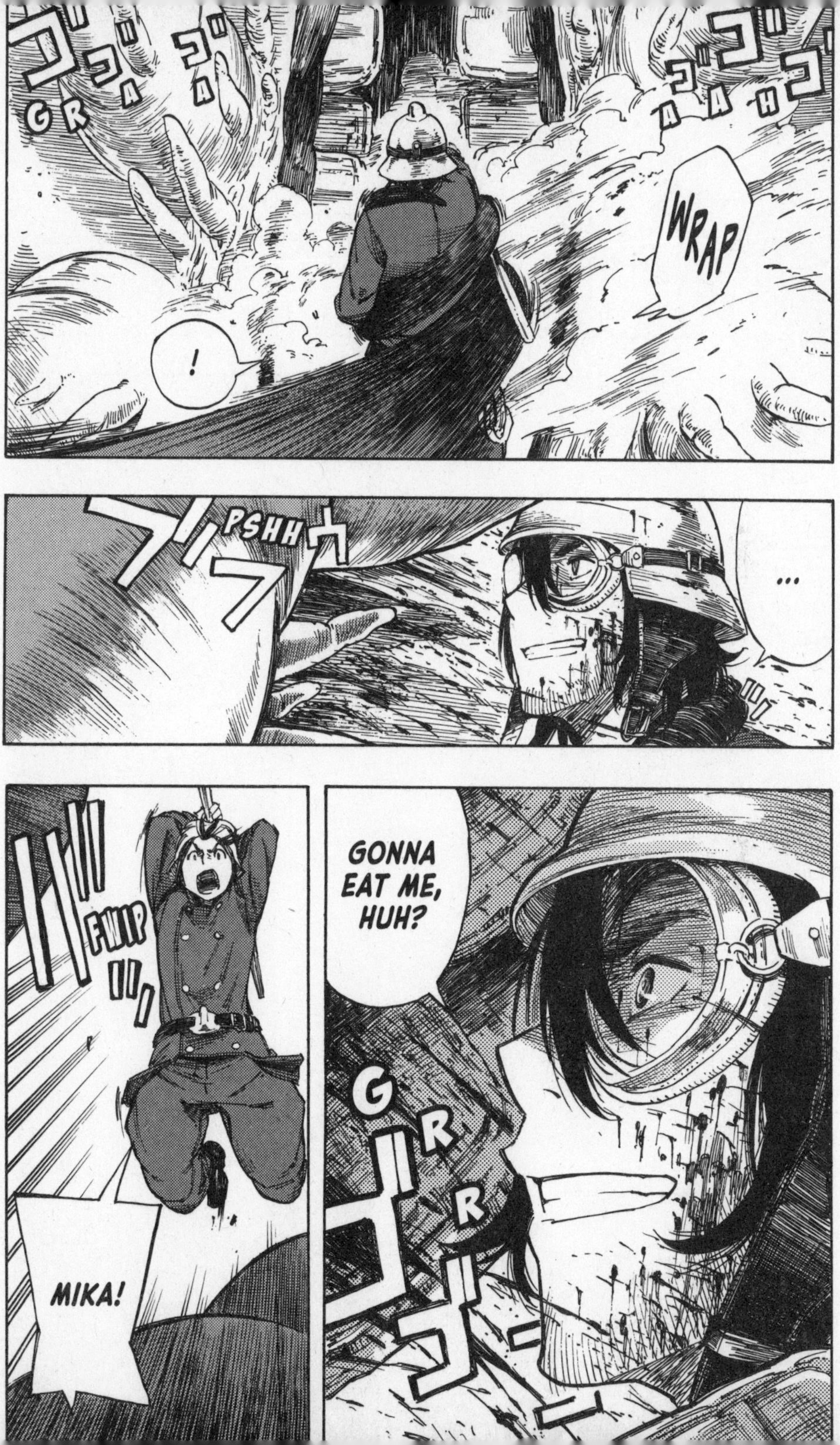

GRAAAH
WRAP
!
GRAA
PSHH
...
GONNA EAT ME, HUH?
GRRR
FWIP
MIKA!

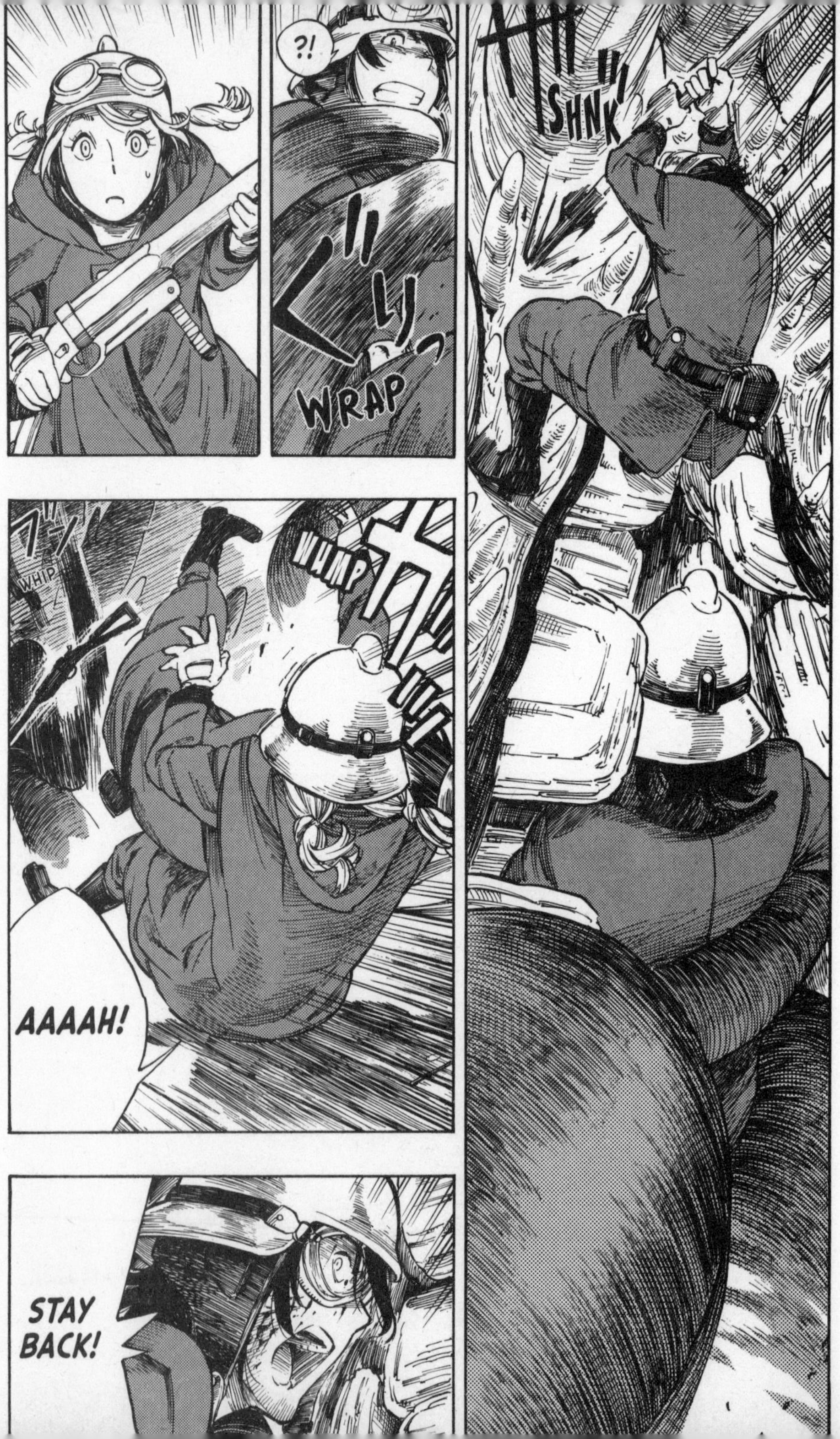
SHNK
?!
WRAP
WUMP
WHIP
AAAAH!
STAY BACK!

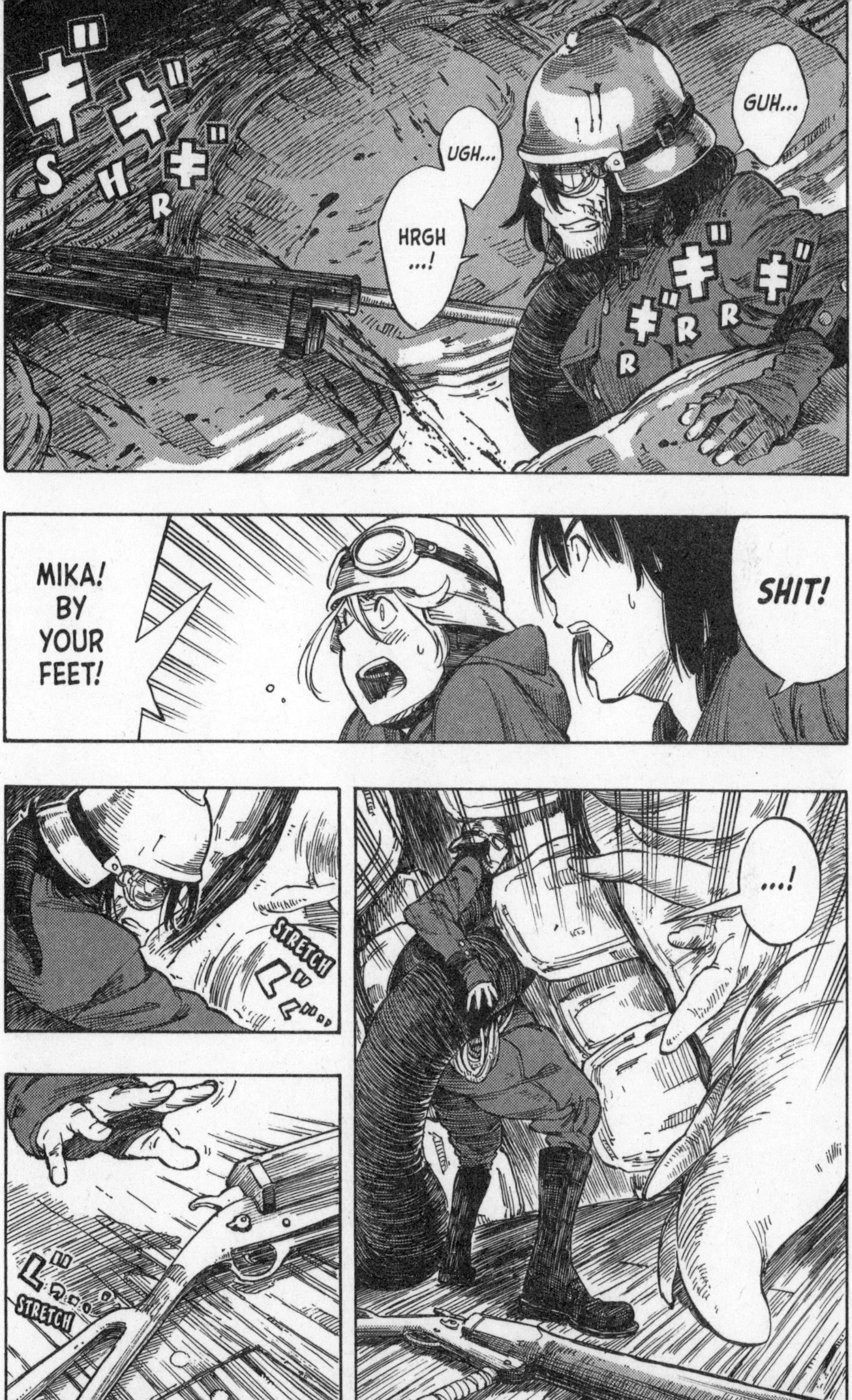
GUH...
UGH...
HRGH ...!
SHR
R R R R
SHIT!
MIKA! BY YOUR FEET!
...!
STRETCH
STRETCH

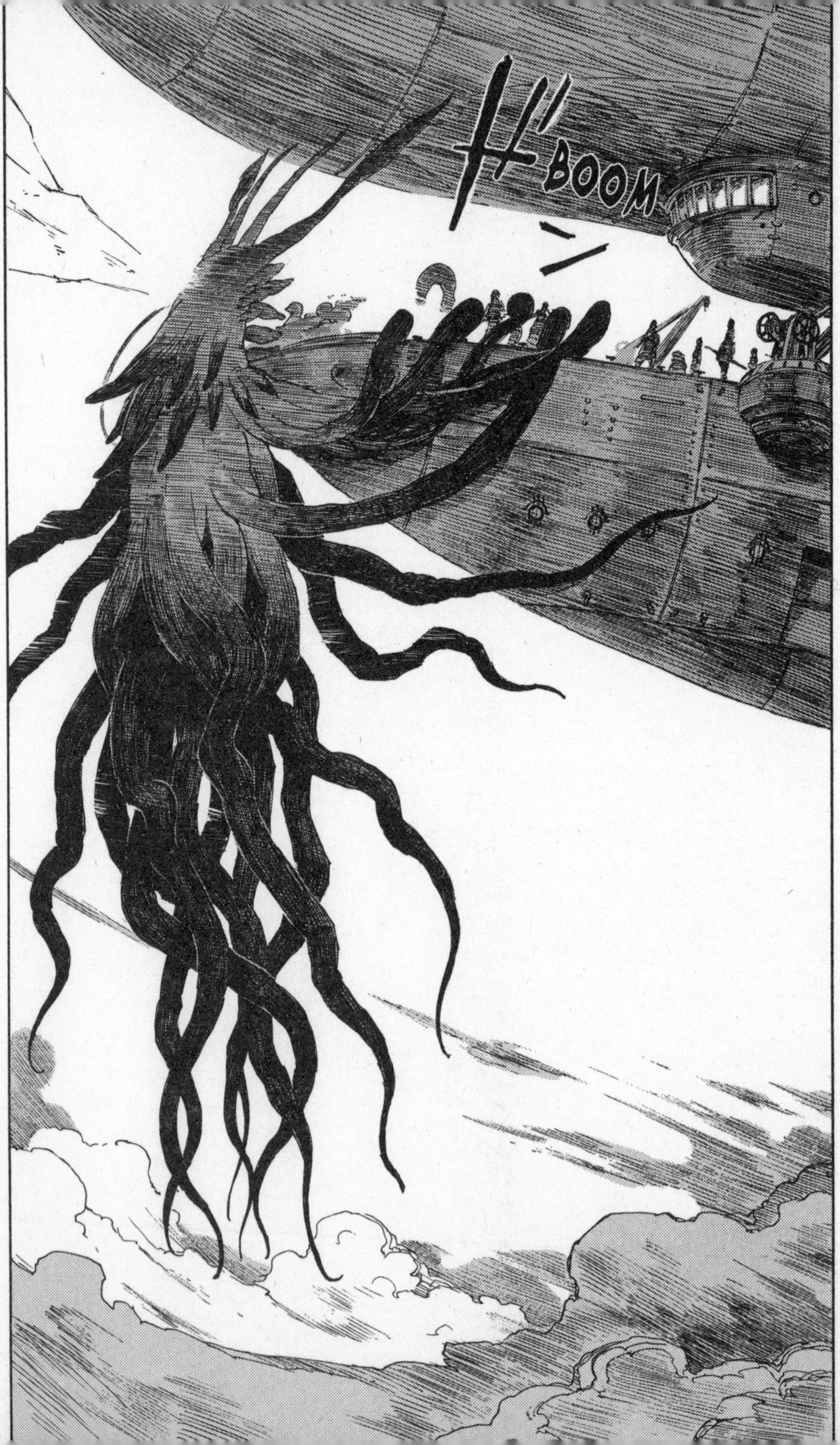
BOOM

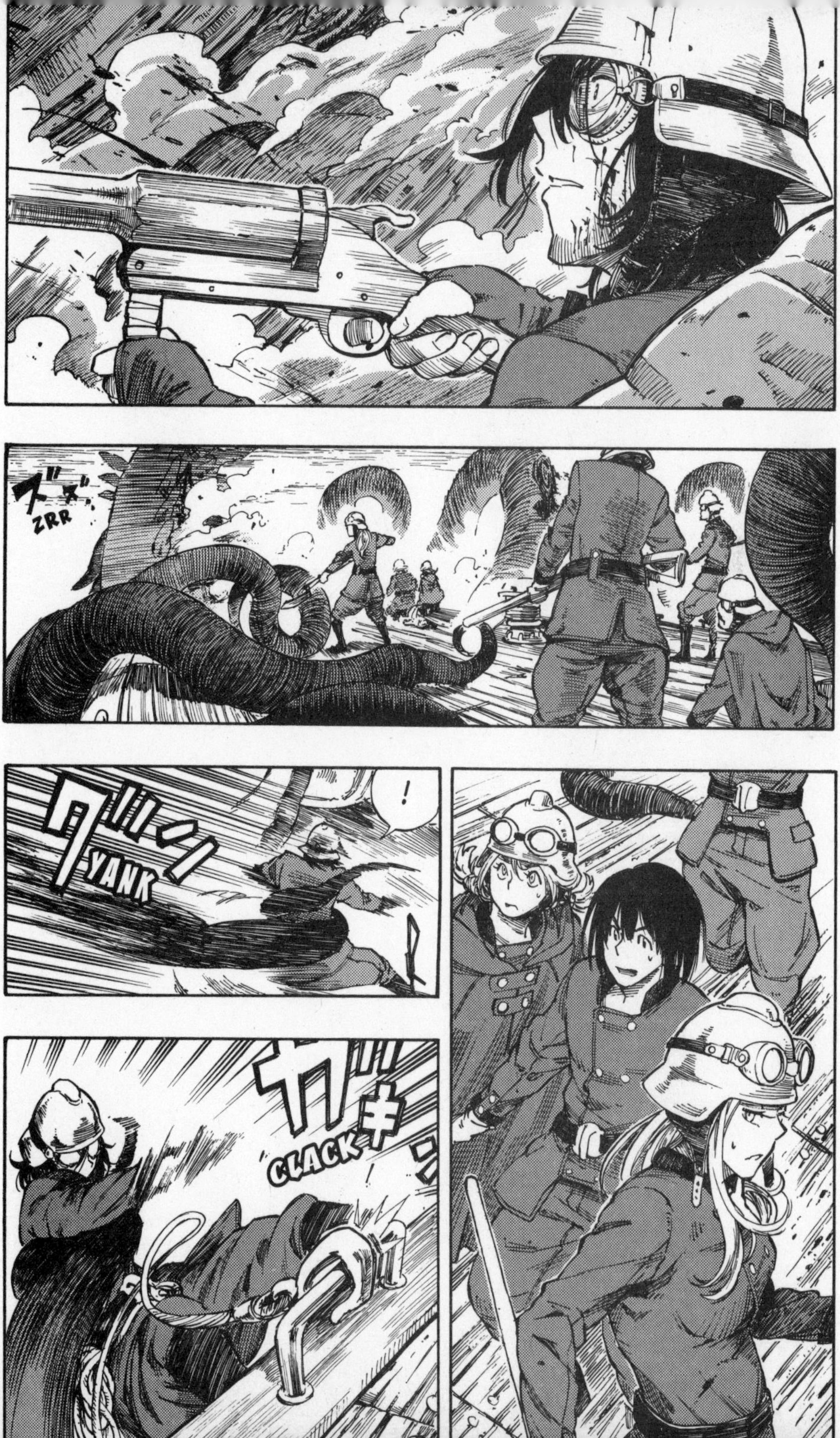
ズズ
ZRR
グイッ
YANK
!
ガキッ
CLACK

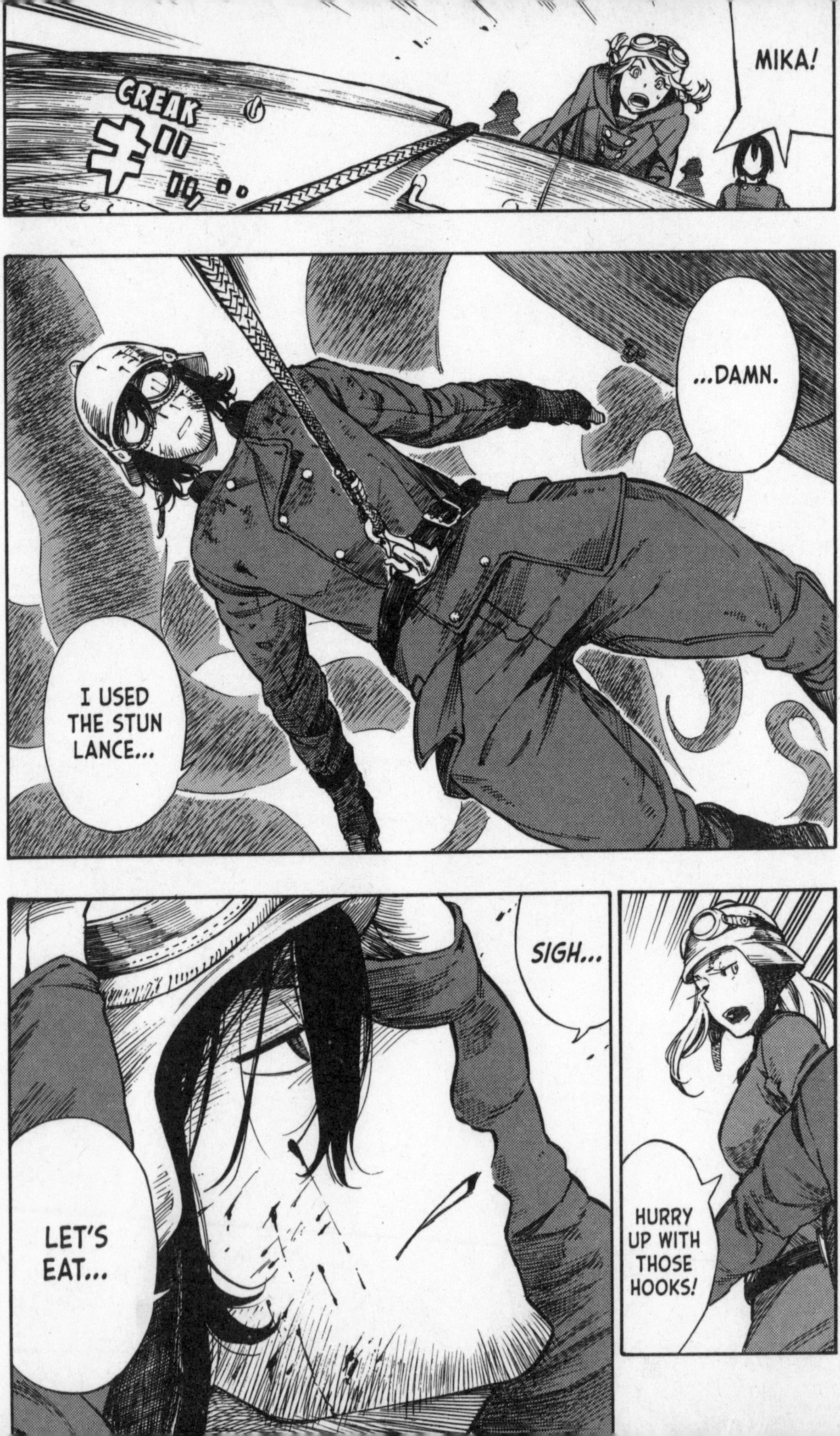
MIKA!
CREAK
...DAMN.
I USED THE STUN LANCE...
HURRY UP WITH THOSE HOOKS!
SIGH...
LET'S EAT...

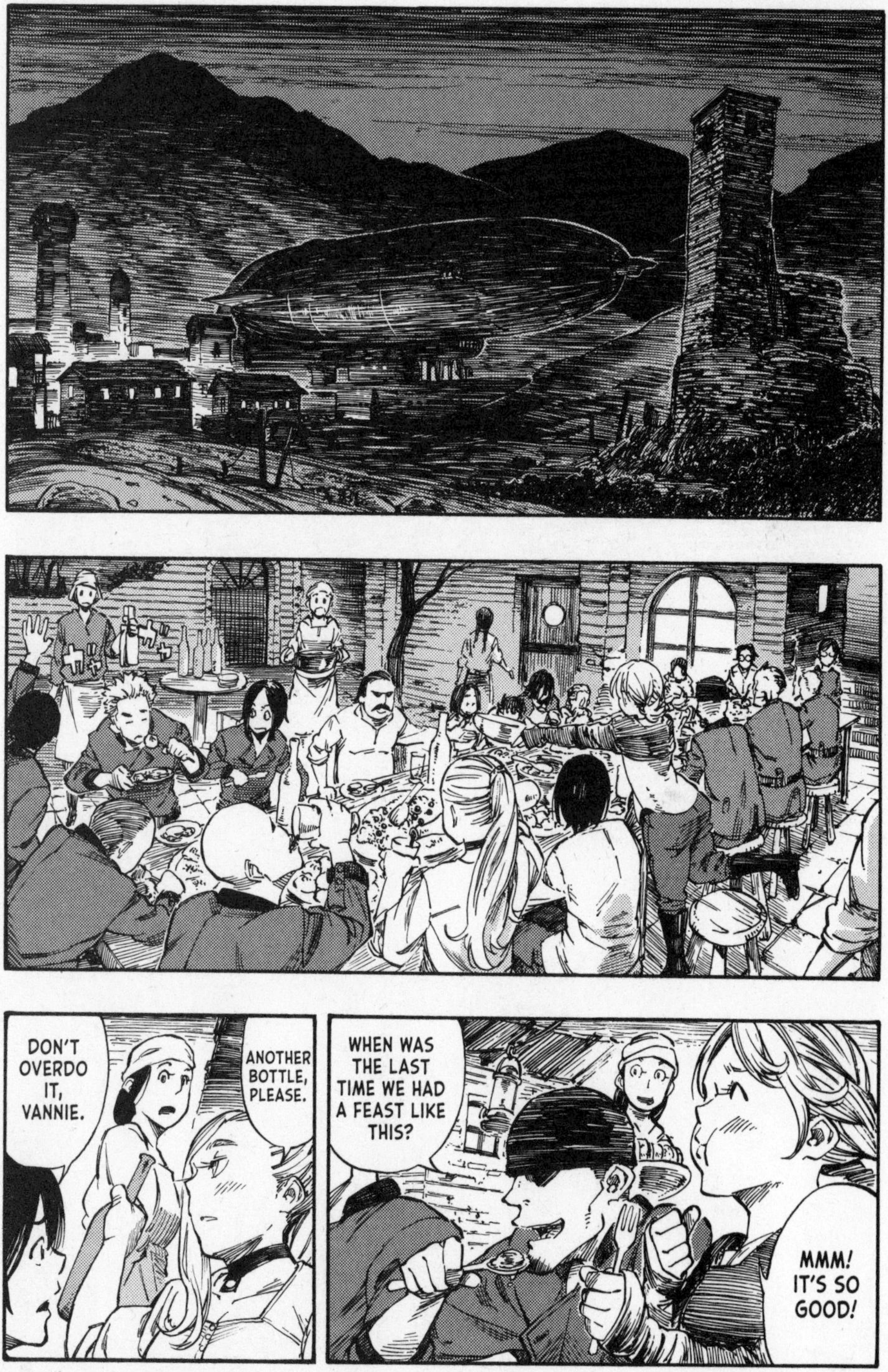
WHEN WAS THE LAST TIME WE HAD A FEAST LIKE THIS?
MMM! IT'S SO GOOD!
ANOTHER BOTTLE, PLEASE.
DON'T OVERDO IT, VANNIE.

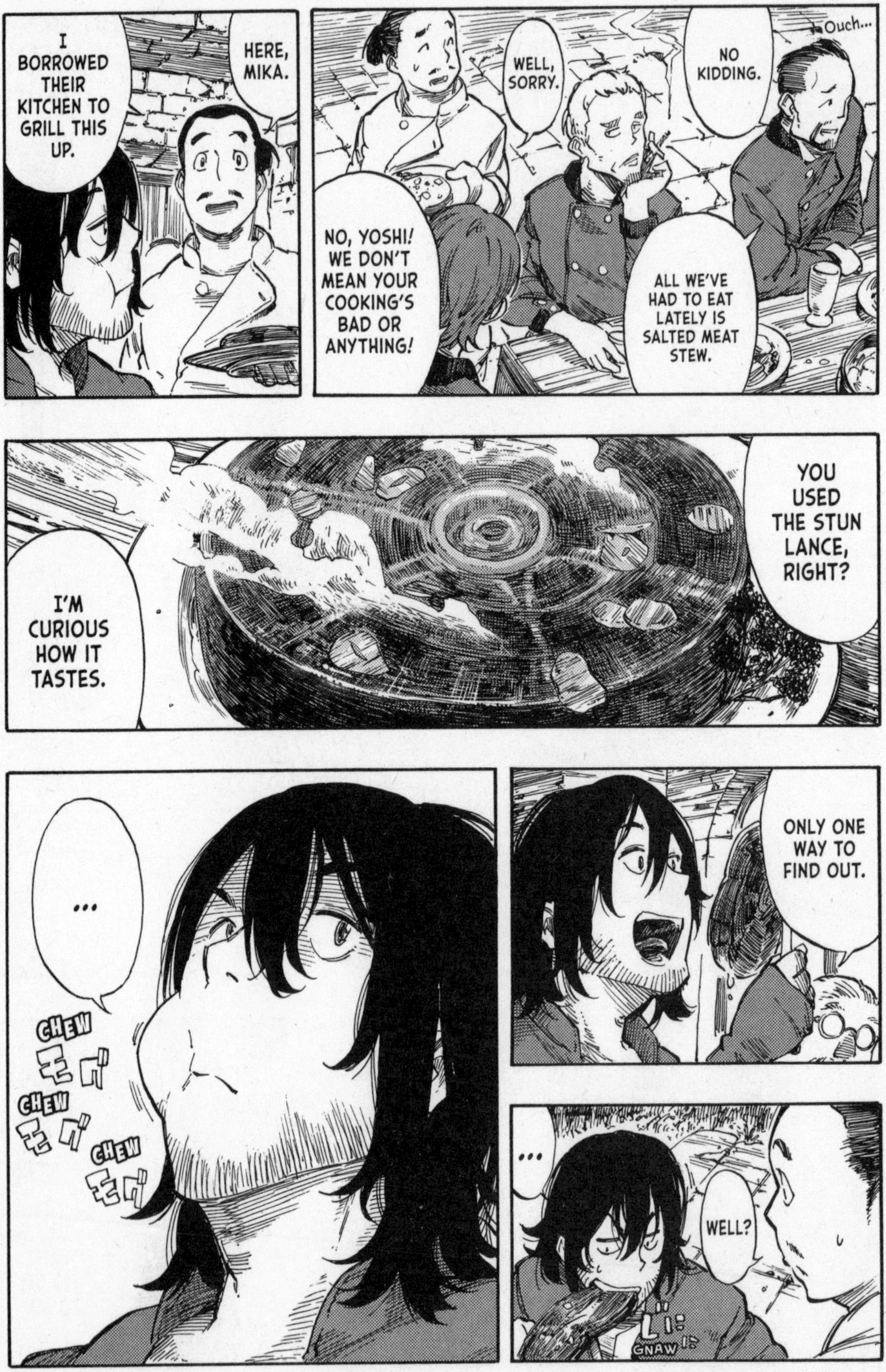
Ouch...
NO KIDDING.
WELL, SORRY.
ALL WE'VE HAD TO EAT LATELY IS SALTED MEAT STEW.
NO, YOSHI! WE DON'T MEAN YOUR COOKING'S BAD OR ANYTHING!
HERE, MIKA.
I BORROWED THEIR KITCHEN TO GRILL THIS UP.
YOU USED THE STUN LANCE, RIGHT?
I'M CURIOUS HOW IT TASTES.
ONLY ONE WAY TO FIND OUT.
WELL?
...
GNAW
...
CHEW
CHEW
CHEW

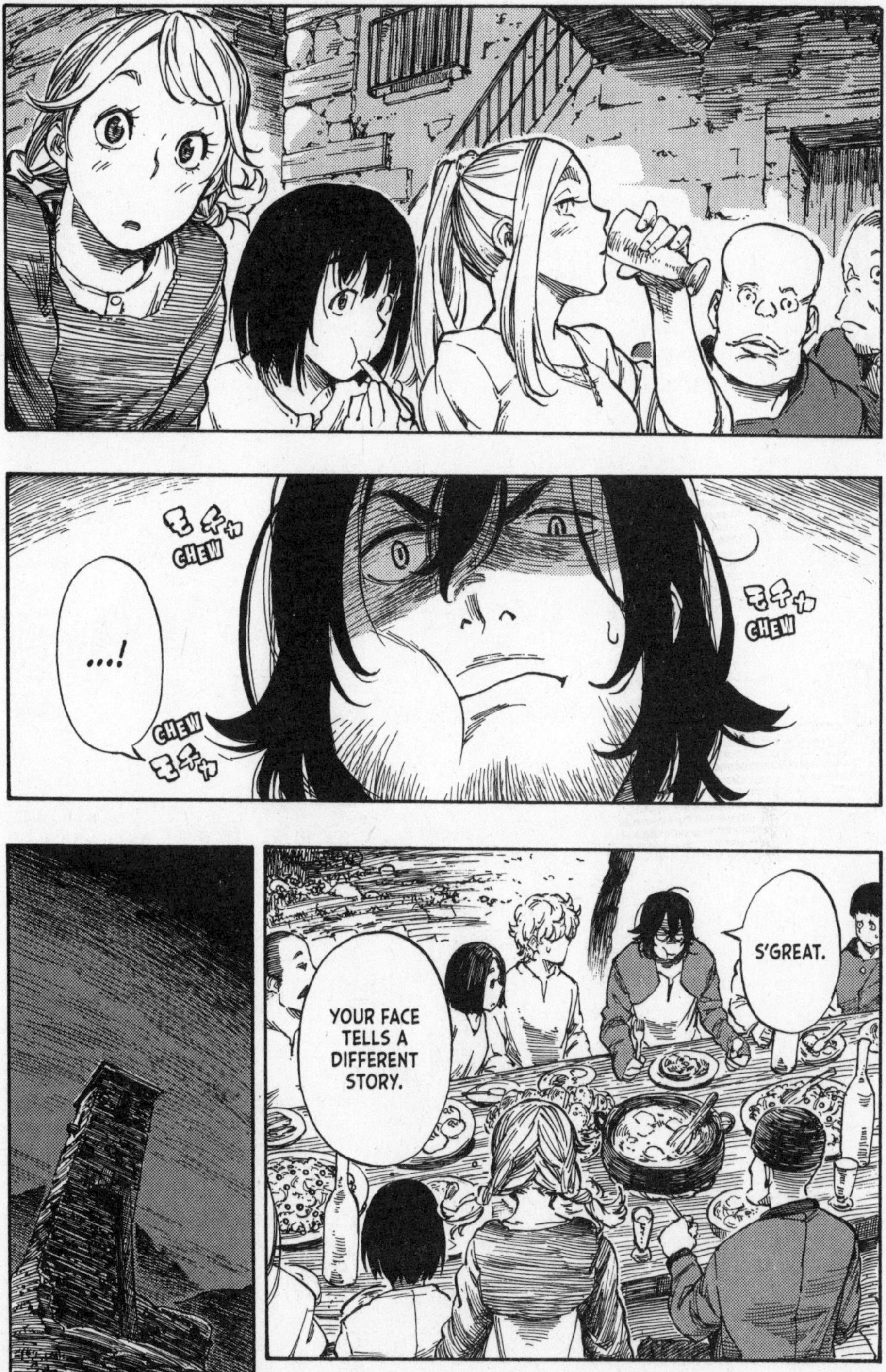
CHEW
CHEW
...!
CHEW
S'GREAT.
YOUR FACE TELLS A DIFFERENT STORY.

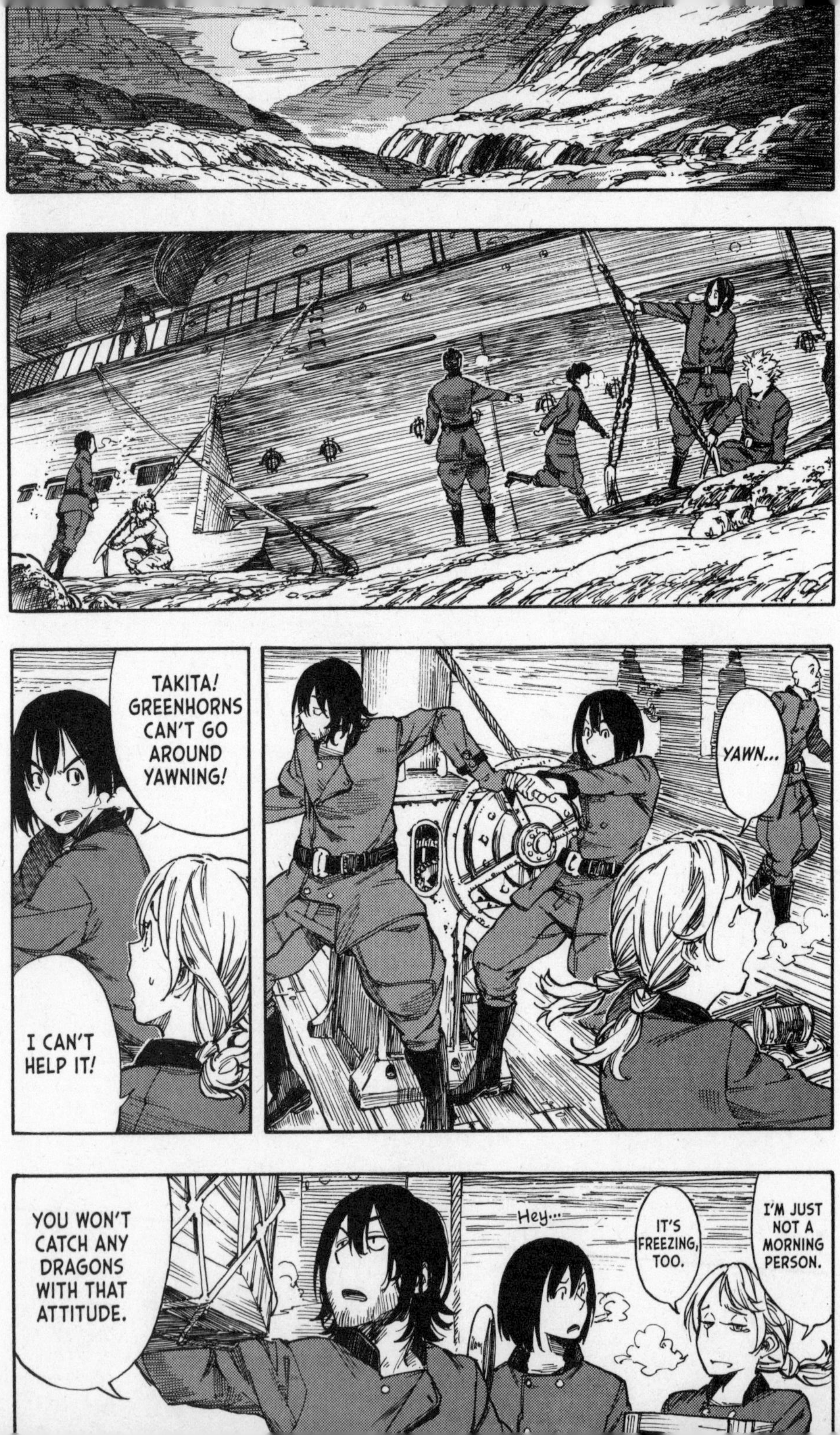
YAWN...
TAKITA! GREENHORNS CAN'T GO AROUND YAWNING!
I CAN'T HELP IT!
I'M JUST NOT A MORNING PERSON.
IT'S FREEZING, TOO.
Hey...
YOU WON'T CATCH ANY DRAGONS WITH THAT ATTITUDE.

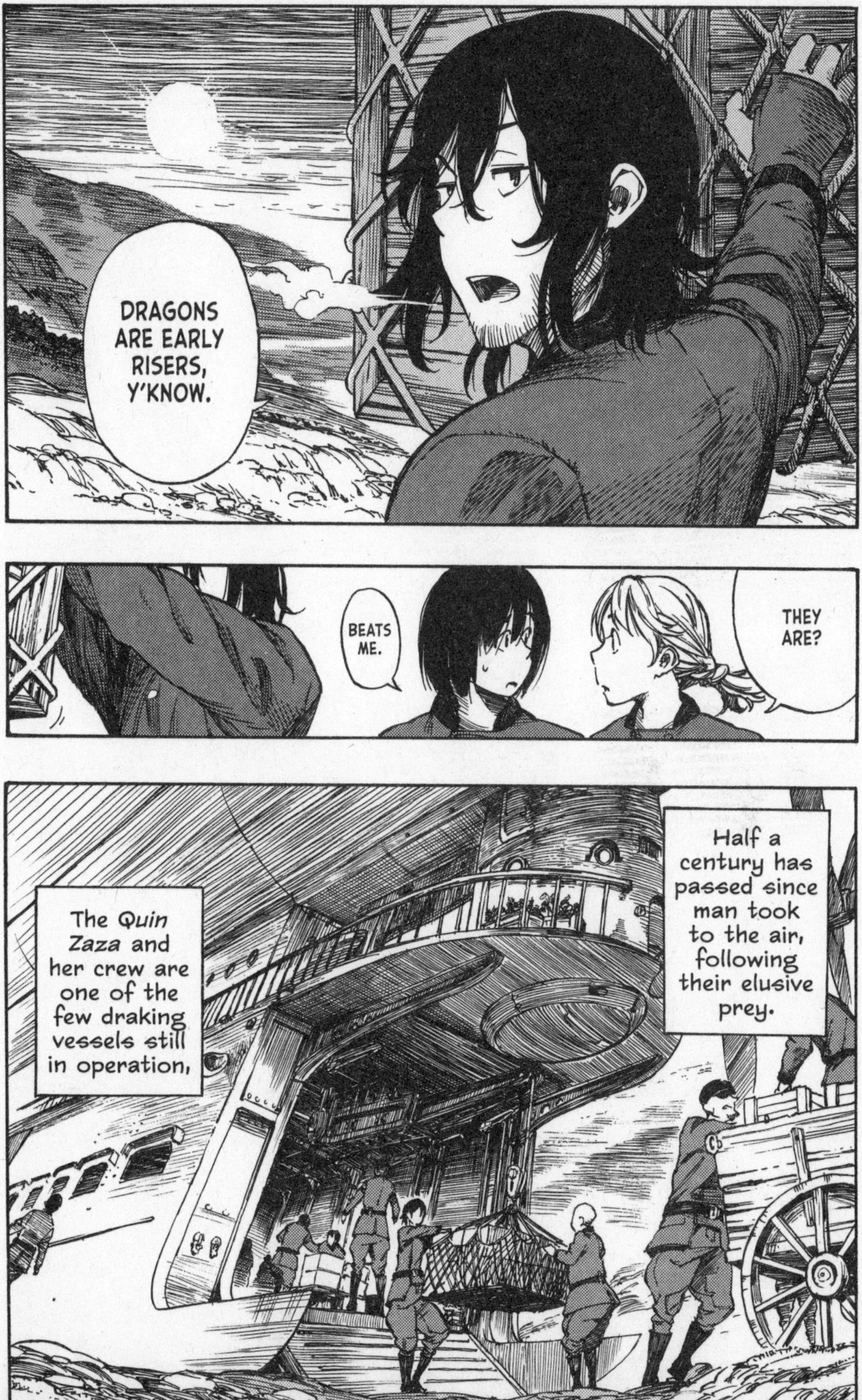
DRAGONS ARE EARLY RISERS, Y'KNOW.
THEY ARE?
BEATS ME.
Half a century has passed since man took to the air, following their elusive prey.
The *Quin Zaza* and her crew are one of the few draking vessels still in operation,

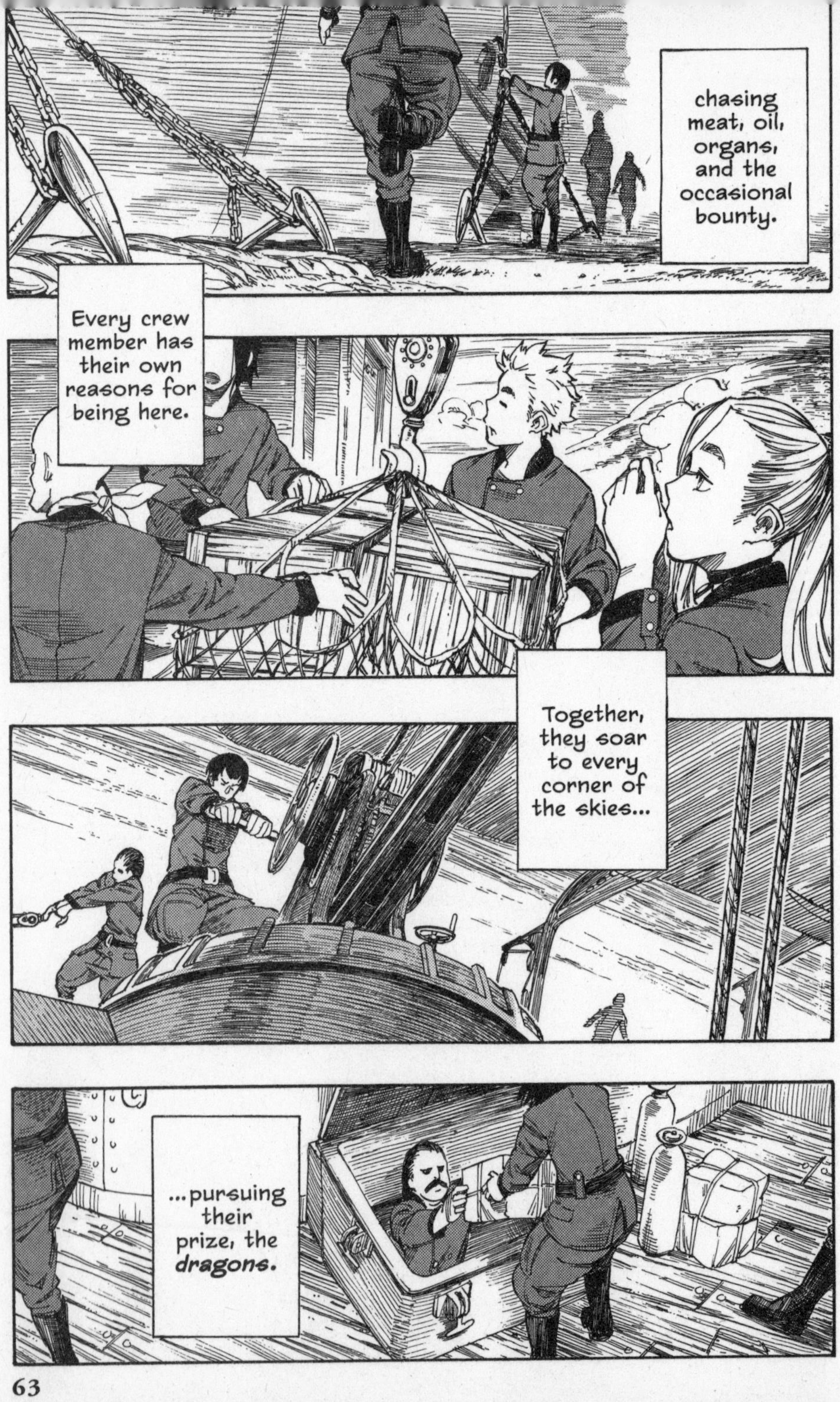
chasing meat, oil, organs, and the occasional bounty.
Every crew member has their own reasons for being here.
Together, they soar to every corner of the skies...
...pursuing their prize, the *dragons*.

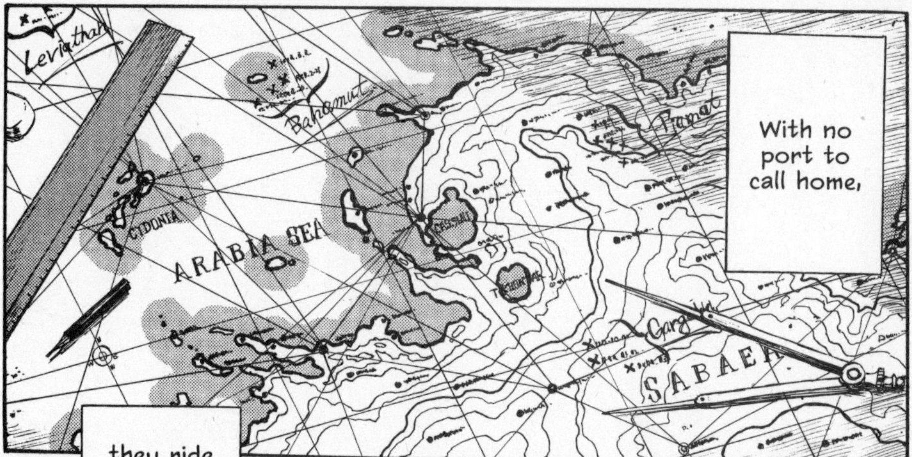
With no port to call home,
Leviathan
Bahamut
CYDONIA
ARABIA SEA

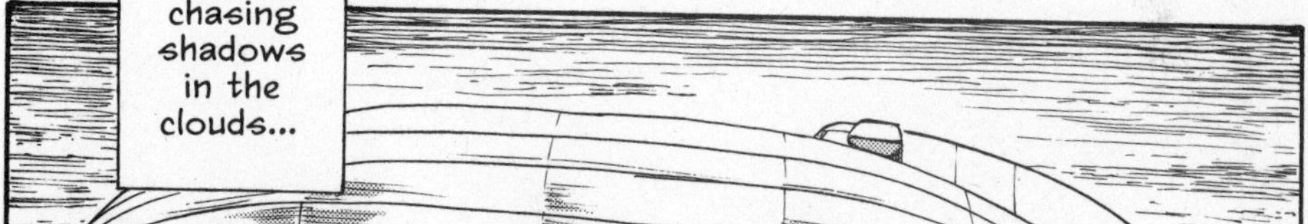
they ride the winds, chasing shadows in the clouds...

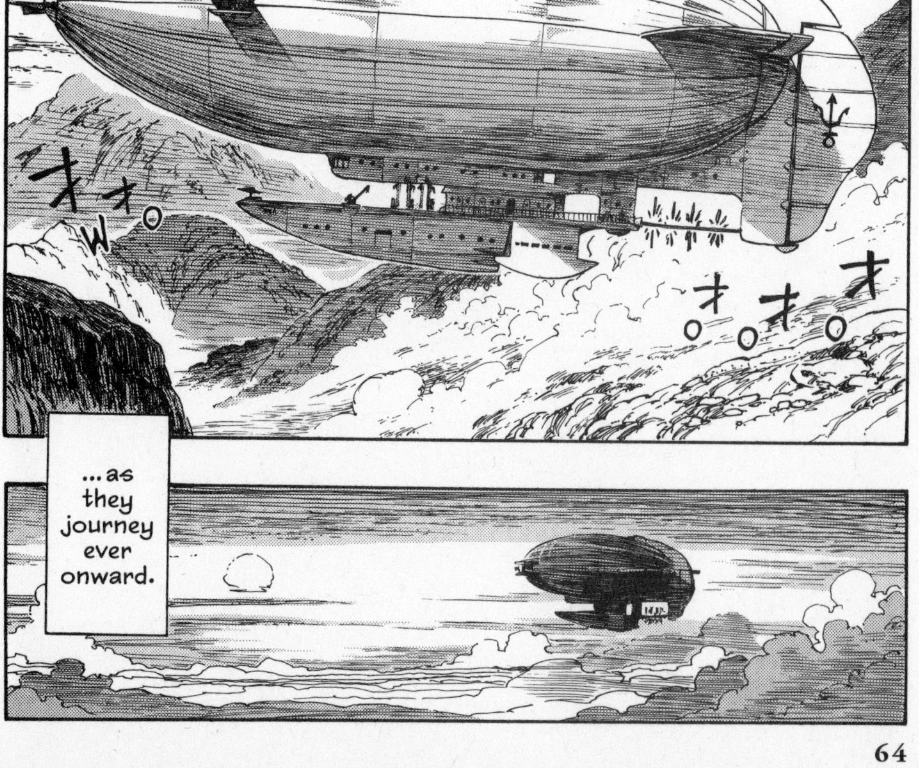
...as they journey ever onward.

Dragon Tail Sandwich

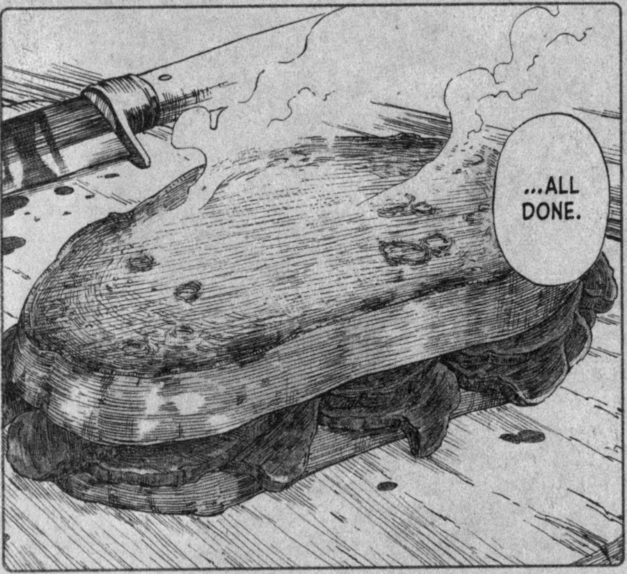
...ALL DONE.

Ingredients (One Serving)

- ✦ 250g Dragon tail meat (from the base of the tail)
- ✦ Dragon hide fat as needed
- ✦ A dash of rock salt
- ✦ A splash of Wine-vodka (can substitute brandy or whiskey)
- ✦ Pepper to taste
- ✦ 2 slices, bread of choice

01
Arrange the fire so that the griddle has areas of high and low heat.

02
Season both sides of the steak with salt and pepper and grease the pan with the fat.

03
Place meat on the griddle. Cook over high heat for 1 minute, then low heat for an additional minute.

04
Flip the meat over. Cook over high heat for 30 seconds, then over low heat for 1 minute and 30 seconds.

05
Add a splash of wine-vodka and cook out the alcohol.

06
Slice the finished steak, sandwich between toasted slices of bread and enjoy.

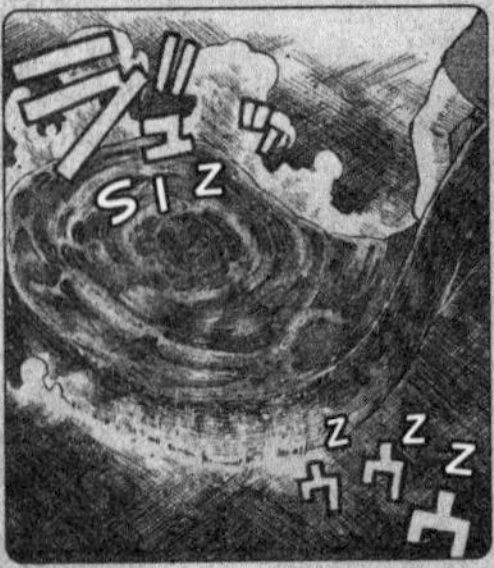
SIZ
Z Z Z

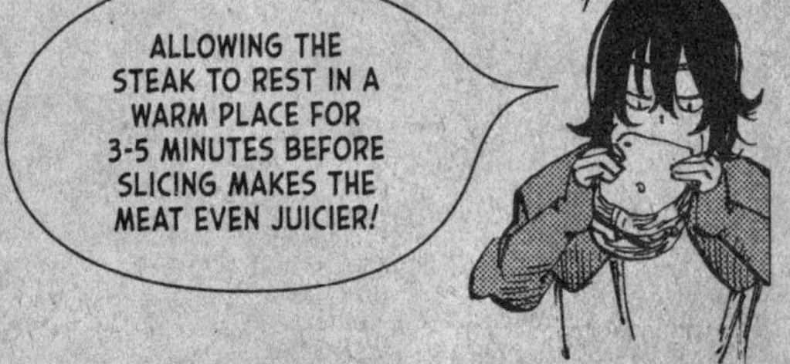
ALLOWING THE STEAK TO REST IN A WARM PLACE FOR 3-5 MINUTES BEFORE SLICING MAKES THE MEAT EVEN JUICIER!

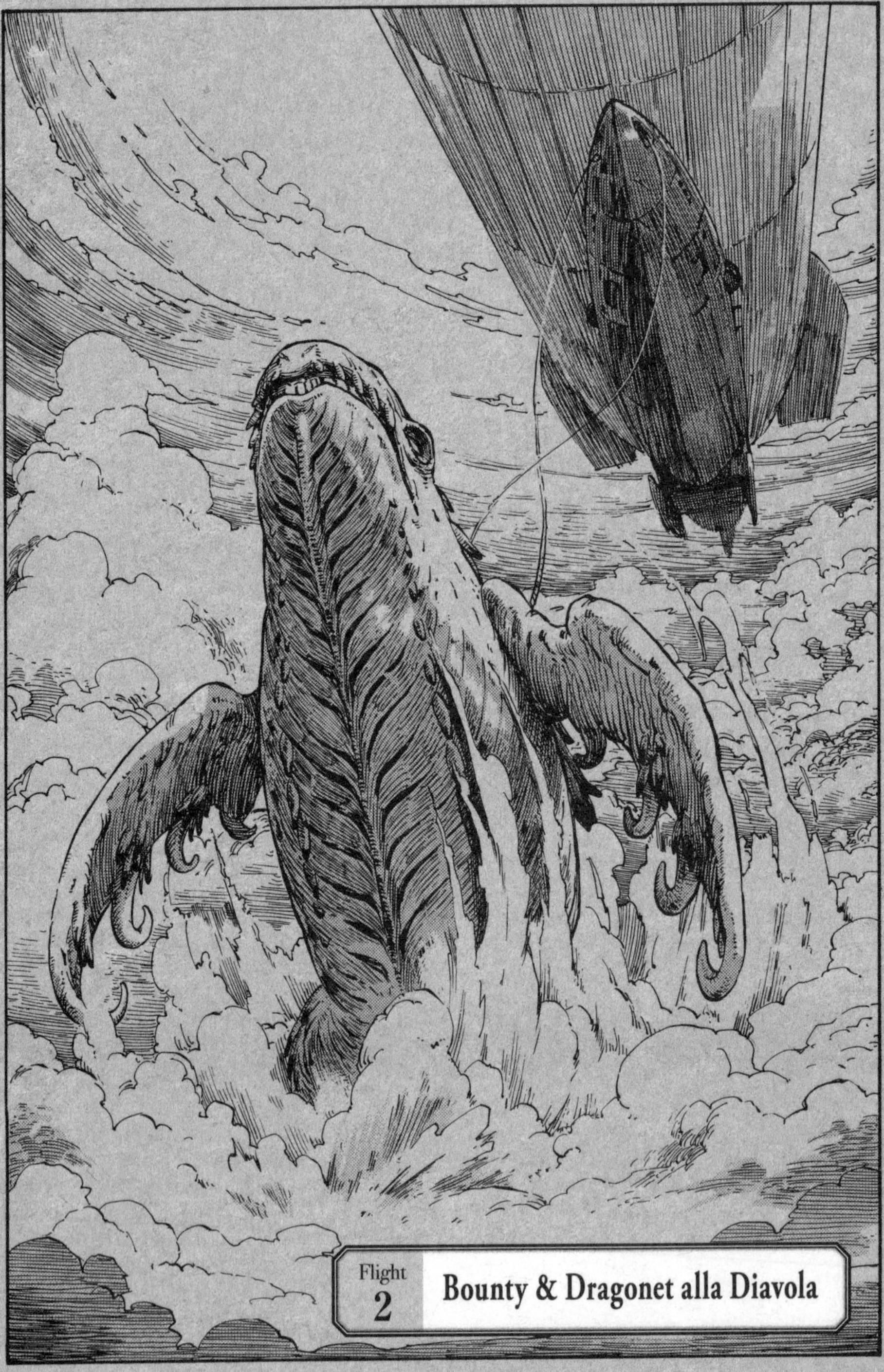
Flight
2
Bounty & Dragonet alla Diavola

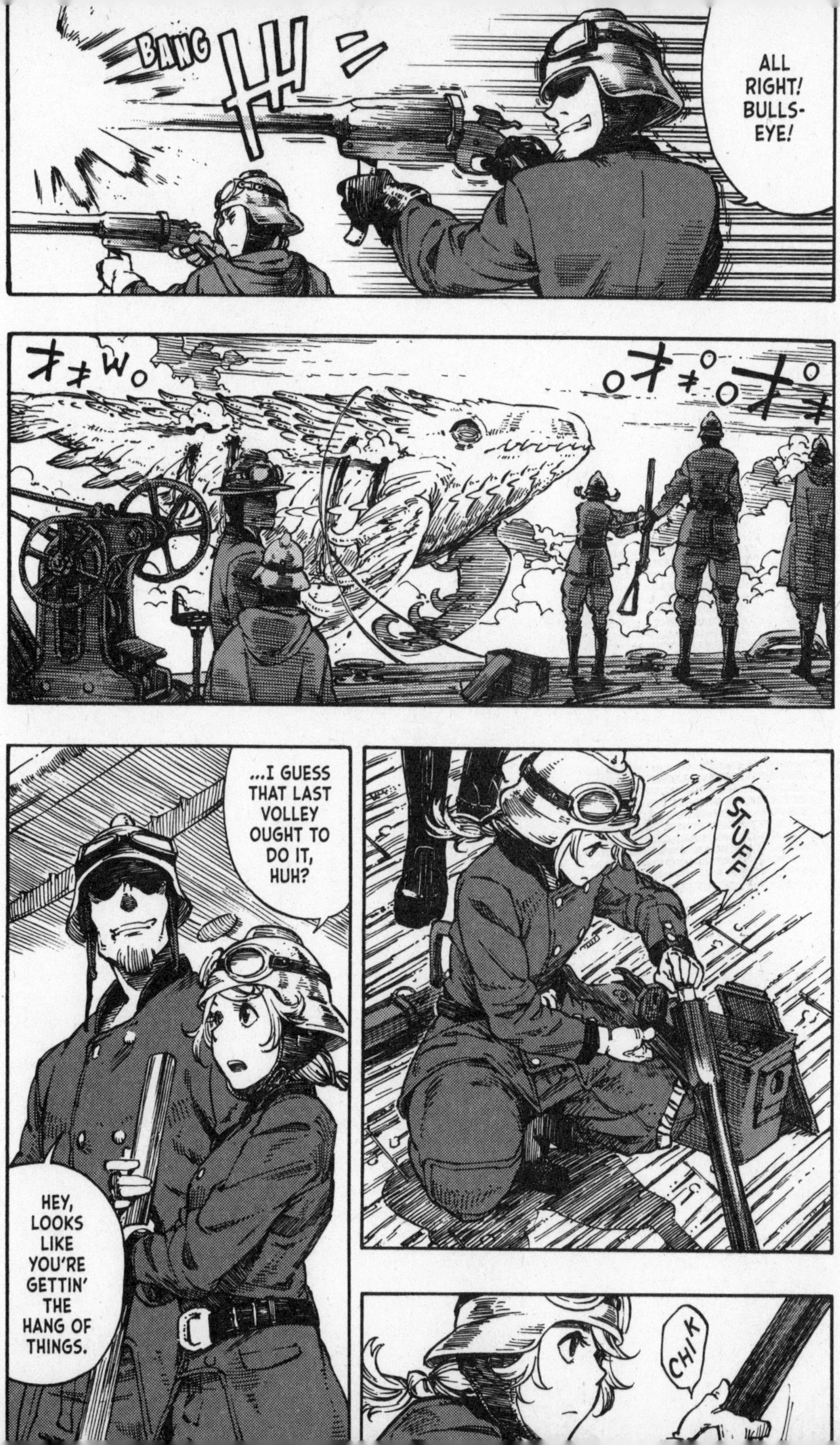
ALL RIGHT! BULLS-EYE!
BANG
STUFF
CHIK
...I GUESS THAT LAST VOLLEY OUGHT TO DO IT, HUH?
HEY, LOOKS LIKE YOU'RE GETTIN' THE HANG OF THINGS.

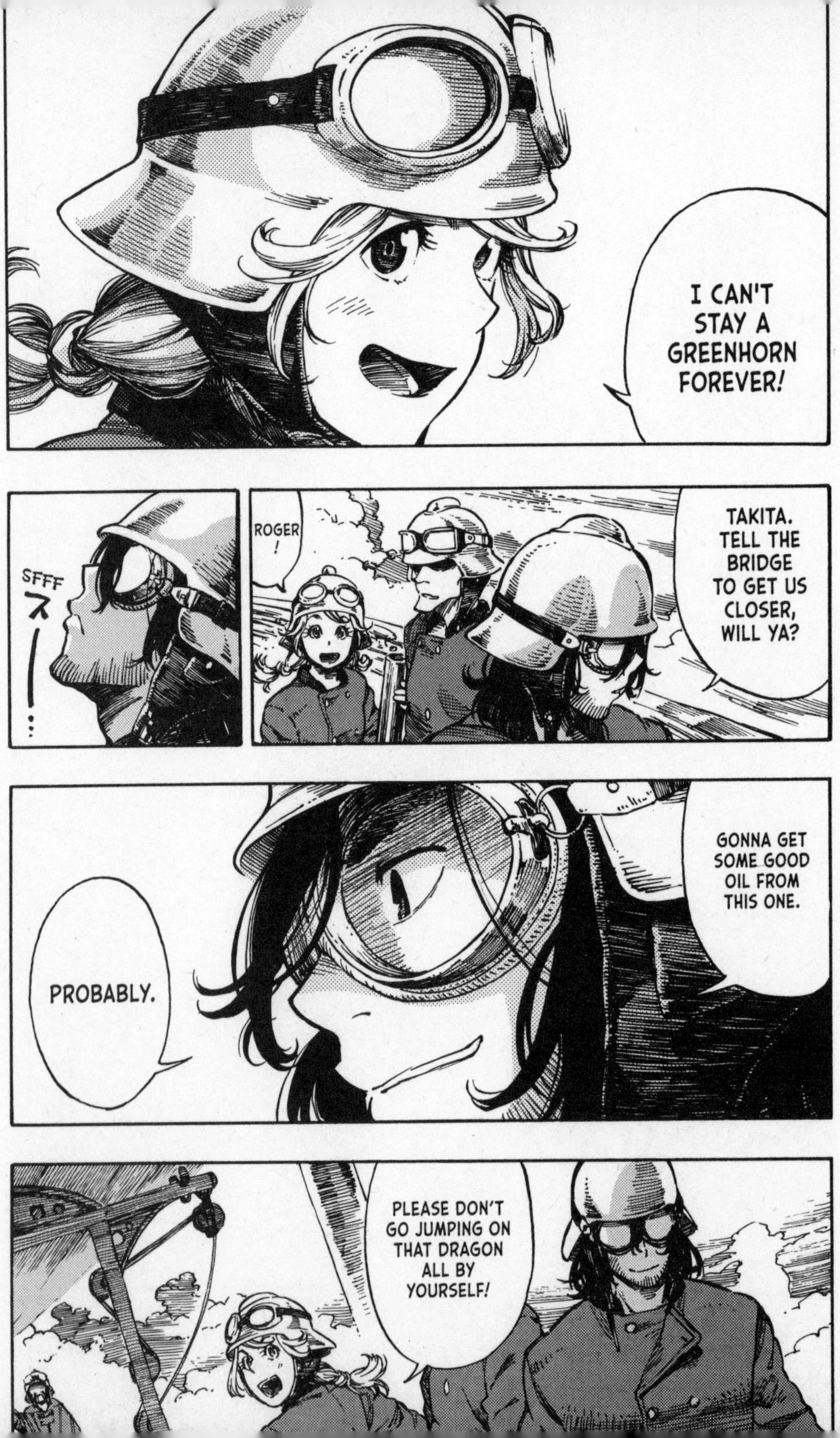
I CAN'T STAY A GREENHORN FOREVER!
TAKITA. TELL THE BRIDGE TO GET US CLOSER, WILL YA?
ROGER!
SFFF
ス―…
GONNA GET SOME GOOD OIL FROM THIS ONE.
PROBABLY.
PLEASE DON'T GO JUMPING ON THAT DRAGON ALL BY YOURSELF!

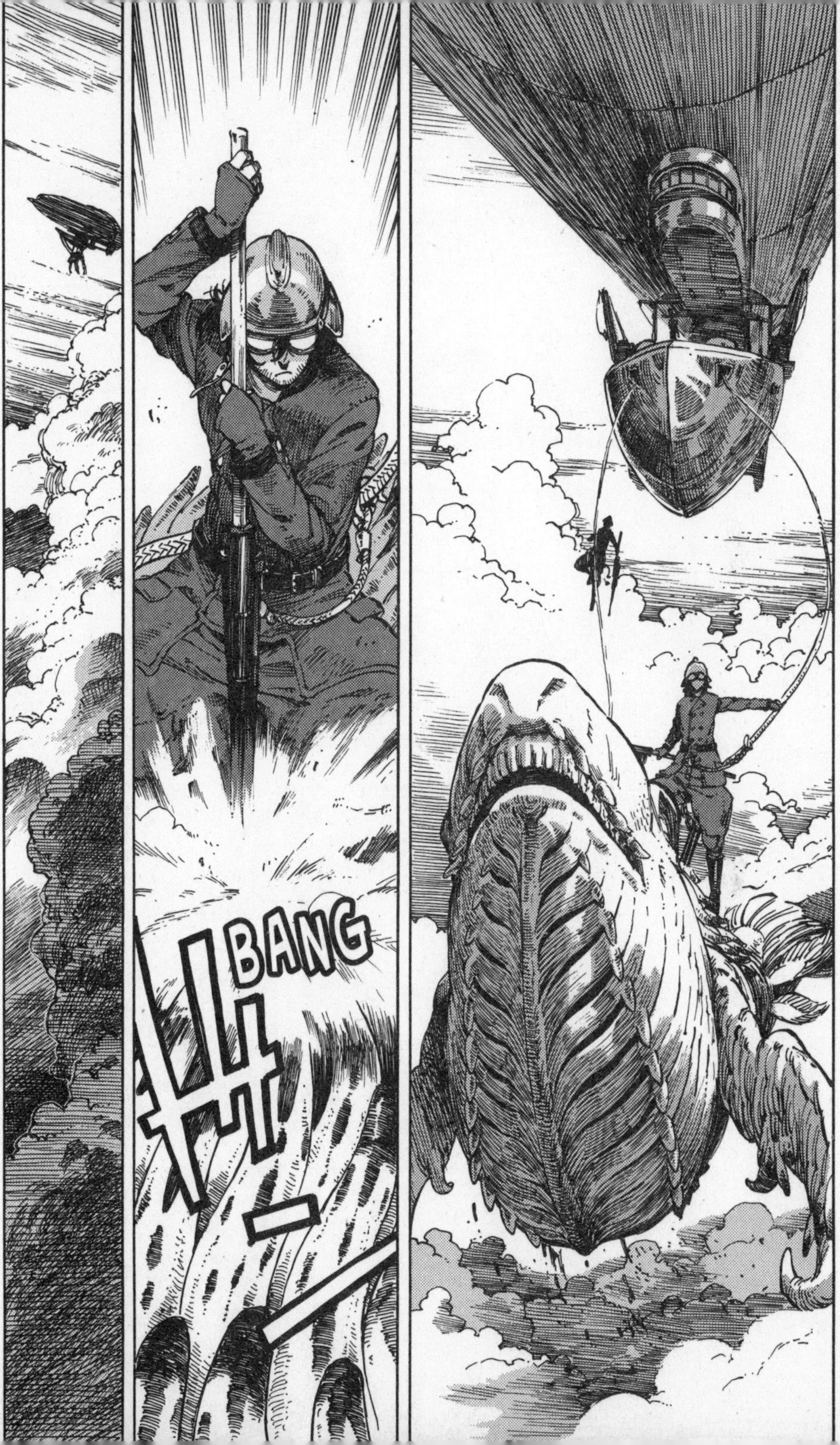
BANG

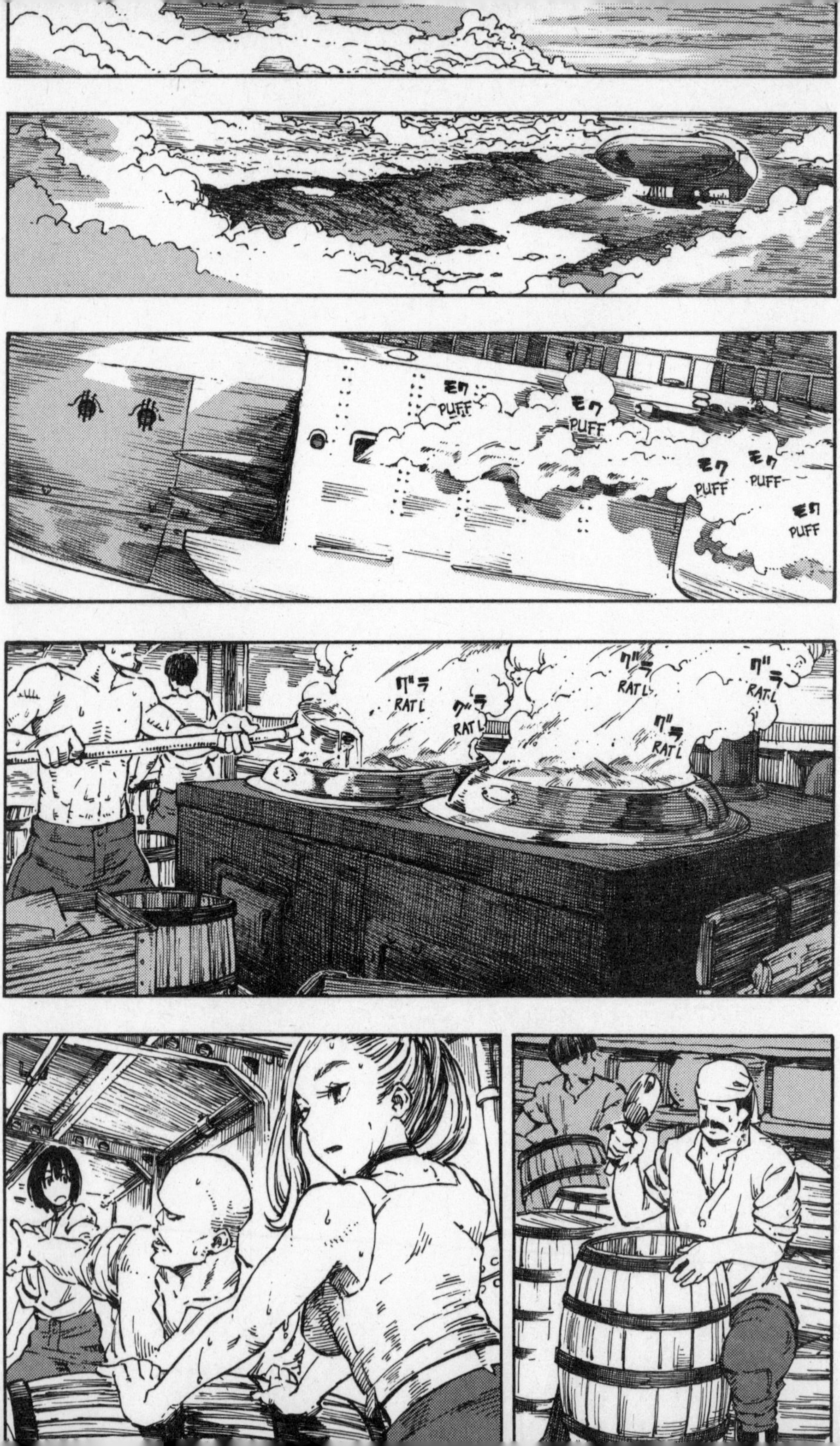
モク
PUFF
モク
PUFF
モク
PUFF
モク
PUFF
モク
PUFF
グラ
RATL
グラ
RATL
グラ
RATL
グラ
RATL
グラ
RATL

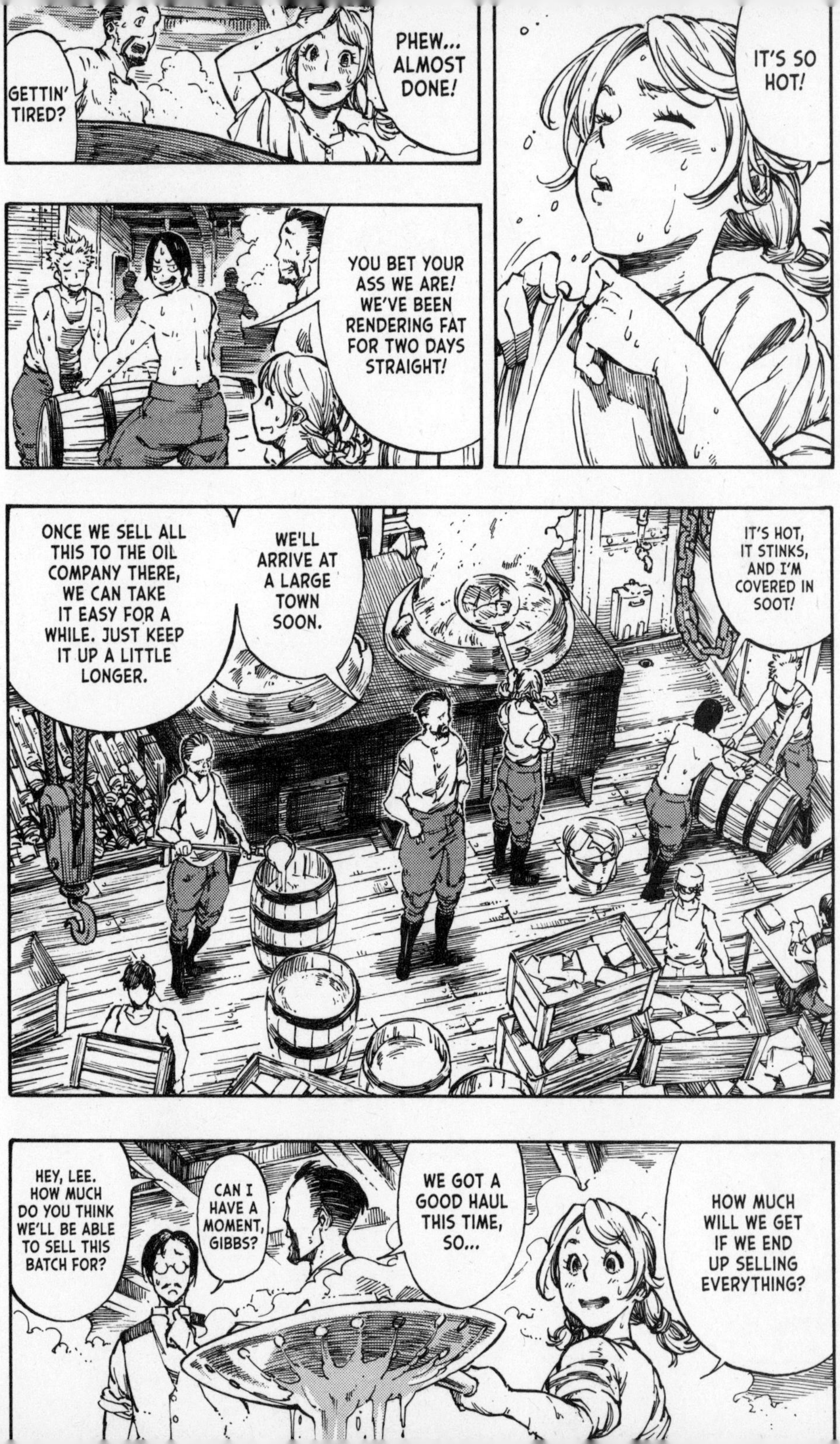

IT'S SO HOT!
PHEW... ALMOST DONE!
GETTIN' TIRED?
YOU BET YOUR ASS WE ARE! WE'VE BEEN RENDERING FAT FOR TWO DAYS STRAIGHT!
IT'S HOT, IT STINKS, AND I'M COVERED IN SOOT!
WE'LL ARRIVE AT A LARGE TOWN SOON.
ONCE WE SELL ALL THIS TO THE OIL COMPANY THERE, WE CAN TAKE IT EASY FOR A WHILE. JUST KEEP IT UP A LITTLE LONGER.
HOW MUCH WILL WE GET IF WE END UP SELLING EVERYTHING?
WE GOT A GOOD HAUL THIS TIME, SO...
CAN I HAVE A MOMENT, GIBBS?
HEY, LEE. HOW MUCH DO YOU THINK WE'LL BE ABLE TO SELL THIS BATCH FOR?

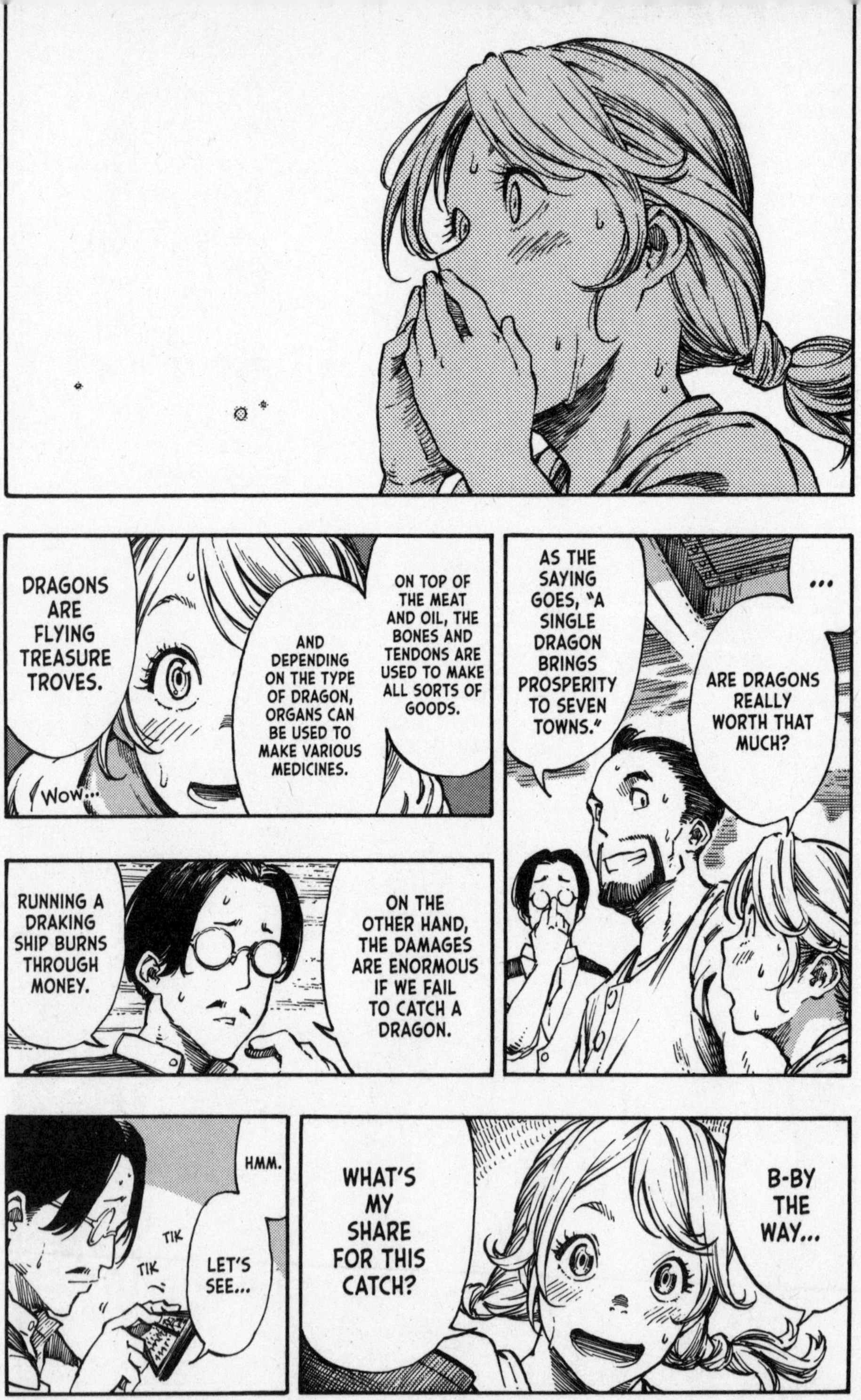
...
ARE DRAGONS REALLY WORTH THAT MUCH?
AS THE SAYING GOES, "A SINGLE DRAGON BRINGS PROSPERITY TO SEVEN TOWNS."
ON TOP OF THE MEAT AND OIL, THE BONES AND TENDONS ARE USED TO MAKE ALL SORTS OF GOODS.
AND DEPENDING ON THE TYPE OF DRAGON, ORGANS CAN BE USED TO MAKE VARIOUS MEDICINES.
DRAGONS ARE FLYING TREASURE TROVES.
WOW...
ON THE OTHER HAND, THE DAMAGES ARE ENORMOUS IF WE FAIL TO CATCH A DRAGON.
RUNNING A DRAKING SHIP BURNS THROUGH MONEY.
B-BY THE WAY...
WHAT'S MY SHARE FOR THIS CATCH?
HMM.
LET'S SEE...
TIK
TIK

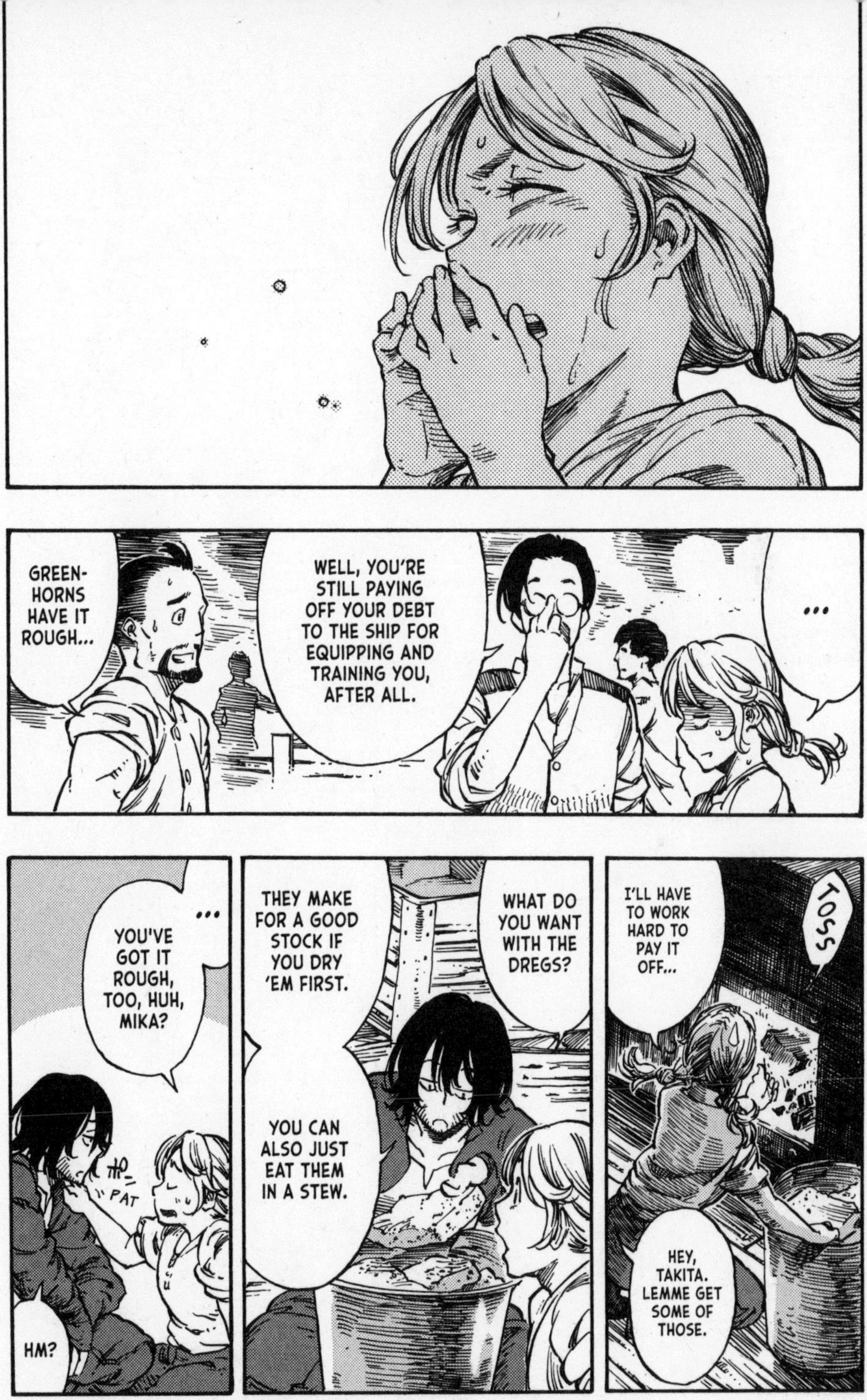
...
WELL, YOU'RE STILL PAYING OFF YOUR DEBT TO THE SHIP FOR EQUIPPING AND TRAINING YOU, AFTER ALL.
GREEN-HORNS HAVE IT ROUGH...
TOSS
I'LL HAVE TO WORK HARD TO PAY IT OFF...
HEY, TAKITA. LEMME GET SOME OF THOSE.
WHAT DO YOU WANT WITH THE DREGS?
THEY MAKE FOR A GOOD STOCK IF YOU DRY 'EM FIRST.
YOU CAN ALSO JUST EAT THEM IN A STEW.
...
YOU'VE GOT IT ROUGH, TOO, HUH, MIKA?
PAT
HM?

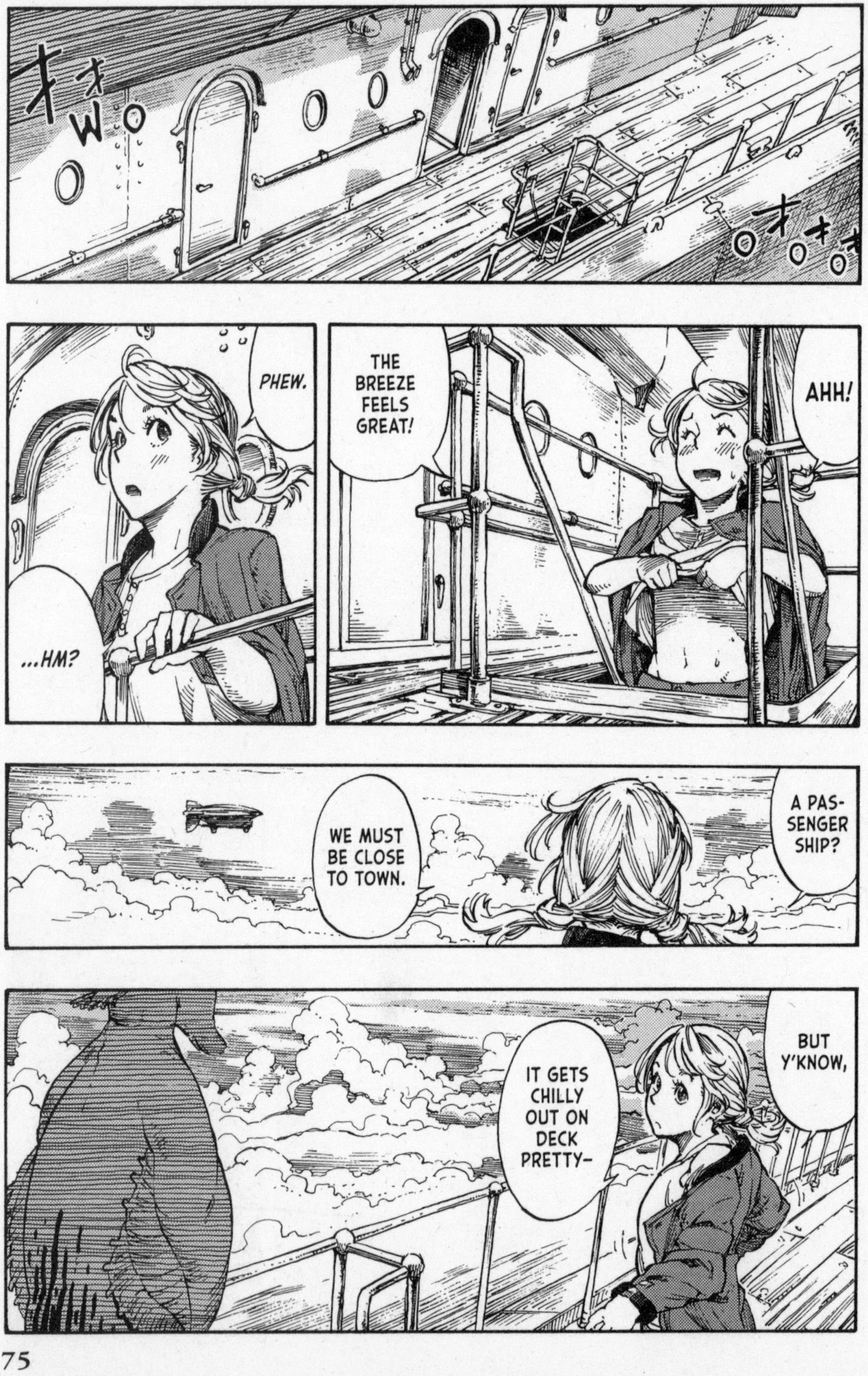
WO
AHH!
THE BREEZE FEELS GREAT!
PHEW.
...HM?
A PAS-SENGER SHIP?
WE MUST BE CLOSE TO TOWN.
BUT Y'KNOW,
IT GETS CHILLY OUT ON DECK PRETTY–

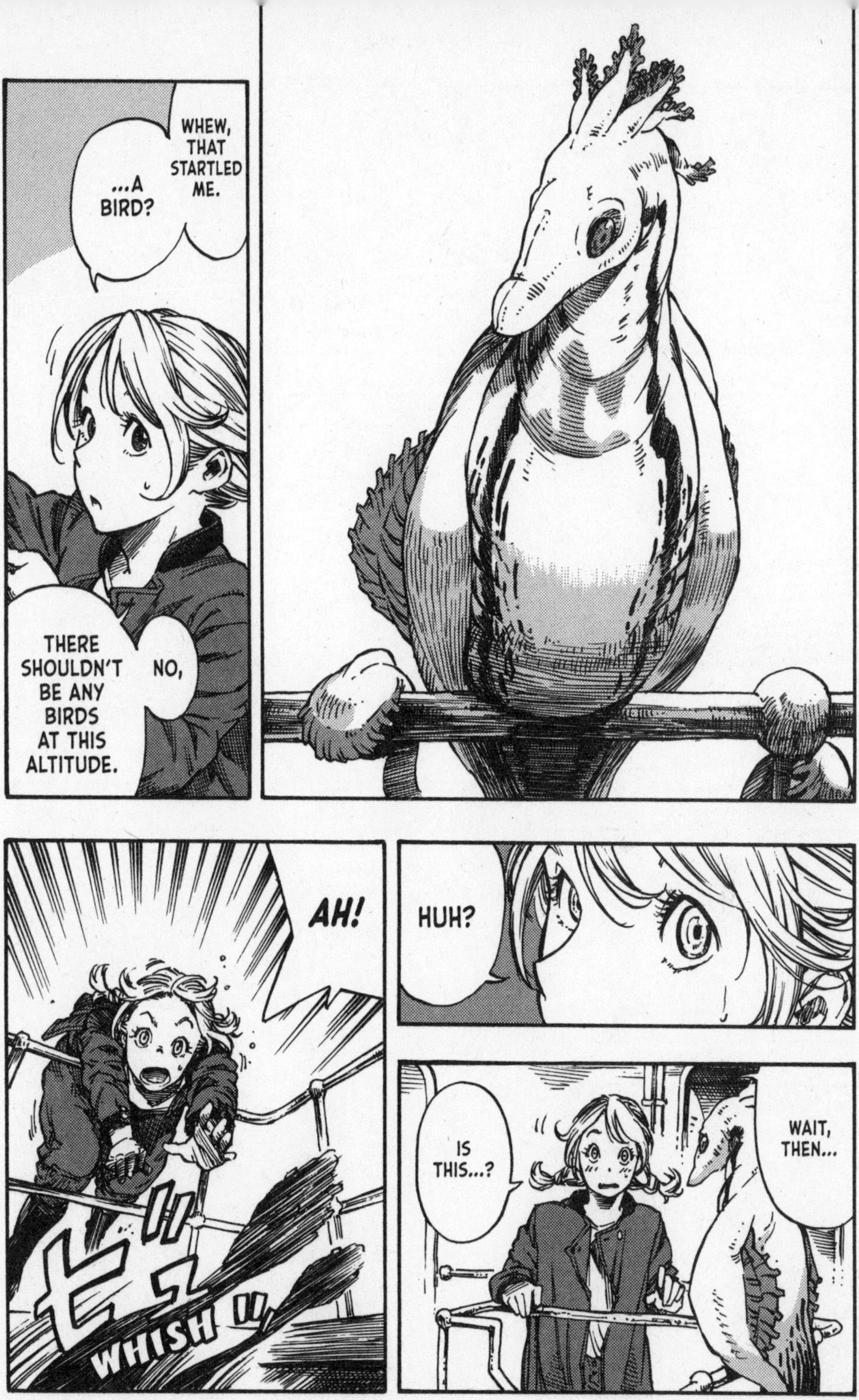
WHEW, THAT STARTLED ME.
...A BIRD?
NO,
THERE SHOULDN'T BE ANY BIRDS AT THIS ALTITUDE.
HUH?
WAIT, THEN...
IS THIS...?
AH!
WHISH

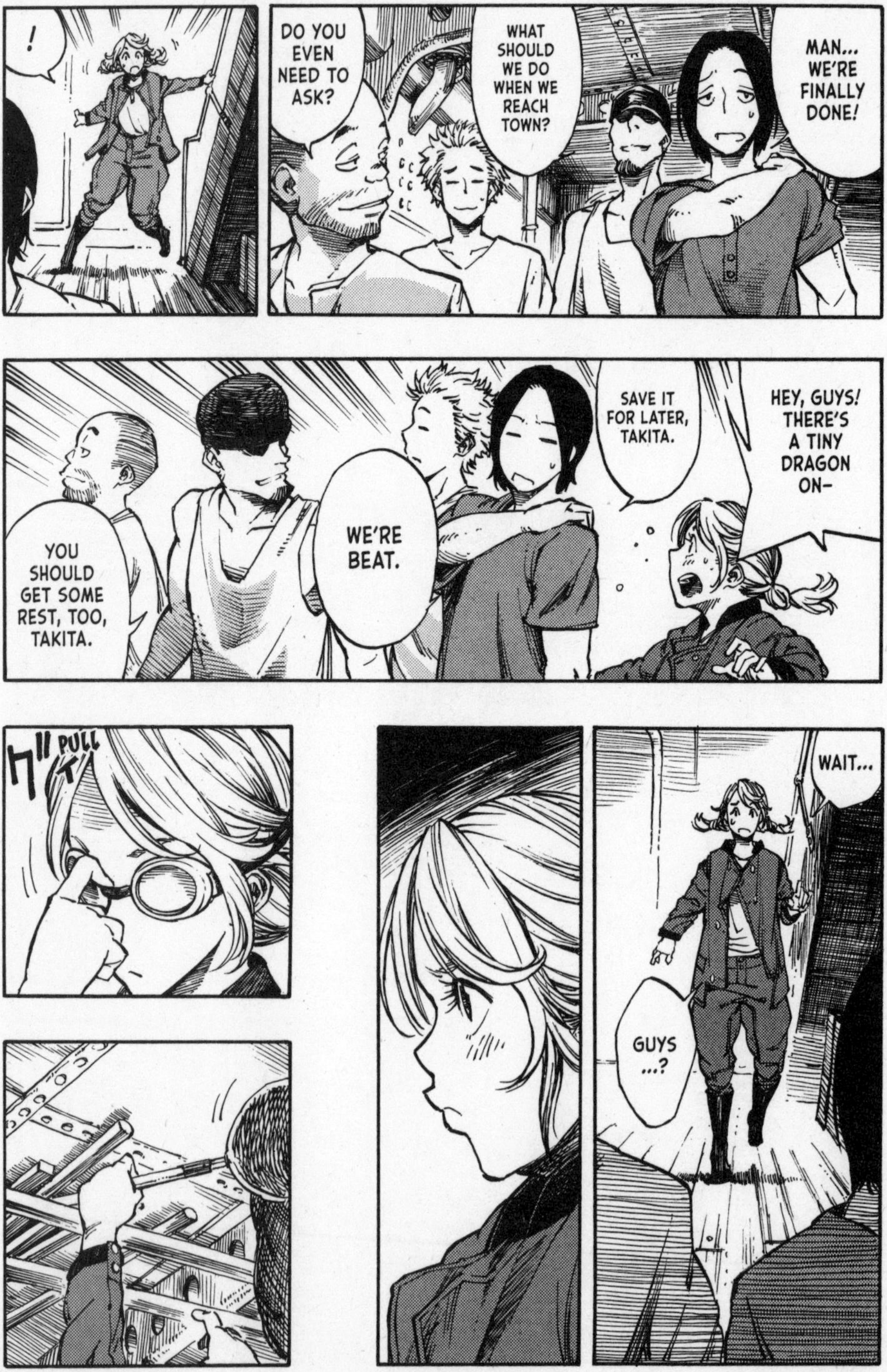

MAN... WE'RE FINALLY DONE!
WHAT SHOULD WE DO WHEN WE REACH TOWN?
DO YOU EVEN NEED TO ASK?
!
HEY, GUYS! THERE'S A TINY DRAGON ON–
SAVE IT FOR LATER, TAKITA.
WE'RE BEAT.
YOU SHOULD GET SOME REST, TOO, TAKITA.
WAIT...
GUYS ...?
PULL

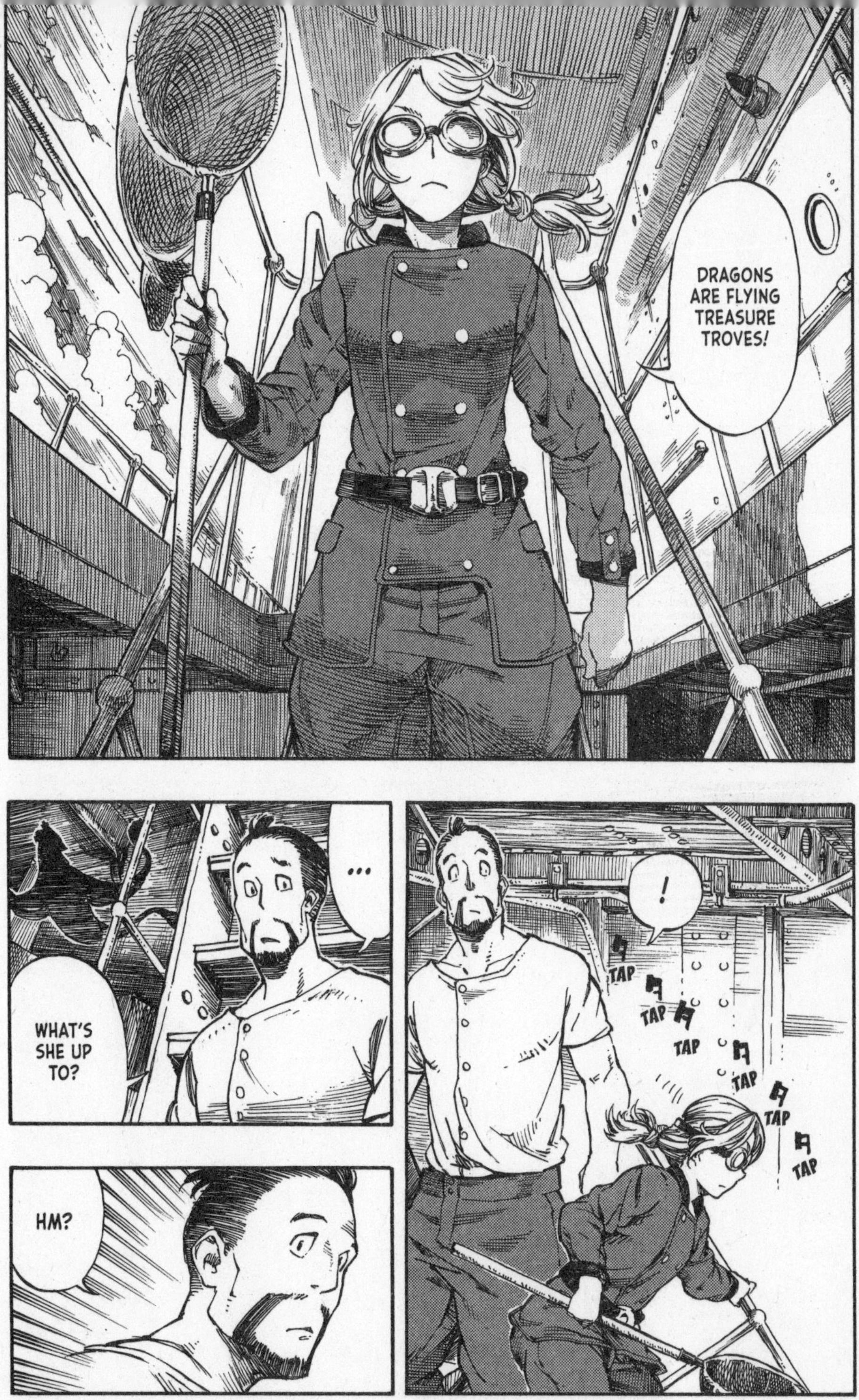
DRAGONS ARE FLYING TREASURE TROVES!
!
TAP
TAP
TAP
TAP
TAP
TAP
...
WHAT'S SHE UP TO?
HM?

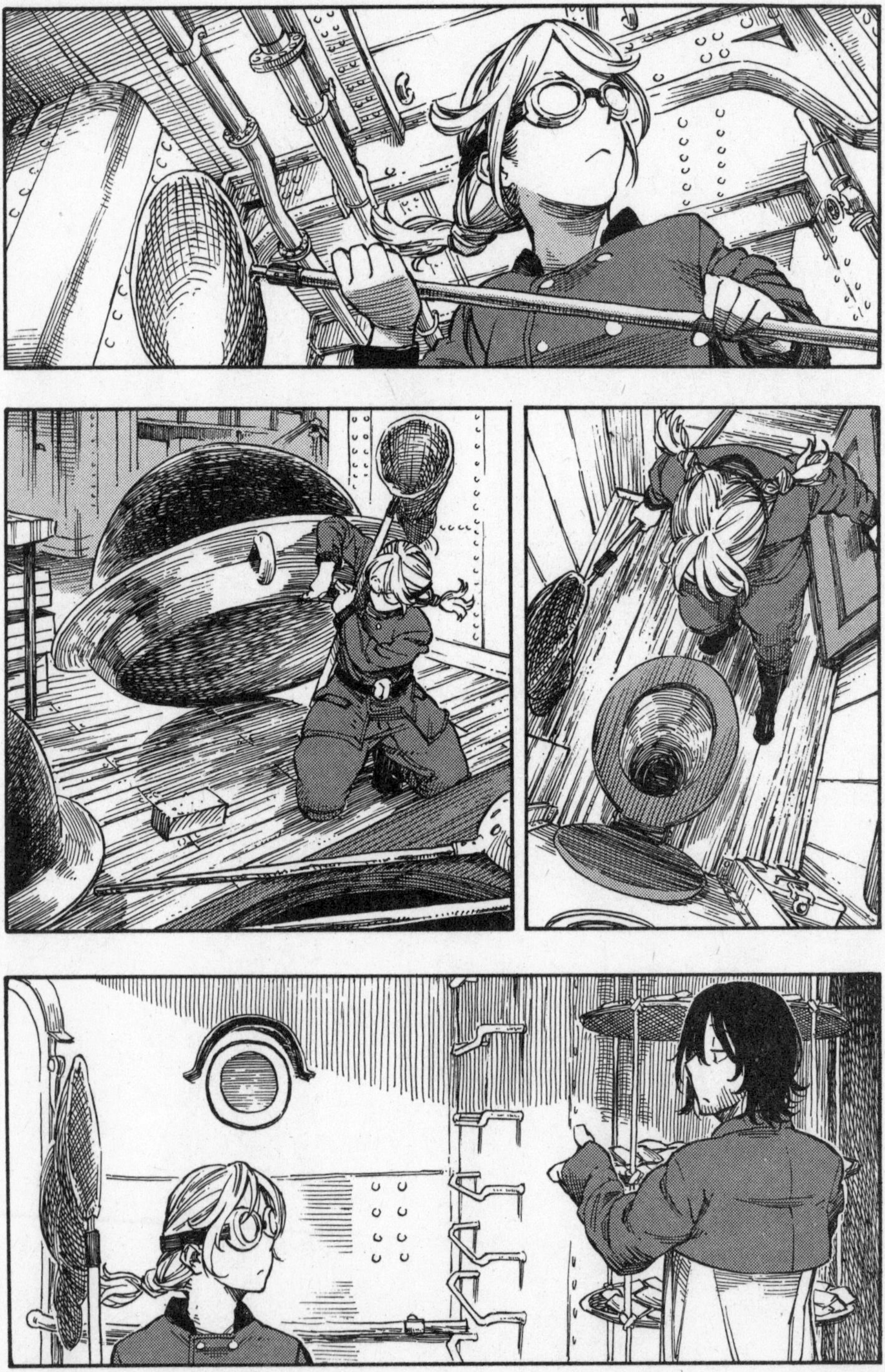

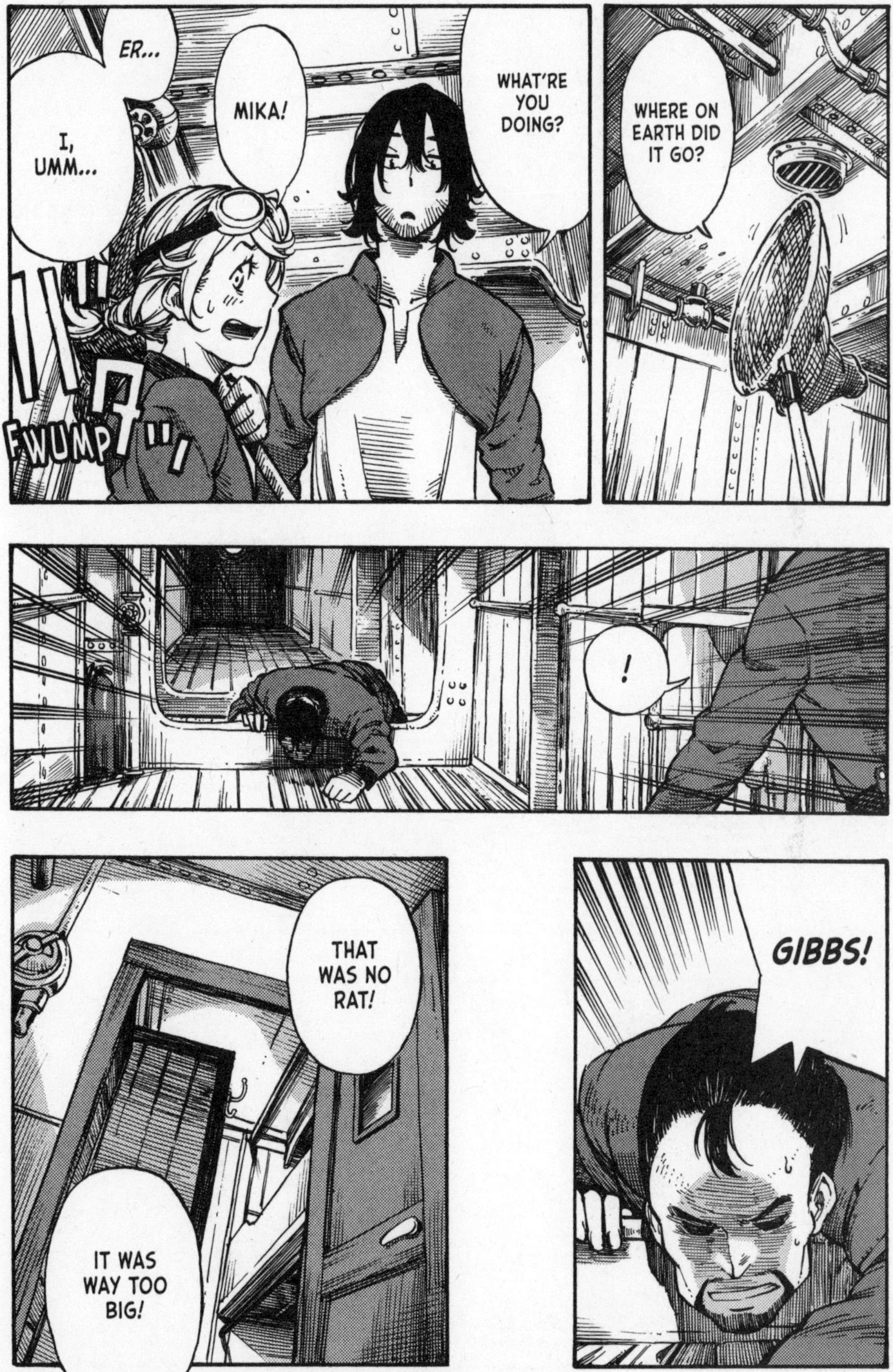
WHERE ON EARTH DID IT GO?
WHAT'RE YOU DOING?
MIKA!
ER...
I, UMM...
FWUMP
!
GIBBS!
THAT WAS NO RAT!
IT WAS WAY TOO BIG!

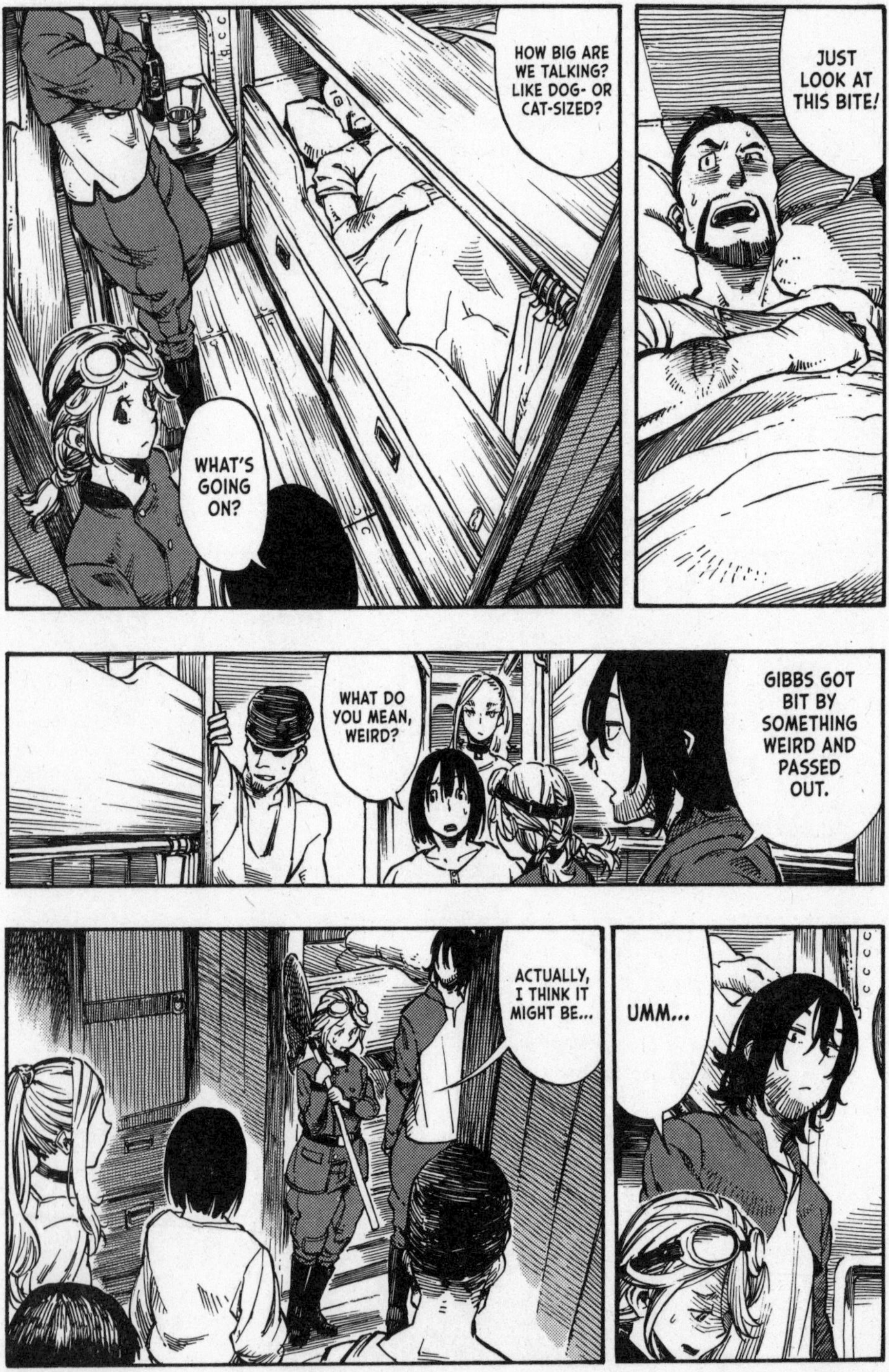
JUST LOOK AT THIS BITE!
HOW BIG ARE WE TALKING? LIKE DOG- OR CAT-SIZED?
WHAT'S GOING ON?
GIBBS GOT BIT BY SOMETHING WEIRD AND PASSED OUT.
WHAT DO YOU MEAN, WEIRD?
UMM...
ACTUALLY, I THINK IT MIGHT BE...

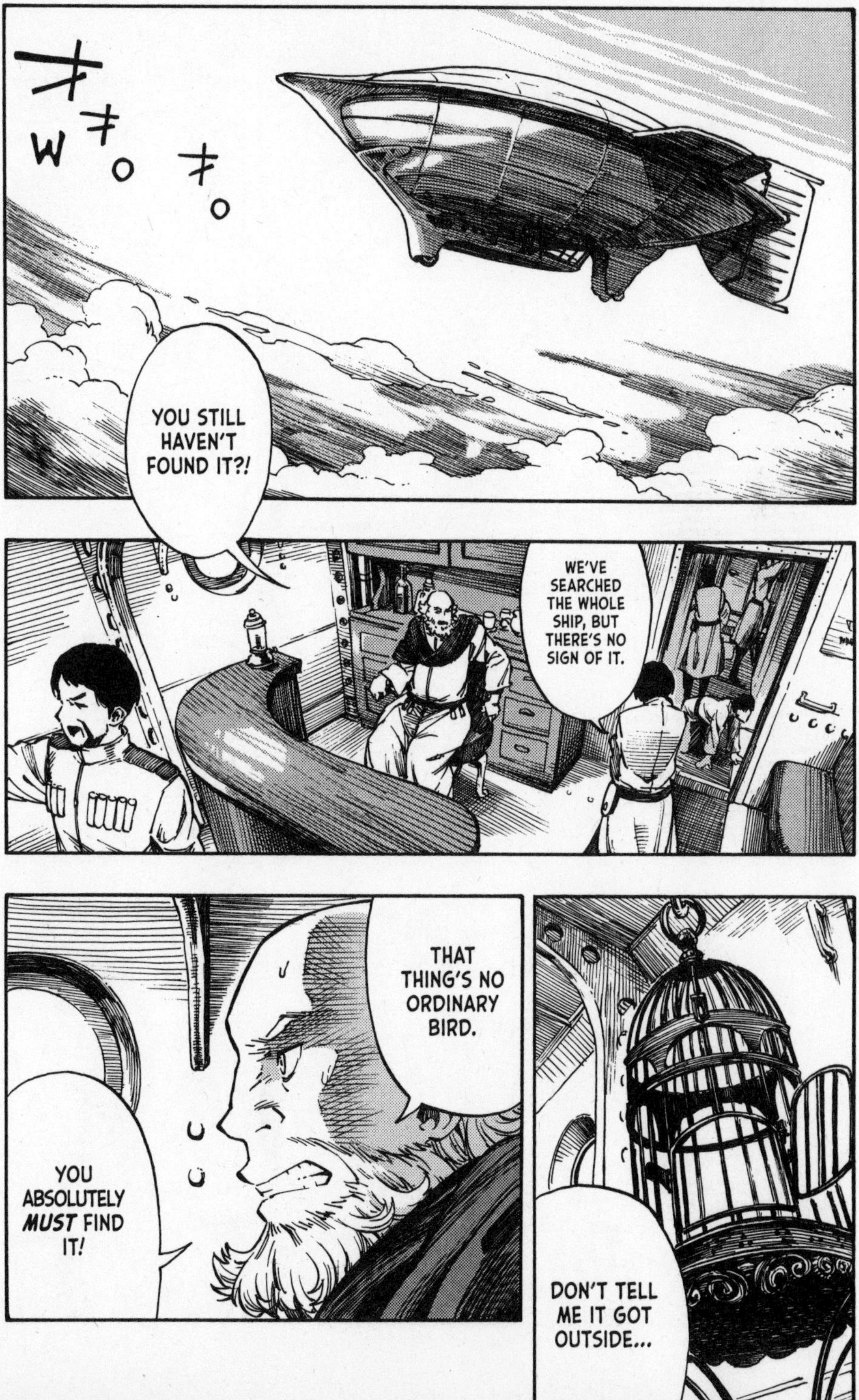
Woo
YOU STILL HAVEN'T FOUND IT?!
WE'VE SEARCHED THE WHOLE SHIP, BUT THERE'S NO SIGN OF IT.
DON'T TELL ME IT GOT OUTSIDE...
THAT THING'S NO ORDINARY BIRD.
YOU ABSOLUTELY *MUST* FIND IT!

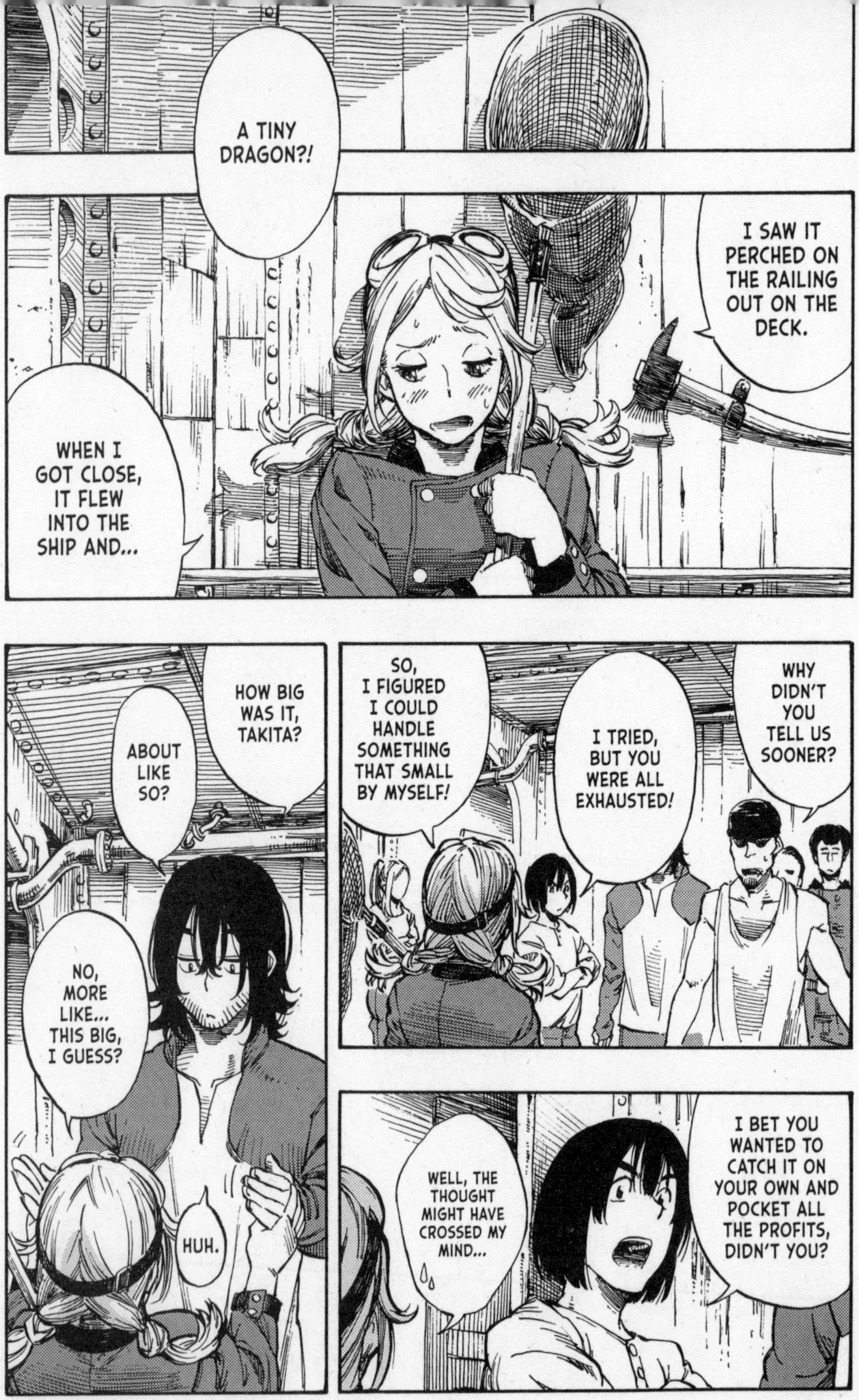
A TINY DRAGON?!
I SAW IT PERCHED ON THE RAILING OUT ON THE DECK.
WHEN I GOT CLOSE, IT FLEW INTO THE SHIP AND...
WHY DIDN'T YOU TELL US SOONER?
I TRIED, BUT YOU WERE ALL EXHAUSTED!
SO, I FIGURED I COULD HANDLE SOMETHING THAT SMALL BY MYSELF!
I BET YOU WANTED TO CATCH IT ON YOUR OWN AND POCKET ALL THE PROFITS, DIDN'T YOU?
WELL, THE THOUGHT MIGHT HAVE CROSSED MY MIND...
HOW BIG WAS IT, TAKITA?
ABOUT LIKE SO?
NO, MORE LIKE... THIS BIG, I GUESS?
HUH.

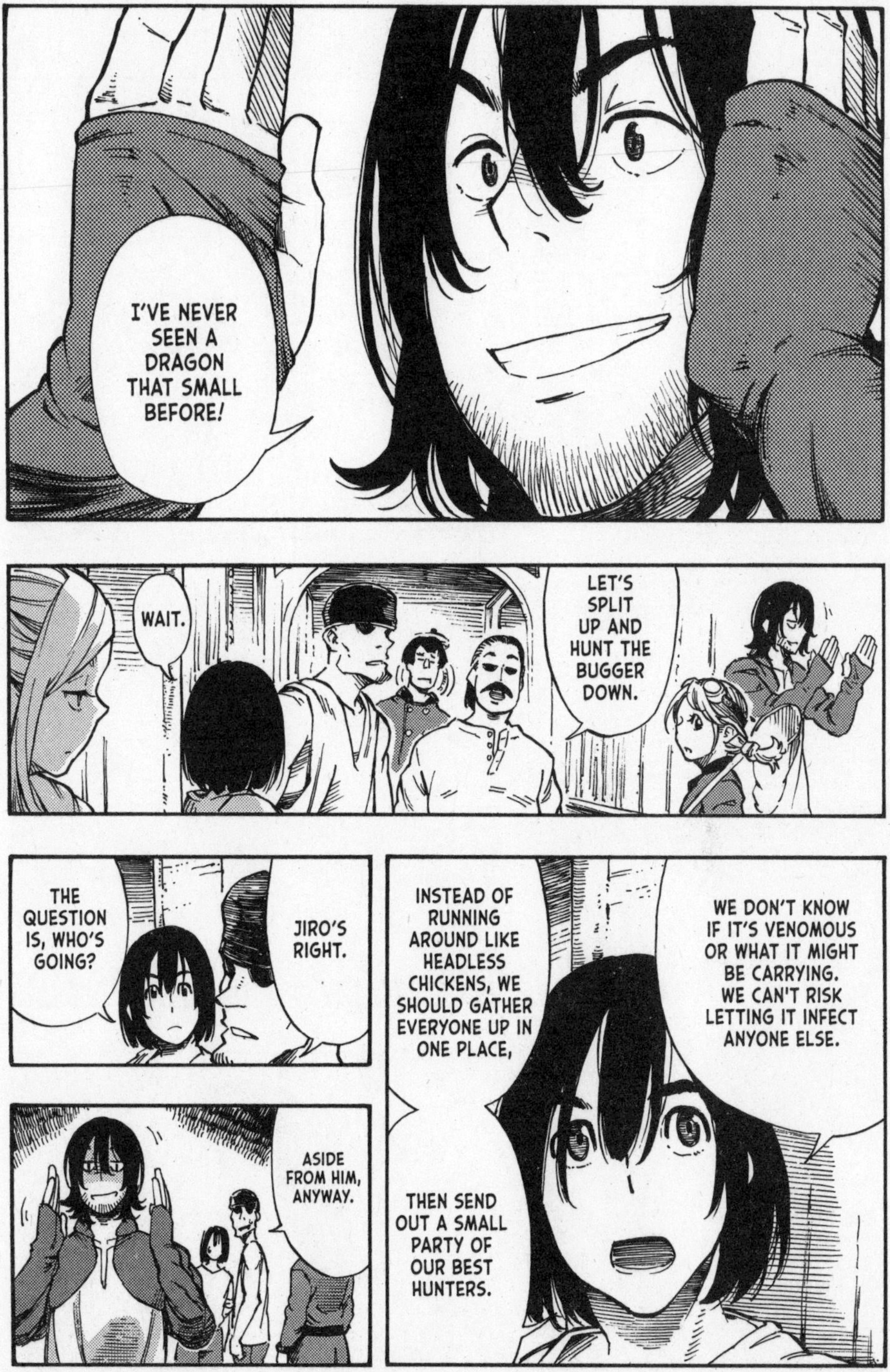
I'VE NEVER SEEN A DRAGON THAT SMALL BEFORE!
LET'S SPLIT UP AND HUNT THE BUGGER DOWN.
WAIT.
WE DON'T KNOW IF IT'S VENOMOUS OR WHAT IT MIGHT BE CARRYING. WE CAN'T RISK LETTING IT INFECT ANYONE ELSE.
INSTEAD OF RUNNING AROUND LIKE HEADLESS CHICKENS, WE SHOULD GATHER EVERYONE UP IN ONE PLACE,
THEN SEND OUT A SMALL PARTY OF OUR BEST HUNTERS.
JIRO'S RIGHT.
THE QUESTION IS, WHO'S GOING?
ASIDE FROM HIM, ANYWAY.

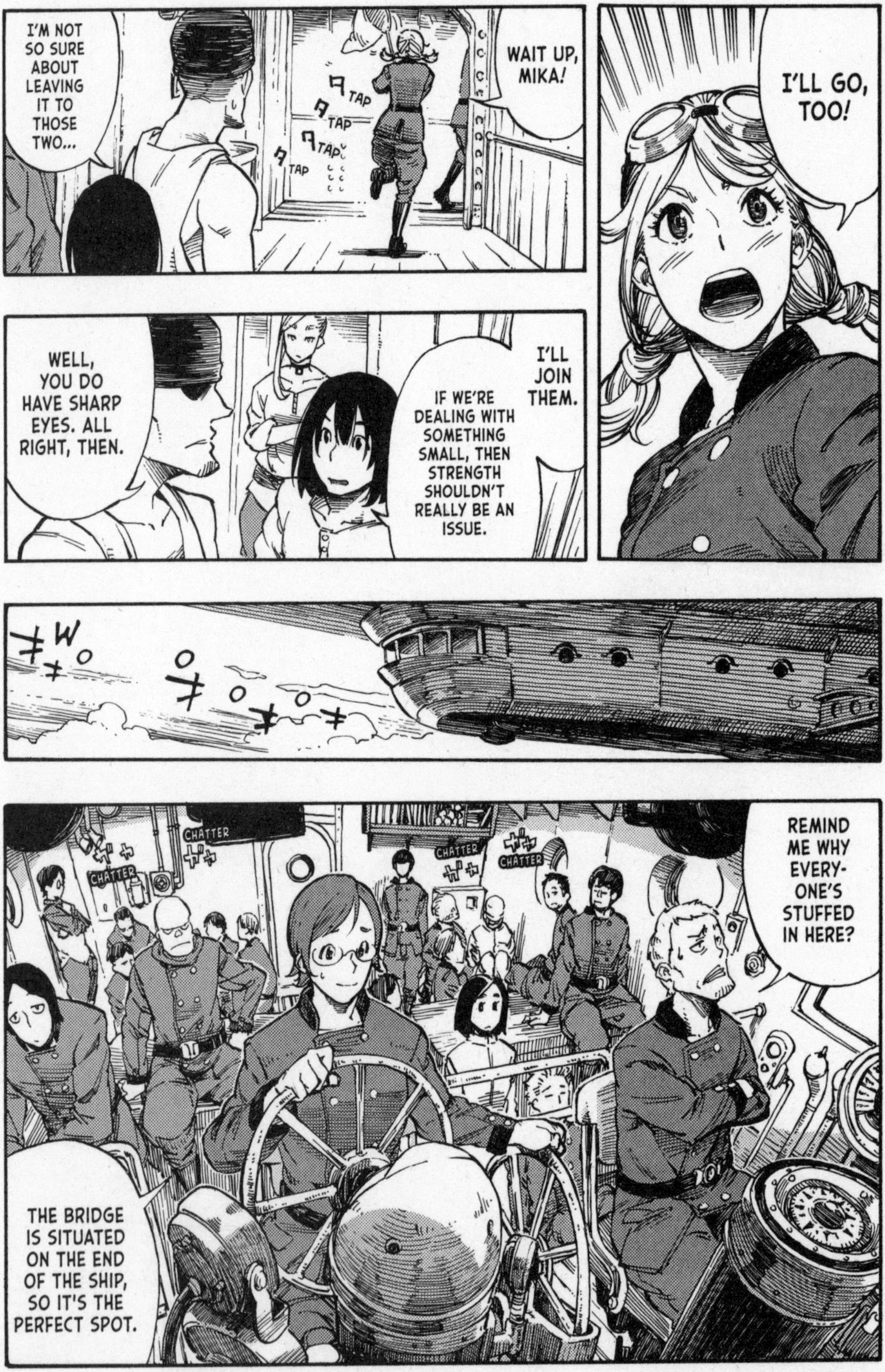
I'LL GO, TOO!
WAIT UP, MIKA!
タ TAP タ TAP タ TAP タ TAP
I'M NOT SO SURE ABOUT LEAVING IT TO THOSE TWO...
I'LL JOIN THEM.
IF WE'RE DEALING WITH SOMETHING SMALL, THEN STRENGTH SHOULDN'T REALLY BE AN ISSUE.
WELL, YOU DO HAVE SHARP EYES. ALL RIGHT, THEN.
W
REMIND ME WHY EVERY-ONE'S STUFFED IN HERE?
CHATTER
CHATTER
CHATTER
CHATTER
THE BRIDGE IS SITUATED ON THE END OF THE SHIP, SO IT'S THE PERFECT SPOT.

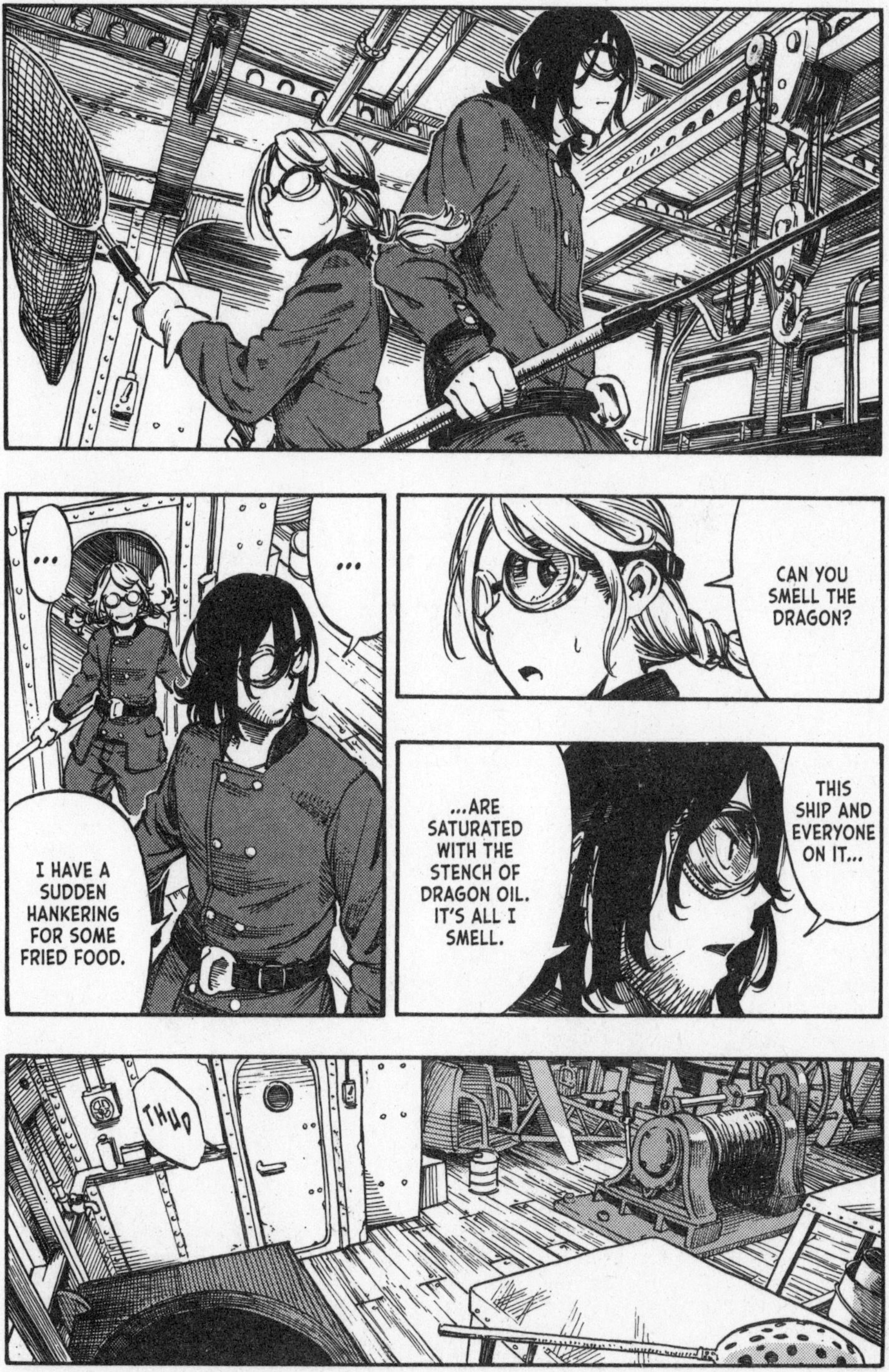
CAN YOU SMELL THE DRAGON?
THIS SHIP AND EVERYONE ON IT...
...ARE SATURATED WITH THE STENCH OF DRAGON OIL. IT'S ALL I SMELL.
...
...
I HAVE A SUDDEN HANKERING FOR SOME FRIED FOOD.
THUD

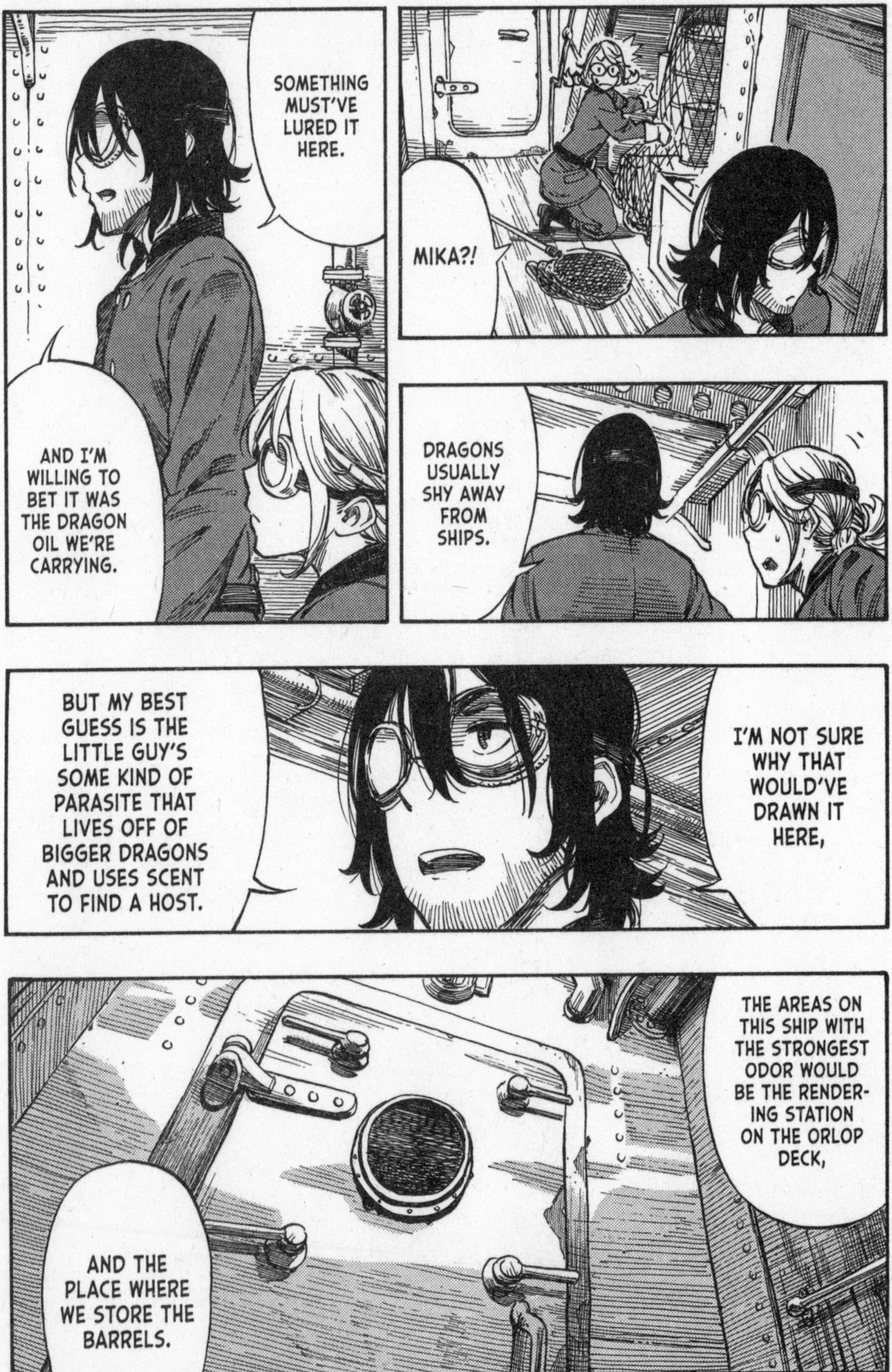
MIKA?!
DRAGONS USUALLY SHY AWAY FROM SHIPS.
SOMETHING MUST'VE LURED IT HERE.
AND I'M WILLING TO BET IT WAS THE DRAGON OIL WE'RE CARRYING.
I'M NOT SURE WHY THAT WOULD'VE DRAWN IT HERE,
BUT MY BEST GUESS IS THE LITTLE GUY'S SOME KIND OF PARASITE THAT LIVES OFF OF BIGGER DRAGONS AND USES SCENT TO FIND A HOST.
THE AREAS ON THIS SHIP WITH THE STRONGEST ODOR WOULD BE THE RENDER-ING STATION ON THE ORLOP DECK,
AND THE PLACE WHERE WE STORE THE BARRELS.

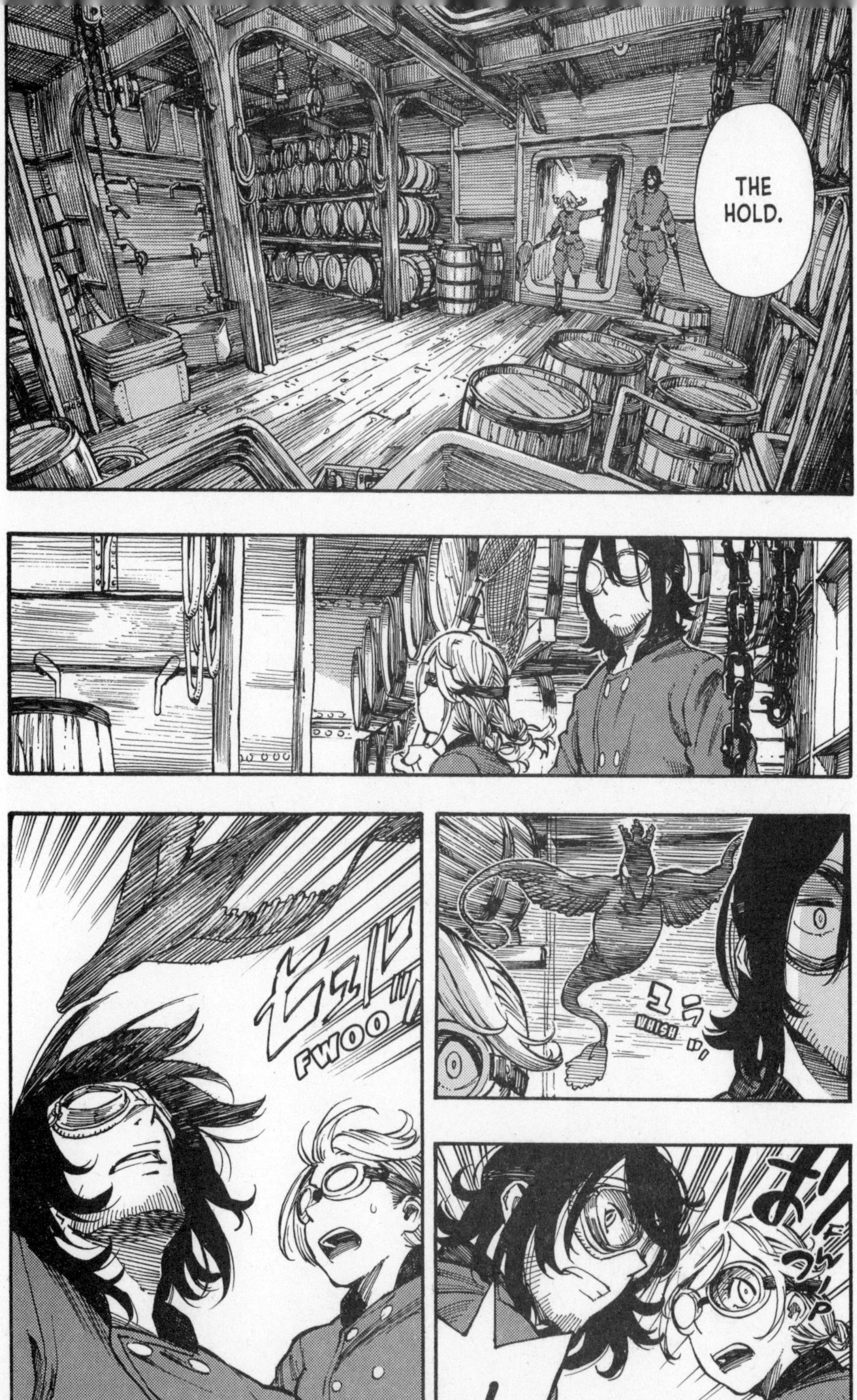
THE HOLD.
WHISH
FWOO

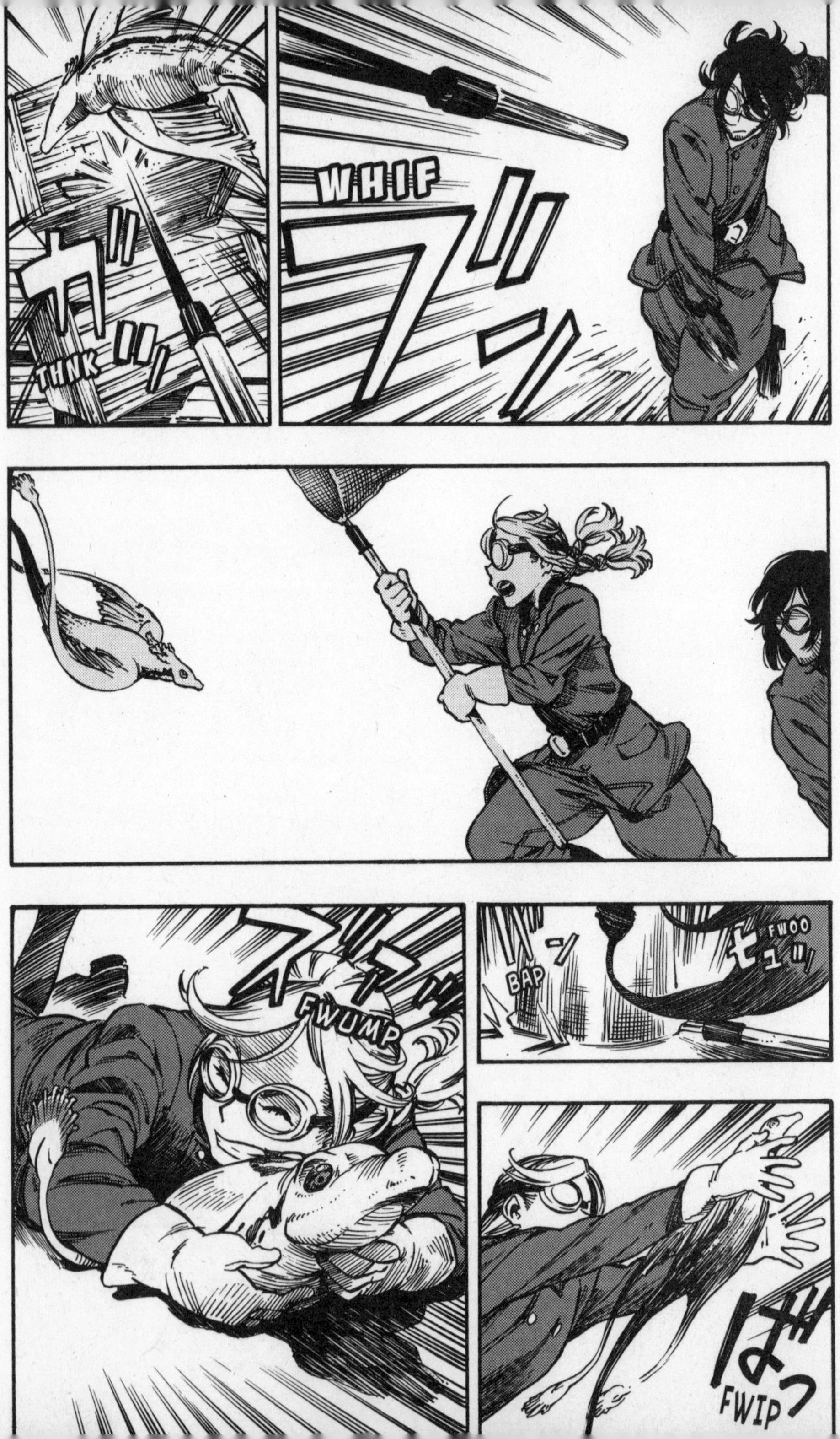
WHIF
THNK
FWOO
BAP
FWIP
FWUMP

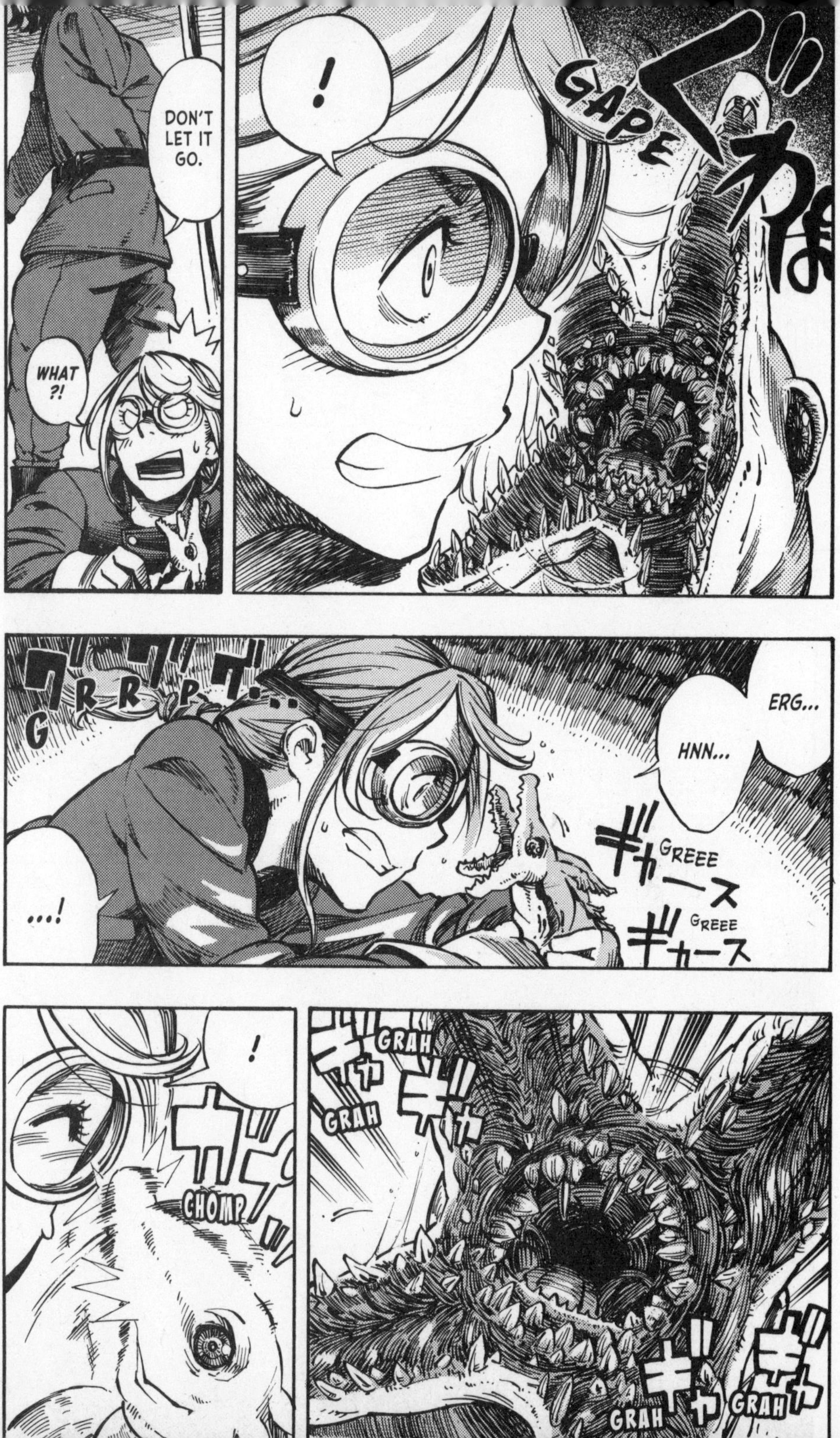
!
GAPE
DON'T LET IT GO.
WHAT ?!
ERG...
HNN...
GREEE
GREEE
GRRP
...!
GRAH
GRAH
GRAH
GRAH
!
CHOMP

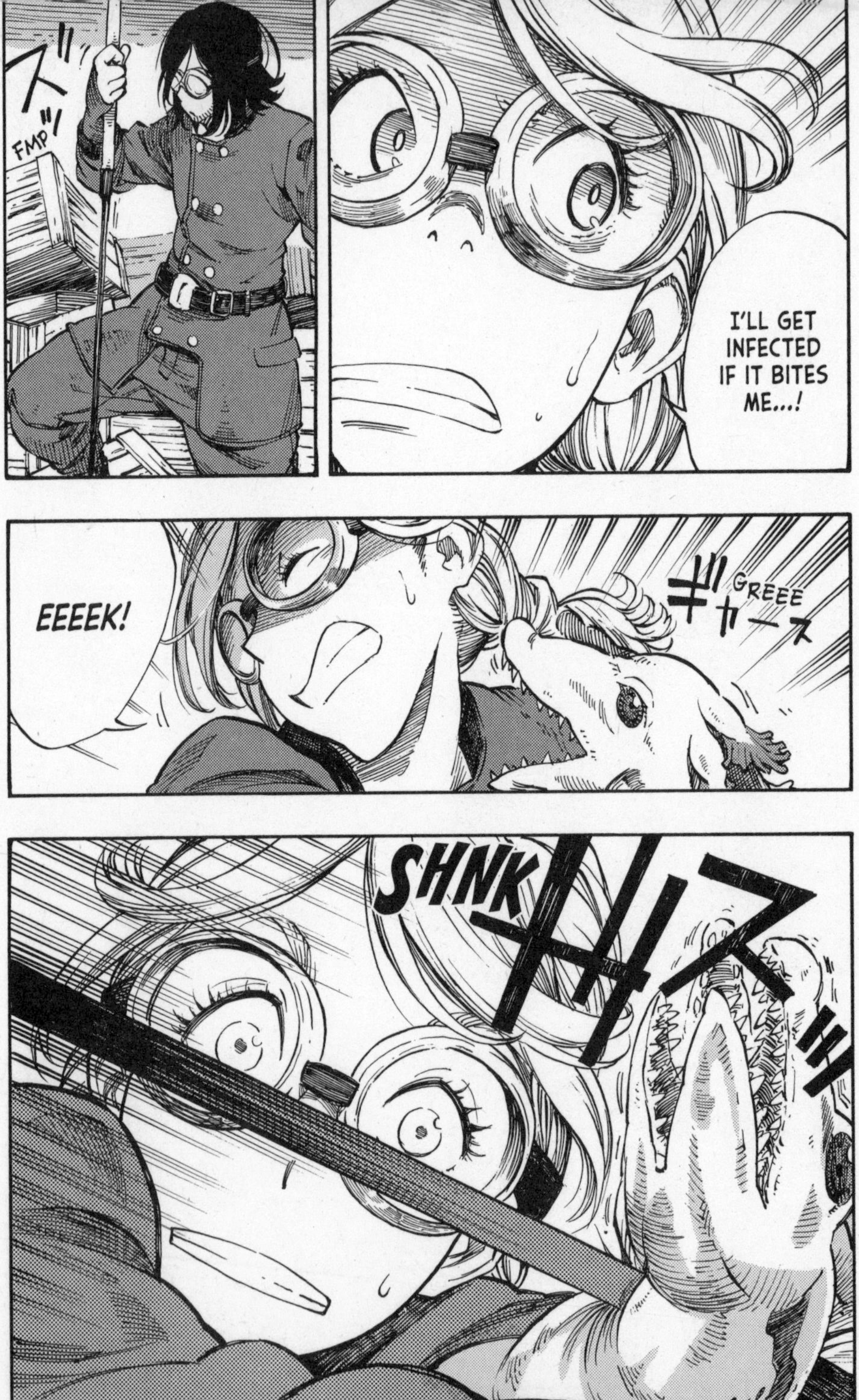
I'LL GET INFECTED IF IT BITES ME...!
ズ
FMP
ギャース
GREEE
EEEEK!
ザスッ
SHNK

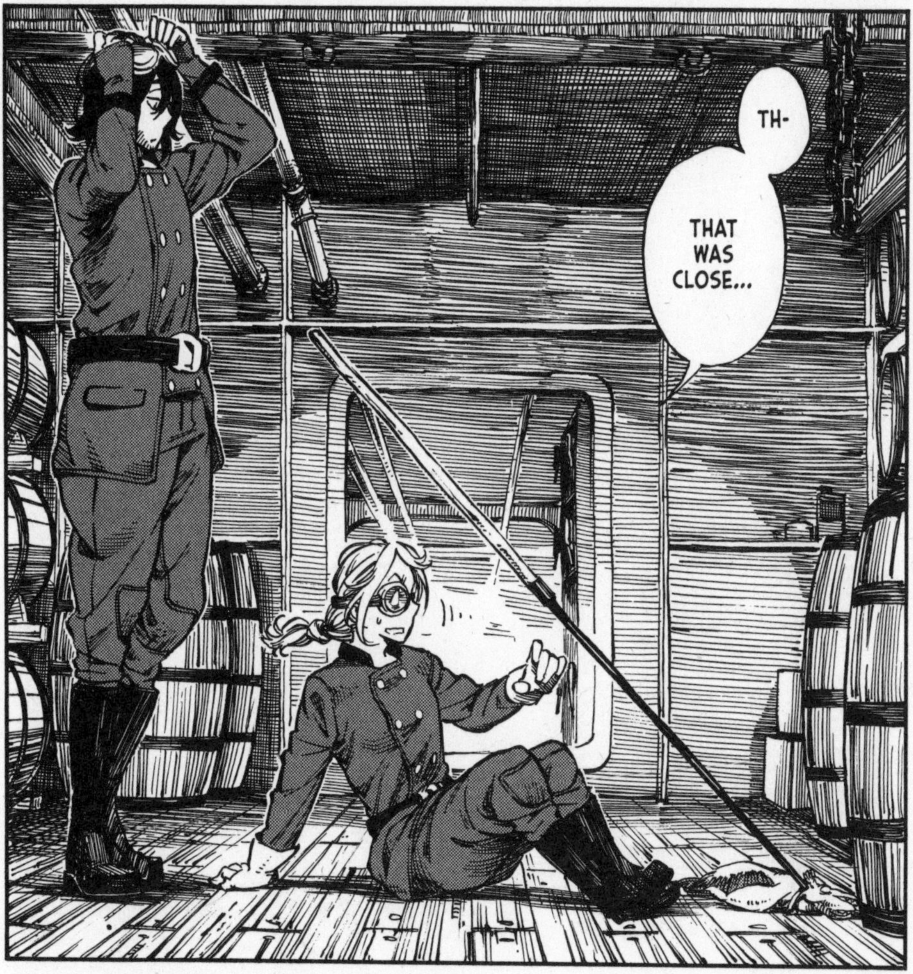
TH-
THAT WAS CLOSE...

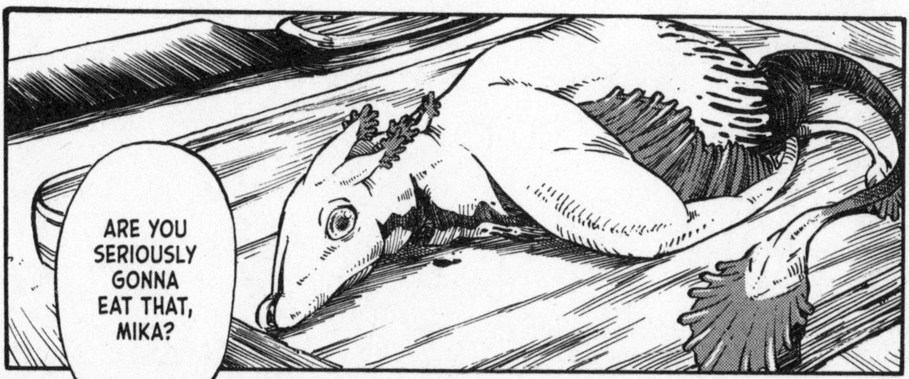
ARE YOU SERIOUSLY GONNA EAT THAT, MIKA?

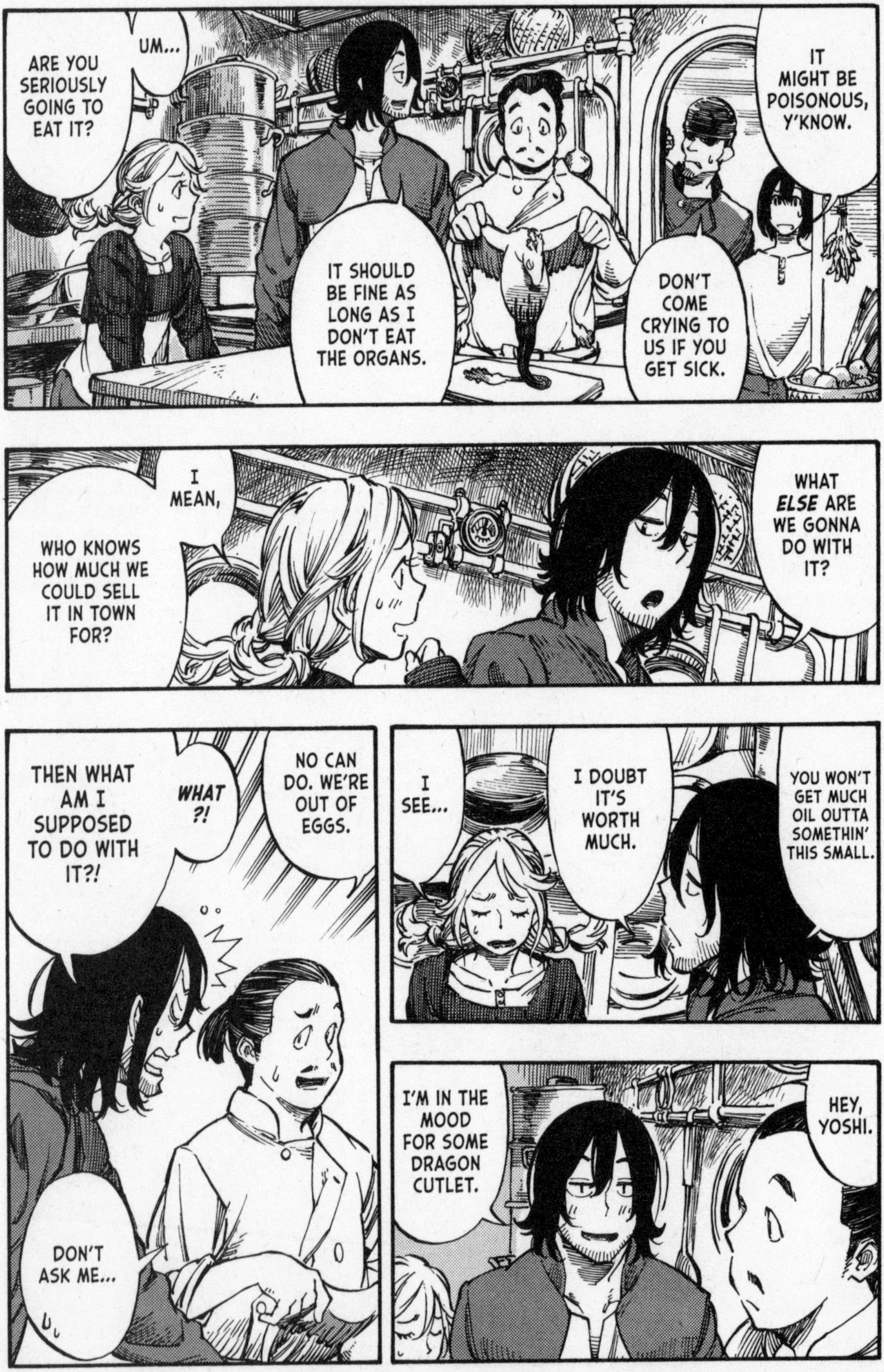
IT MIGHT BE POISONOUS, Y'KNOW.
DON'T COME CRYING TO US IF YOU GET SICK.
IT SHOULD BE FINE AS LONG AS I DON'T EAT THE ORGANS.
UM...
ARE YOU SERIOUSLY GOING TO EAT IT?
WHAT *ELSE* ARE WE GONNA DO WITH IT?
I MEAN,
WHO KNOWS HOW MUCH WE COULD SELL IT IN TOWN FOR?
YOU WON'T GET MUCH OIL OUTTA SOMETHIN' THIS SMALL.
I DOUBT IT'S WORTH MUCH.
I SEE...
HEY, YOSHI.
I'M IN THE MOOD FOR SOME DRAGON CUTLET.
NO CAN DO. WE'RE OUT OF EGGS.
WHAT ?!
THEN WHAT AM I SUPPOSED TO DO WITH IT?!
DON'T ASK ME...

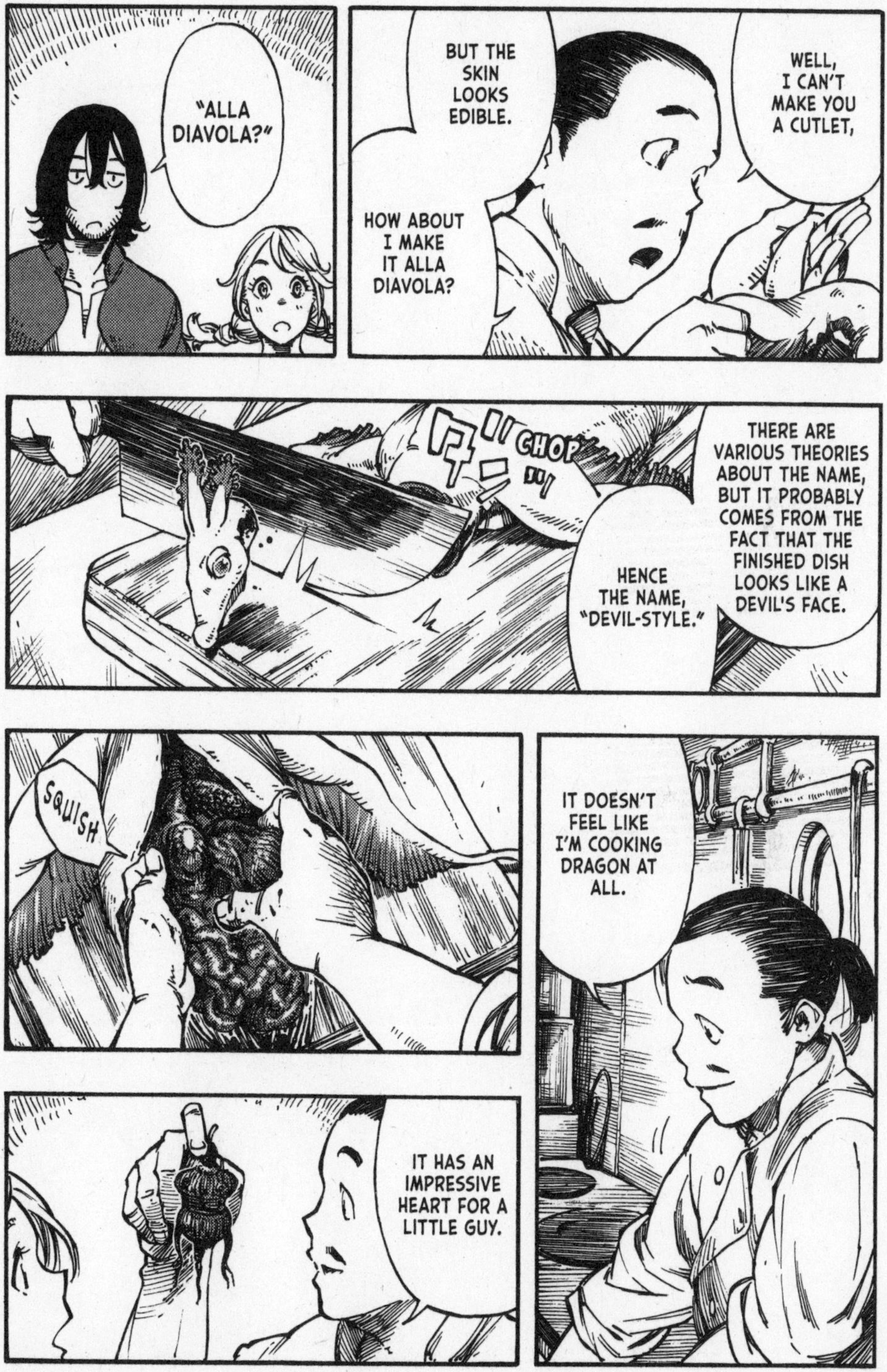
WELL, I CAN'T MAKE YOU A CUTLET,
BUT THE SKIN LOOKS EDIBLE.
HOW ABOUT I MAKE IT ALLA DIAVOLA?
"ALLA DIAVOLA?"
THERE ARE VARIOUS THEORIES ABOUT THE NAME, BUT IT PROBABLY COMES FROM THE FACT THAT THE FINISHED DISH LOOKS LIKE A DEVIL'S FACE.
CHOP
HENCE THE NAME, "DEVIL-STYLE."
IT DOESN'T FEEL LIKE I'M COOKING DRAGON AT ALL.
SQUISH
IT HAS AN IMPRESSIVE HEART FOR A LITTLE GUY.

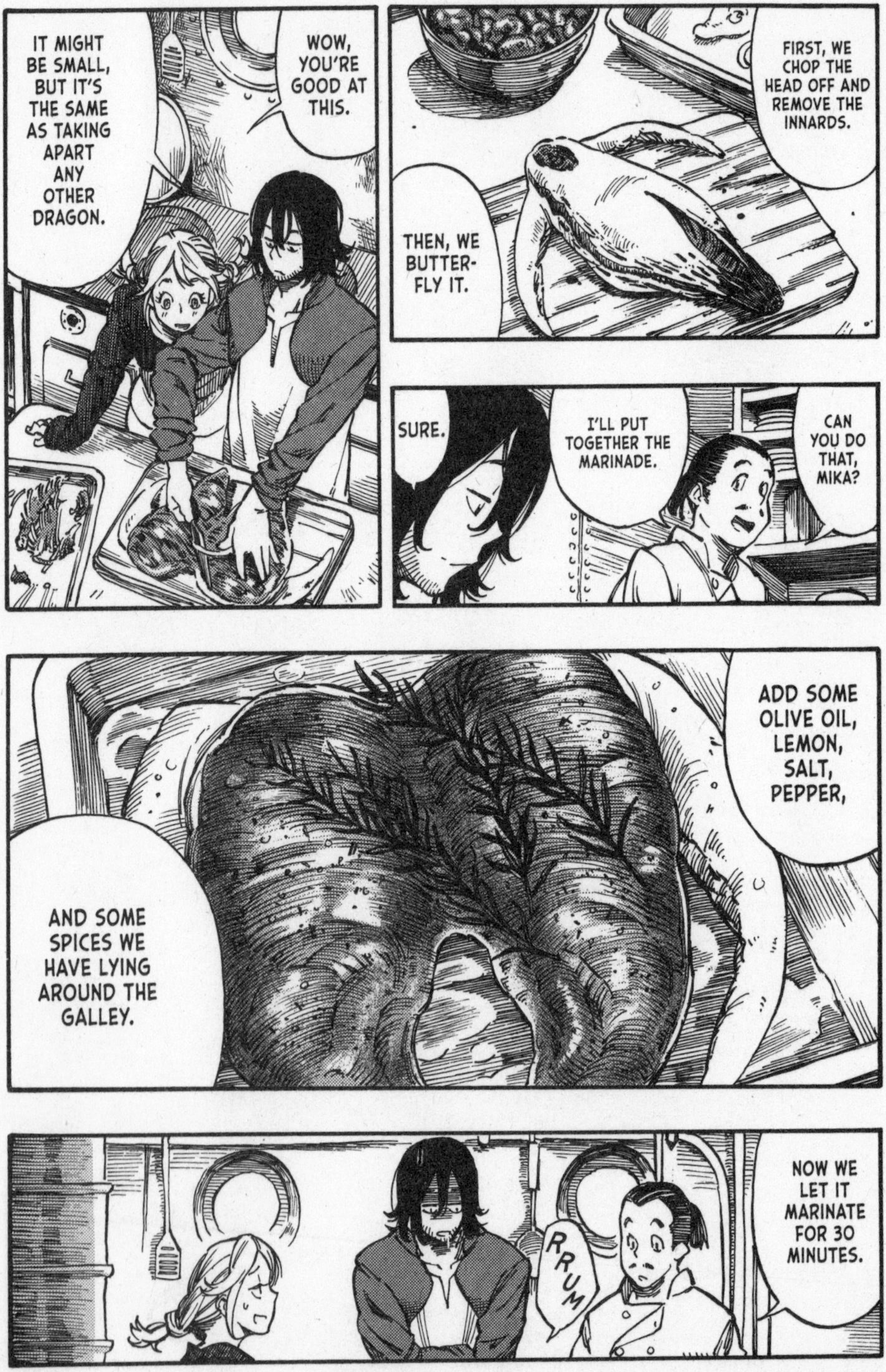
FIRST, WE CHOP THE HEAD OFF AND REMOVE THE INNARDS.
THEN, WE BUTTER-FLY IT.
CAN YOU DO THAT, MIKA?
I'LL PUT TOGETHER THE MARINADE.
SURE.
WOW, YOU'RE GOOD AT THIS.
IT MIGHT BE SMALL, BUT IT'S THE SAME AS TAKING APART ANY OTHER DRAGON.
ADD SOME OLIVE OIL, LEMON, SALT, PEPPER,
AND SOME SPICES WE HAVE LYING AROUND THE GALLEY.
NOW WE LET IT MARINATE FOR 30 MINUTES.
RRUM

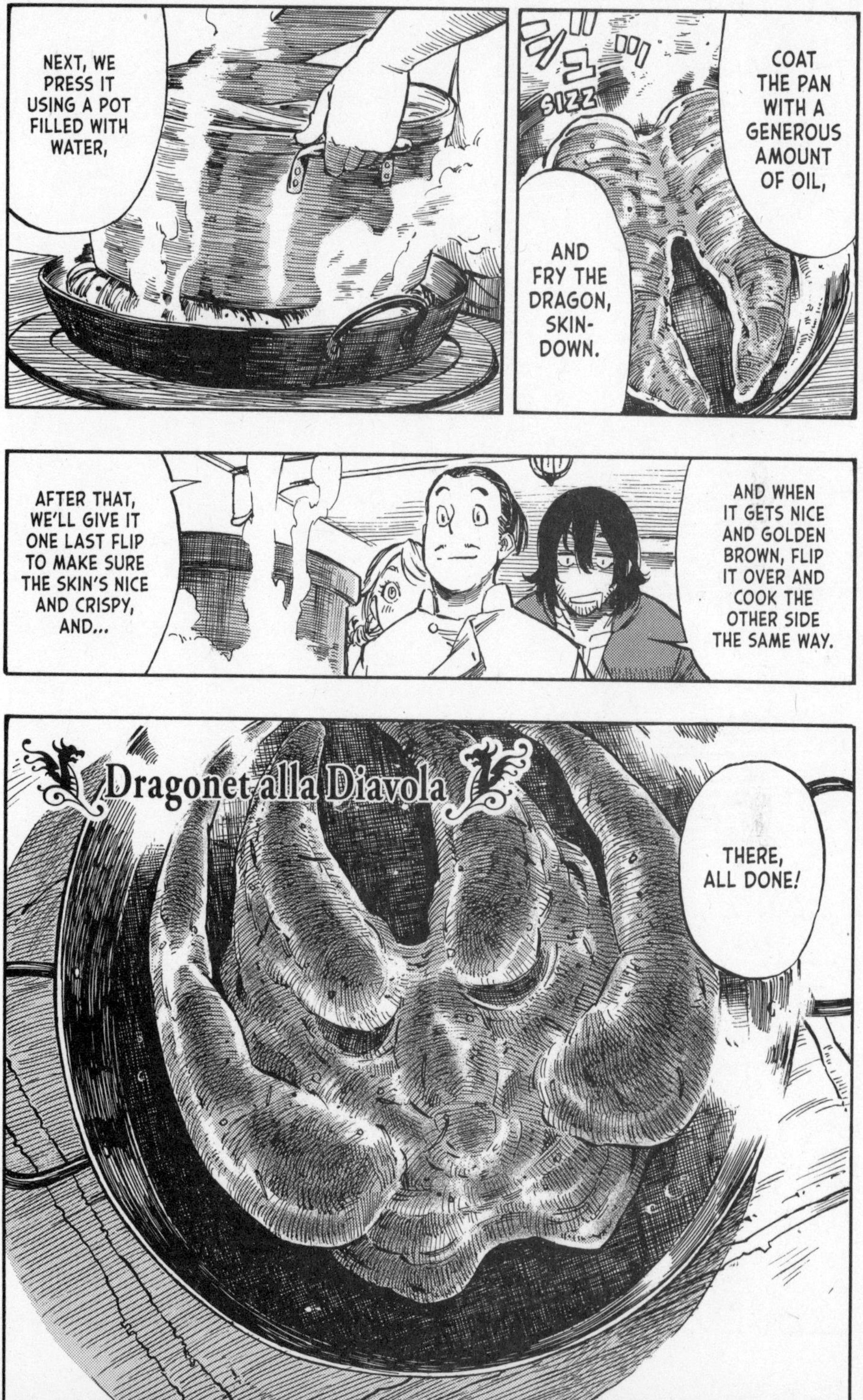
SIZZ
COAT THE PAN WITH A GENEROUS AMOUNT OF OIL,
AND FRY THE DRAGON, SKIN-DOWN.
NEXT, WE PRESS IT USING A POT FILLED WITH WATER,
AND WHEN IT GETS NICE AND GOLDEN BROWN, FLIP IT OVER AND COOK THE OTHER SIDE THE SAME WAY.
AFTER THAT, WE'LL GIVE IT ONE LAST FLIP TO MAKE SURE THE SKIN'S NICE AND CRISPY, AND...
Dragonet alla Diavola
THERE, ALL DONE!

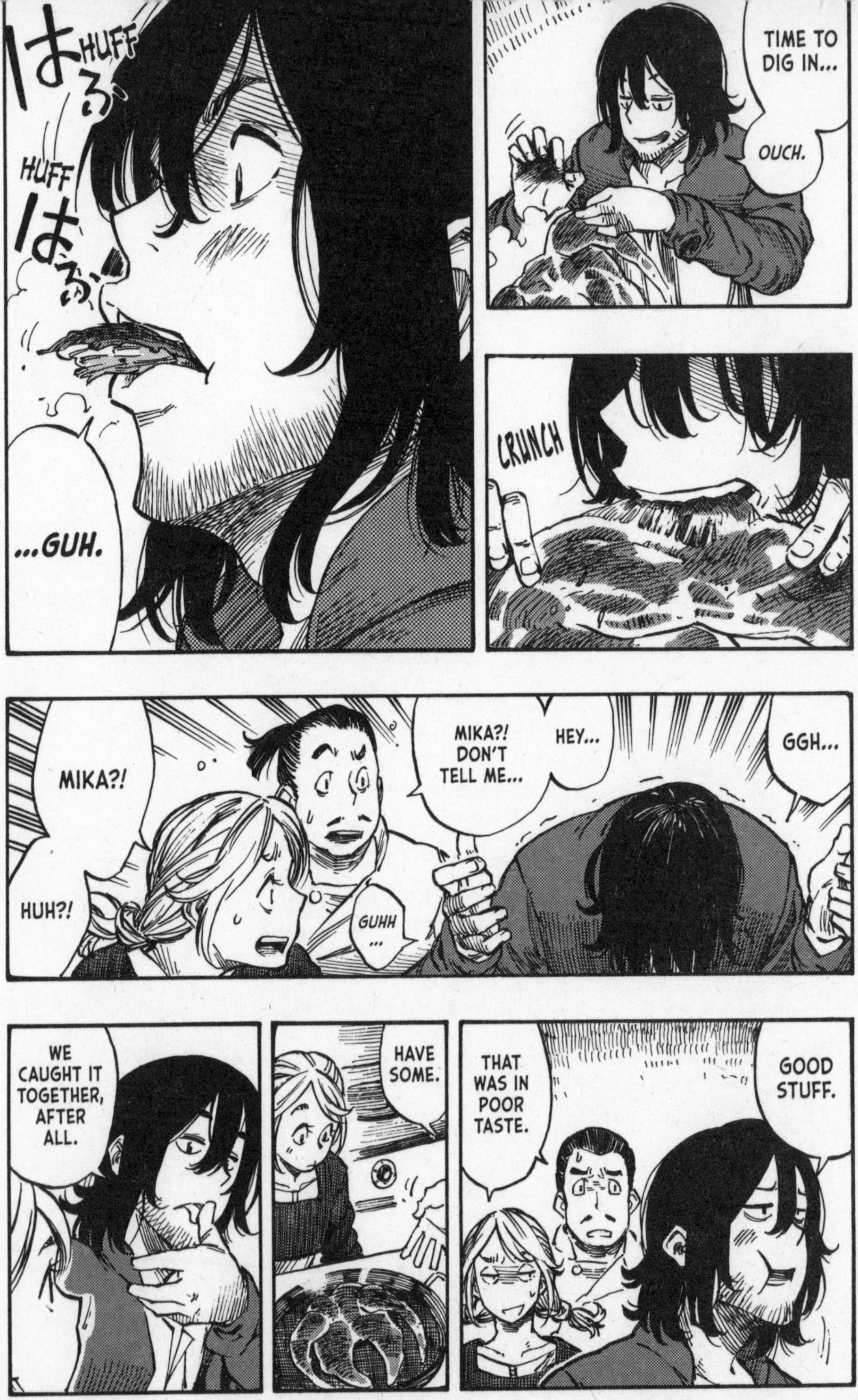
TIME TO DIG IN...
OUCH.
CRUNCH
HUFF
HUFF
...GUH.
GGH...
HEY...
MIKA?! DON'T TELL ME...
GUHH ...
MIKA?!
HUH?!
GOOD STUFF.
THAT WAS IN POOR TASTE.
HAVE SOME.
WE CAUGHT IT TOGETHER, AFTER ALL.

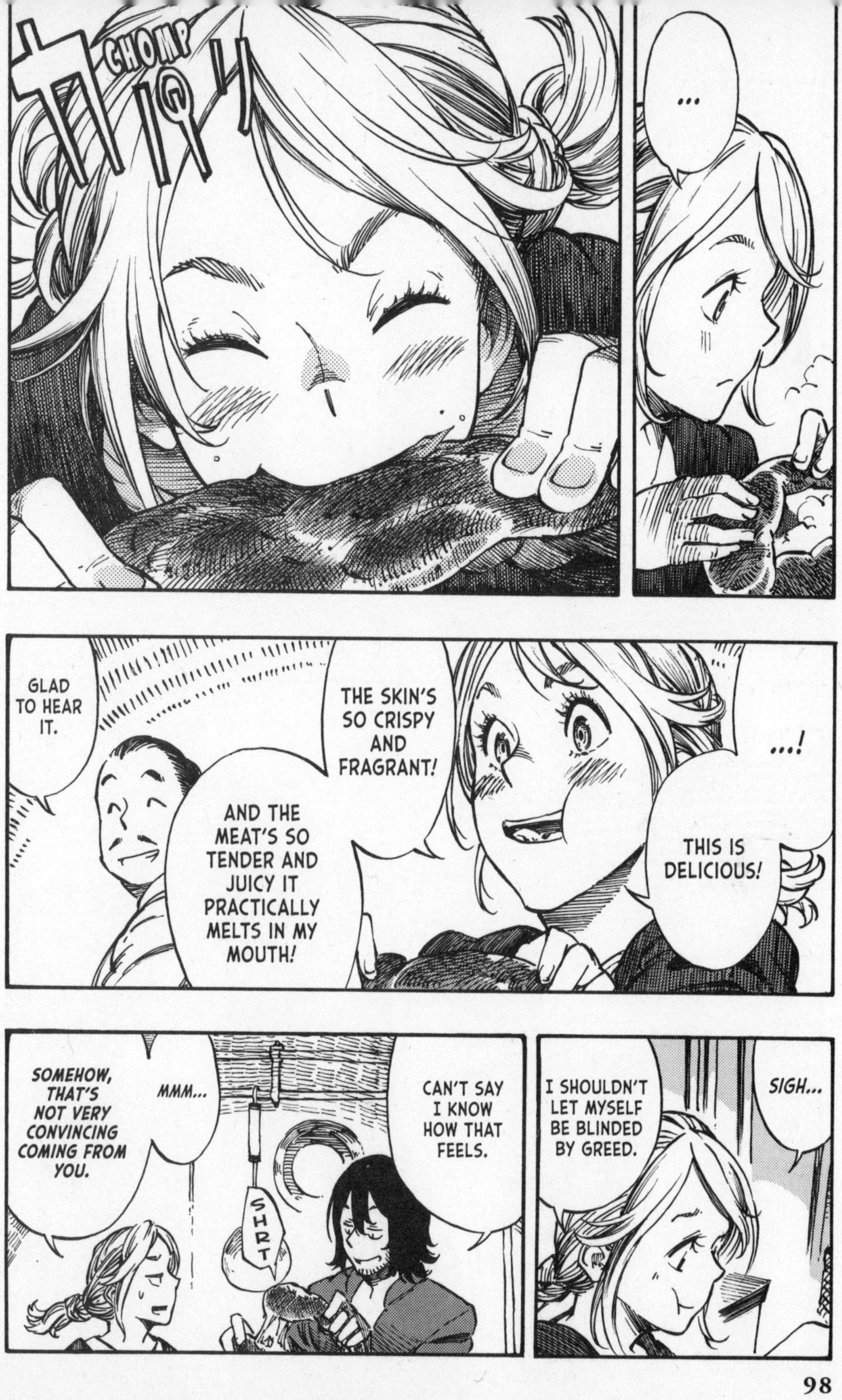
...
CHOMP
...!
THIS IS DELICIOUS!
THE SKIN'S SO CRISPY AND FRAGRANT!
AND THE MEAT'S SO TENDER AND JUICY IT PRACTICALLY MELTS IN MY MOUTH!
GLAD TO HEAR IT.
SIGH...
I SHOULDN'T LET MYSELF BE BLINDED BY GREED.
CAN'T SAY I KNOW HOW THAT FEELS.
SHRT
MMM...
SOMEHOW, THAT'S NOT VERY CONVINCING COMING FROM YOU.

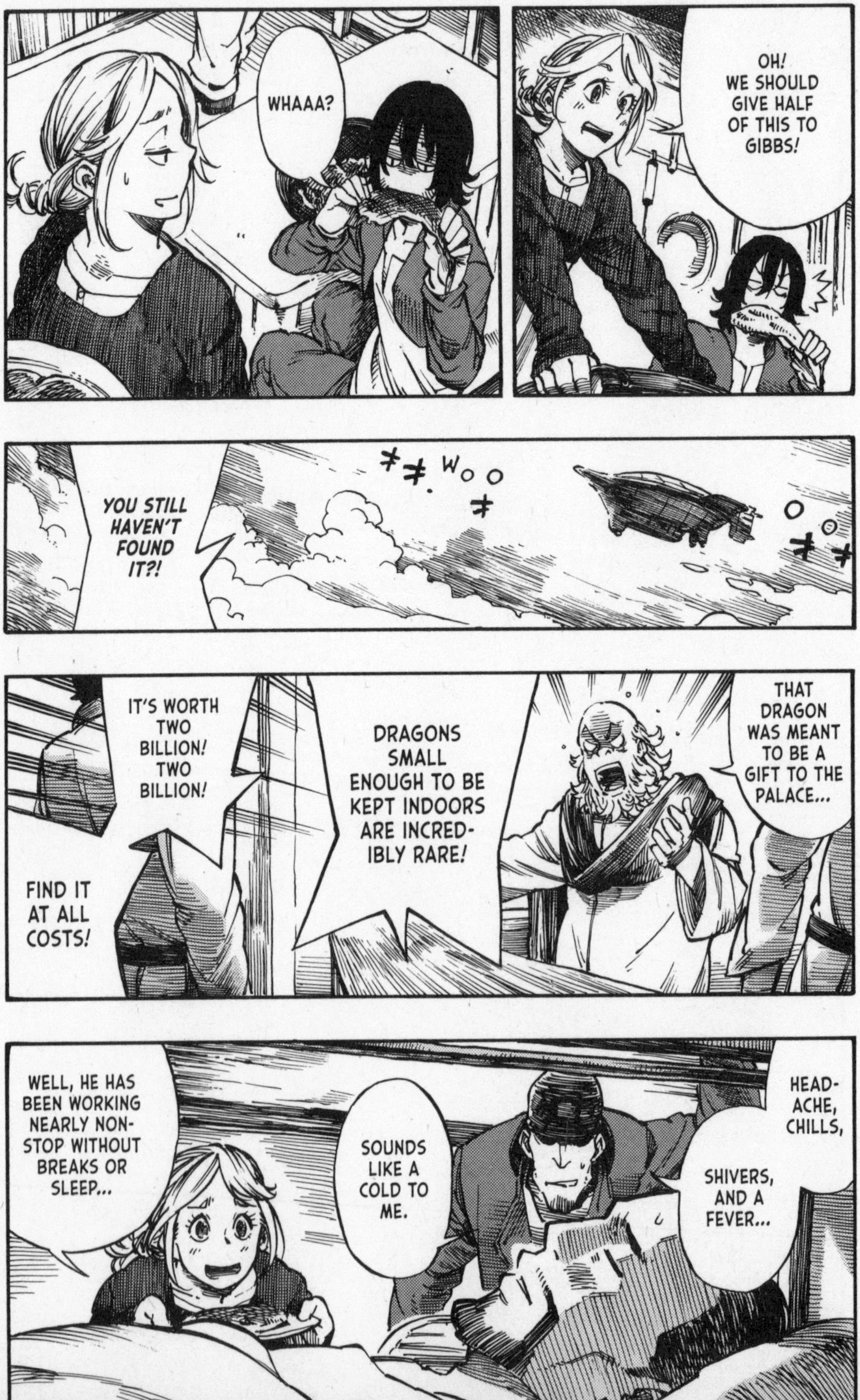
OH! WE SHOULD GIVE HALF OF THIS TO GIBBS!
WHAAA?
YOU STILL HAVEN'T FOUND IT?!
THAT DRAGON WAS MEANT TO BE A GIFT TO THE PALACE...
DRAGONS SMALL ENOUGH TO BE KEPT INDOORS ARE INCRED-IBLY RARE!
IT'S WORTH TWO BILLION! TWO BILLION!
FIND IT AT ALL COSTS!
HEAD-ACHE, CHILLS,
SHIVERS, AND A FEVER...
SOUNDS LIKE A COLD TO ME.
WELL, HE HAS BEEN WORKING NEARLY NON-STOP WITHOUT BREAKS OR SLEEP...

Dragonet alla Diavola

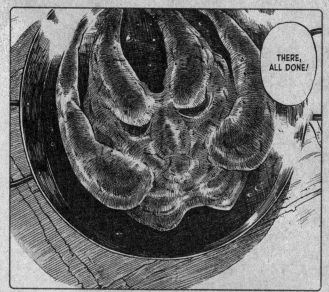

THERE, ALL DONE!

Ingredients (Servers 2-3)

- ✦ 1 whole dragonet
- ✦ Olive oil as needed
- ✦ Salt to taste
- ✦ Pepper to taste
- ✦ 1 lemon
- ✦ 3 sprigs rosemary
- ✦ ½ tsp cayenne pepper
- ✦ 1 clove garlic

01

Chop off the head and antennae, remove the organs, and butterfly the carcass.

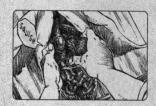

SQUISH

02

Mix together minced garlic, olive oil, lemon juice, cayenne pepper, salt, pepper, and rosemary in a bowl, then, after patting the meat dry, thoroughly coat with the marinade and let sit for 30 minutes to 1 hour.

03

Heat oil (or marinade) in a pan. Fry the meat skin-side down and weigh down with a water-filled pot or other weight.

04

Once the skin becomes golden brown, flip and repeat the cooking process on the other side.

05

Place garlic and rosemary from the marinade into the pan. Cook skin-side down once more on high heat until crisp.

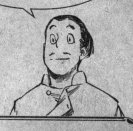

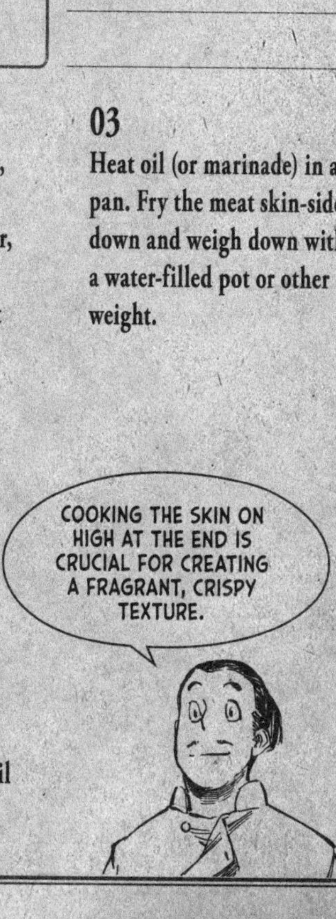

COOKING THE SKIN ON HIGH AT THE END IS CRUCIAL FOR CREATING A FRAGRANT, CRISPY TEXTURE.

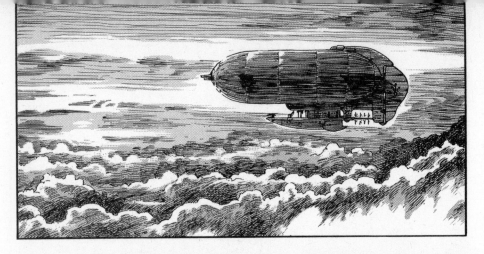

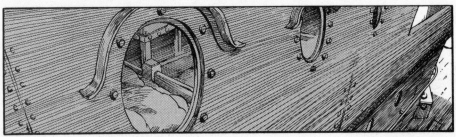

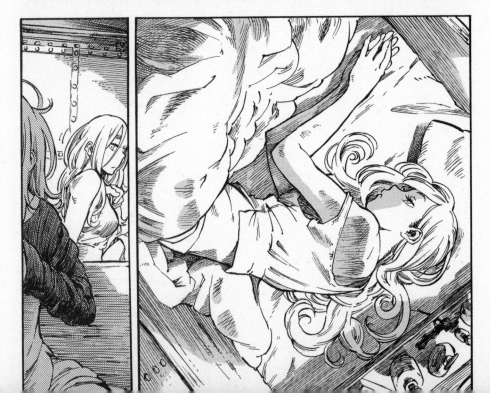

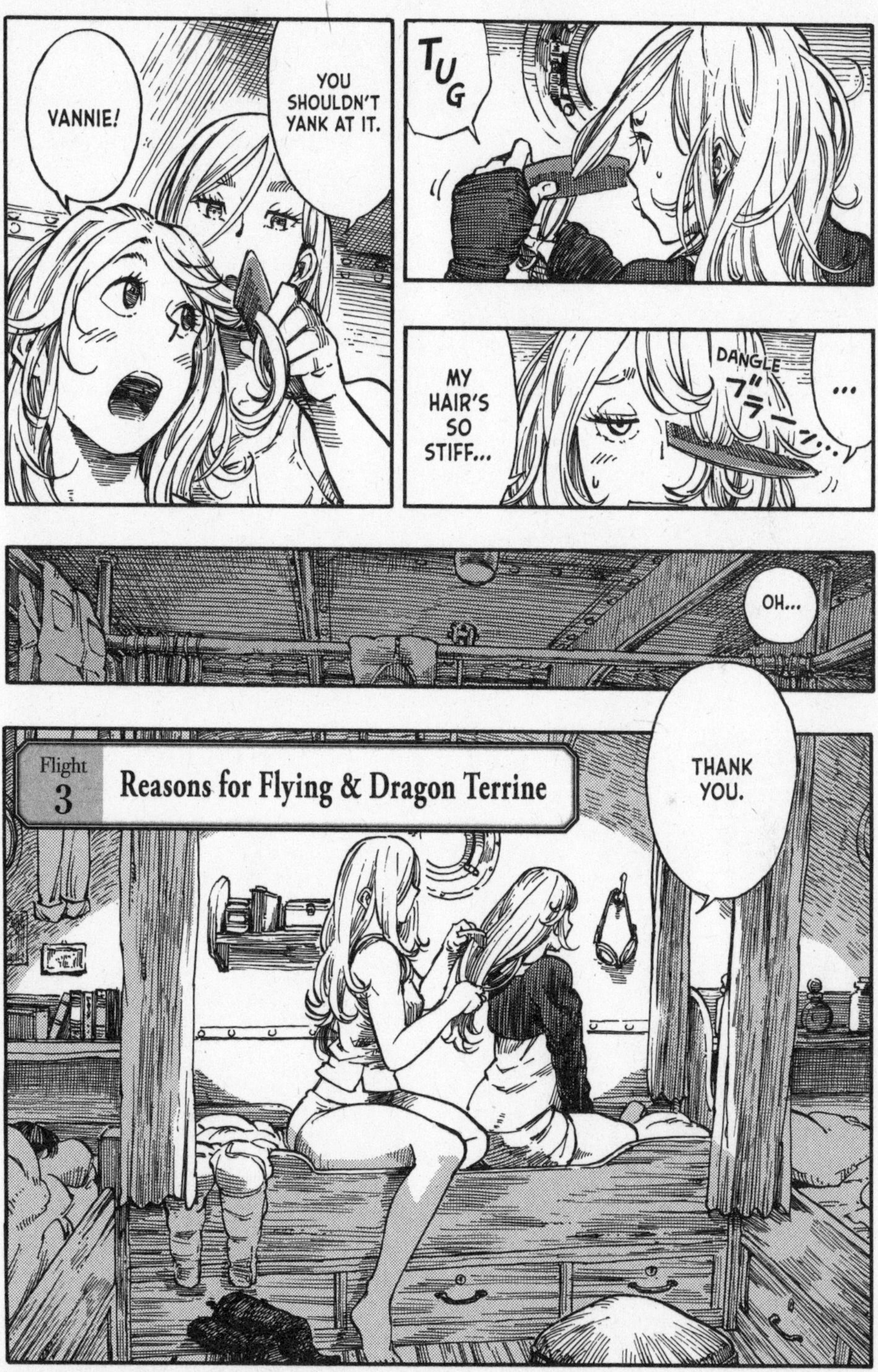
TUG
...
DANGLE
ブラーン…
MY HAIR'S SO STIFF...
YOU SHOULDN'T YANK AT IT.
VANNIE!
OH...
THANK YOU.
Flight 3
Reasons for Flying & Dragon Terrine

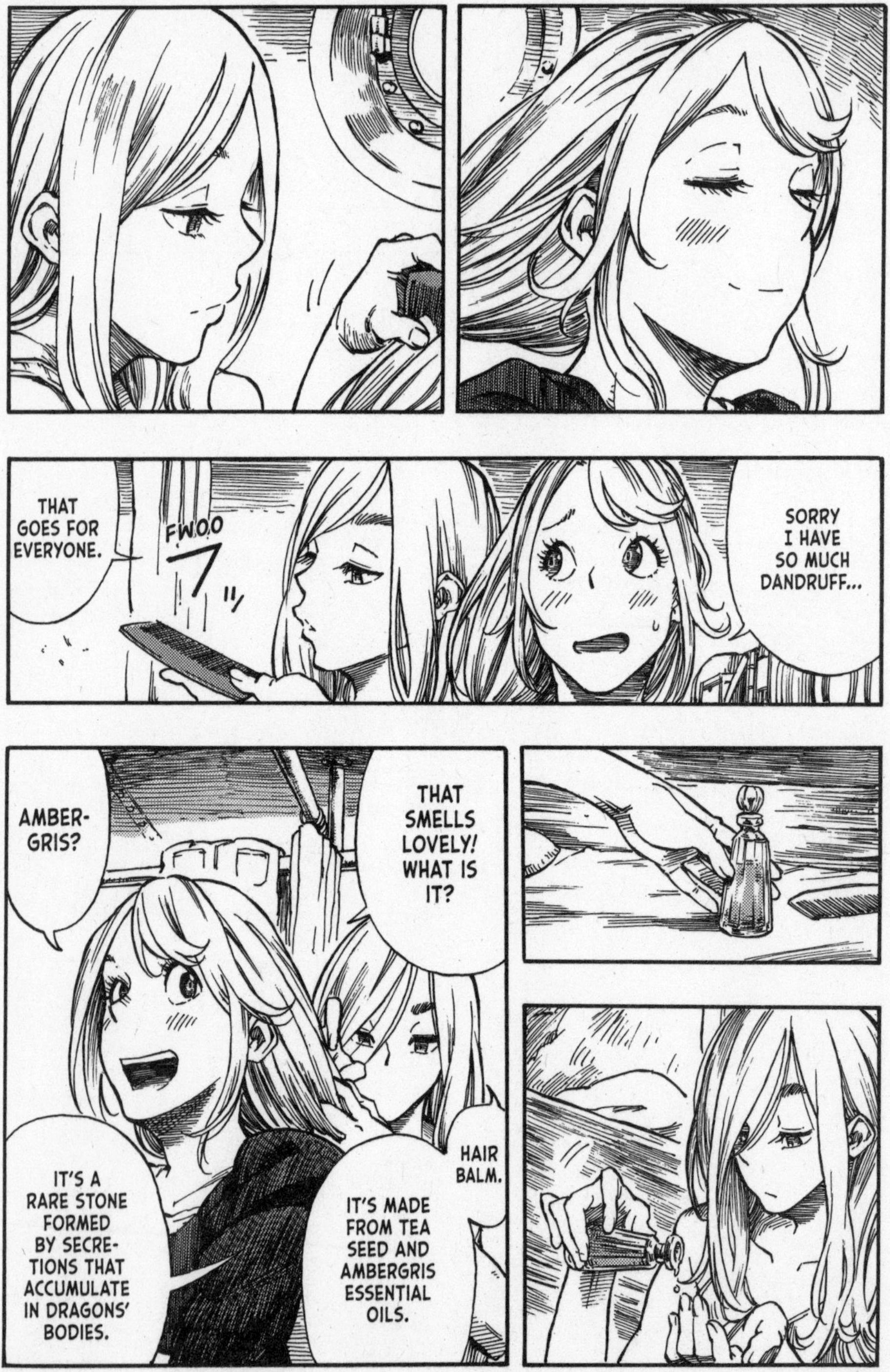
SORRY I HAVE SO MUCH DANDRUFF...
FWOO
THAT GOES FOR EVERYONE.
THAT SMELLS LOVELY! WHAT IS IT?
HAIR BALM.
IT'S MADE FROM TEA SEED AND AMBERGRIS ESSENTIAL OILS.
AMBERGRIS?
IT'S A RARE STONE FORMED BY SECRETIONS THAT ACCUMULATE IN DRAGONS' BODIES.

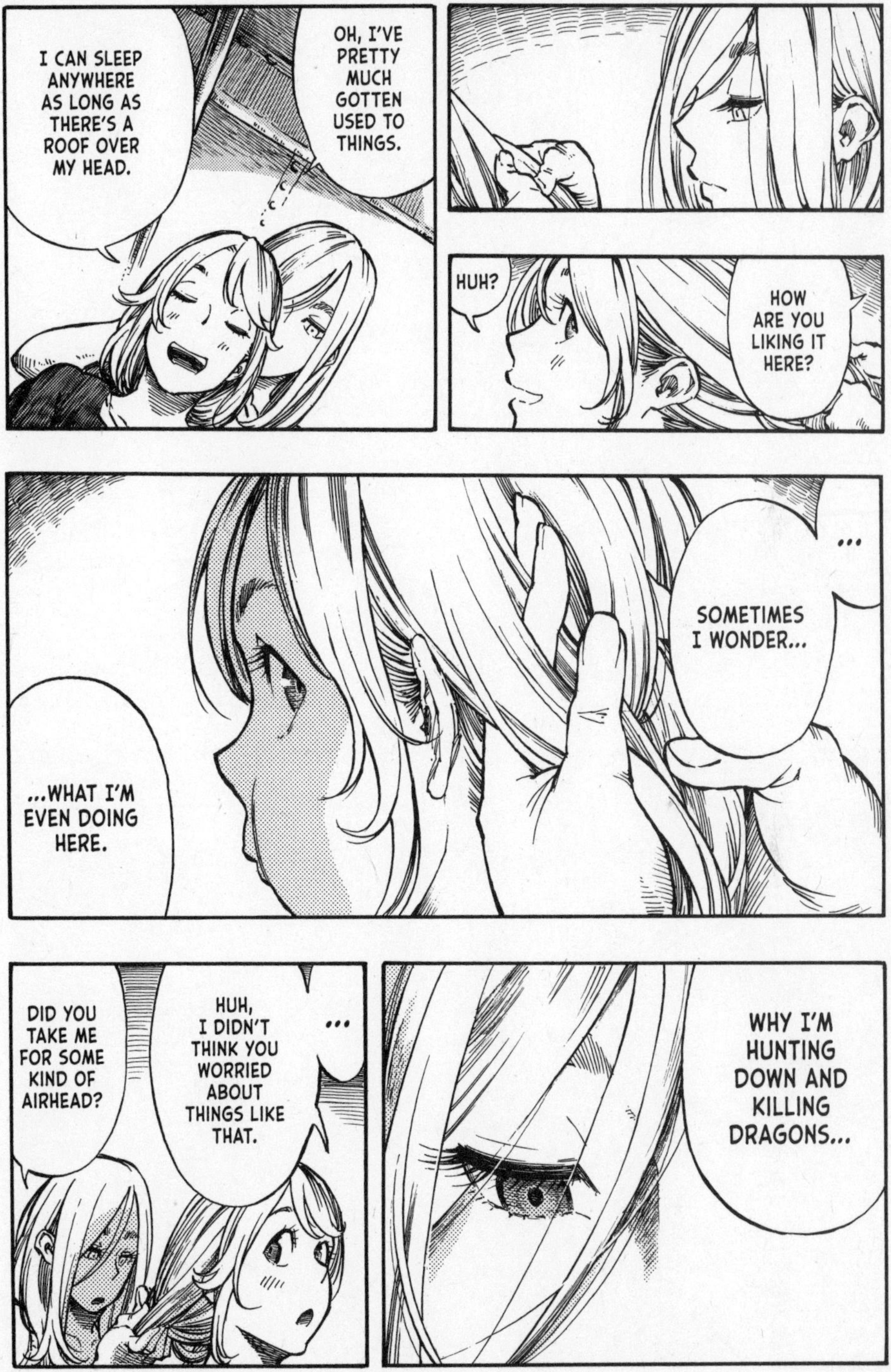
HOW ARE YOU LIKING IT HERE?
HUH?
OH, I'VE PRETTY MUCH GOTTEN USED TO THINGS.
I CAN SLEEP ANYWHERE AS LONG AS THERE'S A ROOF OVER MY HEAD.
...
SOMETIMES I WONDER...
...WHAT I'M EVEN DOING HERE.
WHY I'M HUNTING DOWN AND KILLING DRAGONS...
...
HUH, I DIDN'T THINK YOU WORRIED ABOUT THINGS LIKE THAT.
DID YOU TAKE ME FOR SOME KIND OF AIRHEAD?

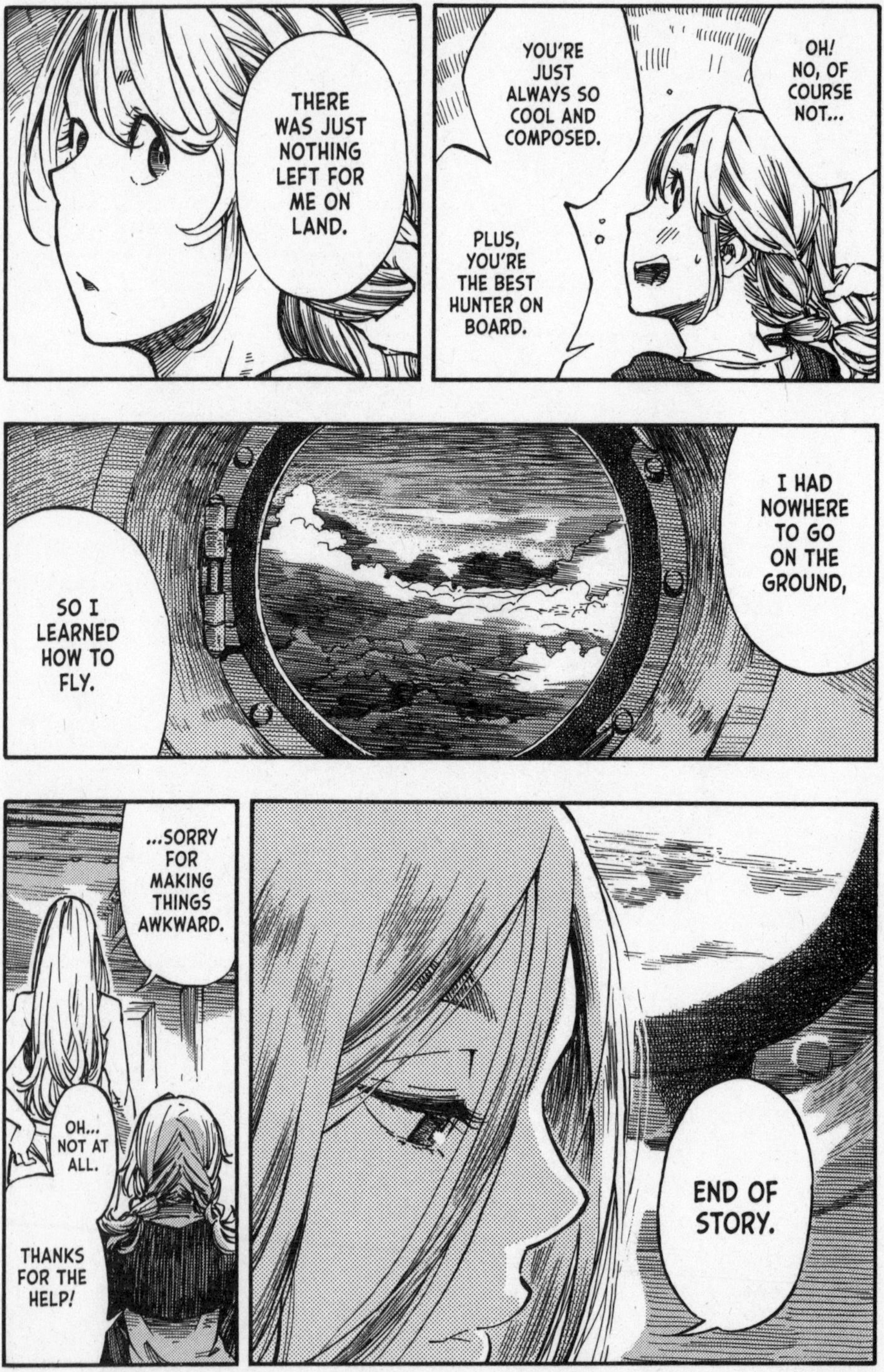
OH! NO, OF COURSE NOT...
YOU'RE JUST ALWAYS SO COOL AND COMPOSED.
PLUS, YOU'RE THE BEST HUNTER ON BOARD.
THERE WAS JUST NOTHING LEFT FOR ME ON LAND.
I HAD NOWHERE TO GO ON THE GROUND,
SO I LEARNED HOW TO FLY.
END OF STORY.
...SORRY FOR MAKING THINGS AWKWARD.
OH... NOT AT ALL.
THANKS FOR THE HELP!

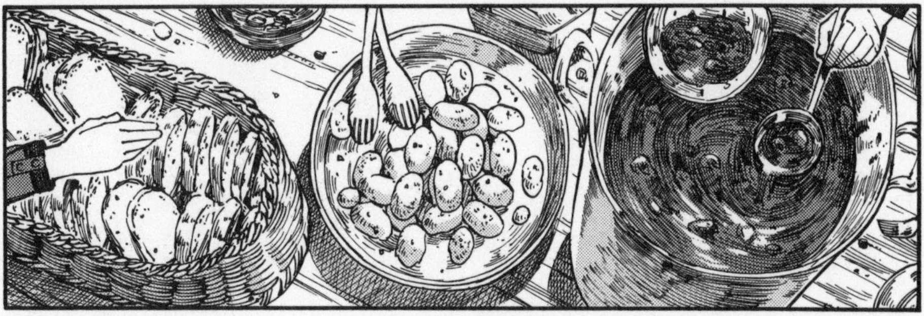

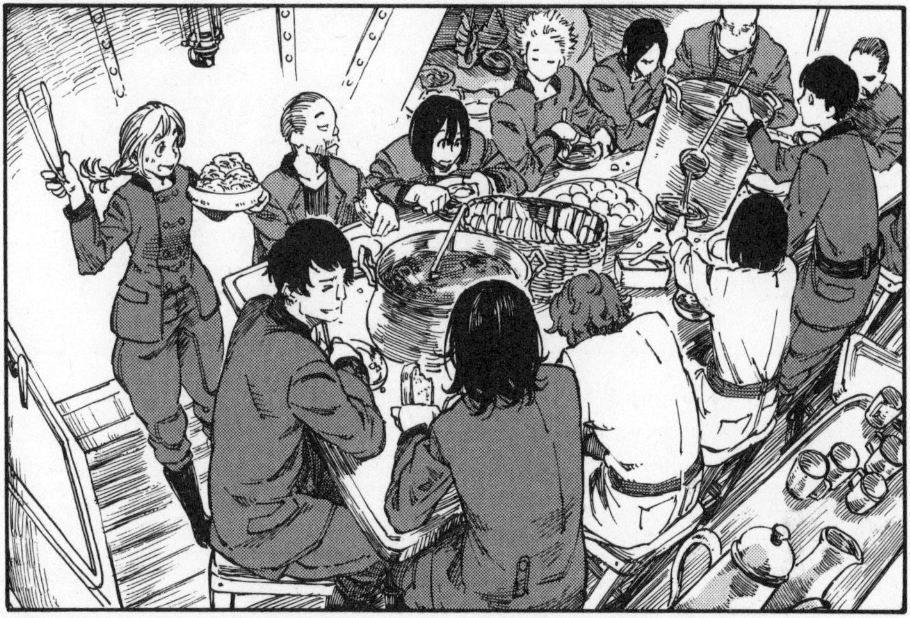

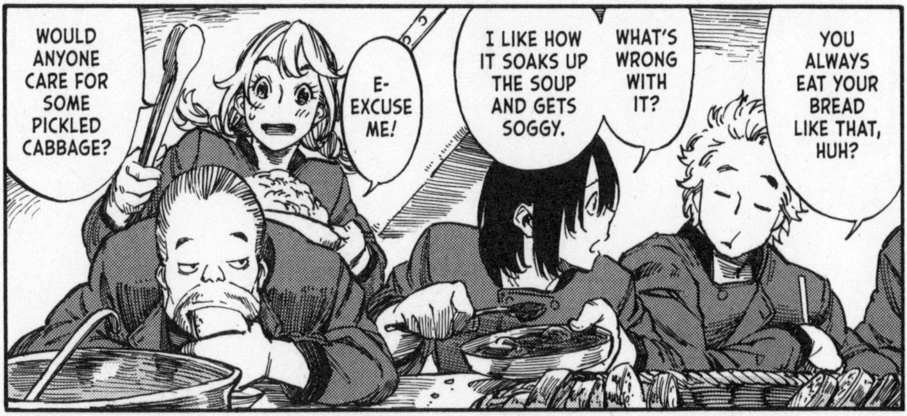
YOU ALWAYS EAT YOUR BREAD LIKE THAT, HUH?
WHAT'S WRONG WITH IT?
I LIKE HOW IT SOAKS UP THE SOUP AND GETS SOGGY.
E-EXCUSE ME!
WOULD ANYONE CARE FOR SOME PICKLED CABBAGE?

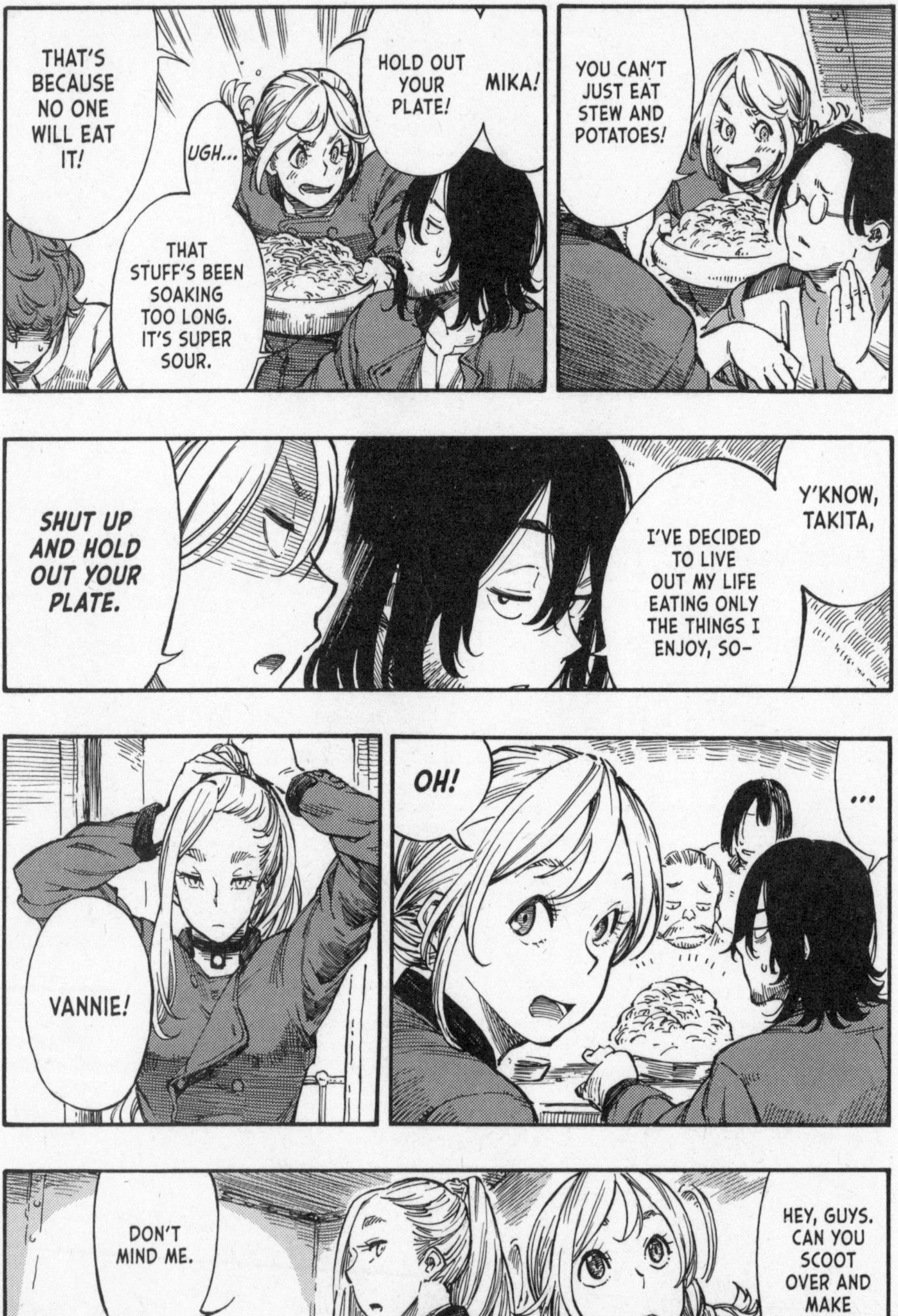
YOU CAN'T JUST EAT STEW AND POTATOES!
MIKA!
HOLD OUT YOUR PLATE!
THAT'S BECAUSE NO ONE WILL EAT IT!
UGH...
THAT STUFF'S BEEN SOAKING TOO LONG. IT'S SUPER SOUR.
Y'KNOW, TAKITA,
I'VE DECIDED TO LIVE OUT MY LIFE EATING ONLY THE THINGS I ENJOY, SO–
SHUT UP AND HOLD OUT YOUR PLATE.
...
OH!
VANNIE!
HEY, GUYS. CAN YOU SCOOT OVER AND MAKE ROOM?
DON'T MIND ME.

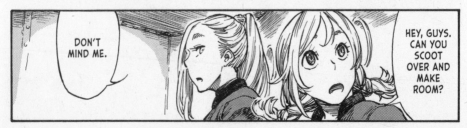

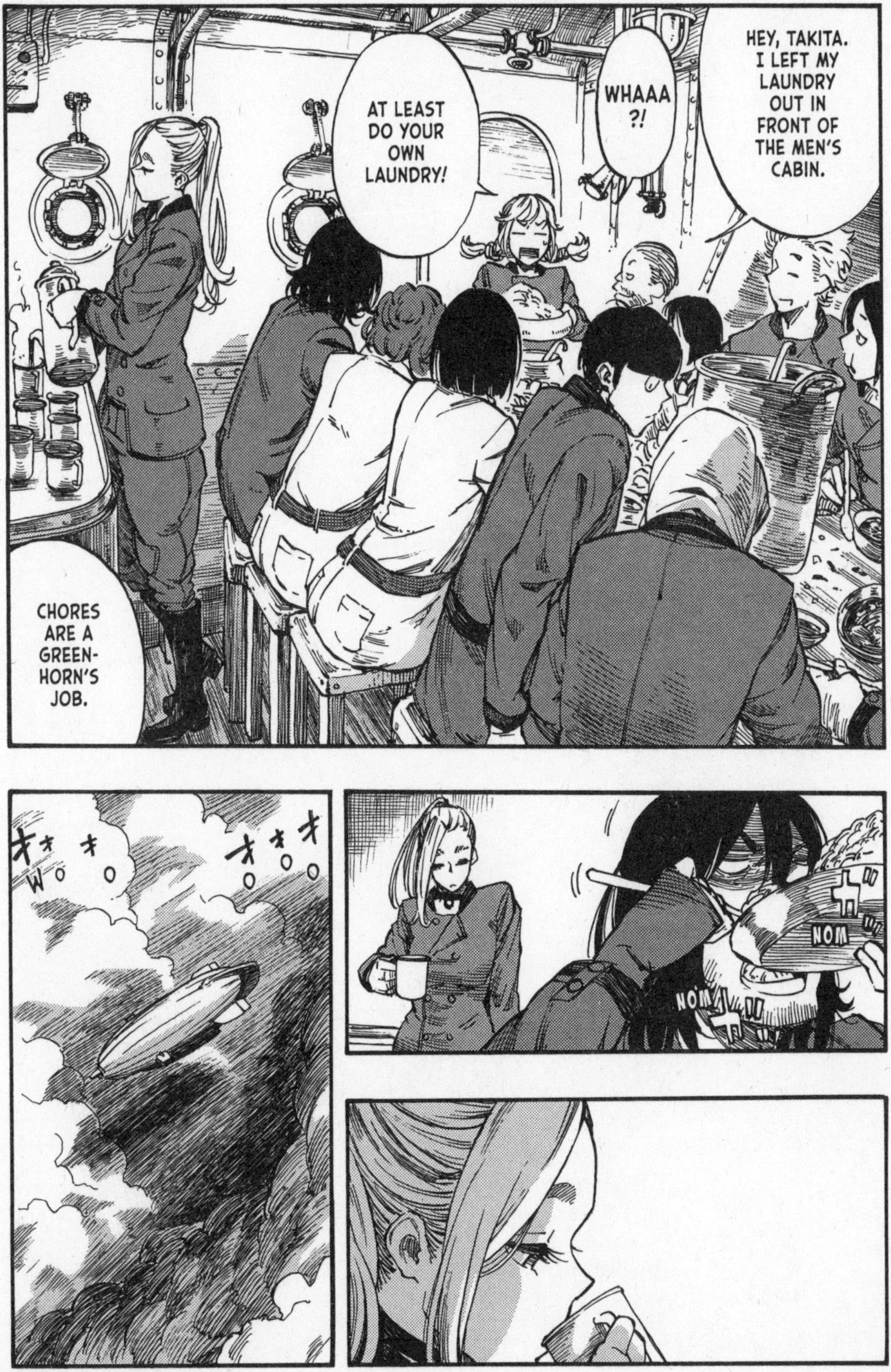
HEY, TAKITA. I LEFT MY LAUNDRY OUT IN FRONT OF THE MEN'S CABIN.
WHAAA?!
AT LEAST DO YOUR OWN LAUNDRY!
CHORES ARE A GREEN-HORN'S JOB.
NOM
NOM
WOO
OOO

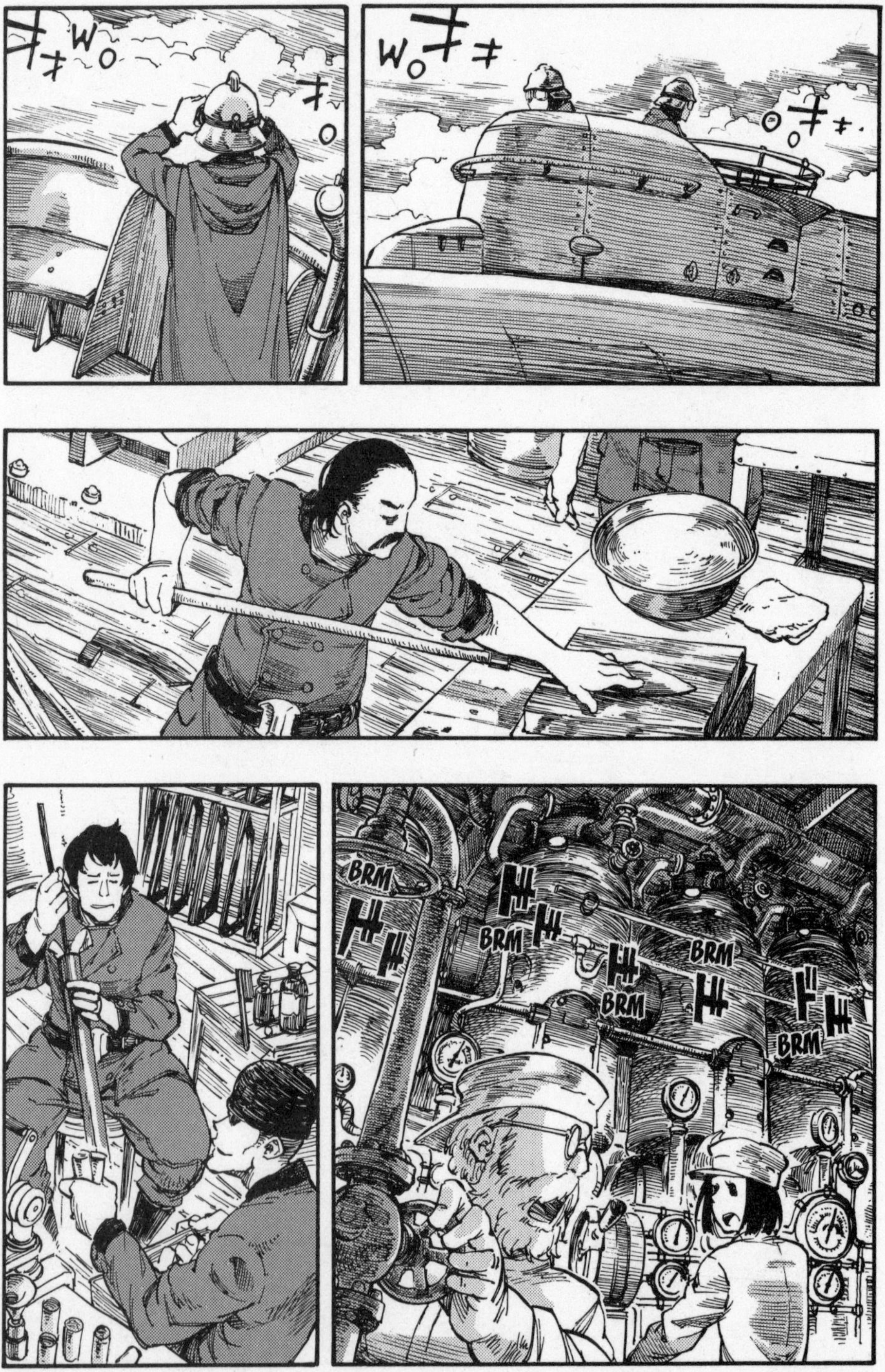
WO
WO
BRM
BRM
BRM
BRM
BRM

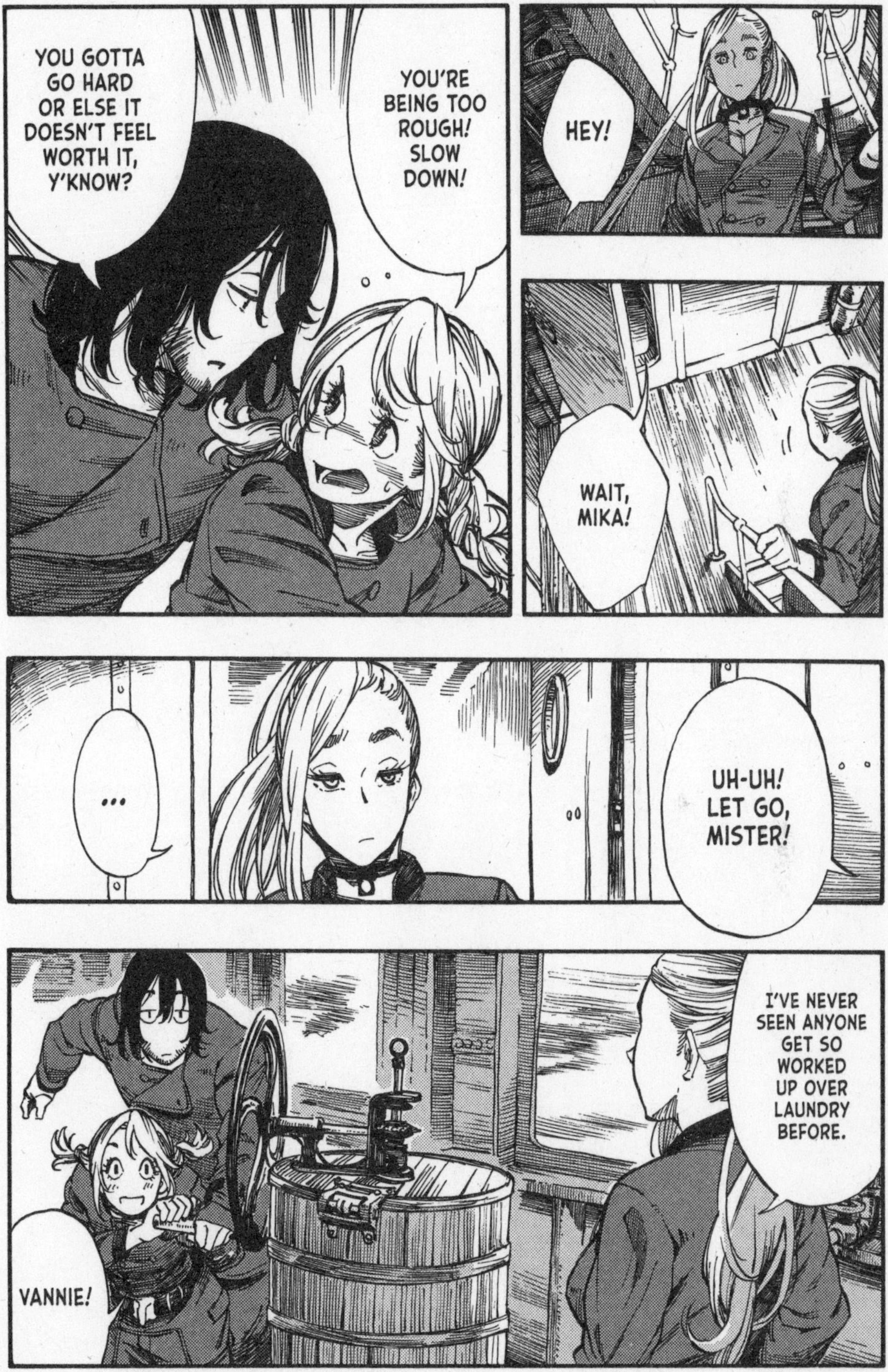
HEY!
WAIT, MIKA!
YOU'RE BEING TOO ROUGH! SLOW DOWN!
YOU GOTTA GO HARD OR ELSE IT DOESN'T FEEL WORTH IT, Y'KNOW?
UH-UH! LET GO, MISTER!
...
I'VE NEVER SEEN ANYONE GET SO WORKED UP OVER LAUNDRY BEFORE.
VANNIE!

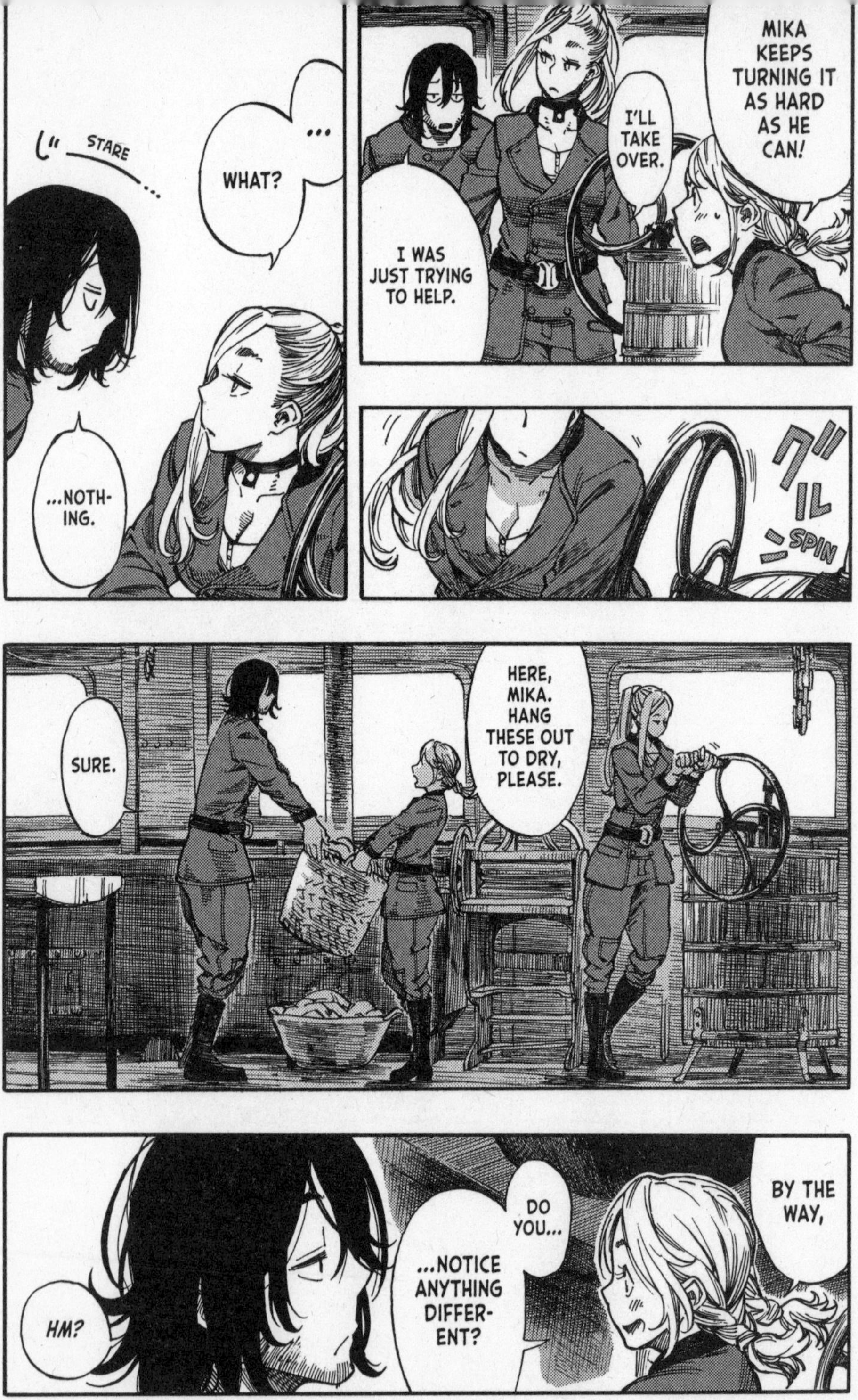

MIKA KEEPS TURNING IT AS HARD AS HE CAN!
I'LL TAKE OVER.
I WAS JUST TRYING TO HELP.
グルン
SPIN
... WHAT?
じ"
STARE...
...NOTH-ING.
HERE, MIKA. HANG THESE OUT TO DRY, PLEASE.
SURE.
BY THE WAY,
DO YOU...
...NOTICE ANYTHING DIFFER-ENT?
HM?

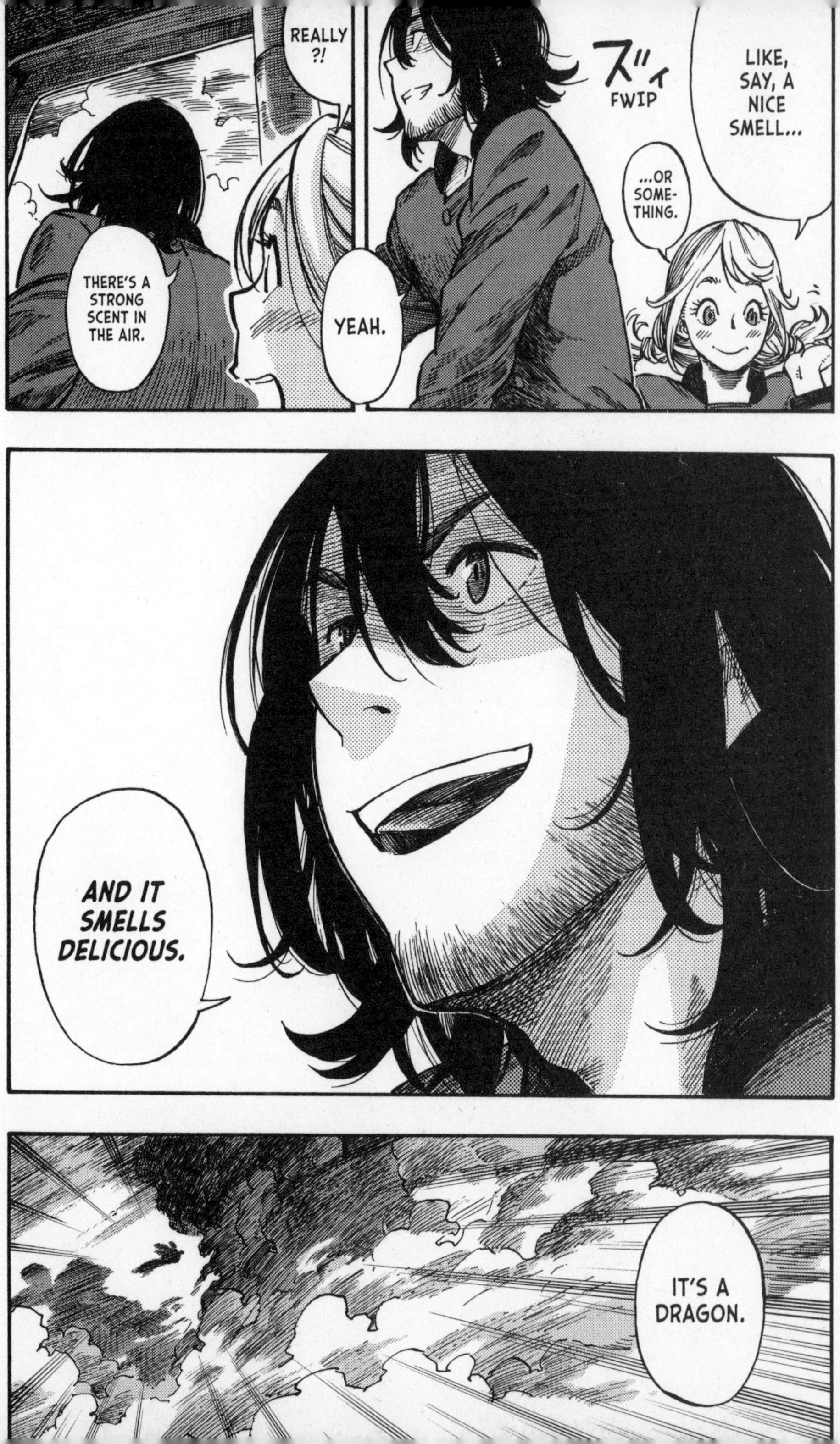

LIKE, SAY, A NICE SMELL...
ズィ
FWIP
...OR SOMETHING.
YEAH.
REALLY?!
THERE'S A STRONG SCENT IN THE AIR.
AND IT SMELLS DELICIOUS.
IT'S A DRAGON.

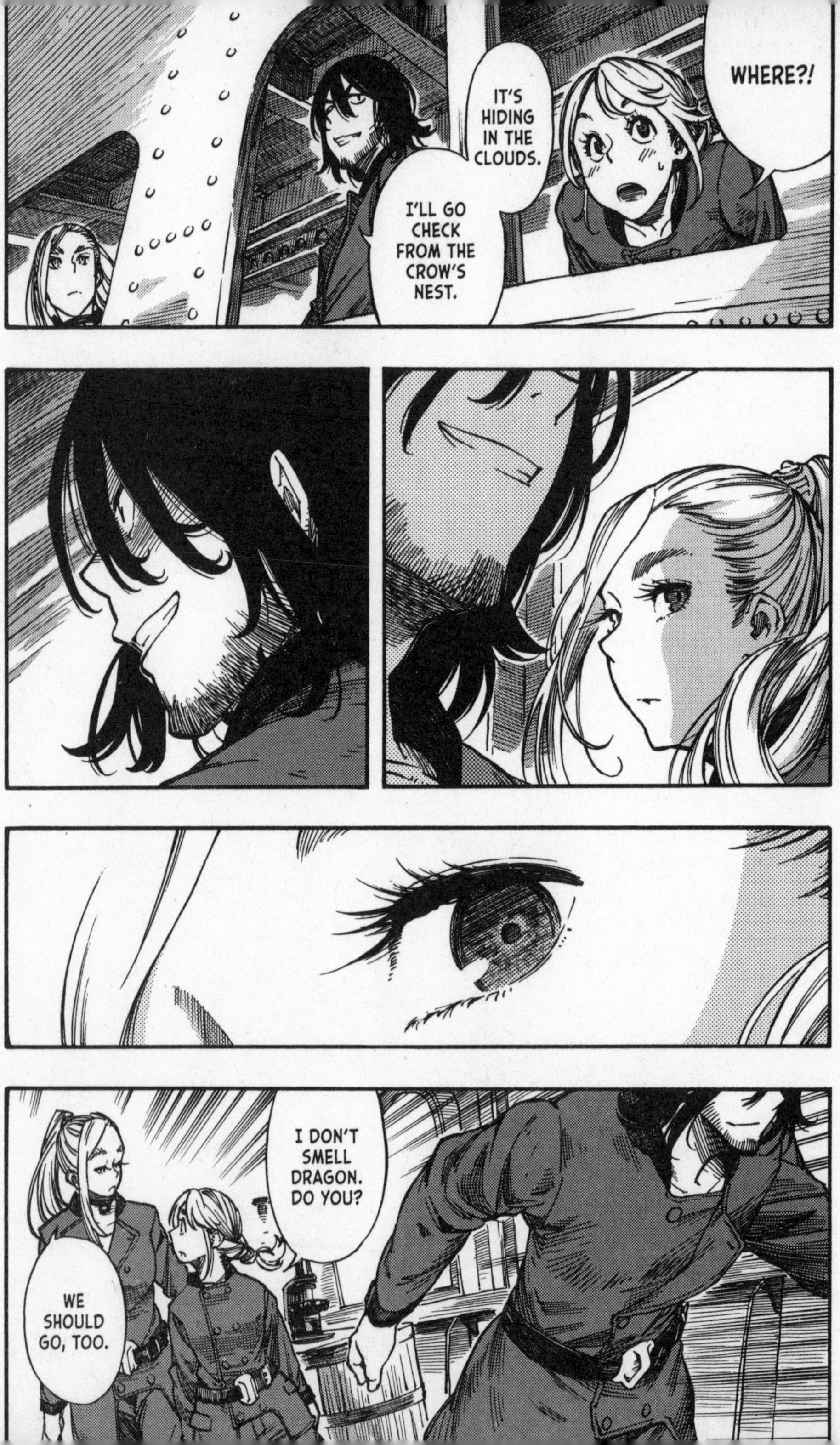
WHERE?!
IT'S HIDING IN THE CLOUDS.
I'LL GO CHECK FROM THE CROW'S NEST.
I DON'T SMELL DRAGON. DO YOU?
WE SHOULD GO, TOO.

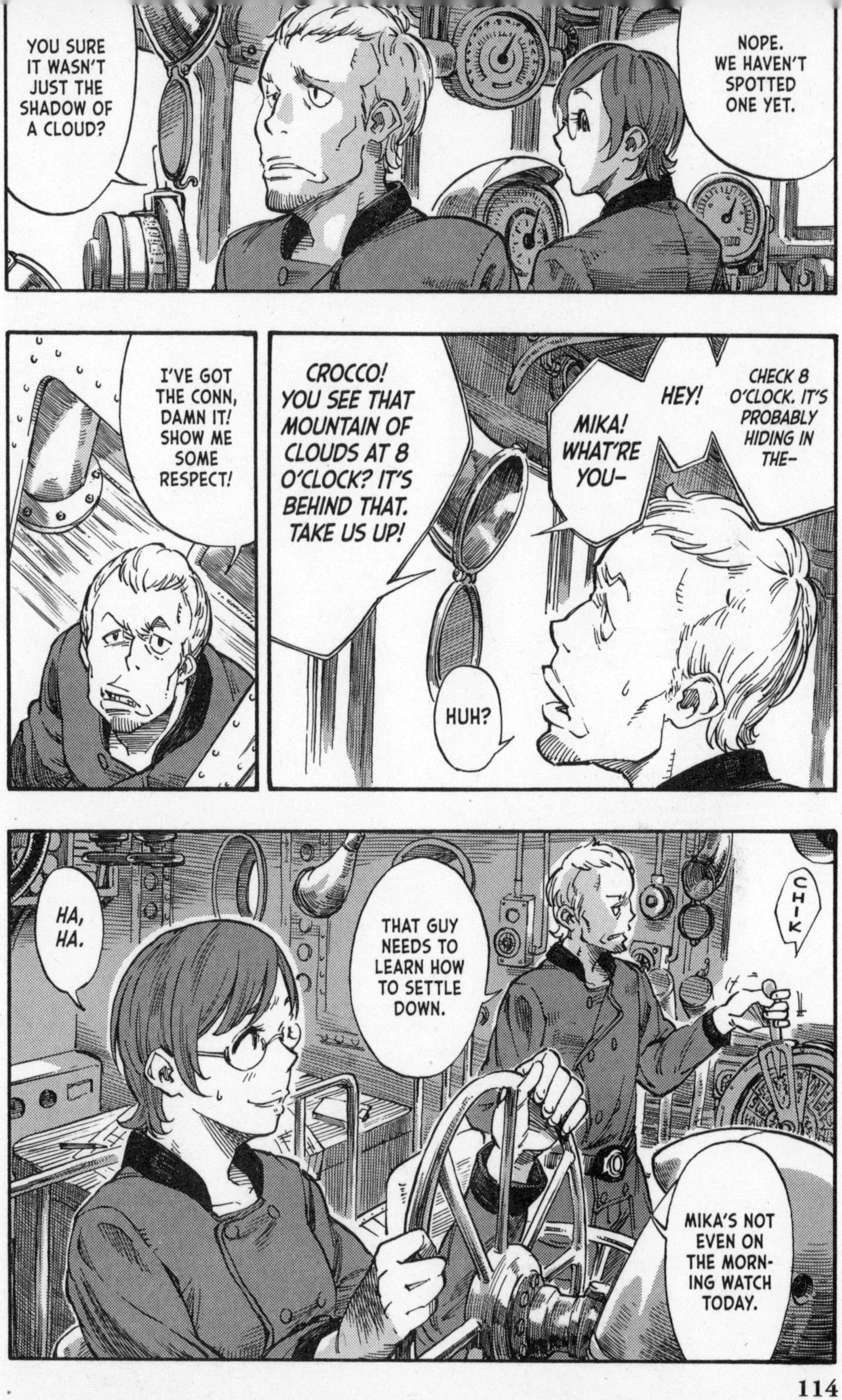
NOPE. WE HAVEN'T SPOTTED ONE YET.
YOU SURE IT WASN'T JUST THE SHADOW OF A CLOUD?
CHECK 8 O'CLOCK. IT'S PROBABLY HIDING IN THE–
HEY!
MIKA! WHAT'RE YOU–
CROCCO! YOU SEE THAT MOUNTAIN OF CLOUDS AT 8 O'CLOCK? IT'S BEHIND THAT. TAKE US UP!
HUH?
I'VE GOT THE CONN, DAMN IT! SHOW ME SOME RESPECT!
CHIK
MIKA'S NOT EVEN ON THE MORN-ING WATCH TODAY.
THAT GUY NEEDS TO LEARN HOW TO SETTLE DOWN.
HA, HA.

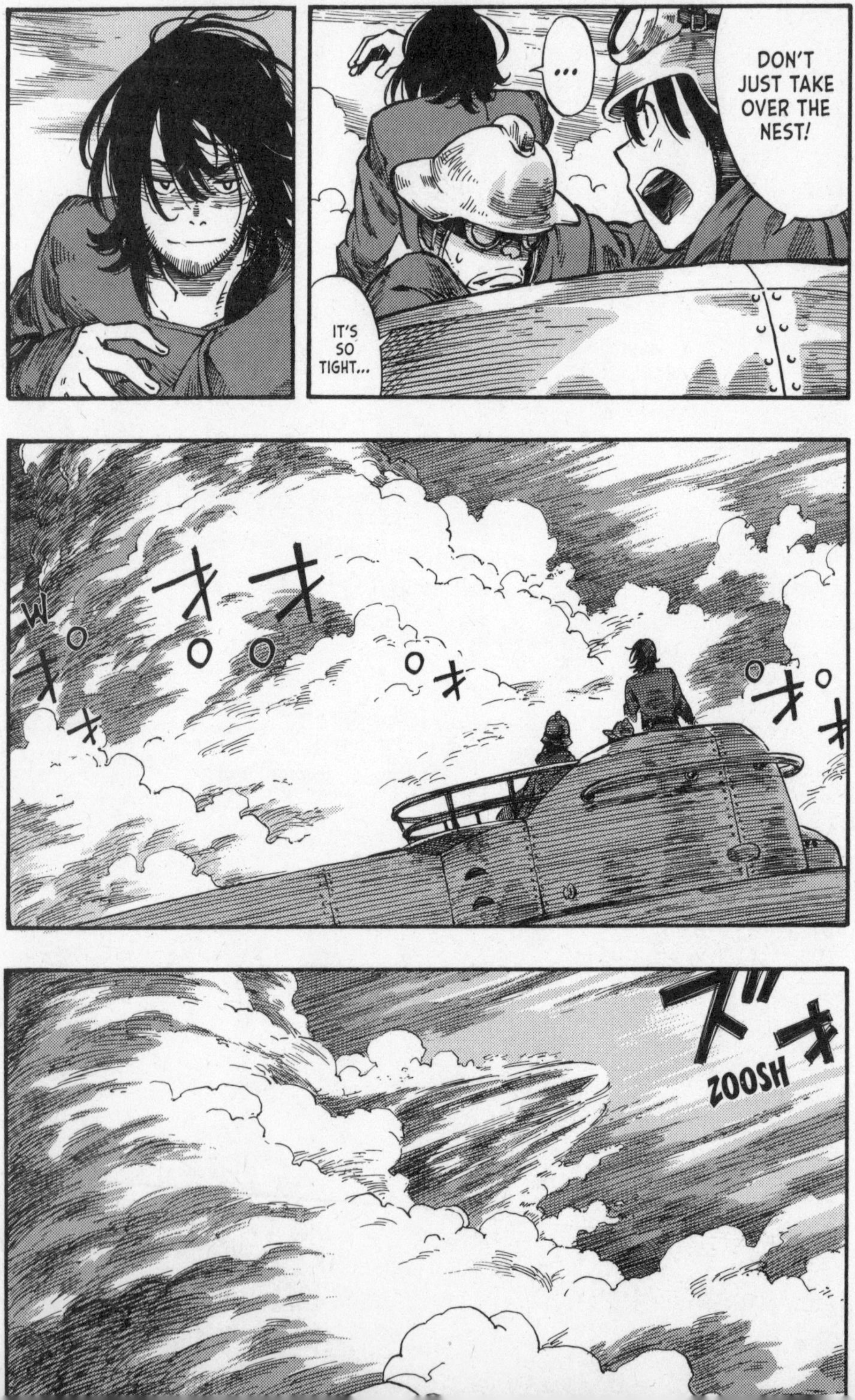
DON'T JUST TAKE OVER THE NEST!
...
IT'S SO TIGHT...
ZOOSH

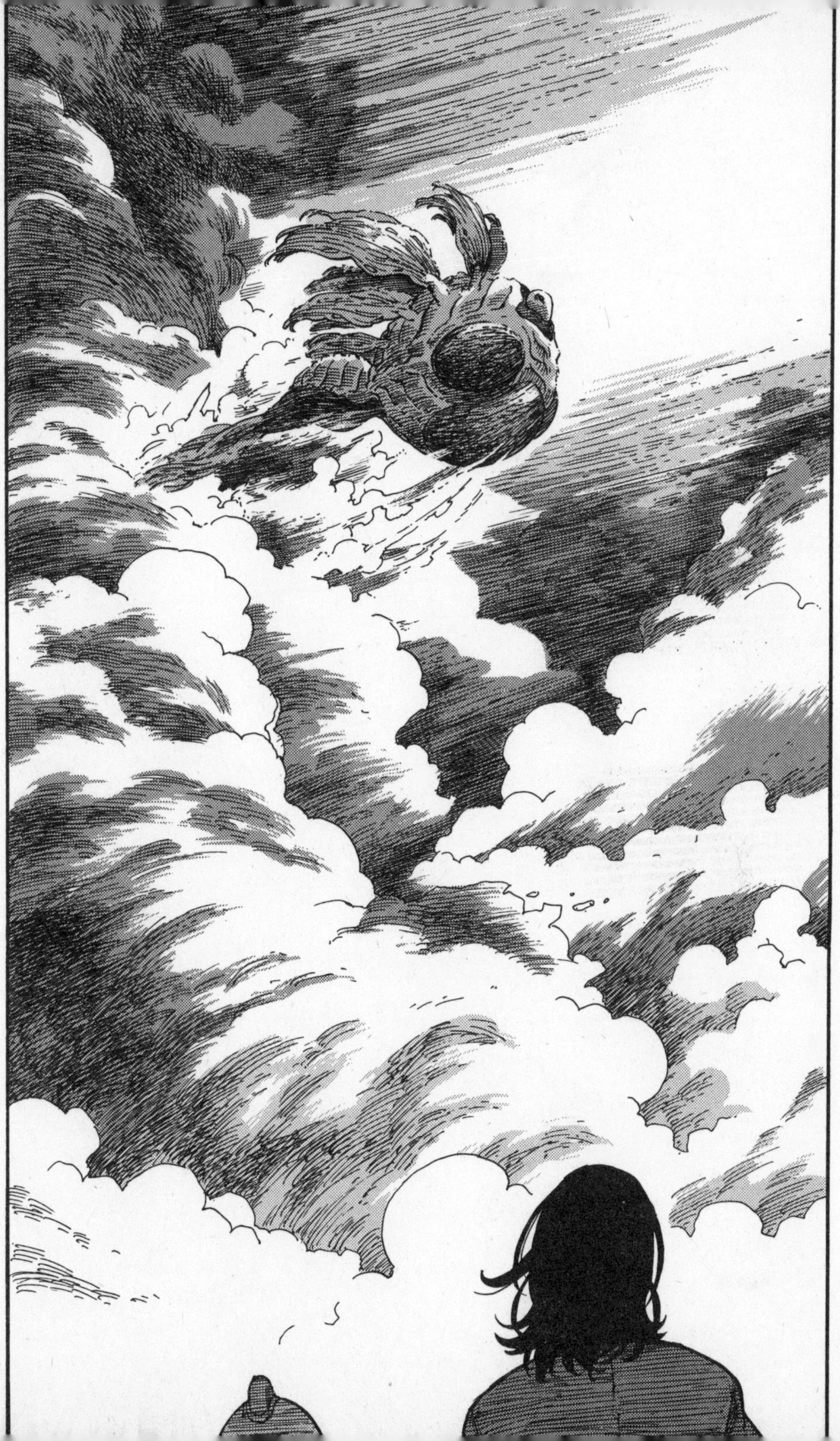

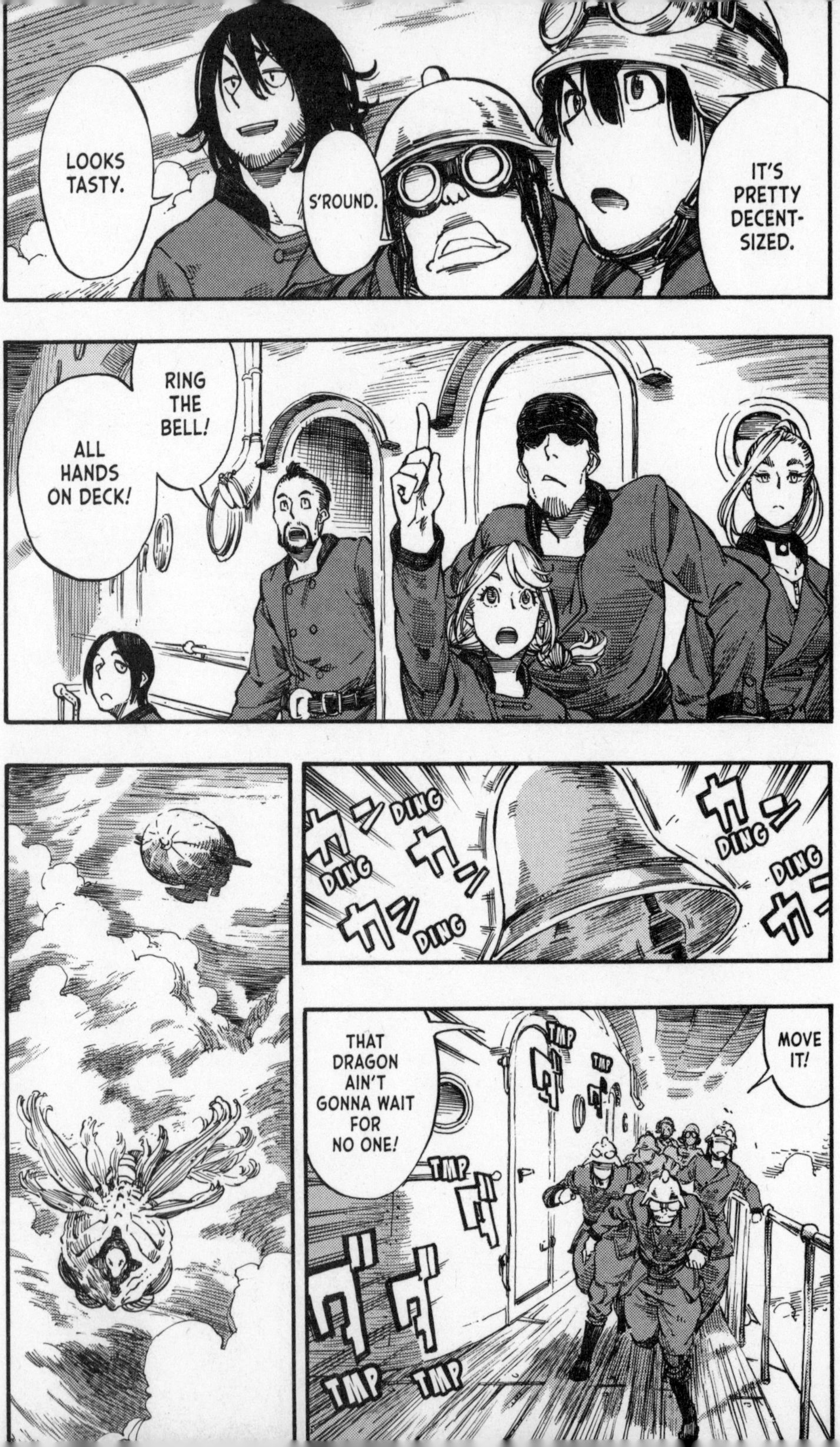
IT'S PRETTY DECENT-SIZED.
S'ROUND.
LOOKS TASTY.
RING THE BELL!
ALL HANDS ON DECK!
DING DING DING DING DING DING
MOVE IT!
THAT DRAGON AIN'T GONNA WAIT FOR NO ONE!
TMP TMP TMP TMP TMP

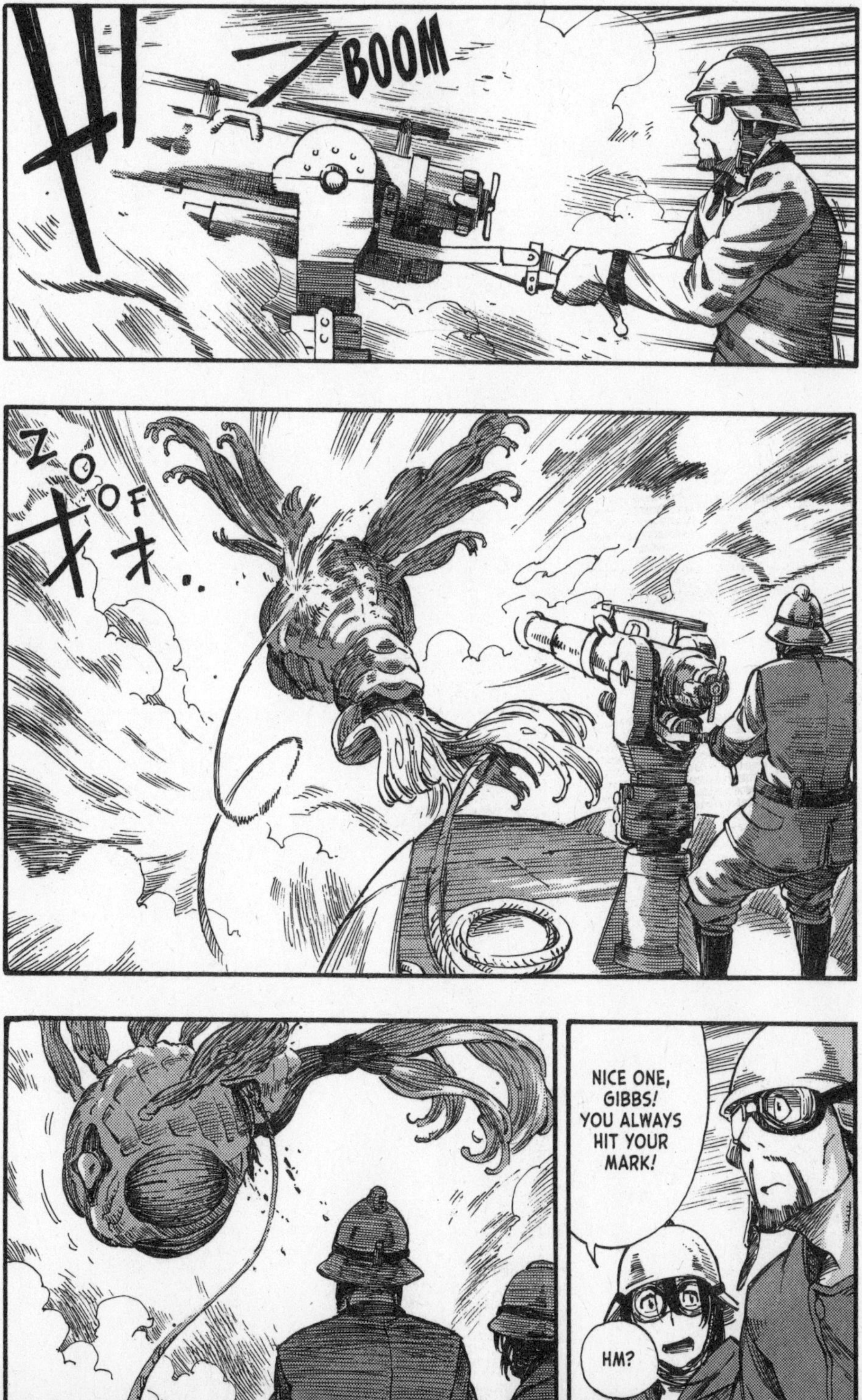
BOOM
ZOOF
NICE ONE, GIBBS! YOU ALWAYS HIT YOUR MARK!
HM?

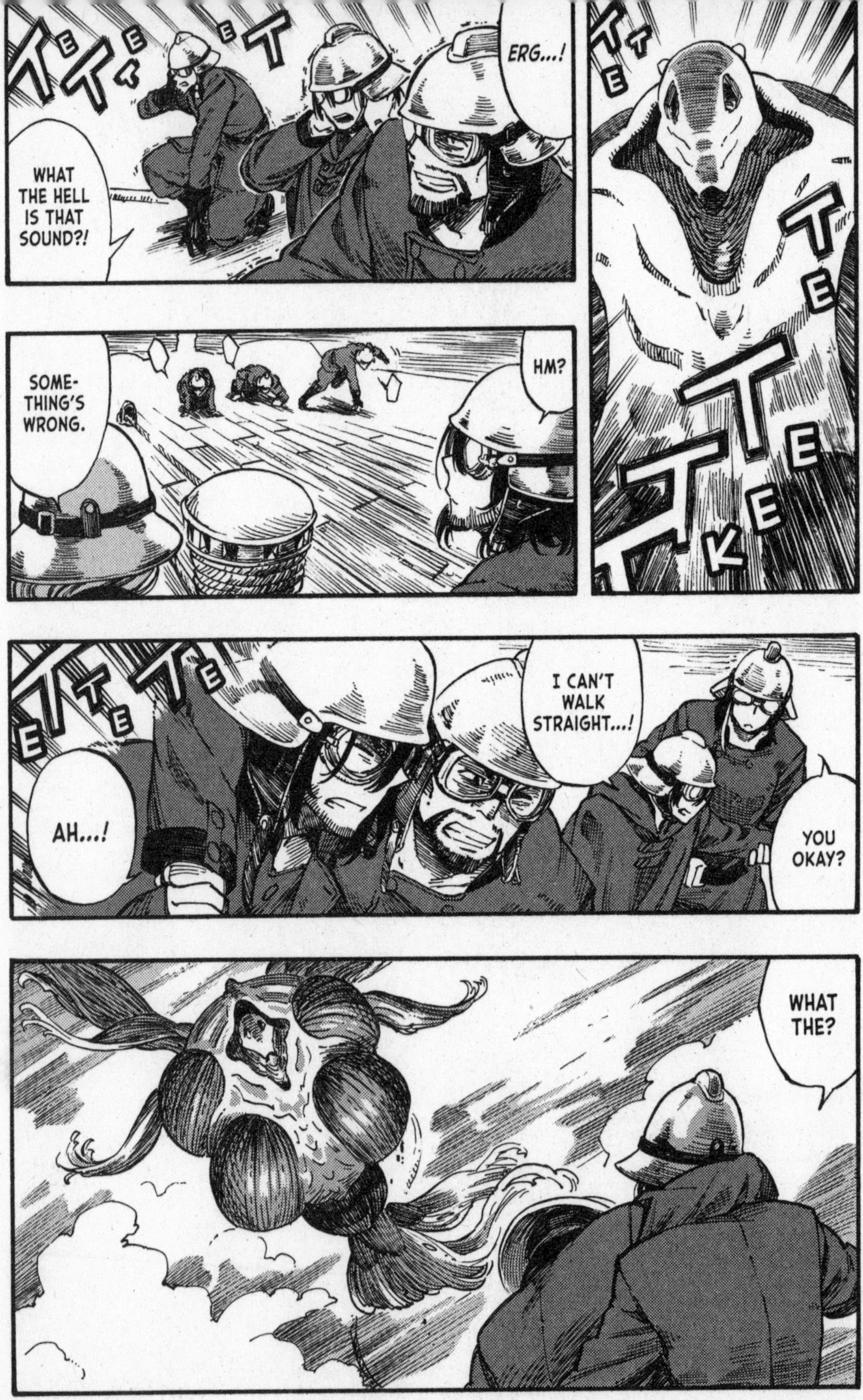
ERG...!
WHAT THE HELL IS THAT SOUND?!
HM?
SOME-THING'S WRONG.
I CAN'T WALK STRAIGHT...!
YOU OKAY?
AH...!
WHAT THE?

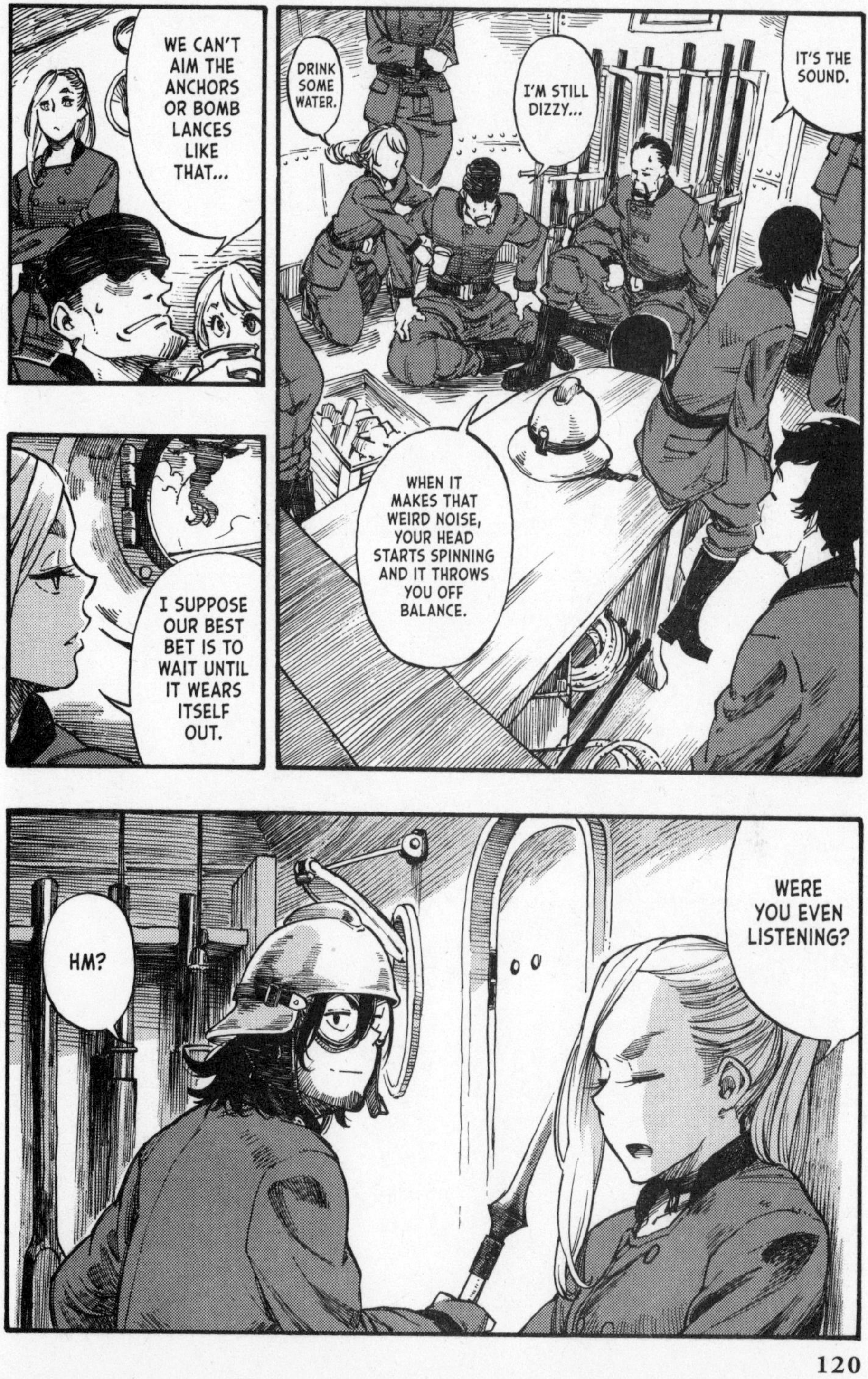
IT'S THE SOUND.
I'M STILL DIZZY...
DRINK SOME WATER.
WHEN IT MAKES THAT WEIRD NOISE, YOUR HEAD STARTS SPINNING AND IT THROWS YOU OFF BALANCE.
WE CAN'T AIM THE ANCHORS OR BOMB LANCES LIKE THAT...
I SUPPOSE OUR BEST BET IS TO WAIT UNTIL IT WEARS ITSELF OUT.
WERE YOU EVEN LISTENING?
HM?

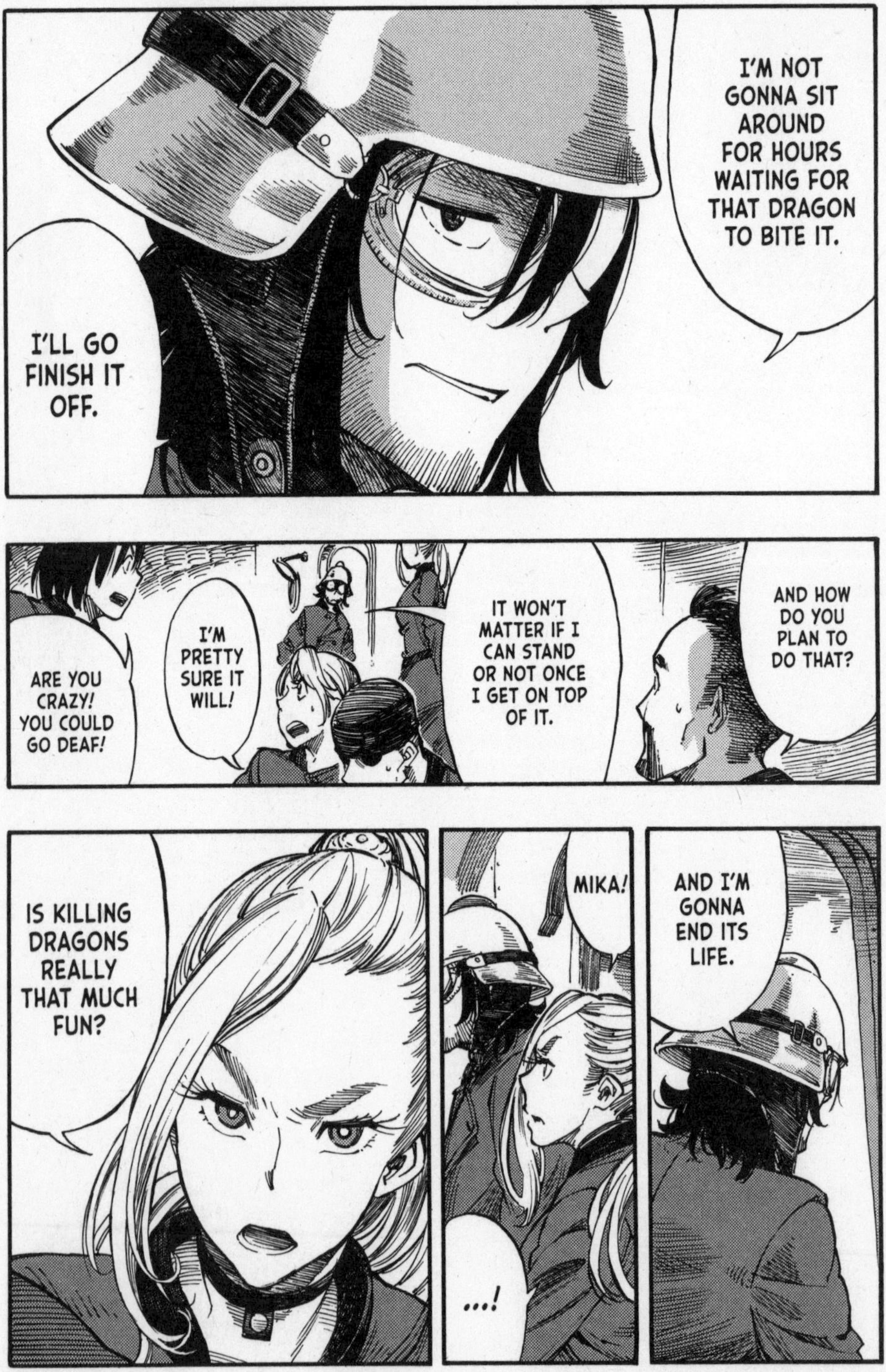
I'M NOT GONNA SIT AROUND FOR HOURS WAITING FOR THAT DRAGON TO BITE IT.
I'LL GO FINISH IT OFF.
AND HOW DO YOU PLAN TO DO THAT?
IT WON'T MATTER IF I CAN STAND OR NOT ONCE I GET ON TOP OF IT.
I'M PRETTY SURE IT WILL!
ARE YOU CRAZY! YOU COULD GO DEAF!
AND I'M GONNA END ITS LIFE.
MIKA!
...!
IS KILLING DRAGONS REALLY THAT MUCH FUN?

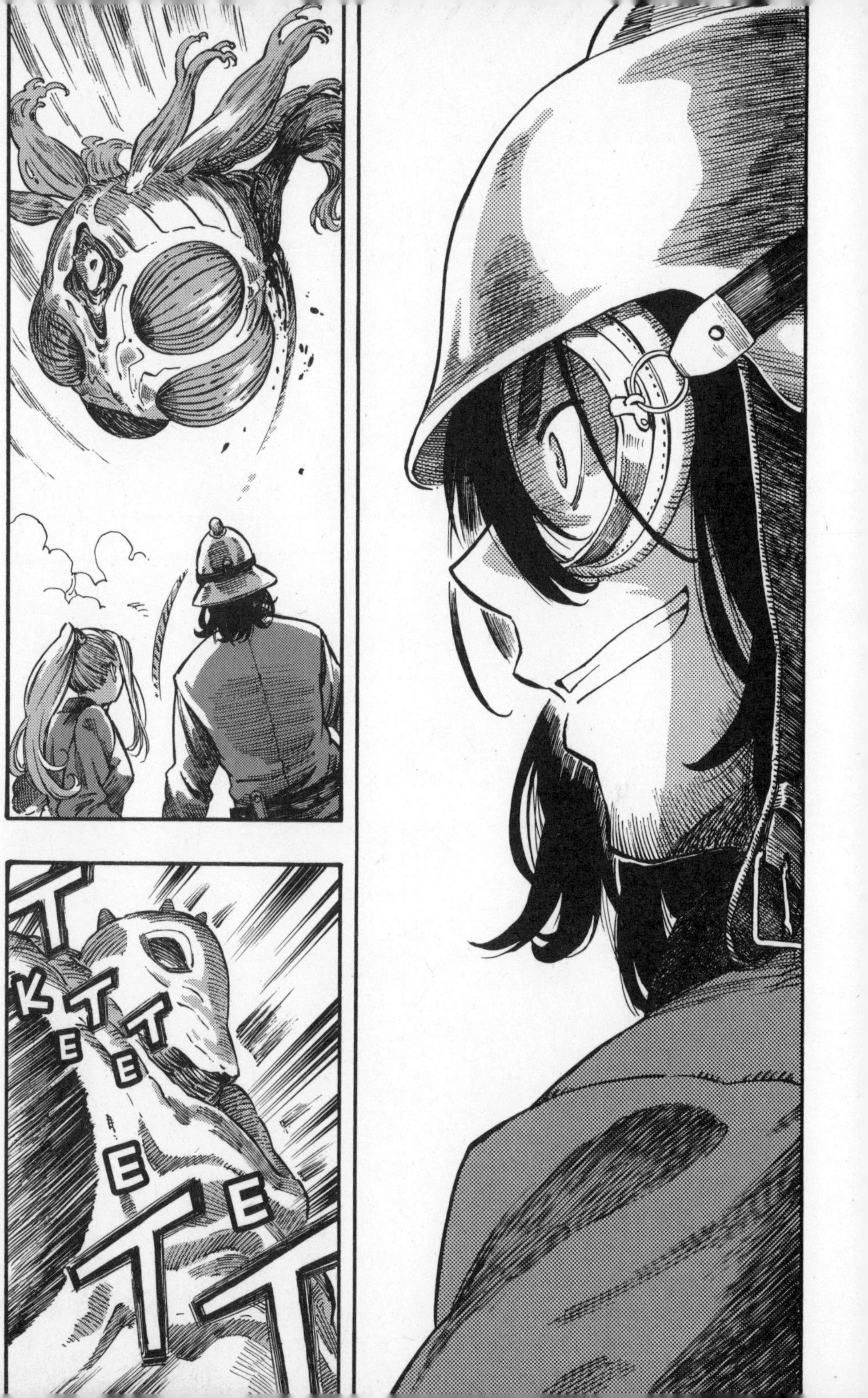
T
KTETE
EETT

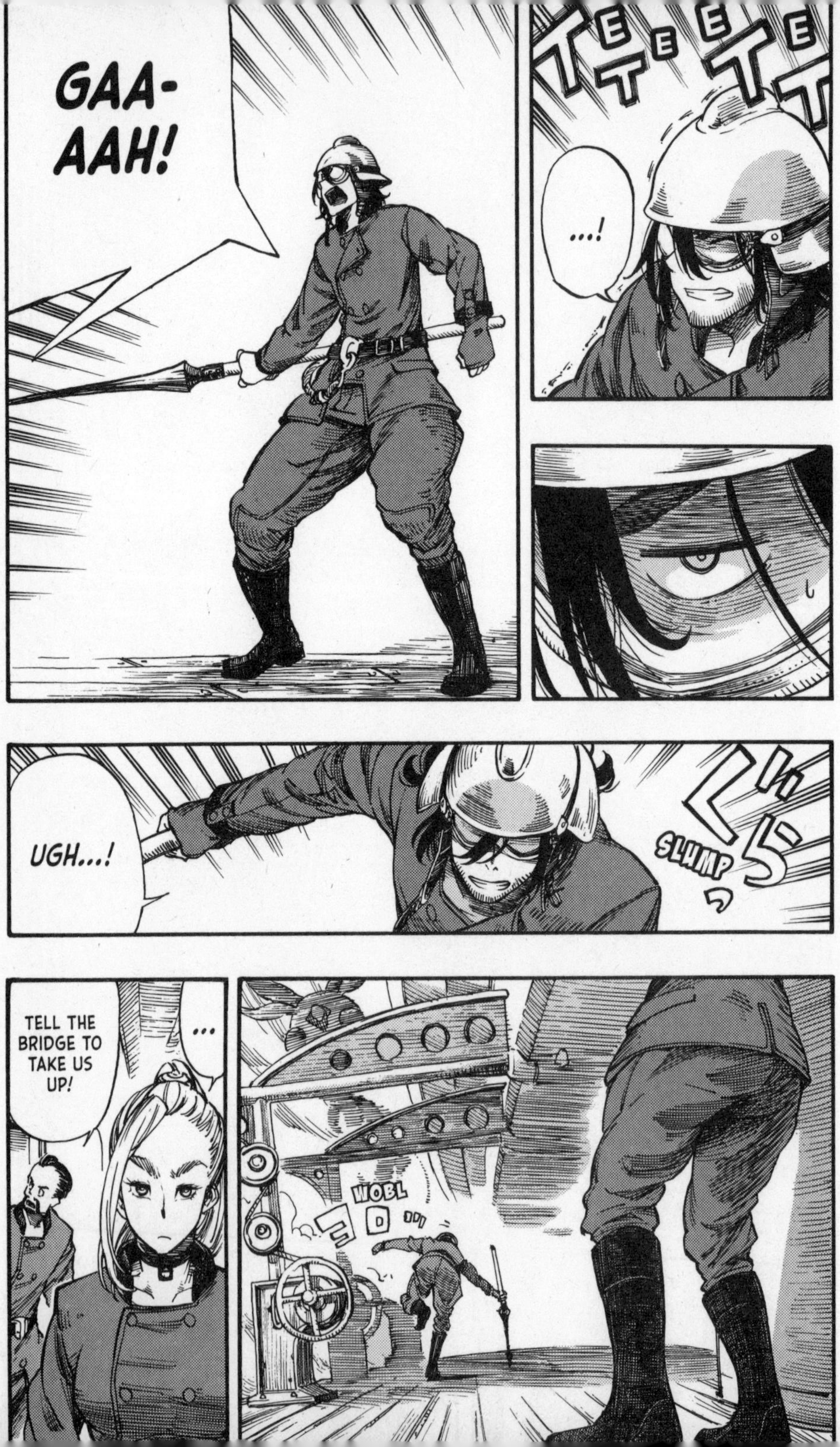
TETEETET
...!
GAA-AAH!
SLUMP
UGH...!
WOBL
...
TELL THE BRIDGE TO TAKE US UP!

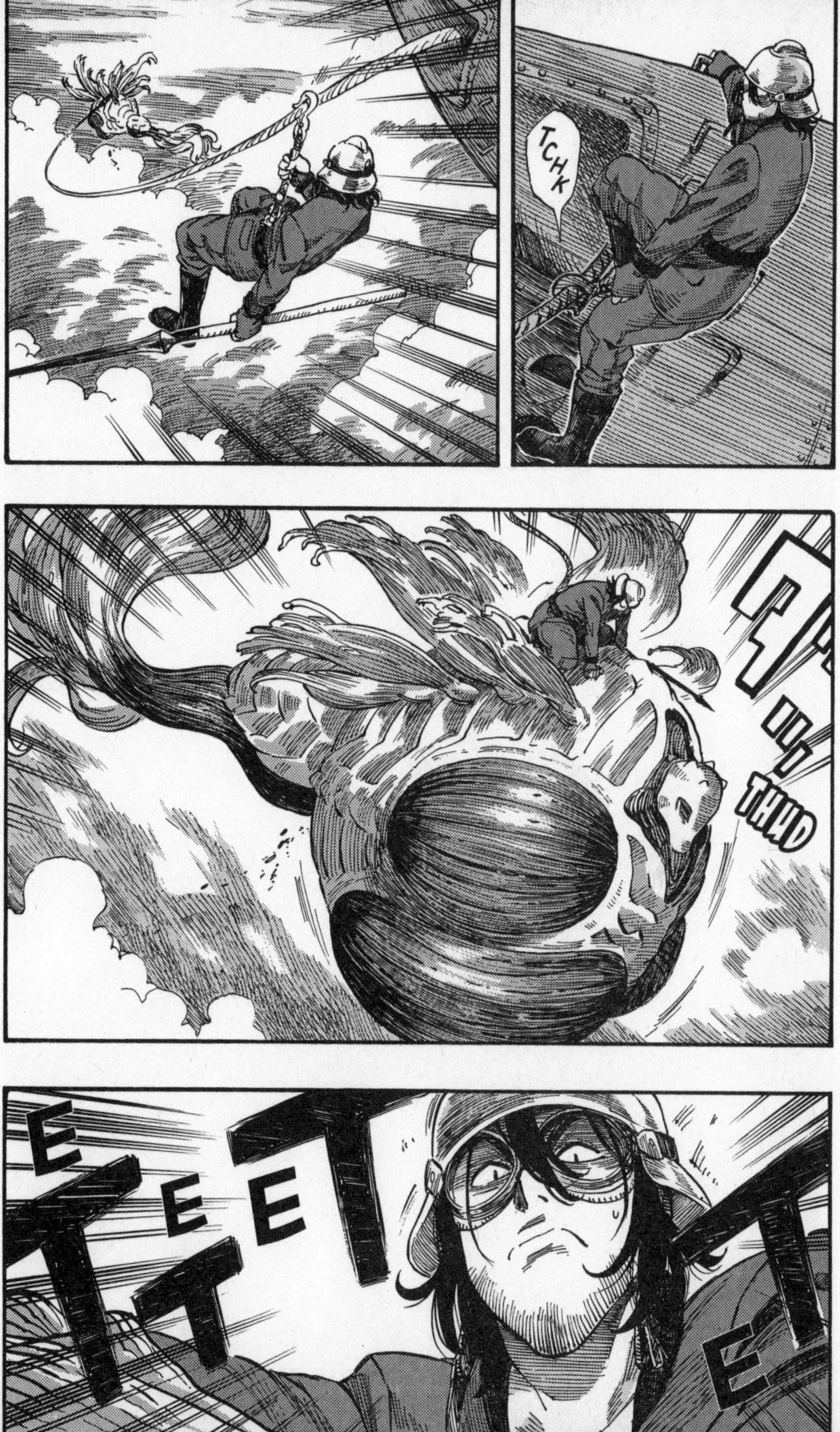
TCHK
THUD

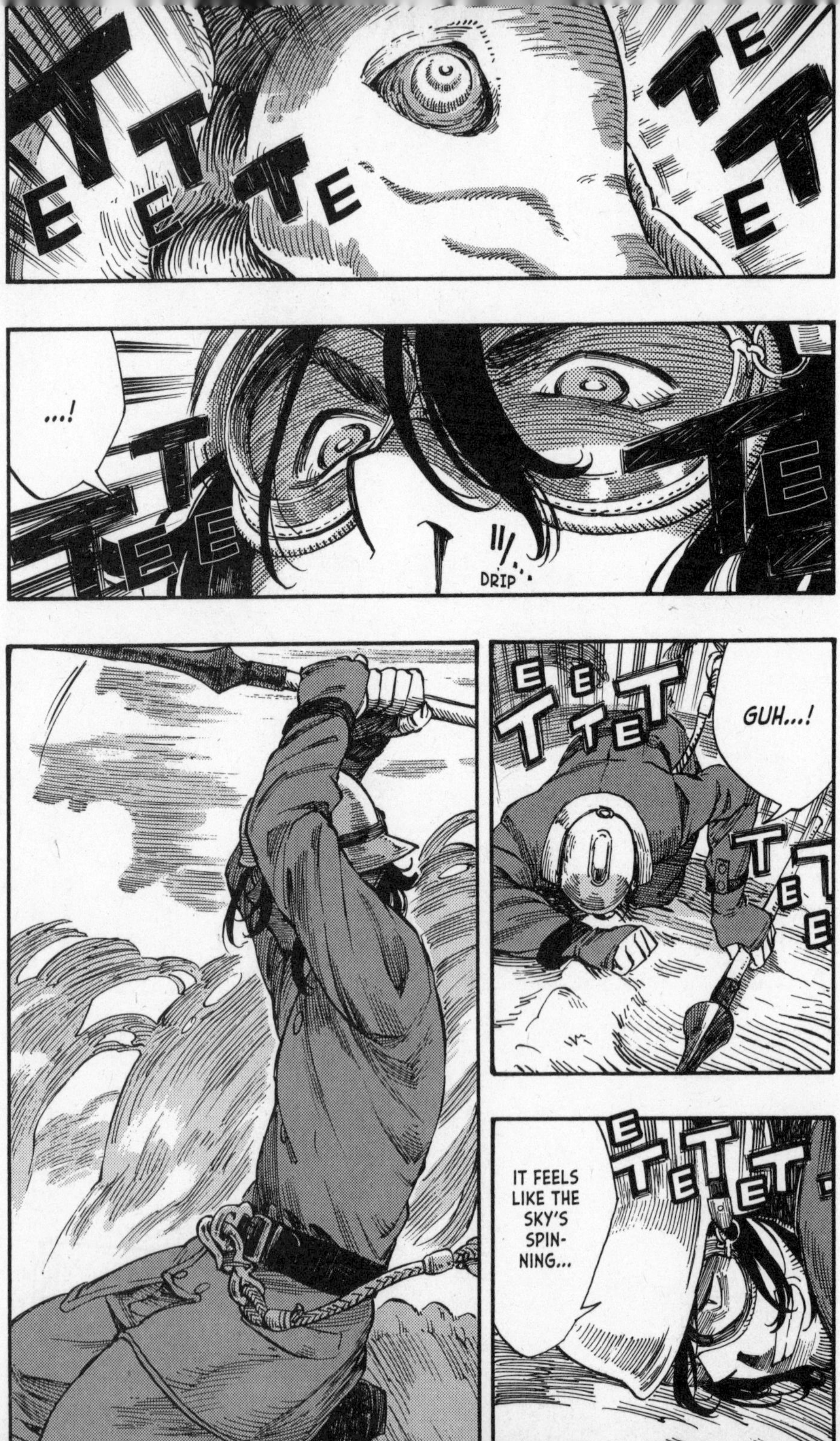
...!
DRIP
GUH...!
IT FEELS LIKE THE SKY'S SPIN-NING...

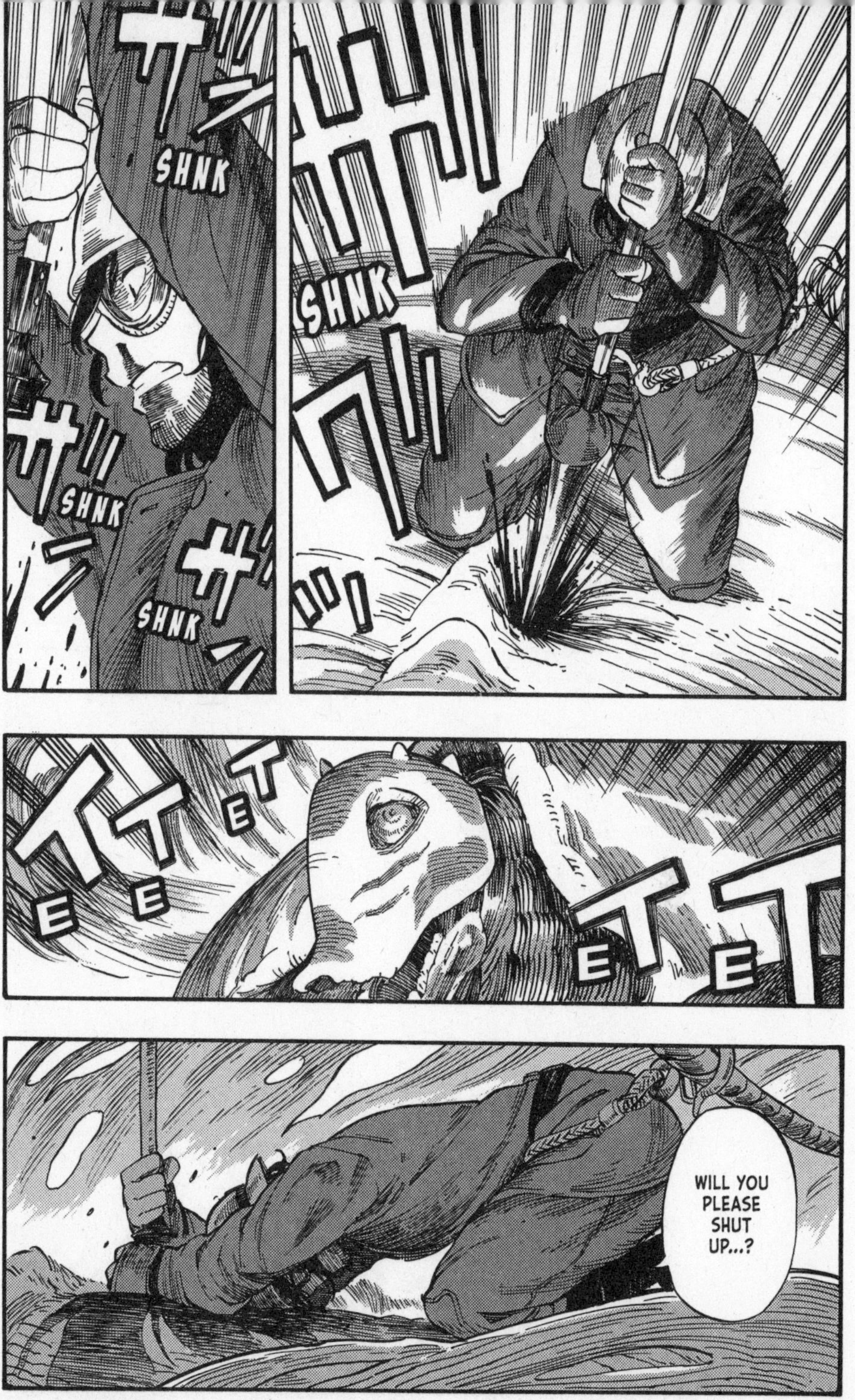
SHNK
SHNK
SHNK
SHNK
WILL YOU PLEASE SHUT UP...?

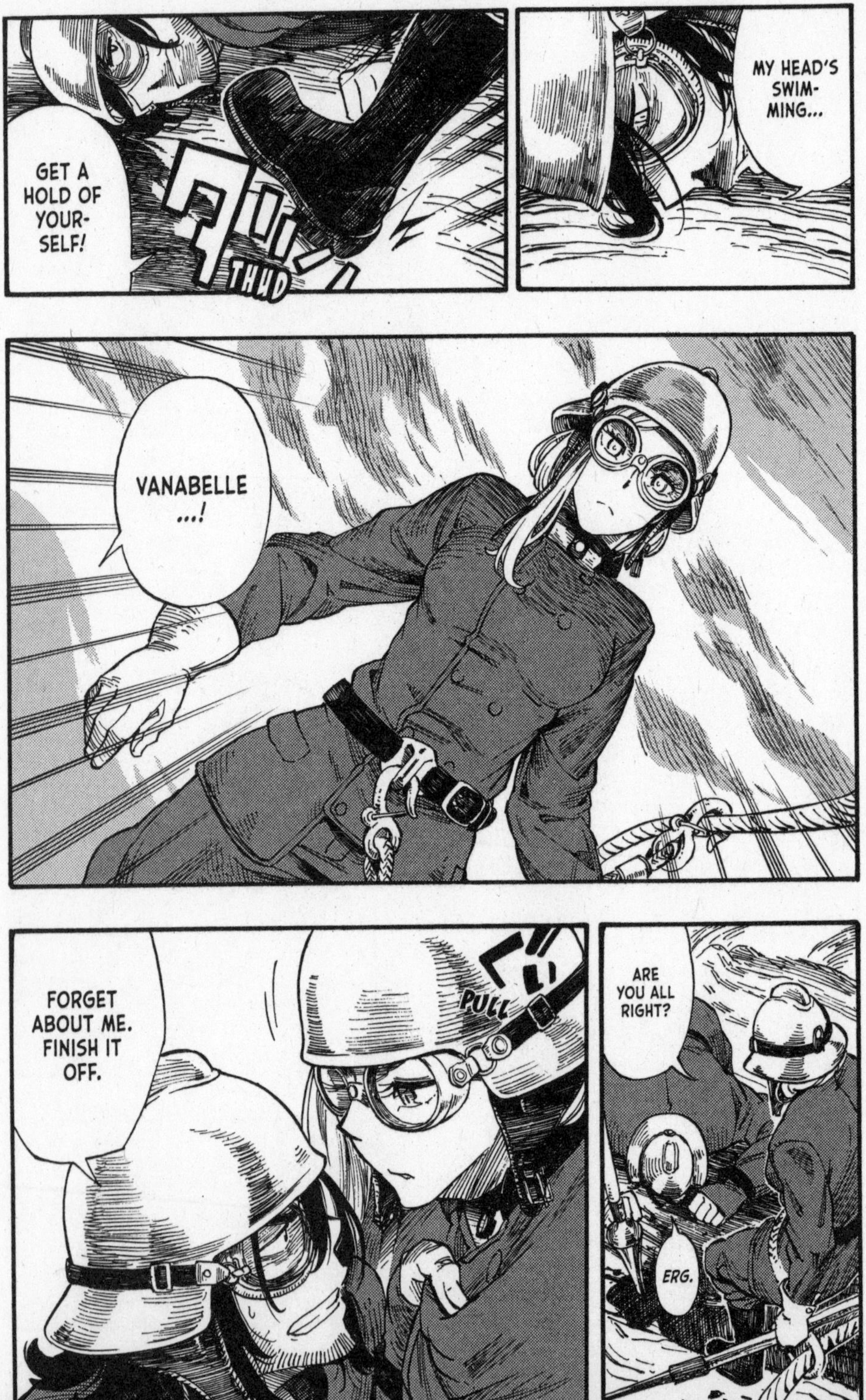
MY HEAD'S SWIMMING...
GET A HOLD OF YOURSELF!
THUD
VANABELLE ...!
ARE YOU ALL RIGHT?
ERG.
PULL
FORGET ABOUT ME. FINISH IT OFF.

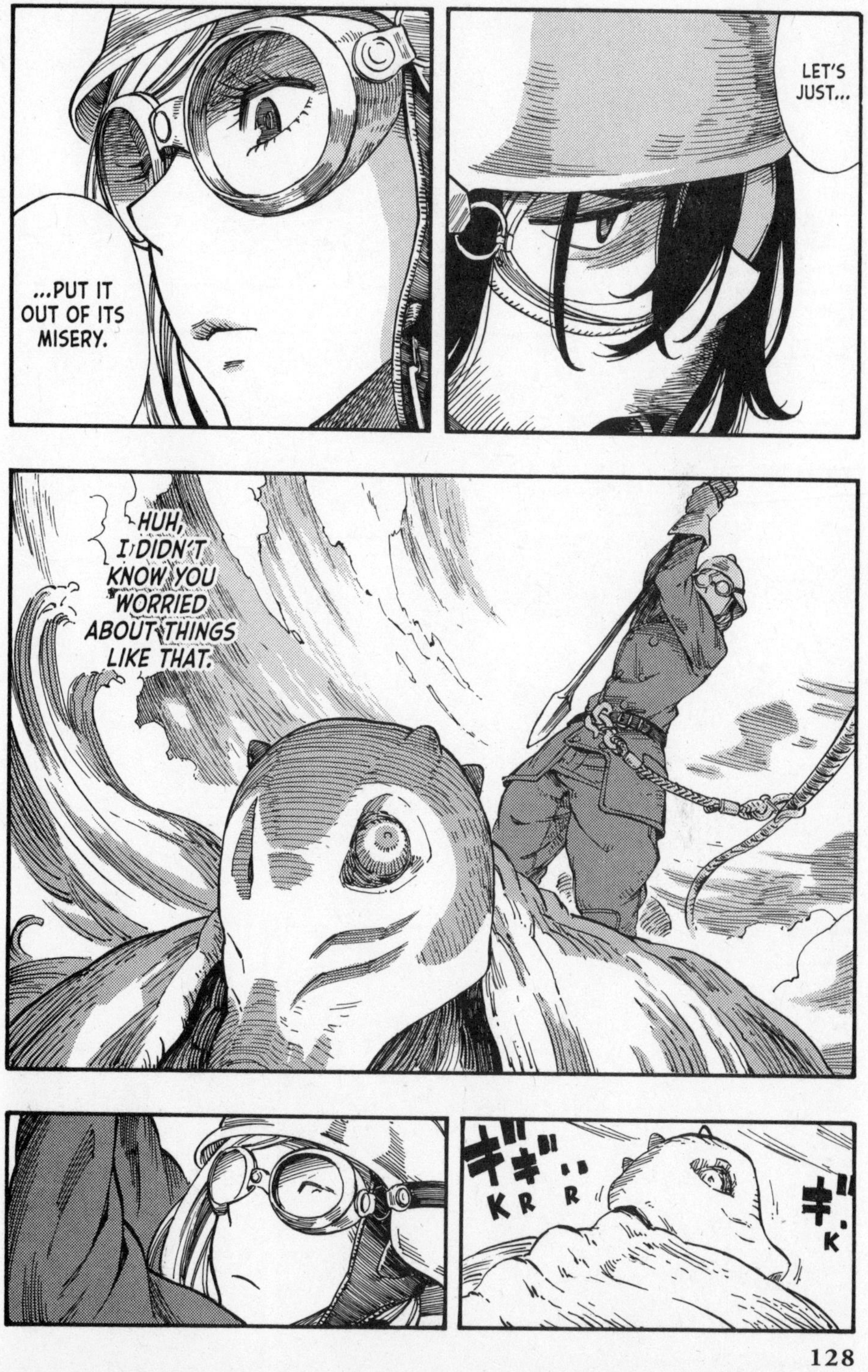
LET'S JUST...
...PUT IT OUT OF ITS MISERY.
HUH, I DIDN'T KNOW YOU WORRIED ABOUT THINGS LIKE THAT.
K R R
K

I HAD NOWHERE TO GO ON THE GROUND,
SO I LEARNED HOW TO FLY.
END OF STORY.

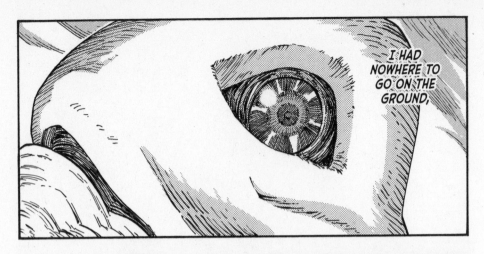

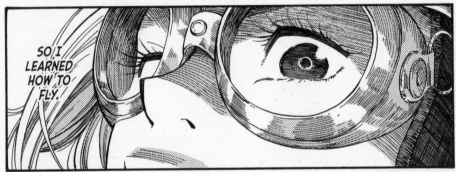

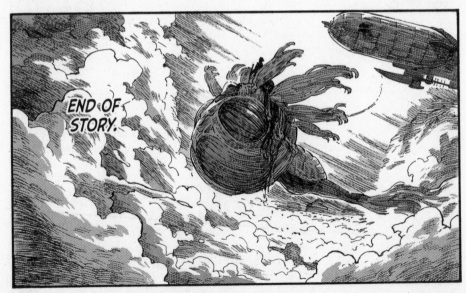

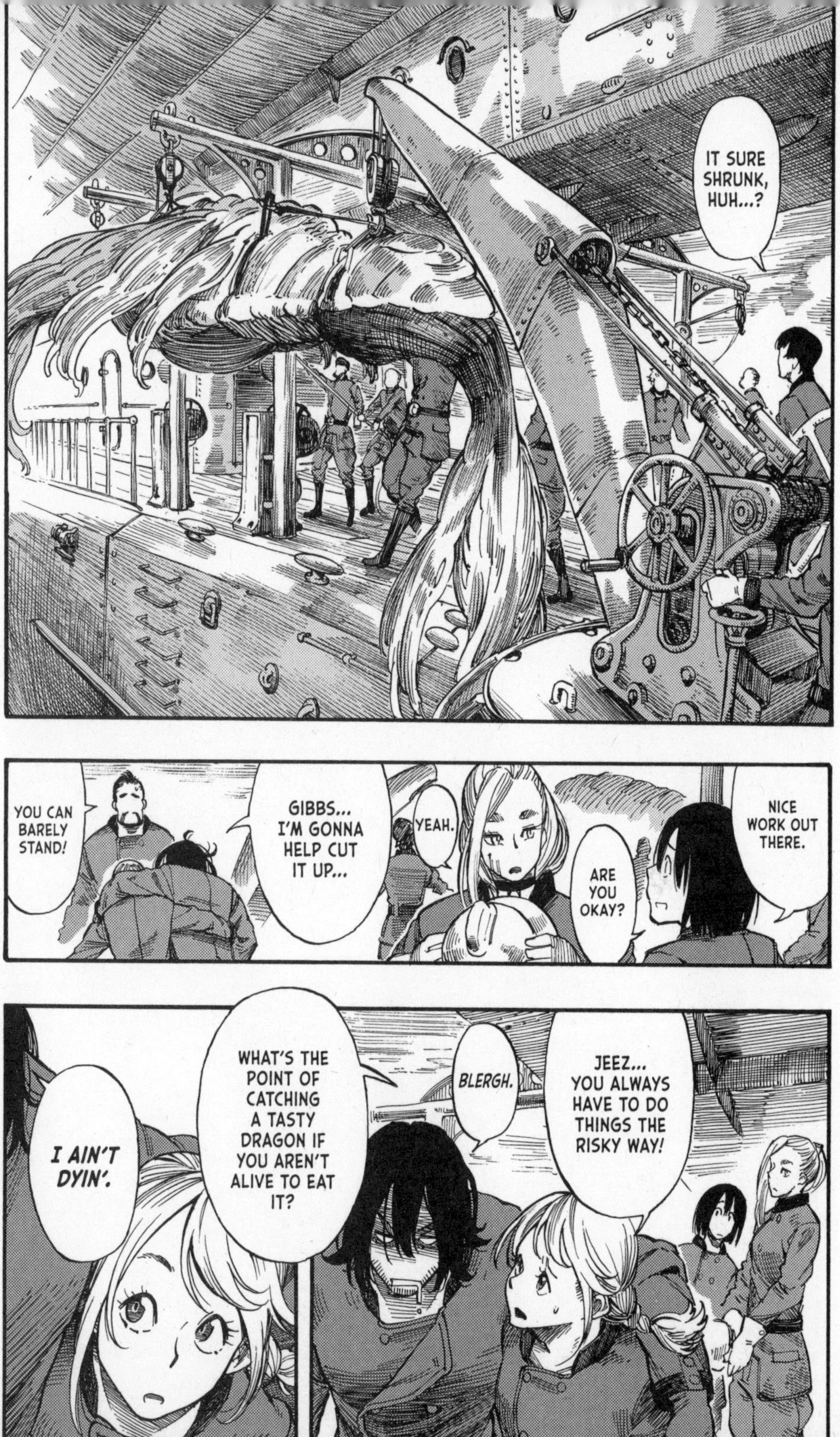
IT SURE SHRUNK, HUH...?
NICE WORK OUT THERE.
ARE YOU OKAY?
YEAH.
GIBBS... I'M GONNA HELP CUT IT UP...
YOU CAN BARELY STAND!
JEEZ... YOU ALWAYS HAVE TO DO THINGS THE RISKY WAY!
BLERGH.
WHAT'S THE POINT OF CATCHING A TASTY DRAGON IF YOU AREN'T ALIVE TO EAT IT?
I AIN'T DYIN'.

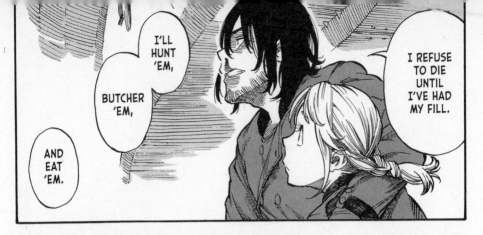

I'LL HUNT 'EM,

BUTCHER 'EM,

AND EAT 'EM.

I REFUSE TO DIE UNTIL I'VE HAD MY FILL.

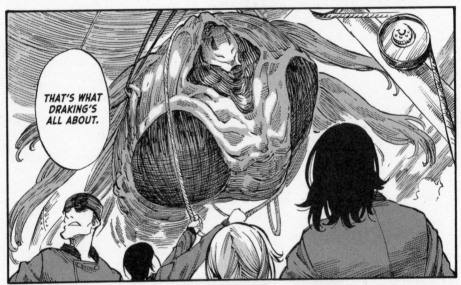

THAT'S WHAT DRAKING'S ALL ABOUT.

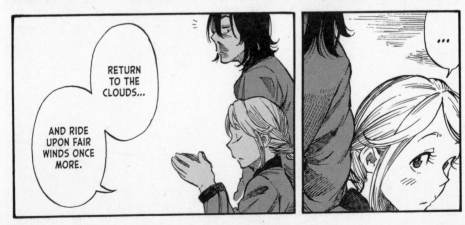

RETURN TO THE CLOUDS...

AND RIDE UPON FAIR WINDS ONCE MORE.

...

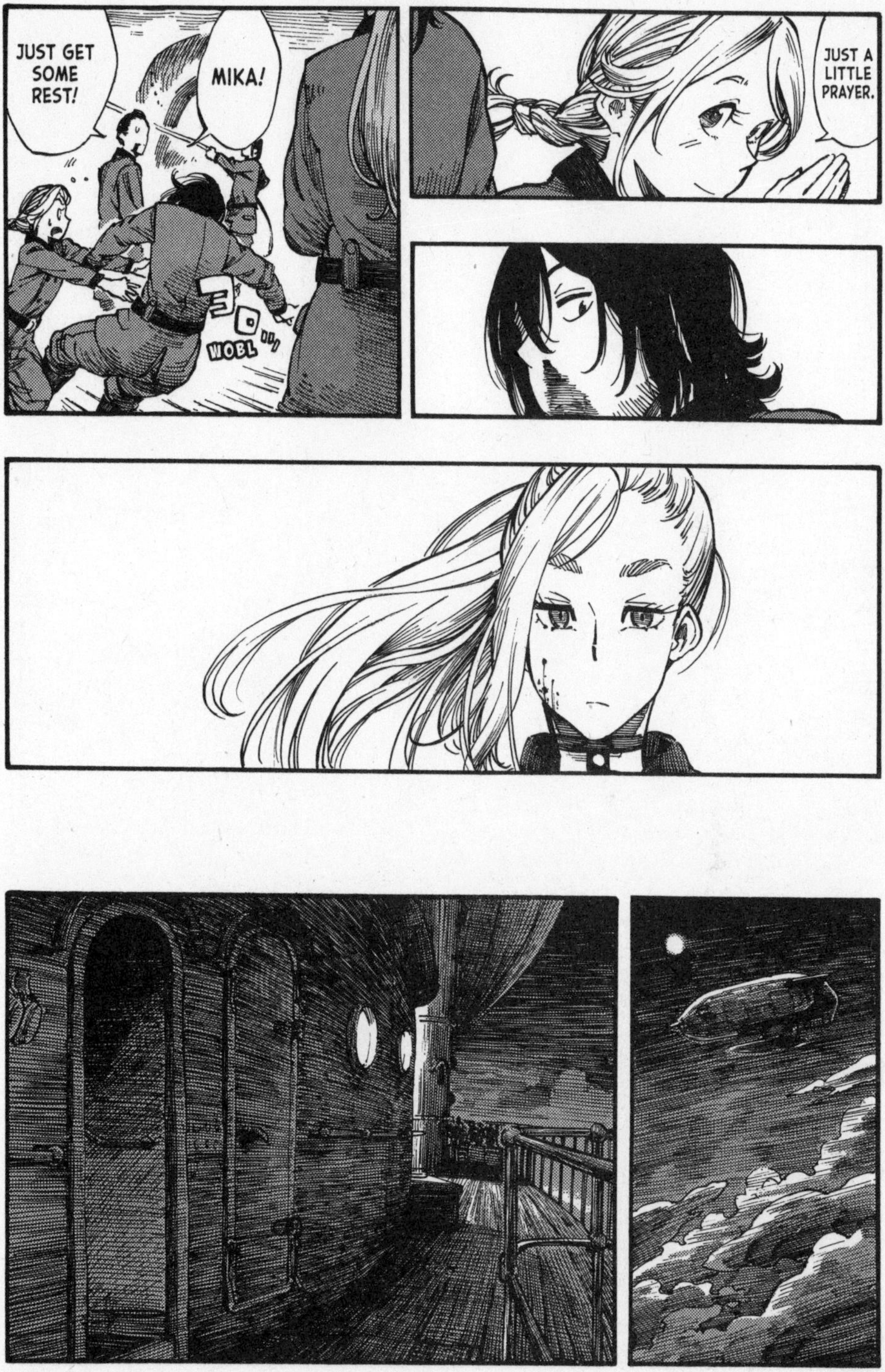
JUST A LITTLE PRAYER.
MIKA!
JUST GET SOME REST!
WOBL

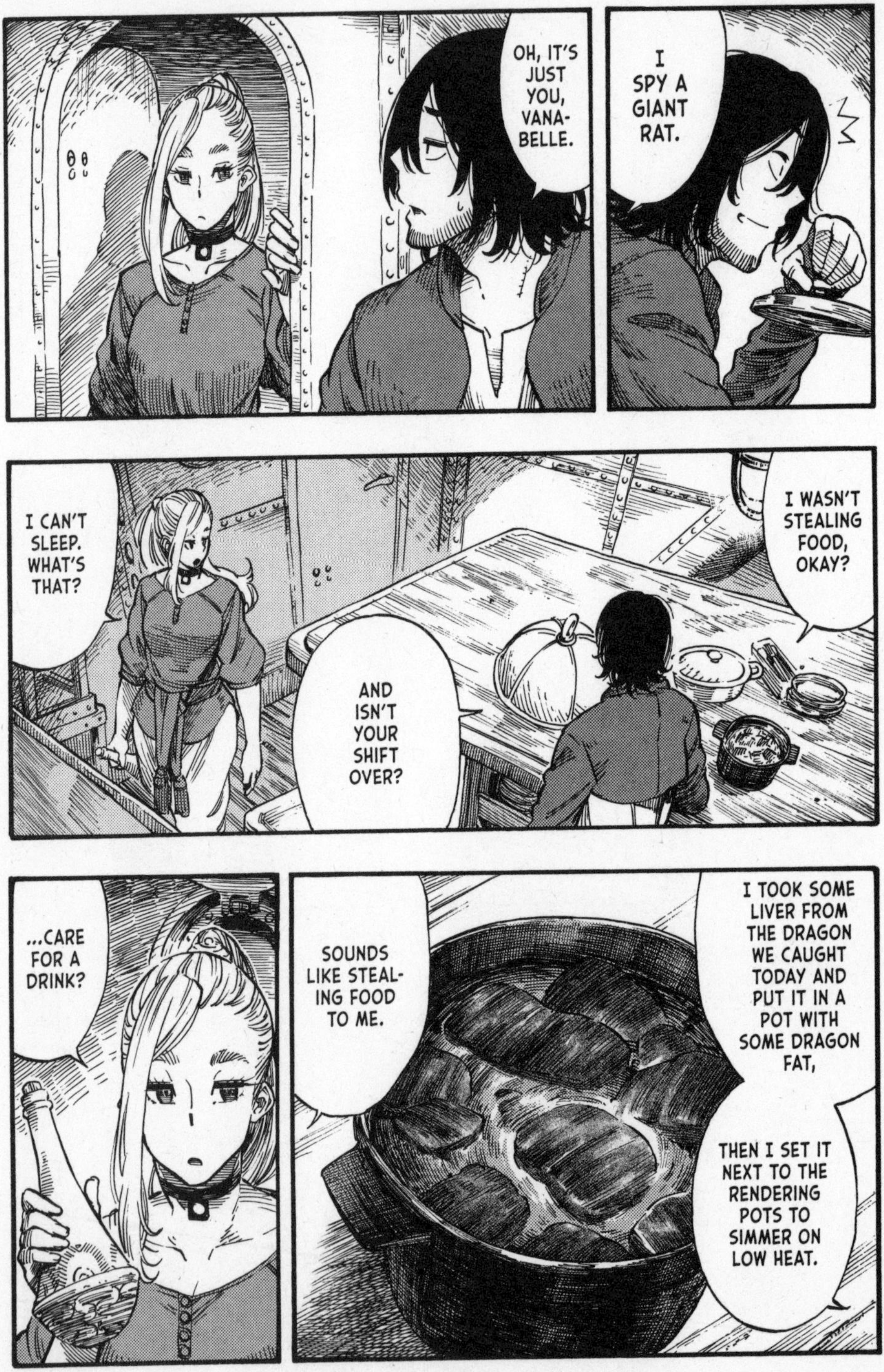
I SPY A GIANT RAT.
OH, IT'S JUST YOU, VANA-BELLE.
I WASN'T STEALING FOOD, OKAY?
AND ISN'T YOUR SHIFT OVER?
I CAN'T SLEEP. WHAT'S THAT?
I TOOK SOME LIVER FROM THE DRAGON WE CAUGHT TODAY AND PUT IT IN A POT WITH SOME DRAGON FAT,
THEN I SET IT NEXT TO THE RENDERING POTS TO SIMMER ON LOW HEAT.
SOUNDS LIKE STEAL-ING FOOD TO ME.
...CARE FOR A DRINK?

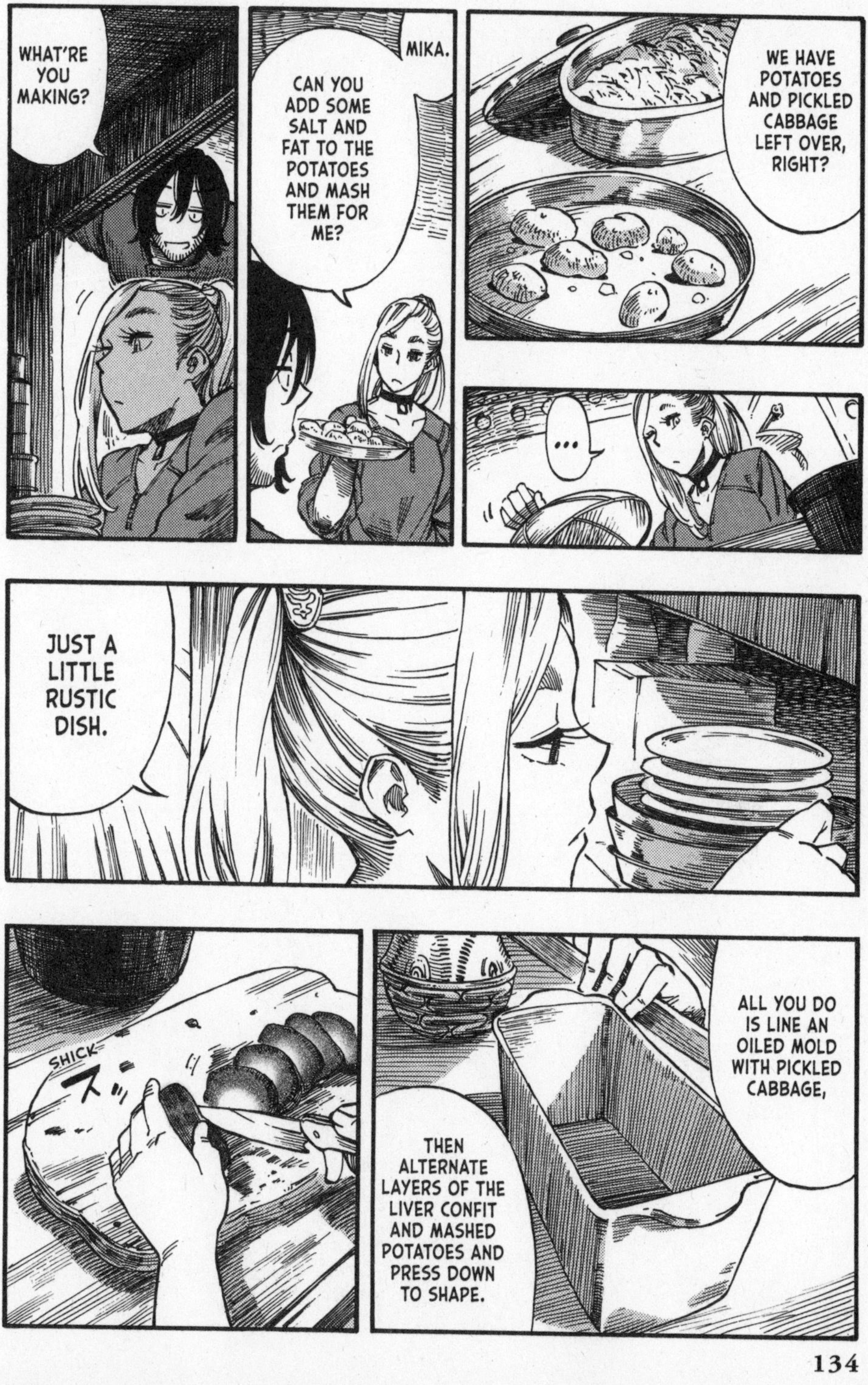
WE HAVE POTATOES AND PICKLED CABBAGE LEFT OVER, RIGHT?
...
MIKA.
CAN YOU ADD SOME SALT AND FAT TO THE POTATOES AND MASH THEM FOR ME?
WHAT'RE YOU MAKING?
JUST A LITTLE RUSTIC DISH.
ALL YOU DO IS LINE AN OILED MOLD WITH PICKLED CABBAGE,
THEN ALTERNATE LAYERS OF THE LIVER CONFIT AND MASHED POTATOES AND PRESS DOWN TO SHAPE.
SHICK

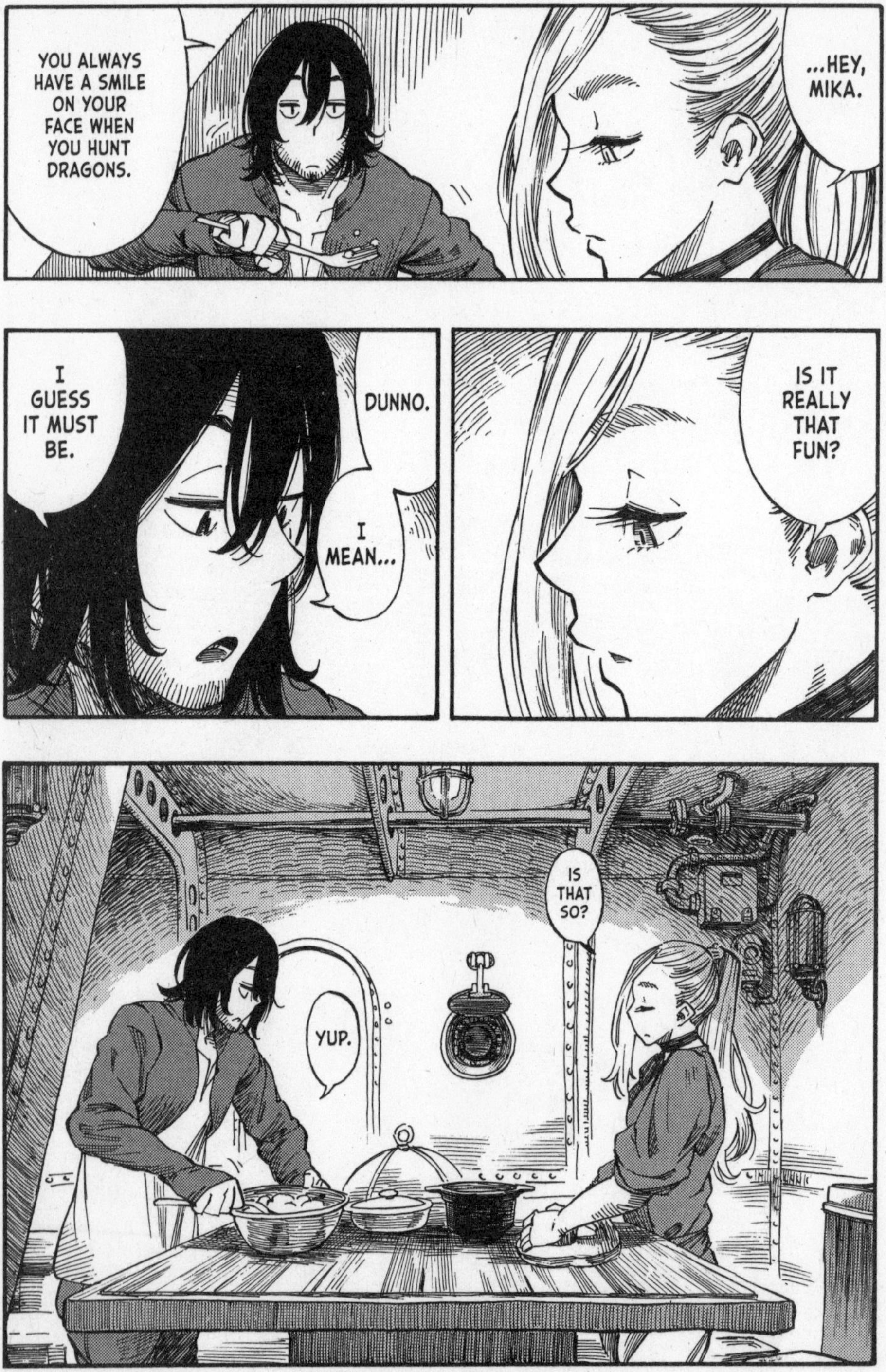
...HEY, MIKA.
YOU ALWAYS HAVE A SMILE ON YOUR FACE WHEN YOU HUNT DRAGONS.
IS IT REALLY THAT FUN?
DUNNO.
I MEAN...
I GUESS IT MUST BE.
IS THAT SO?
YUP.

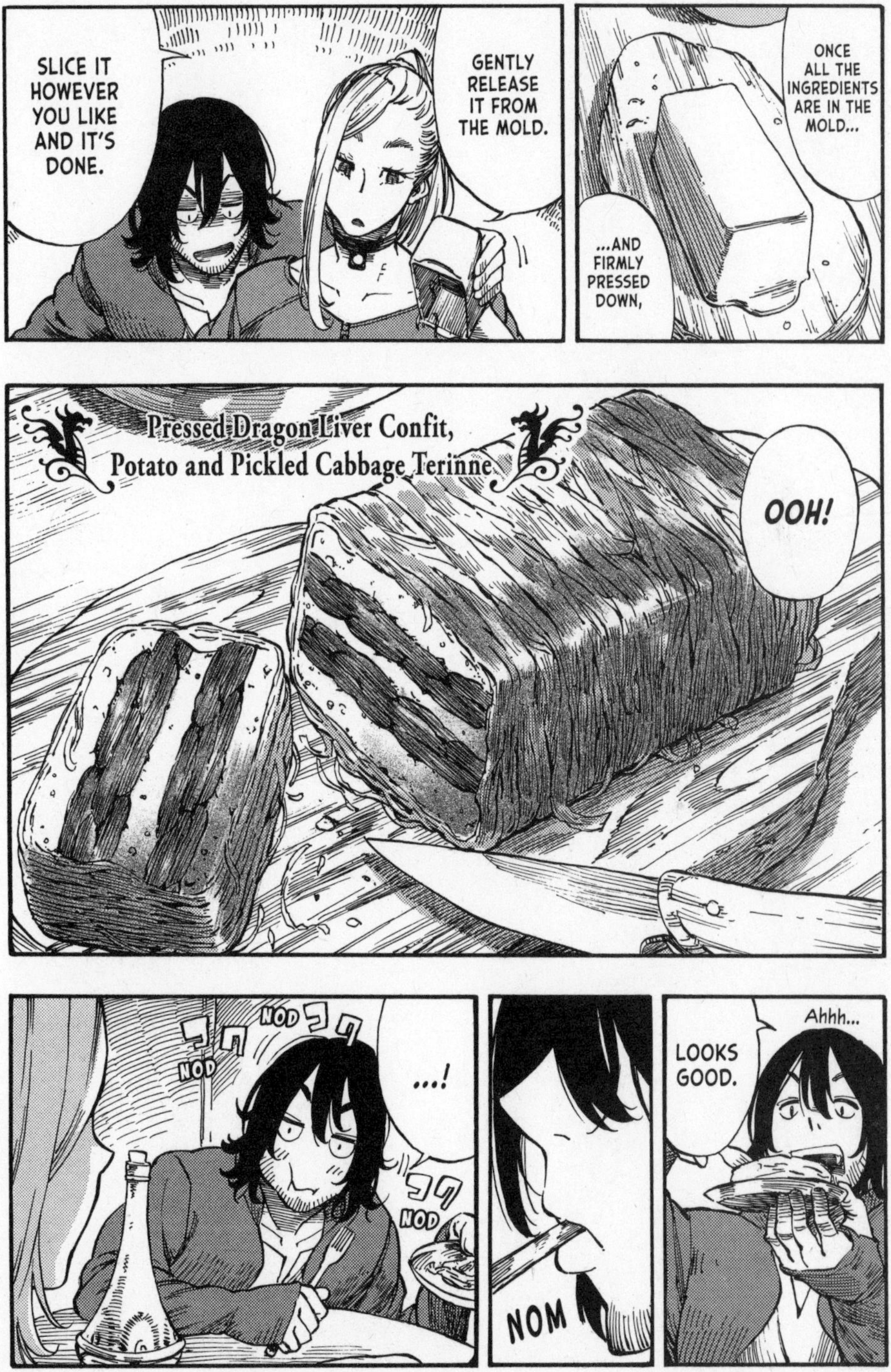
ONCE ALL THE INGREDIENTS ARE IN THE MOLD...
...AND FIRMLY PRESSED DOWN,
GENTLY RELEASE IT FROM THE MOLD.
SLICE IT HOWEVER YOU LIKE AND IT'S DONE.
OOH!
Pressed Dragon Liver Confit, Potato and Pickled Cabbage Terinne
Ahhh...
LOOKS GOOD.
NOM
...!
NOD
NOD
NOD

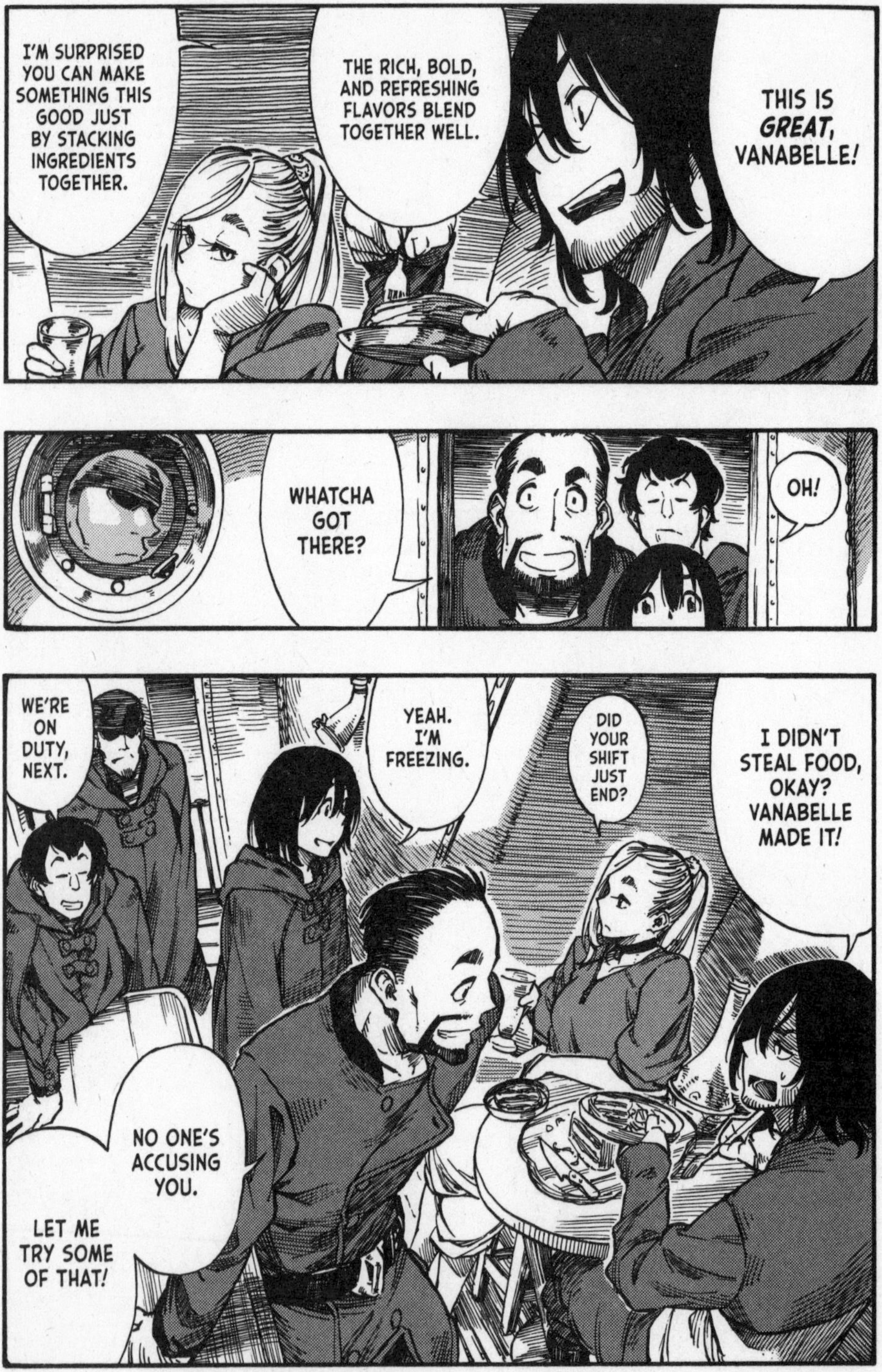
THIS IS GREAT, VANABELLE!
THE RICH, BOLD, AND REFRESHING FLAVORS BLEND TOGETHER WELL.
I'M SURPRISED YOU CAN MAKE SOMETHING THIS GOOD JUST BY STACKING INGREDIENTS TOGETHER.
OH!
WHATCHA GOT THERE?
I DIDN'T STEAL FOOD, OKAY? VANABELLE MADE IT!
DID YOUR SHIFT JUST END?
YEAH. I'M FREEZING.
WE'RE ON DUTY, NEXT.
NO ONE'S ACCUSING YOU.
LET ME TRY SOME OF THAT!

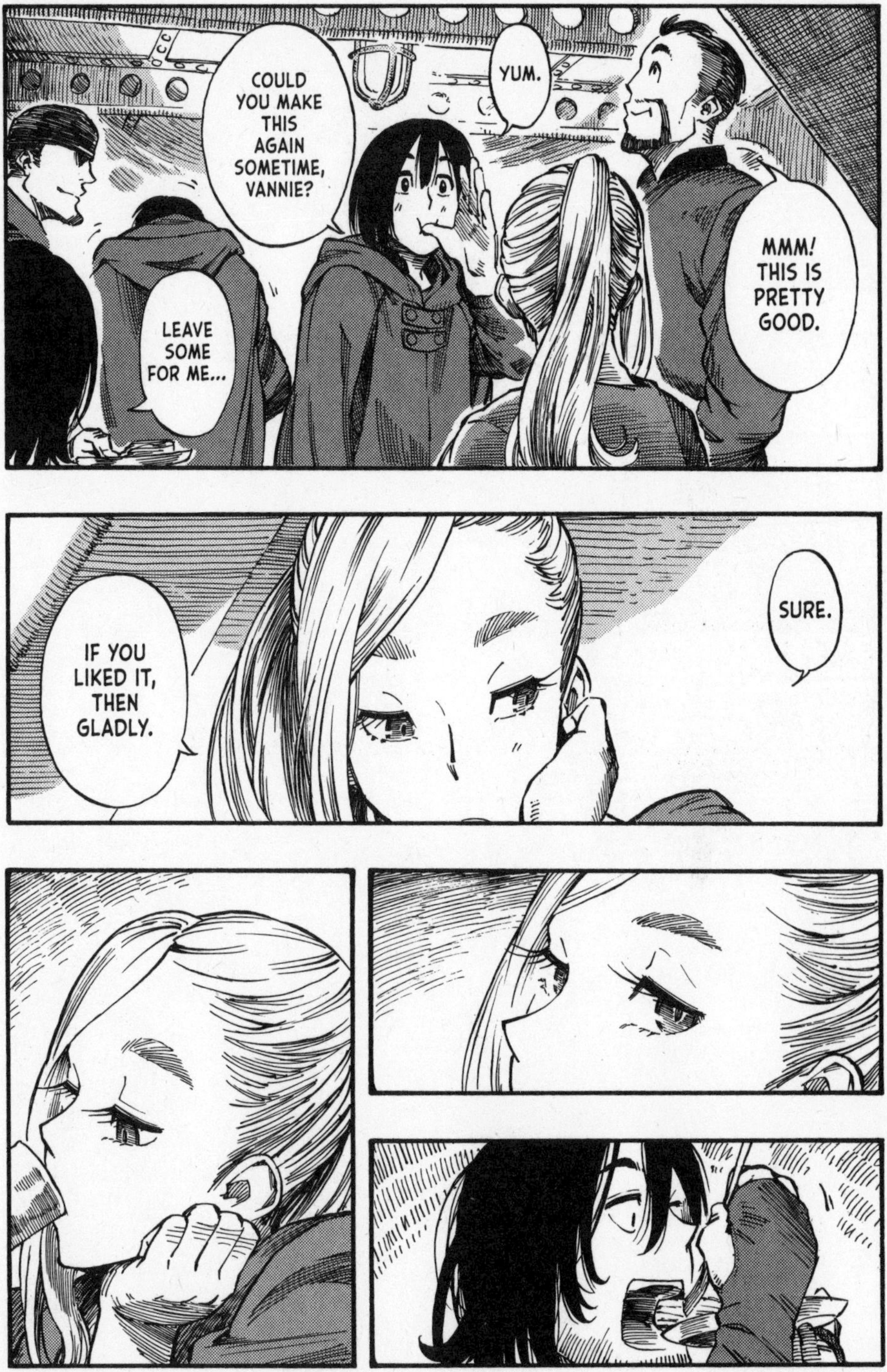
MMM! THIS IS PRETTY GOOD.
YUM.
COULD YOU MAKE THIS AGAIN SOMETIME, VANNIE?
LEAVE SOME FOR ME...
SURE.
IF YOU LIKED IT, THEN GLADLY.

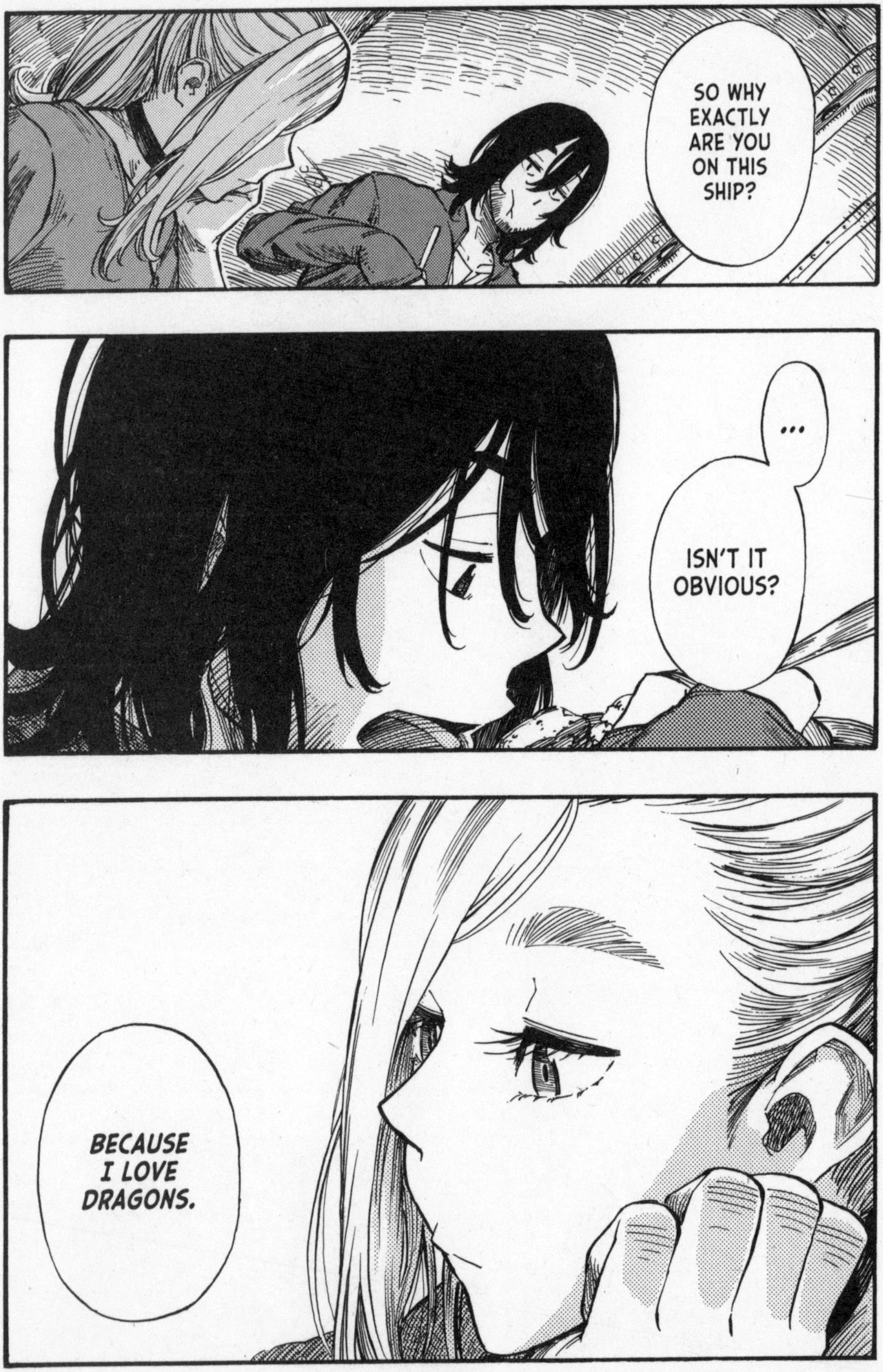
SO WHY EXACTLY ARE YOU ON THIS SHIP?
...
ISN'T IT OBVIOUS?
BECAUSE I LOVE DRAGONS.

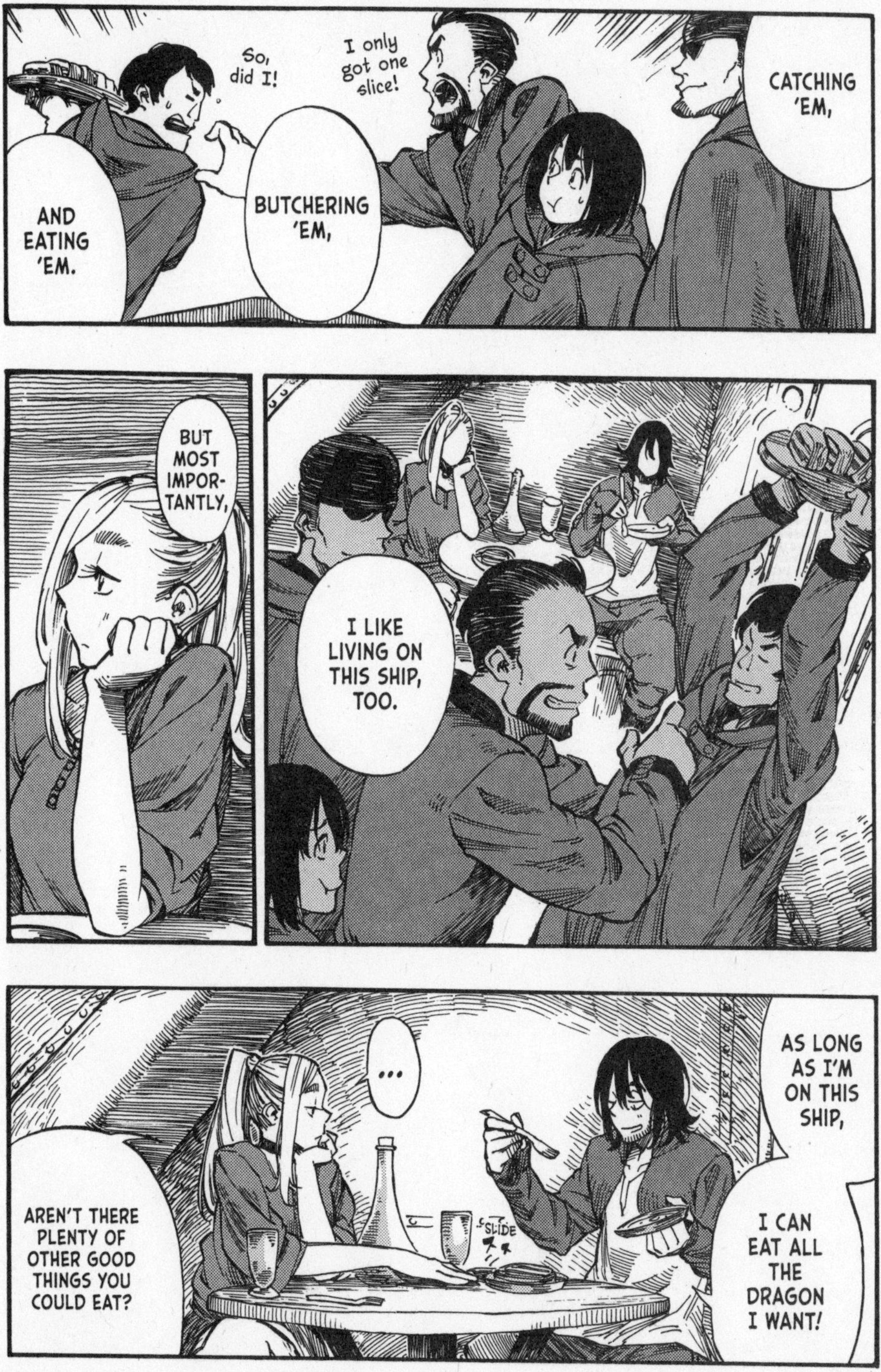
CATCHING 'EM,
I only got one slice!
BUTCHERING 'EM,
So, did I!
AND EATING 'EM.
I LIKE LIVING ON THIS SHIP, TOO.
BUT MOST IMPOR-TANTLY,
AS LONG AS I'M ON THIS SHIP,
I CAN EAT ALL THE DRAGON I WANT!
...
SLIDE
AREN'T THERE PLENTY OF OTHER GOOD THINGS YOU COULD EAT?

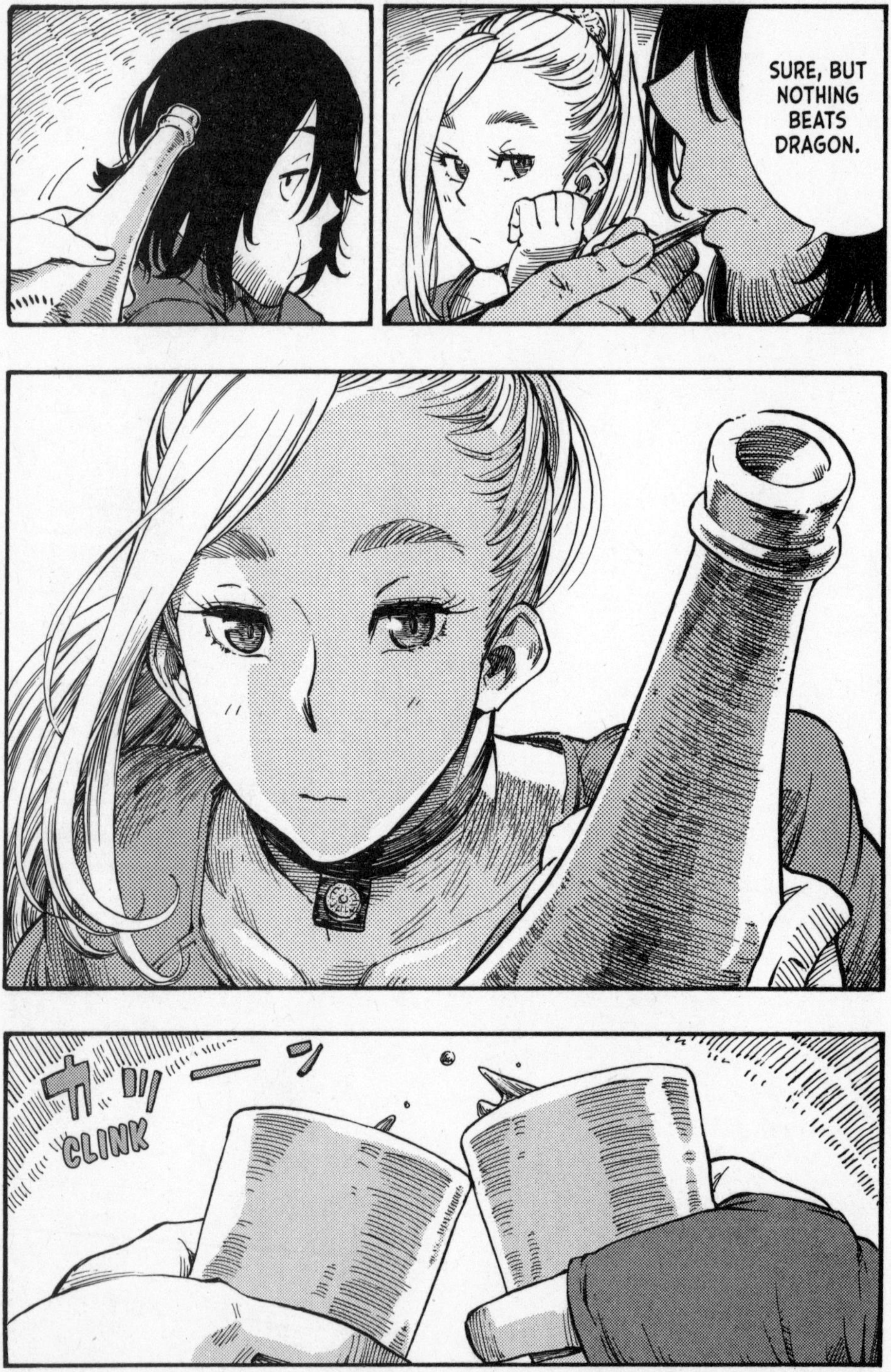
SURE, BUT NOTHING BEATS DRAGON.
カッーーン
CLINK

Pressed Dragon Terrine

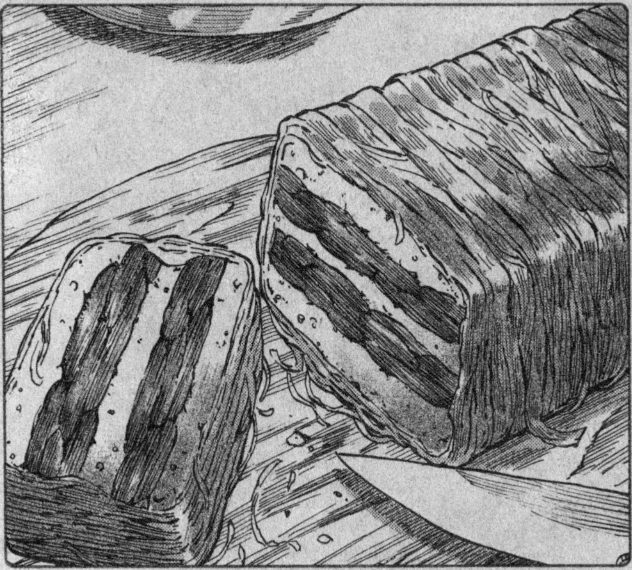

Ingredients (1 loaf)

- ✦ 300 g dragon liver
- ✦ 3-4 potatoes
- ✦ Pickled cabbage
- ✦ Salt to taste
- ✦ Pepper to taste
- ✦ 1-2 cloves garlic
- ✦ Enough dragon fat to submerge liver

01
Season dragon liver with salt, pepper, and minced garlic. Feel free to add herbs and spices.

02
To make the confit, cover the liver with dragon fat in a large pot and simmer at about 175° Fahrenheit for 1.5-2 hours.

03
Mash potatoes and season with salt, pepper, and a dash of confit fat. Mix together well.

04
Line the inside of a mold with pickled cabbage, then layer the mashed potato mixture and sliced liver confit, pressing each layer to remove any air pockets.

05
Fold pickled cabbage over the top of the ingredients and press down firmly (traditionally, a weight is used to press the loaf for 2-3 hours).

06
Slide a knife along the edge of the mold and gently remove the terrine.

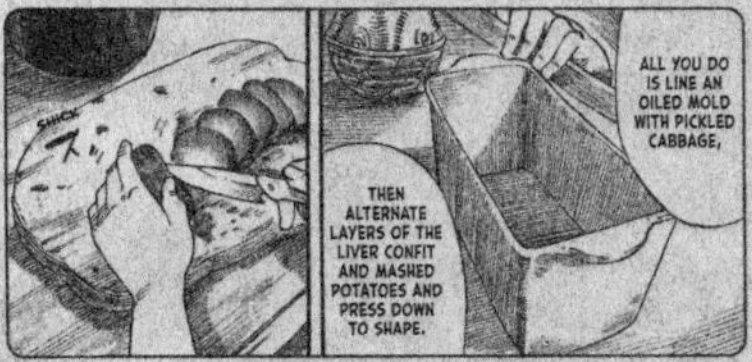
ALL YOU DO IS LINE AN OILED MOLD WITH PICKLED CABBAGE,
THEN ALTERNATE LAYERS OF THE LIVER CONFIT AND MASHED POTATOES AND PRESS DOWN TO SHAPE.
SHICK

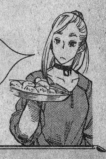

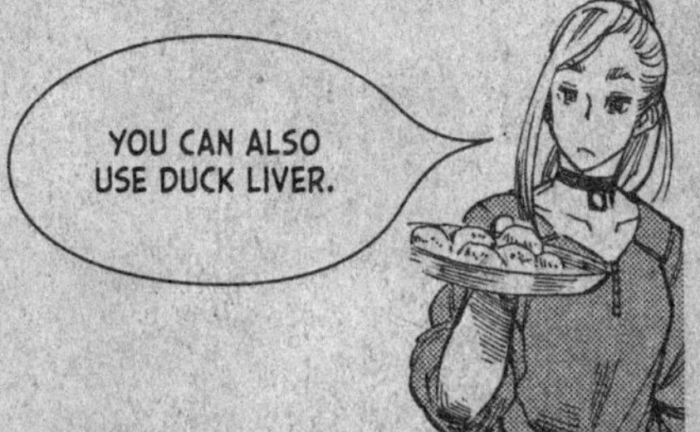
YOU CAN ALSO USE DUCK LIVER.

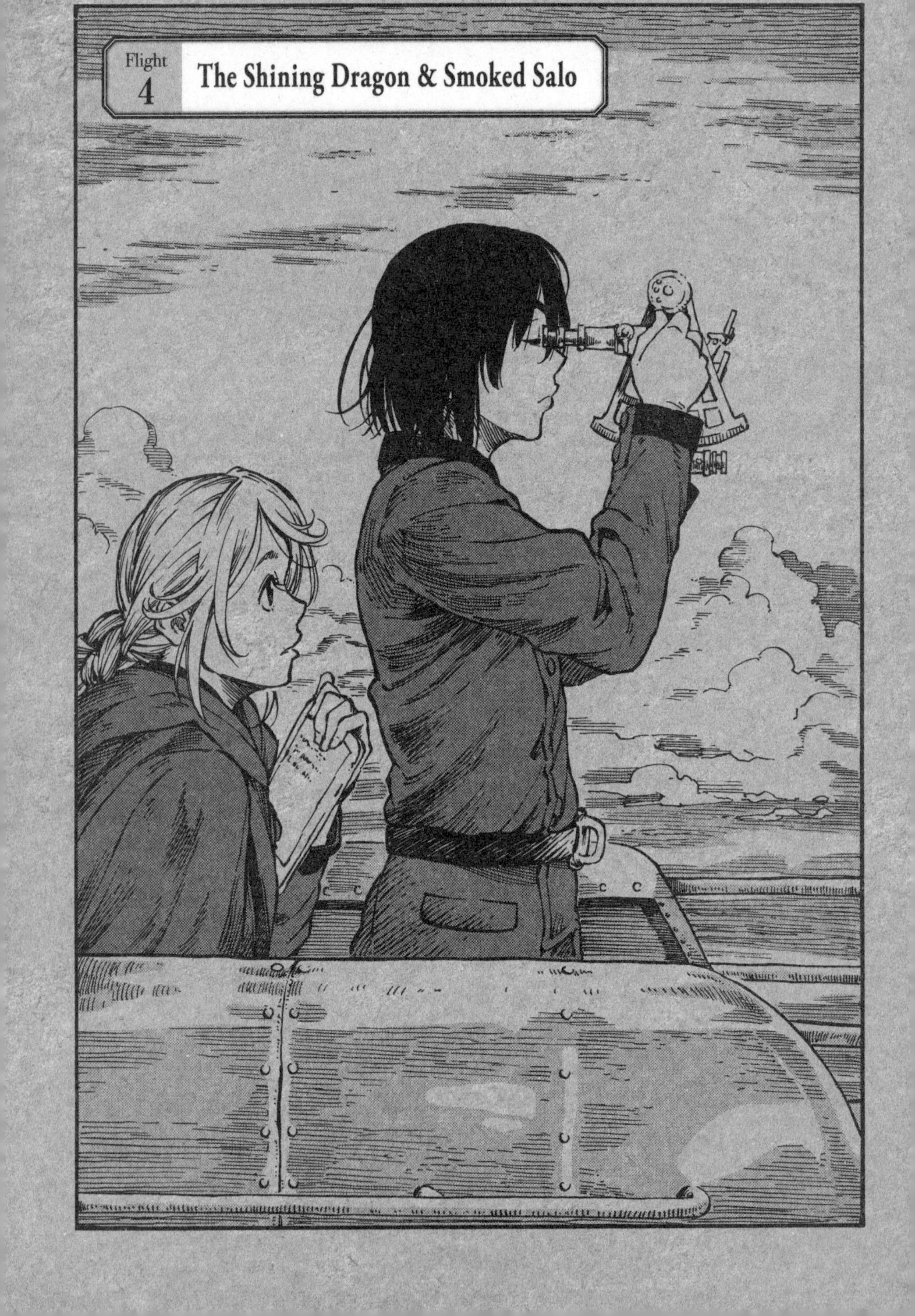
Flight 4
The Shining Dragon & Smoked Salo

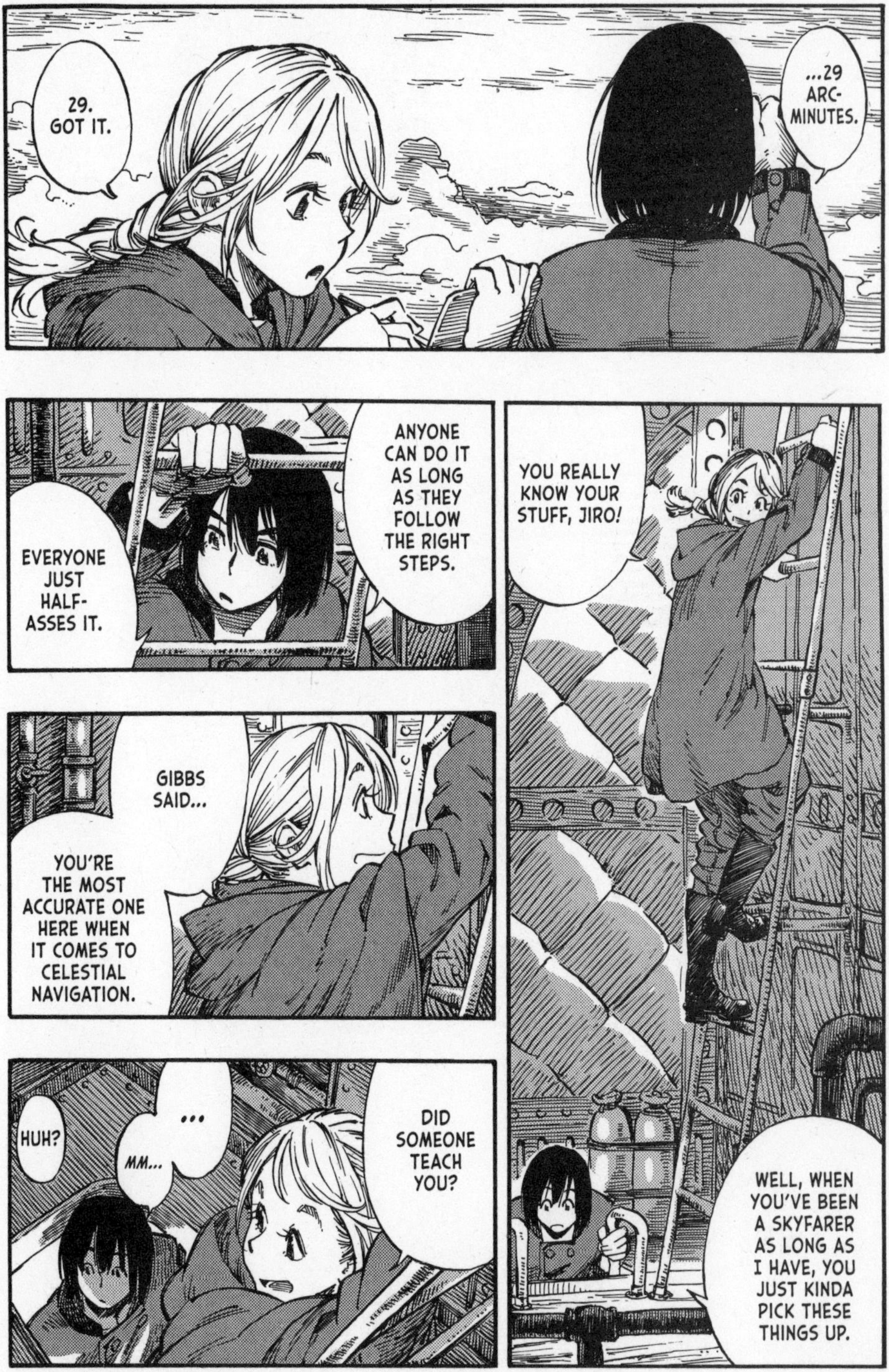
...29 ARC-MINUTES.
29. GOT IT.
YOU REALLY KNOW YOUR STUFF, JIRO!
WELL, WHEN YOU'VE BEEN A SKYFARER AS LONG AS I HAVE, YOU JUST KINDA PICK THESE THINGS UP.
ANYONE CAN DO IT AS LONG AS THEY FOLLOW THE RIGHT STEPS.
EVERYONE JUST HALF-ASSES IT.
GIBBS SAID...
YOU'RE THE MOST ACCURATE ONE HERE WHEN IT COMES TO CELESTIAL NAVIGATION.
DID SOMEONE TEACH YOU?
...
MM...
HUH?

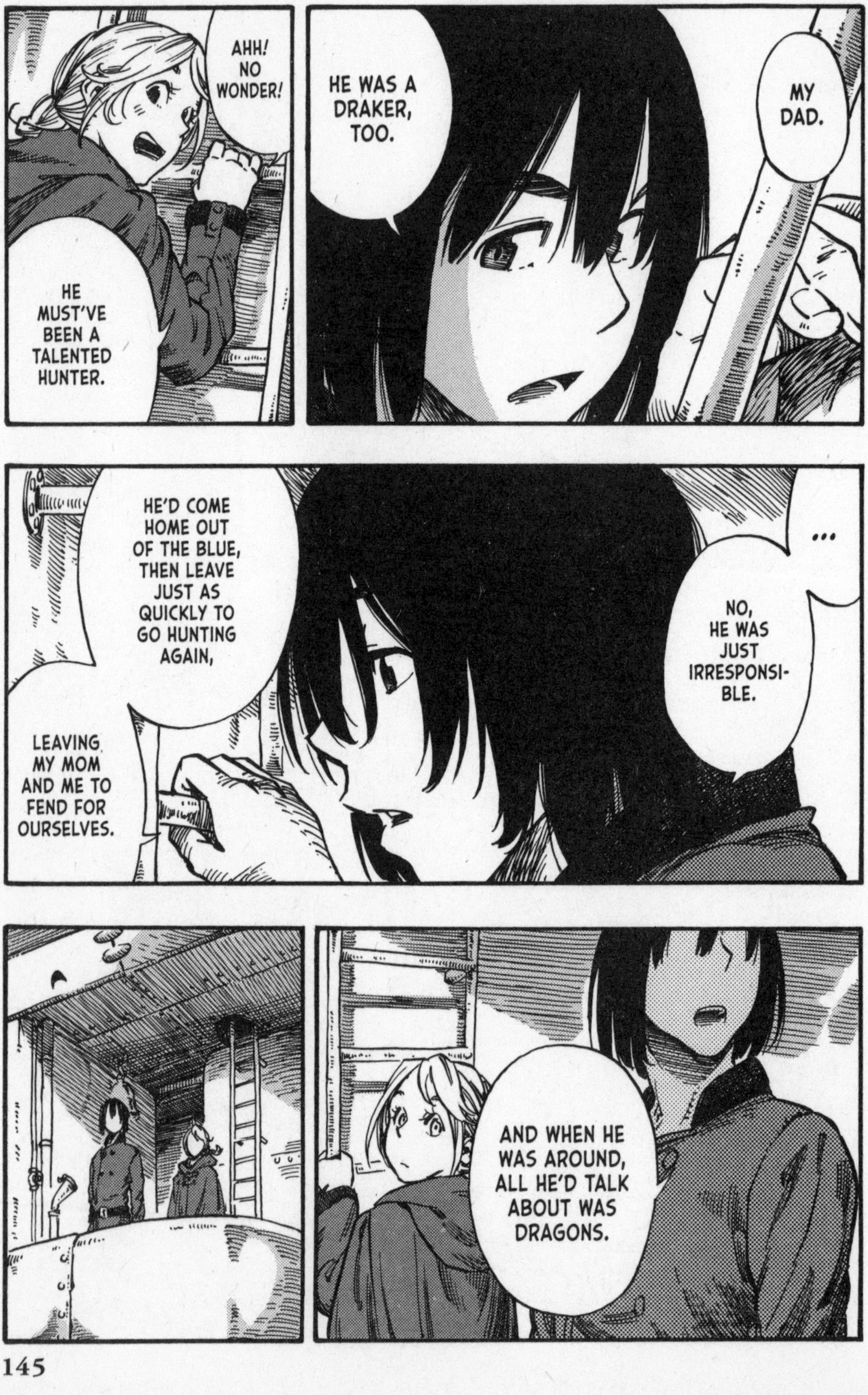
MY DAD.
HE WAS A DRAKER, TOO.
AHH! NO WONDER!
HE MUST'VE BEEN A TALENTED HUNTER.
...
NO, HE WAS JUST IRRESPONSIBLE.
HE'D COME HOME OUT OF THE BLUE, THEN LEAVE JUST AS QUICKLY TO GO HUNTING AGAIN,
LEAVING MY MOM AND ME TO FEND FOR OURSELVES.
AND WHEN HE WAS AROUND, ALL HE'D TALK ABOUT WAS DRAGONS.

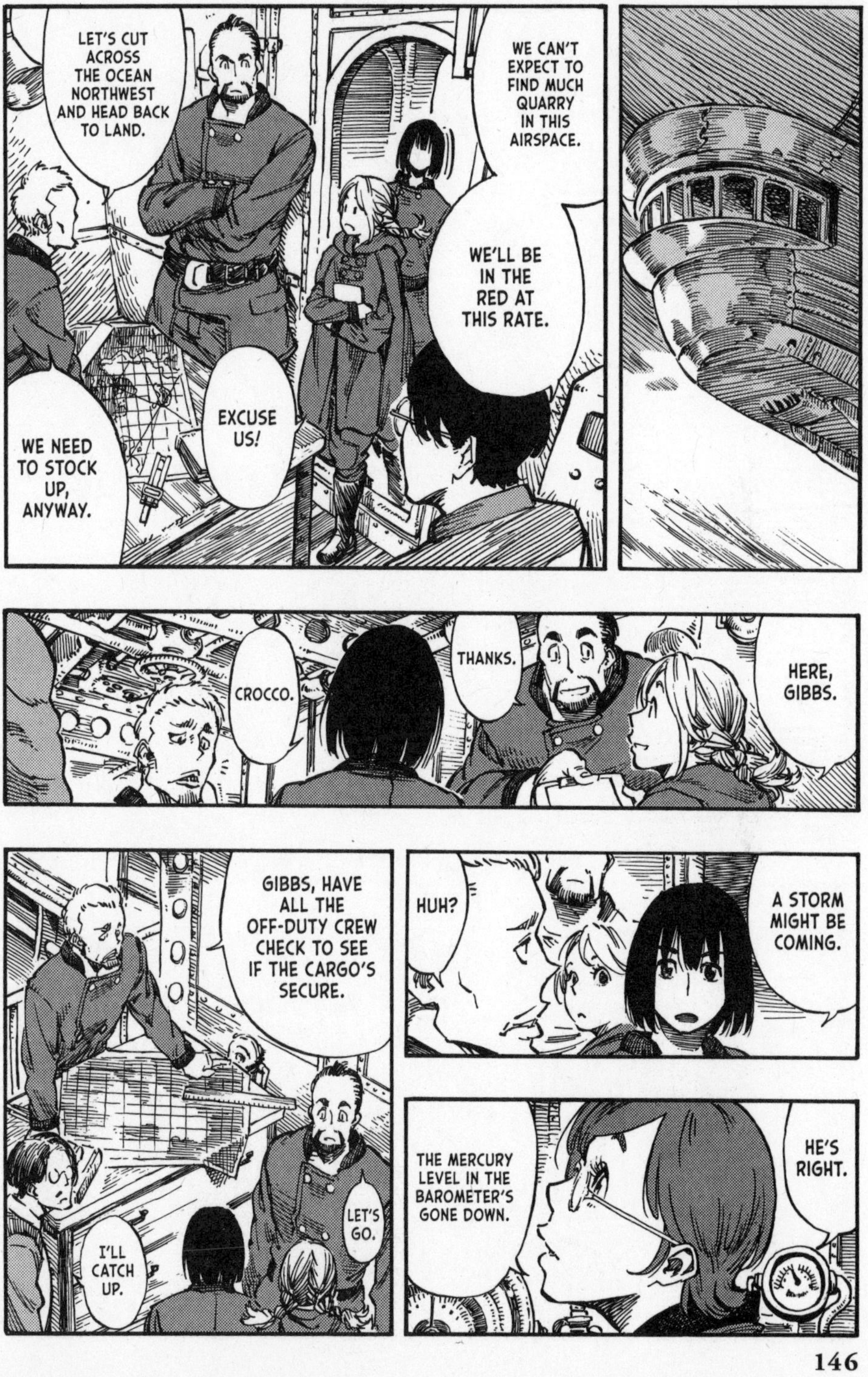
WE CAN'T EXPECT TO FIND MUCH QUARRY IN THIS AIRSPACE.
LET'S CUT ACROSS THE OCEAN NORTHWEST AND HEAD BACK TO LAND.
WE'LL BE IN THE RED AT THIS RATE.
EXCUSE US!
WE NEED TO STOCK UP, ANYWAY.
HERE, GIBBS.
THANKS.
CROCCO.
A STORM MIGHT BE COMING.
HUH?
HE'S RIGHT.
THE MERCURY LEVEL IN THE BAROMETER'S GONE DOWN.
GIBBS, HAVE ALL THE OFF-DUTY CREW CHECK TO SEE IF THE CARGO'S SECURE.
LET'S GO.
I'LL CATCH UP.

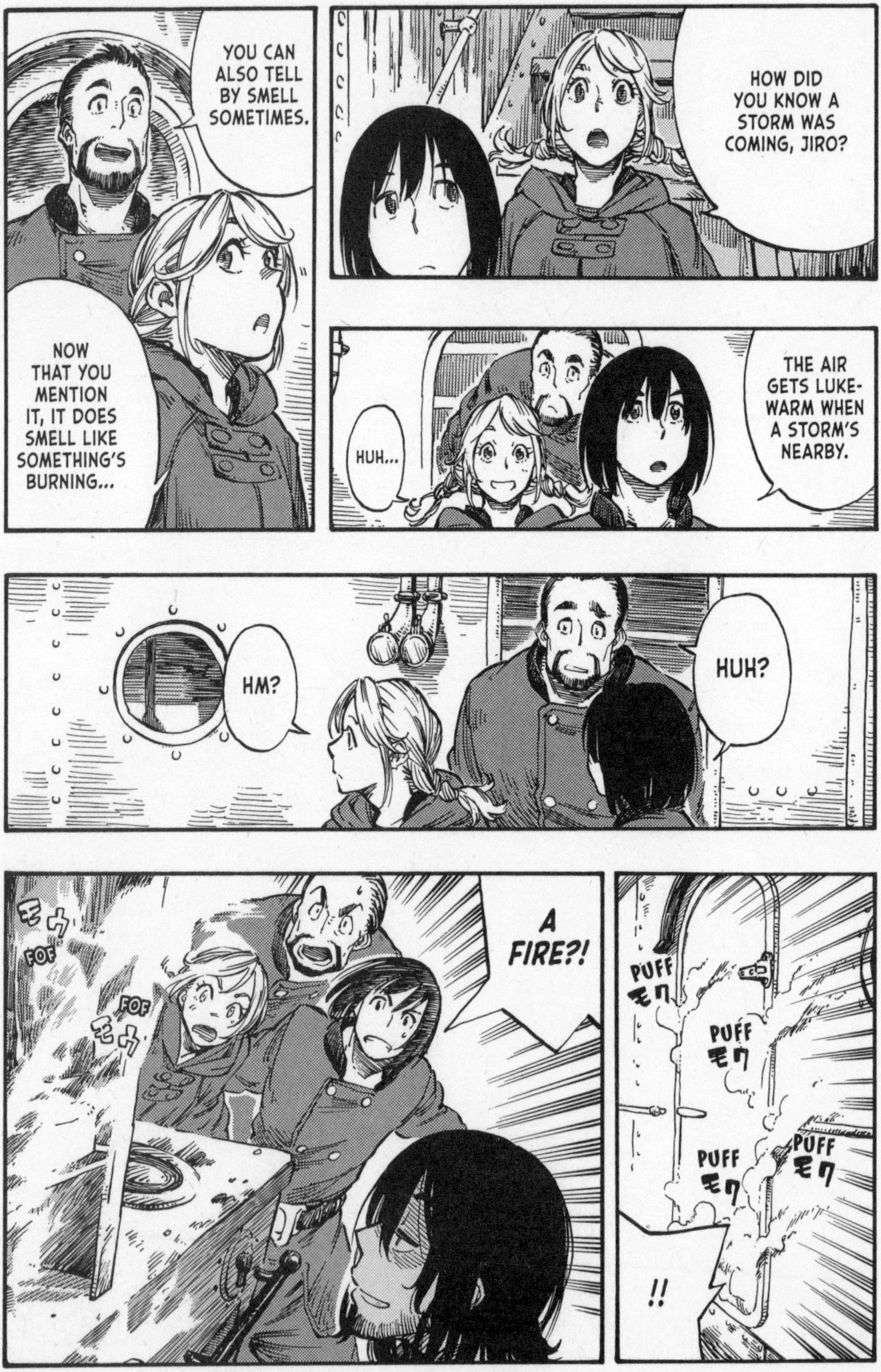
HOW DID YOU KNOW A STORM WAS COMING, JIRO?
THE AIR GETS LUKE-WARM WHEN A STORM'S NEARBY.
HUH...
YOU CAN ALSO TELL BY SMELL SOMETIMES.
NOW THAT YOU MENTION IT, IT DOES SMELL LIKE SOMETHING'S BURNING...
HUH?
HM?
PUFF モク
PUFF モク
PUFF モク
PUFF モク
!!
A FIRE?!
モウ FOF
FOF モウ

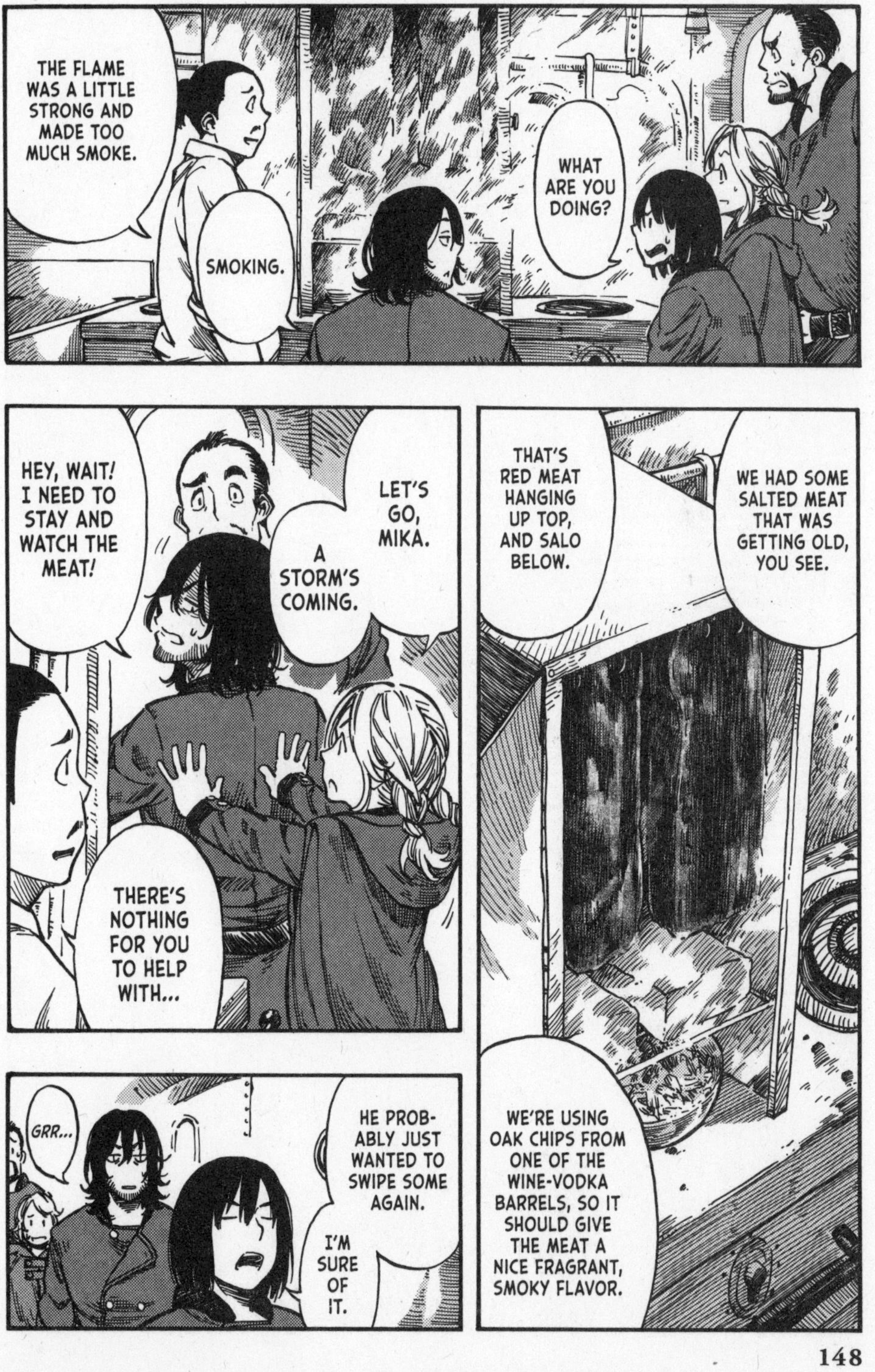
WHAT ARE YOU DOING?
SMOKING.
THE FLAME WAS A LITTLE STRONG AND MADE TOO MUCH SMOKE.
WE HAD SOME SALTED MEAT THAT WAS GETTING OLD, YOU SEE.
THAT'S RED MEAT HANGING UP TOP, AND SALO BELOW.
WE'RE USING OAK CHIPS FROM ONE OF THE WINE-VODKA BARRELS, SO IT SHOULD GIVE THE MEAT A NICE FRAGRANT, SMOKY FLAVOR.
LET'S GO, MIKA.
A STORM'S COMING.
HEY, WAIT! I NEED TO STAY AND WATCH THE MEAT!
THERE'S NOTHING FOR YOU TO HELP WITH...
HE PROBABLY JUST WANTED TO SWIPE SOME AGAIN.
I'M SURE OF IT.
GRR...

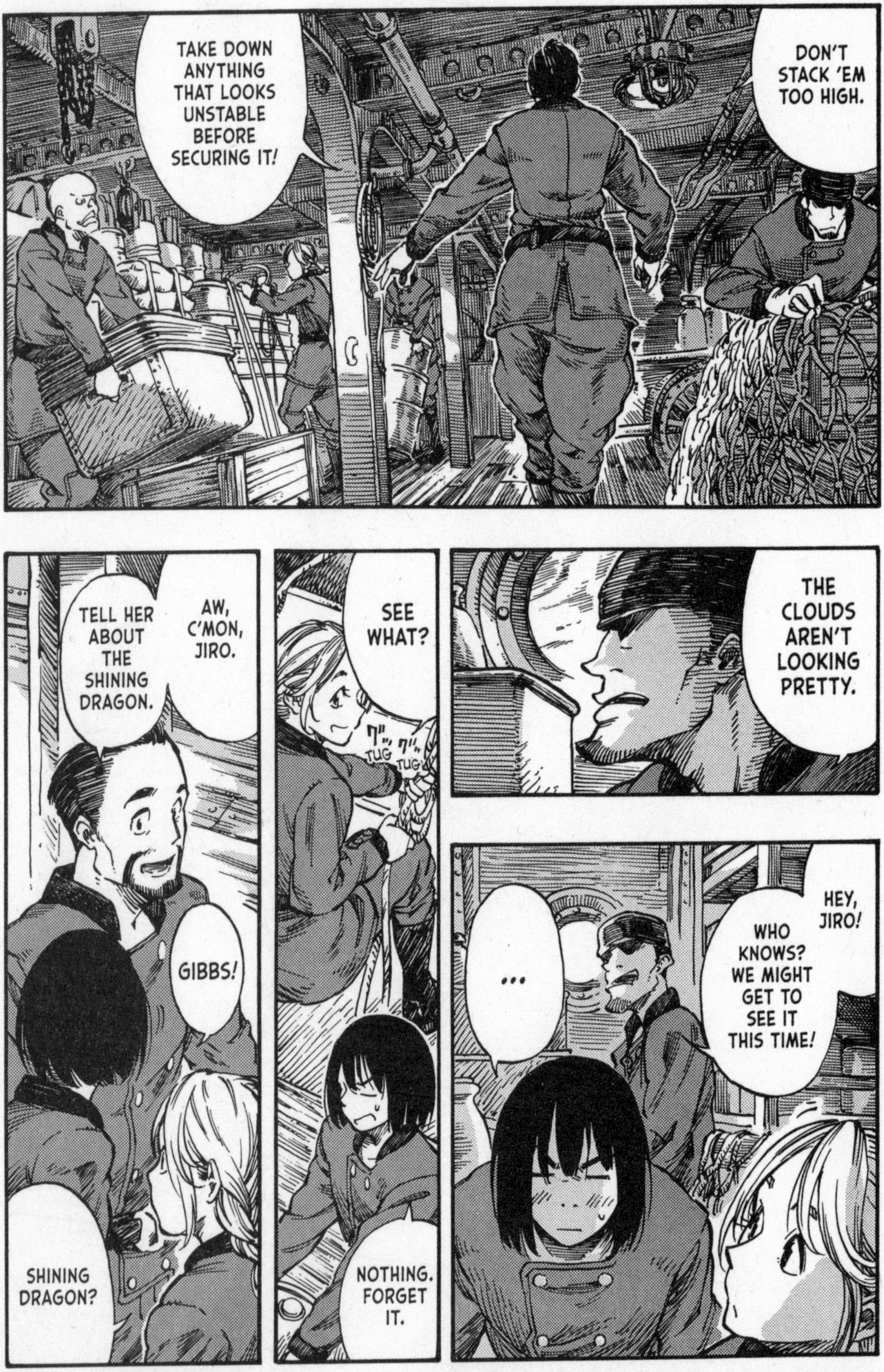
DON'T STACK 'EM TOO HIGH.
TAKE DOWN ANYTHING THAT LOOKS UNSTABLE BEFORE SECURING IT!
THE CLOUDS AREN'T LOOKING PRETTY.
HEY, JIRO!
WHO KNOWS? WE MIGHT GET TO SEE IT THIS TIME!
...
SEE WHAT?
TUG TUG
NOTHING. FORGET IT.
AW, C'MON, JIRO.
TELL HER ABOUT THE SHINING DRAGON.
GIBBS!
SHINING DRAGON?

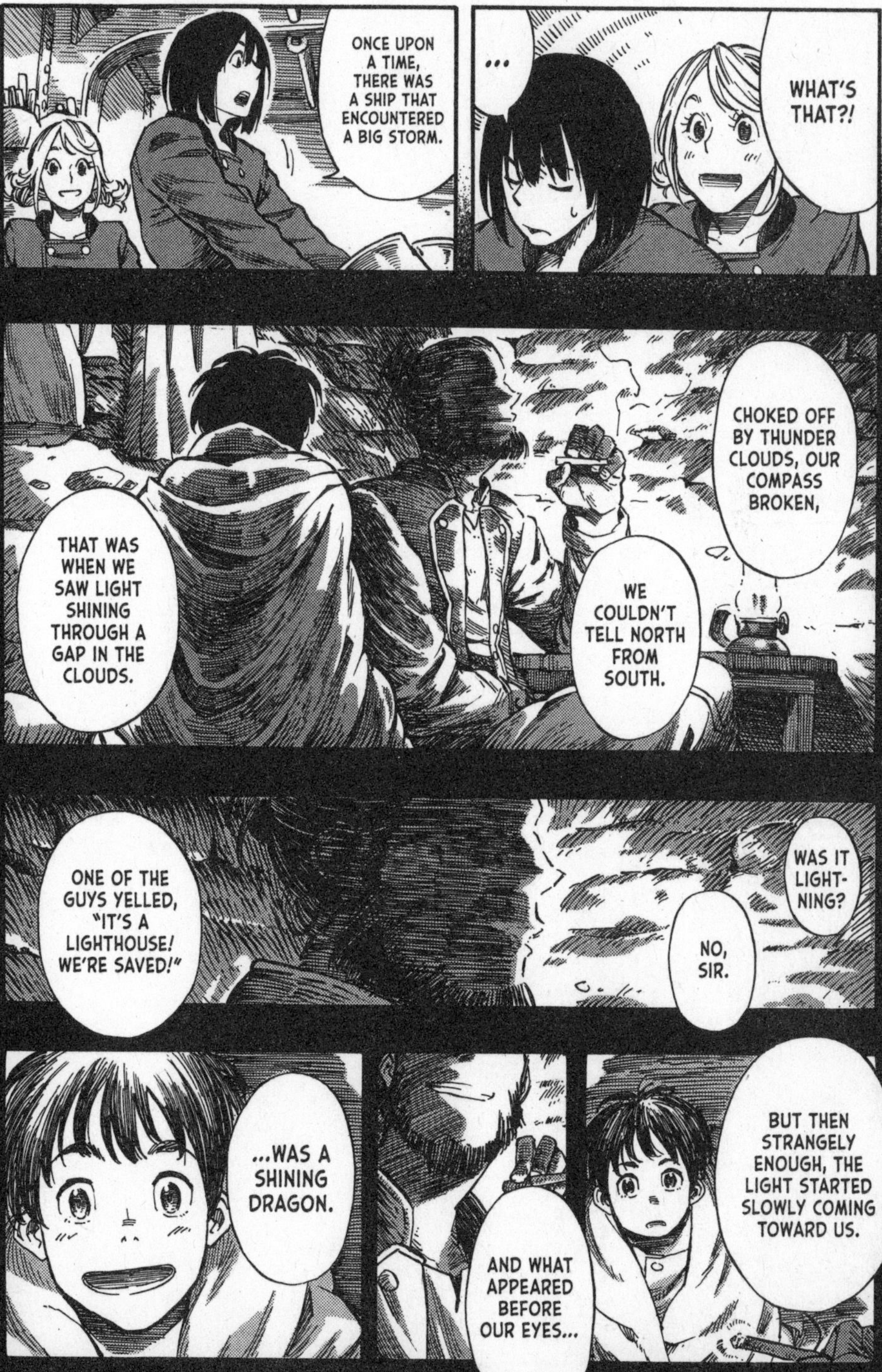
WHAT'S THAT?!
...
ONCE UPON A TIME, THERE WAS A SHIP THAT ENCOUNTERED A BIG STORM.
CHOKED OFF BY THUNDER CLOUDS, OUR COMPASS BROKEN,
WE COULDN'T TELL NORTH FROM SOUTH.
THAT WAS WHEN WE SAW LIGHT SHINING THROUGH A GAP IN THE CLOUDS.
WAS IT LIGHT-NING?
NO, SIR.
ONE OF THE GUYS YELLED, "IT'S A LIGHTHOUSE! WE'RE SAVED!"
BUT THEN STRANGELY ENOUGH, THE LIGHT STARTED SLOWLY COMING TOWARD US.
AND WHAT APPEARED BEFORE OUR EYES...
...WAS A SHINING DRAGON.

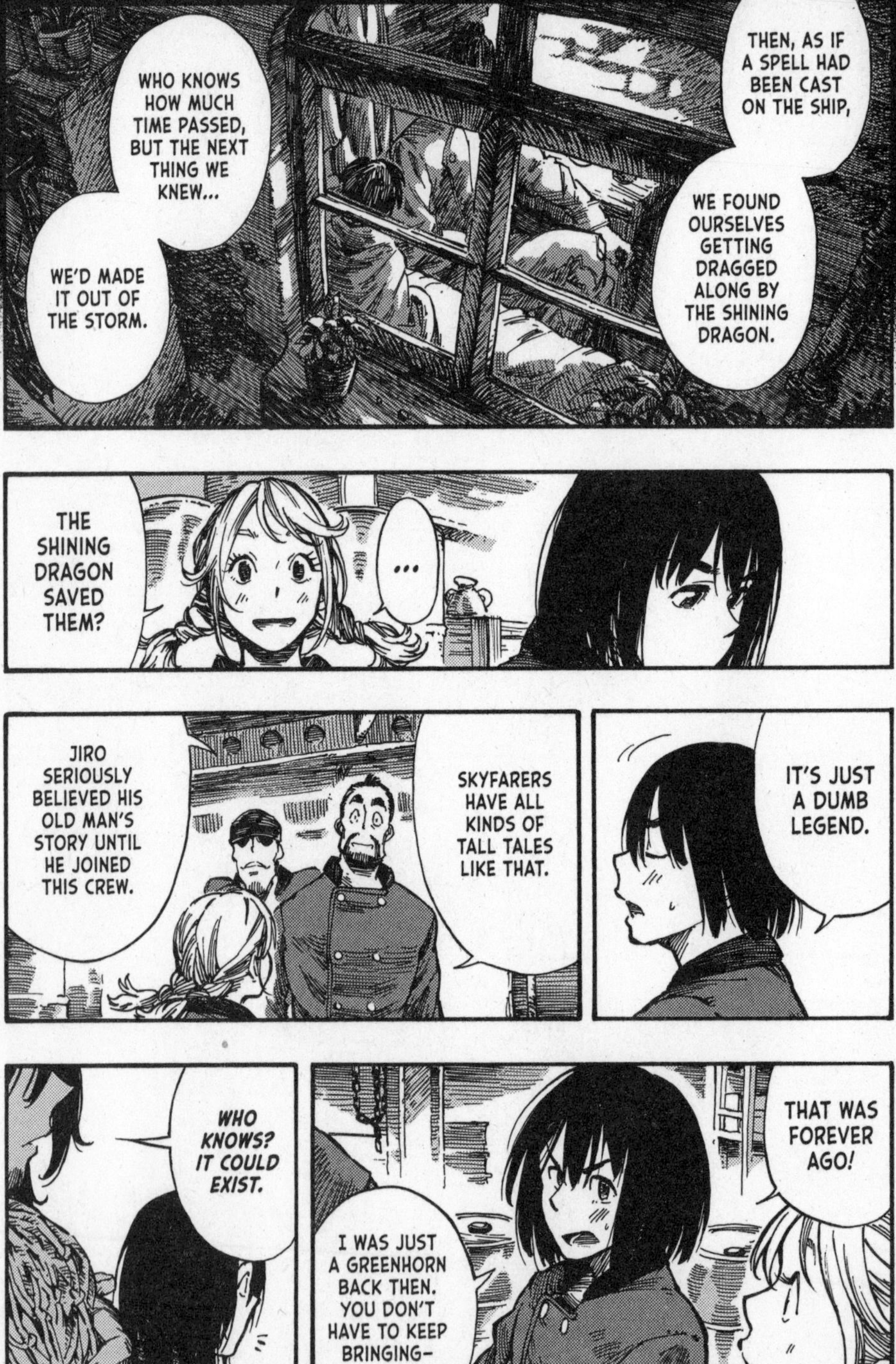
THEN, AS IF A SPELL HAD BEEN CAST ON THE SHIP,
WE FOUND OURSELVES GETTING DRAGGED ALONG BY THE SHINING DRAGON.
WHO KNOWS HOW MUCH TIME PASSED, BUT THE NEXT THING WE KNEW...
WE'D MADE IT OUT OF THE STORM.
...
THE SHINING DRAGON SAVED THEM?
IT'S JUST A DUMB LEGEND.
SKYFARERS HAVE ALL KINDS OF TALL TALES LIKE THAT.
JIRO SERIOUSLY BELIEVED HIS OLD MAN'S STORY UNTIL HE JOINED THIS CREW.
THAT WAS FOREVER AGO!
I WAS JUST A GREENHORN BACK THEN. YOU DON'T HAVE TO KEEP BRINGING-
WHO KNOWS? IT COULD EXIST.

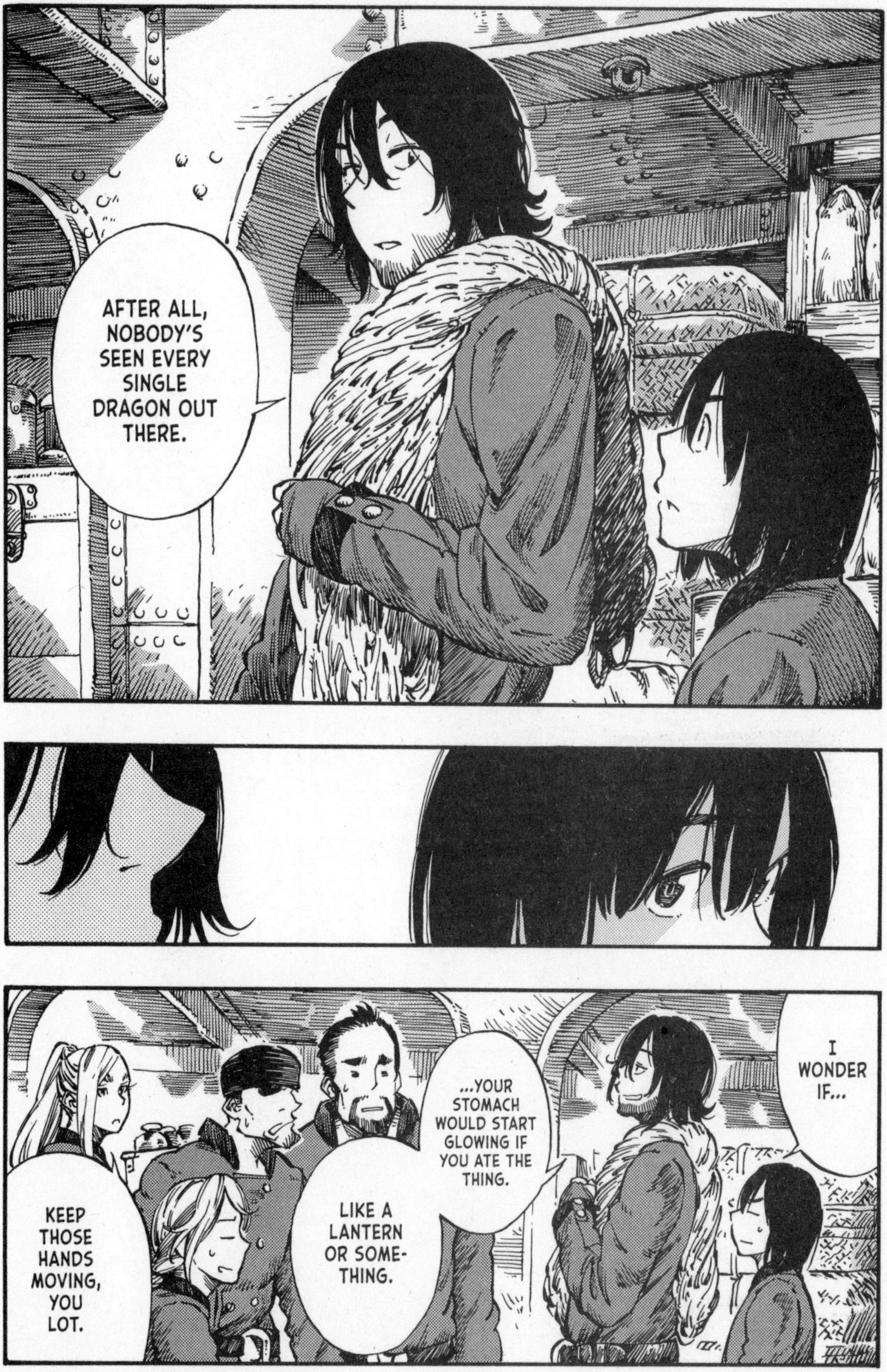
AFTER ALL, NOBODY'S SEEN EVERY SINGLE DRAGON OUT THERE.
I WONDER IF...
...YOUR STOMACH WOULD START GLOWING IF YOU ATE THE THING.
LIKE A LANTERN OR SOME-THING.
KEEP THOSE HANDS MOVING, YOU LOT.

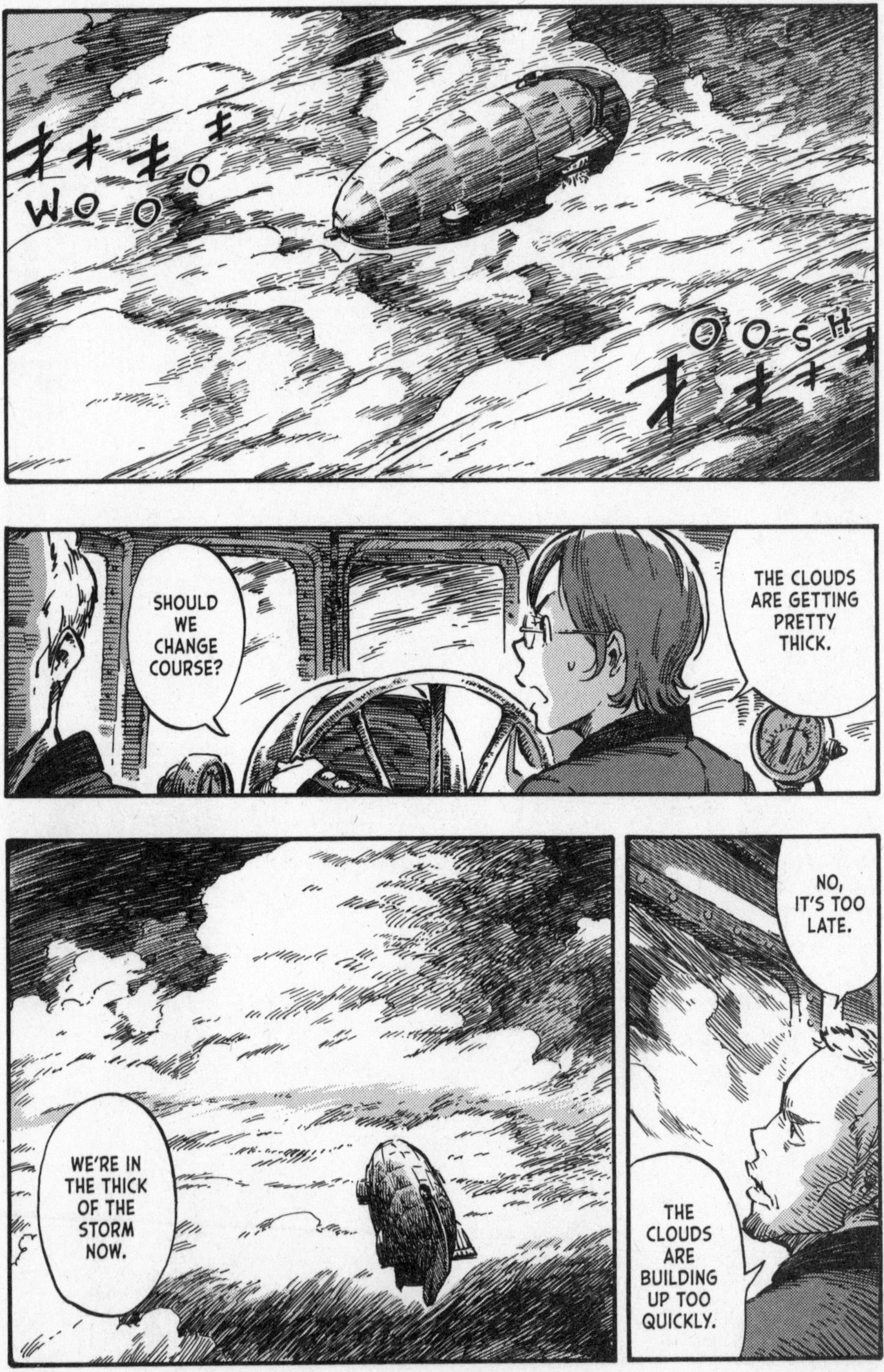
WOOO
OOSH
THE CLOUDS ARE GETTING PRETTY THICK.
SHOULD WE CHANGE COURSE?
NO, IT'S TOO LATE.
THE CLOUDS ARE BUILDING UP TOO QUICKLY.
WE'RE IN THE THICK OF THE STORM NOW.

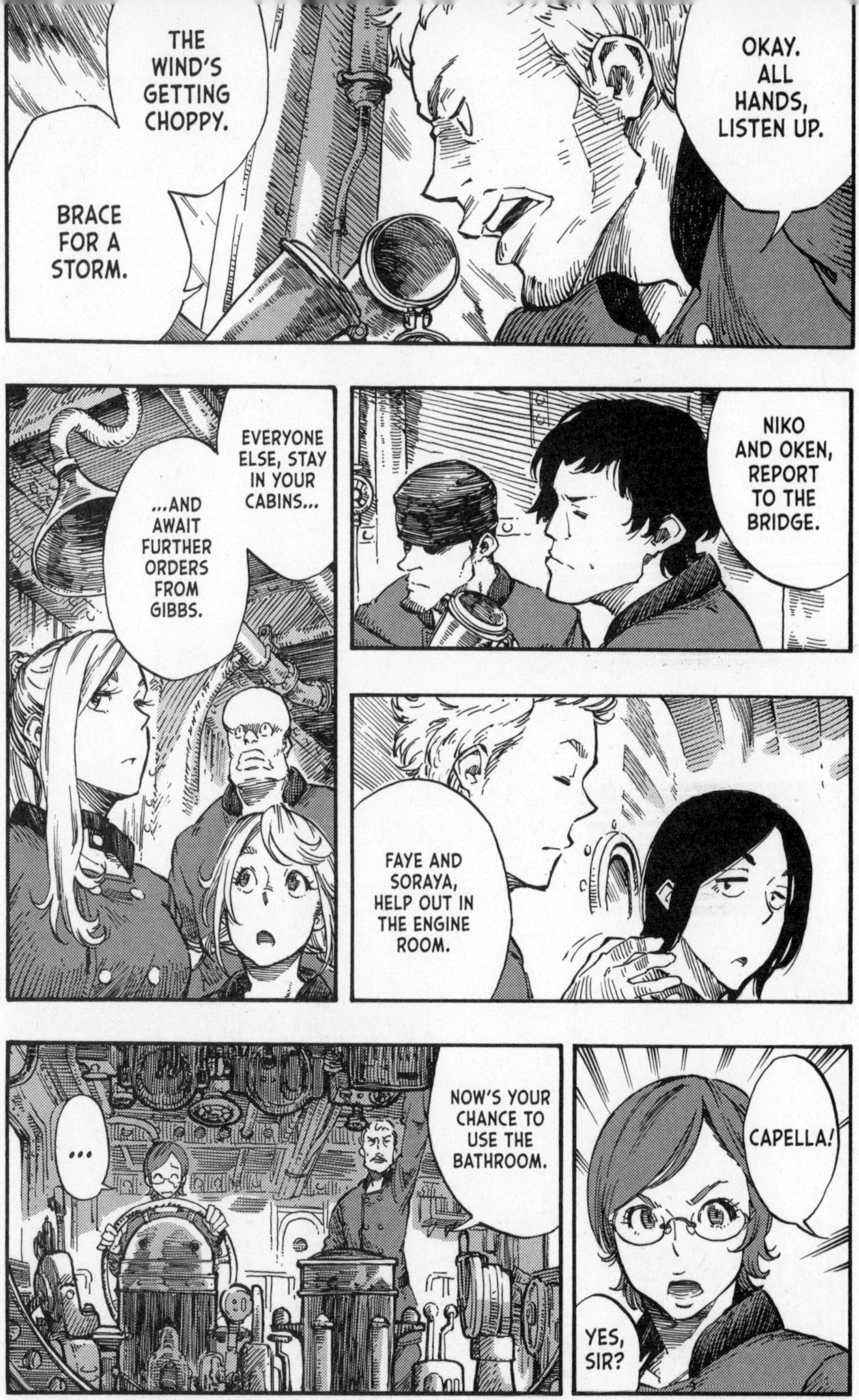
OKAY. ALL HANDS, LISTEN UP.
THE WIND'S GETTING CHOPPY.
BRACE FOR A STORM.
NIKO AND OKEN, REPORT TO THE BRIDGE.
FAYE AND SORAYA, HELP OUT IN THE ENGINE ROOM.
EVERYONE ELSE, STAY IN YOUR CABINS...
...AND AWAIT FURTHER ORDERS FROM GIBBS.
CAPELLA!
YES, SIR?
NOW'S YOUR CHANCE TO USE THE BATHROOM.
...

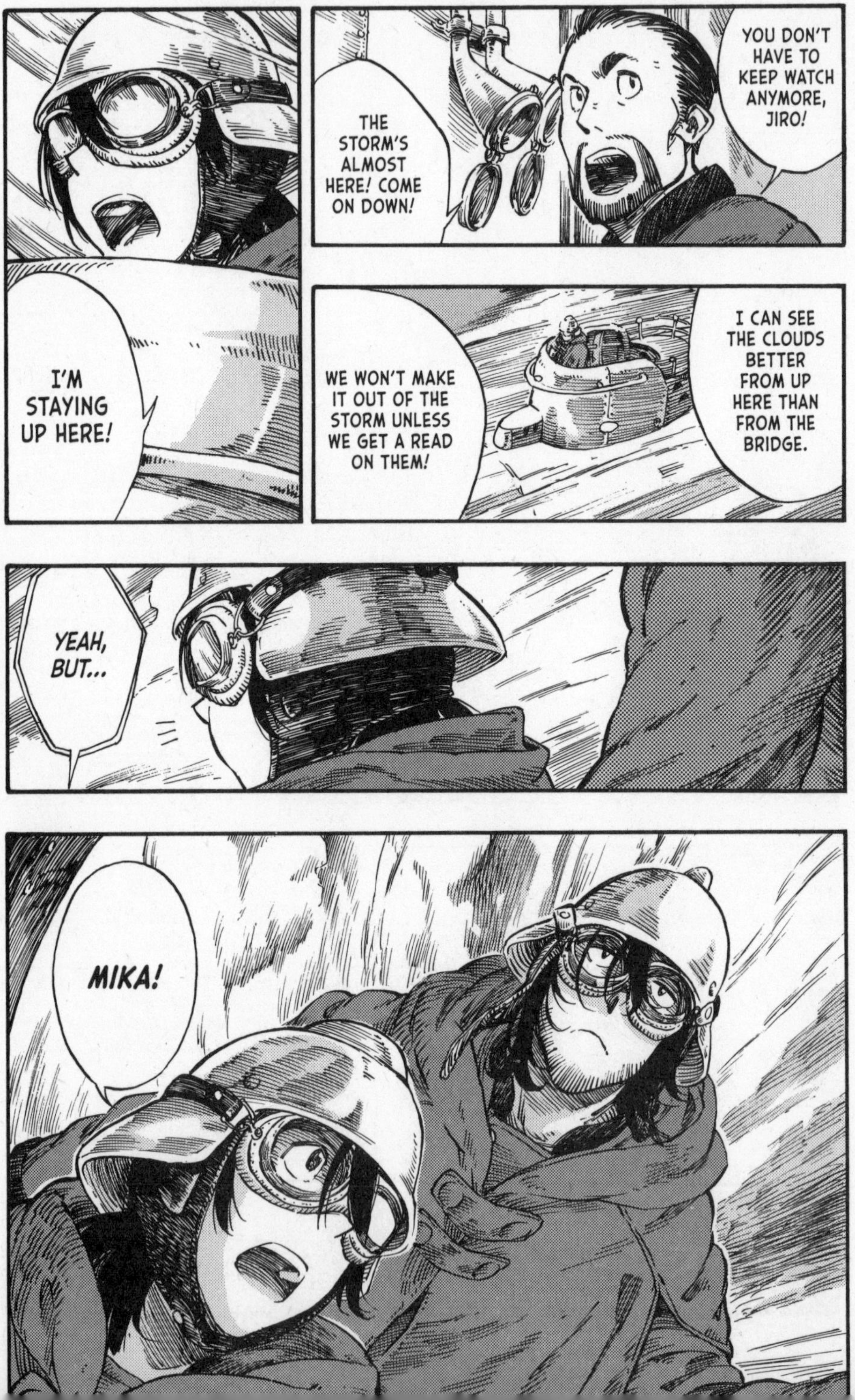
YOU DON'T HAVE TO KEEP WATCH ANYMORE, JIRO!
THE STORM'S ALMOST HERE! COME ON DOWN!
I CAN SEE THE CLOUDS BETTER FROM UP HERE THAN FROM THE BRIDGE.
WE WON'T MAKE IT OUT OF THE STORM UNLESS WE GET A READ ON THEM!
I'M STAYING UP HERE!
YEAH, BUT...
MIKA!

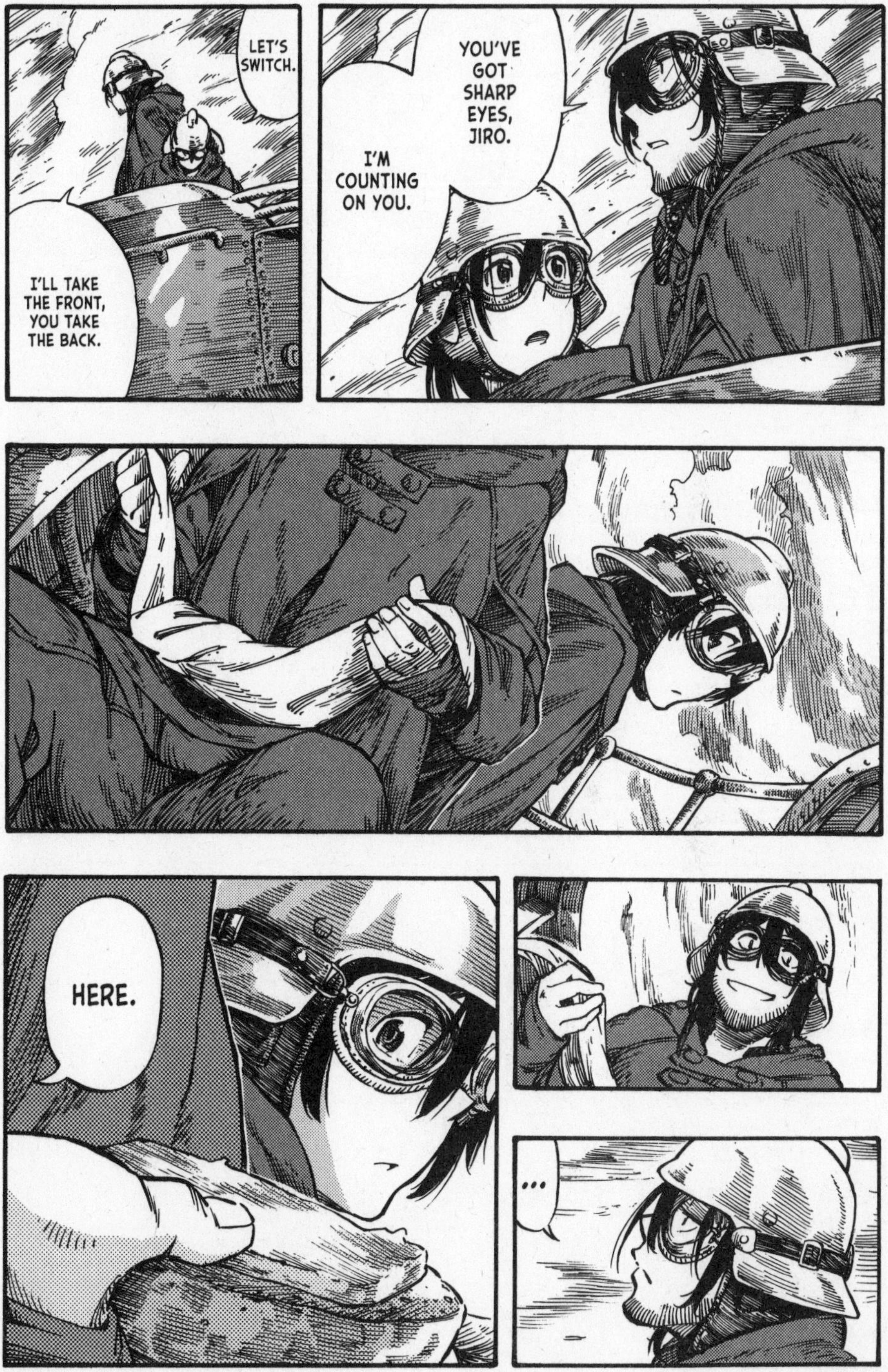
YOU'VE GOT SHARP EYES, JIRO.
I'M COUNTING ON YOU.
LET'S SWITCH.
I'LL TAKE THE FRONT, YOU TAKE THE BACK.
...
HERE.

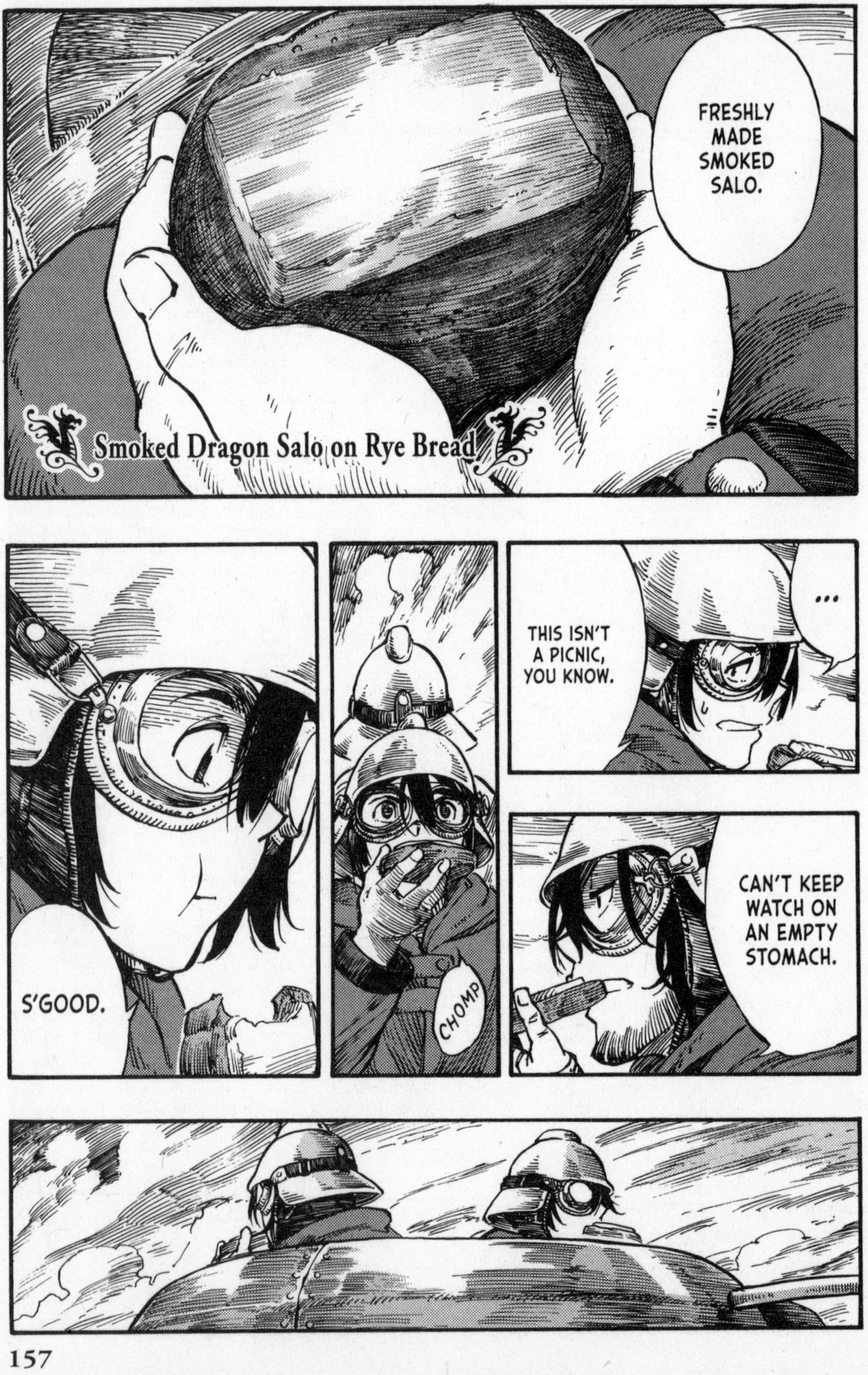
FRESHLY MADE SMOKED SALO.
Smoked Dragon Salo on Rye Bread
...
THIS ISN'T A PICNIC, YOU KNOW.
CAN'T KEEP WATCH ON AN EMPTY STOMACH.
CHOMP
S'GOOD.

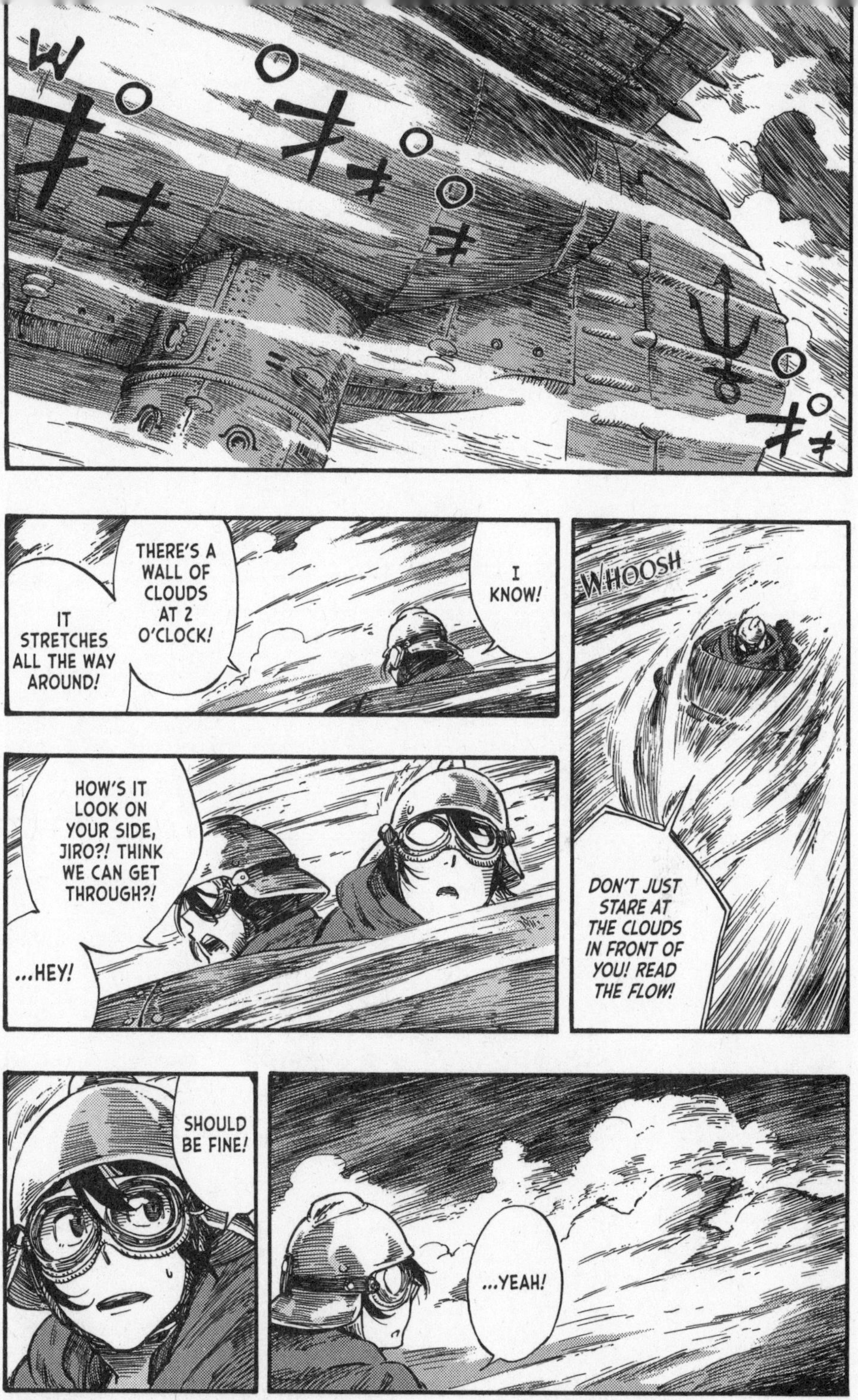
WHOOSH
DON'T JUST STARE AT THE CLOUDS IN FRONT OF YOU! READ THE FLOW!
I KNOW!
THERE'S A WALL OF CLOUDS AT 2 O'CLOCK!
IT STRETCHES ALL THE WAY AROUND!
HOW'S IT LOOK ON YOUR SIDE, JIRO?! THINK WE CAN GET THROUGH?!
...HEY!
...YEAH!
SHOULD BE FINE!

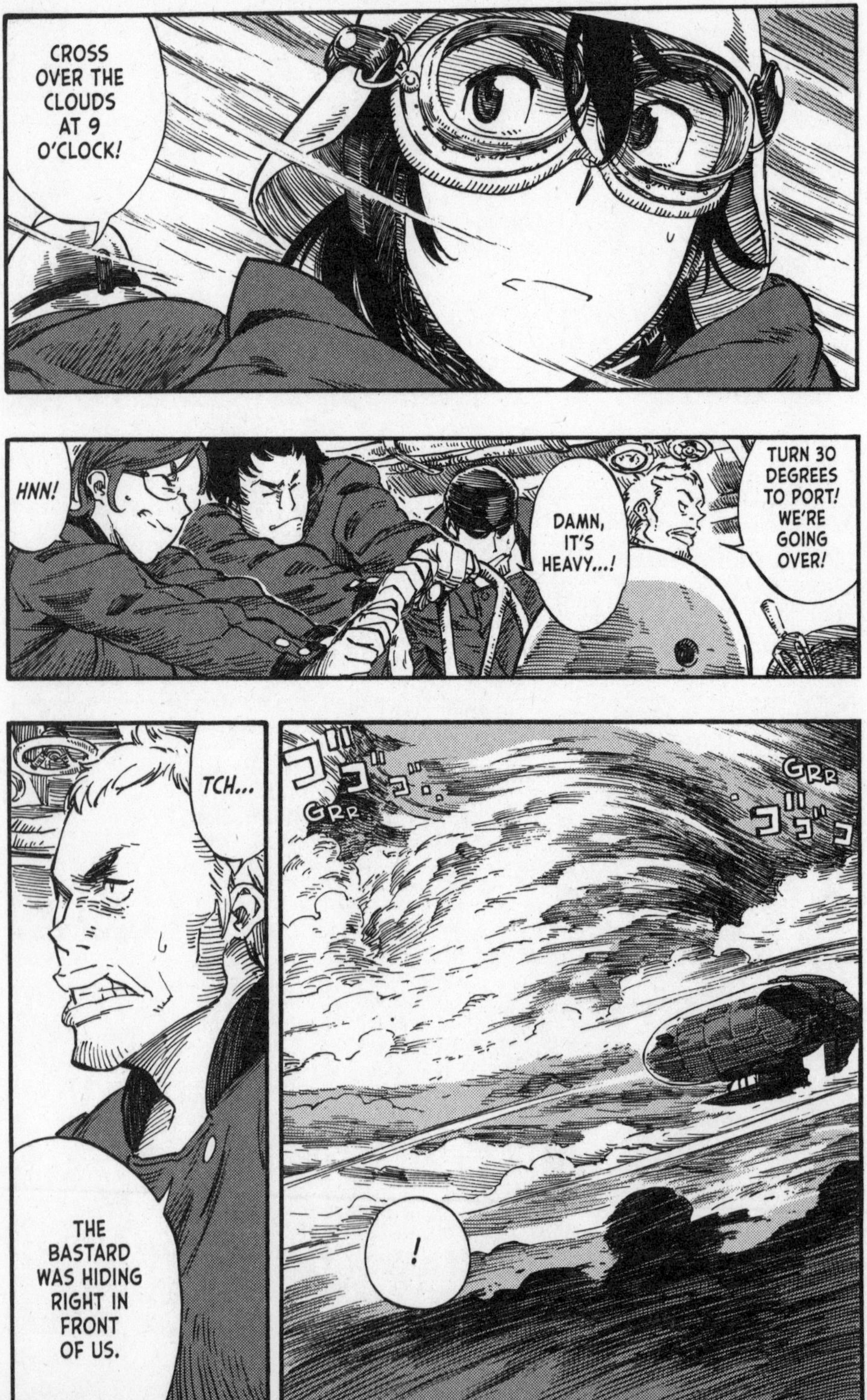
CROSS OVER THE CLOUDS AT 9 O'CLOCK!
TURN 30 DEGREES TO PORT! WE'RE GOING OVER!
DAMN, IT'S HEAVY...!
HNN!
GRR
ゴゴゴ
ゴゴゴ
GRR
!
TCH...
THE BASTARD WAS HIDING RIGHT IN FRONT OF US.

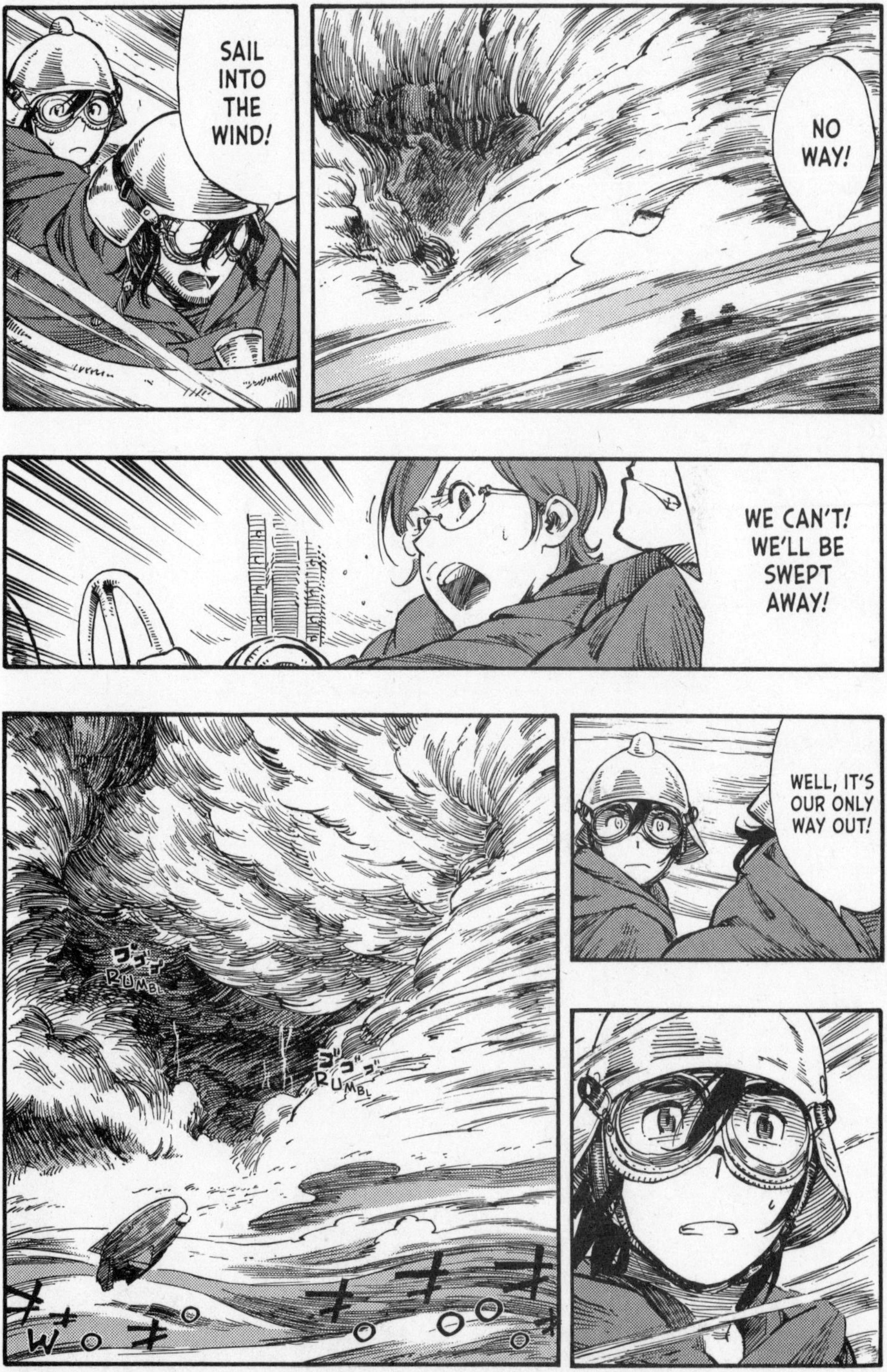
NO WAY!
SAIL INTO THE WIND!
WE CAN'T! WE'LL BE SWEPT AWAY!
WELL, IT'S OUR ONLY WAY OUT!
RUMBL
RUMBL
WOO
OOO

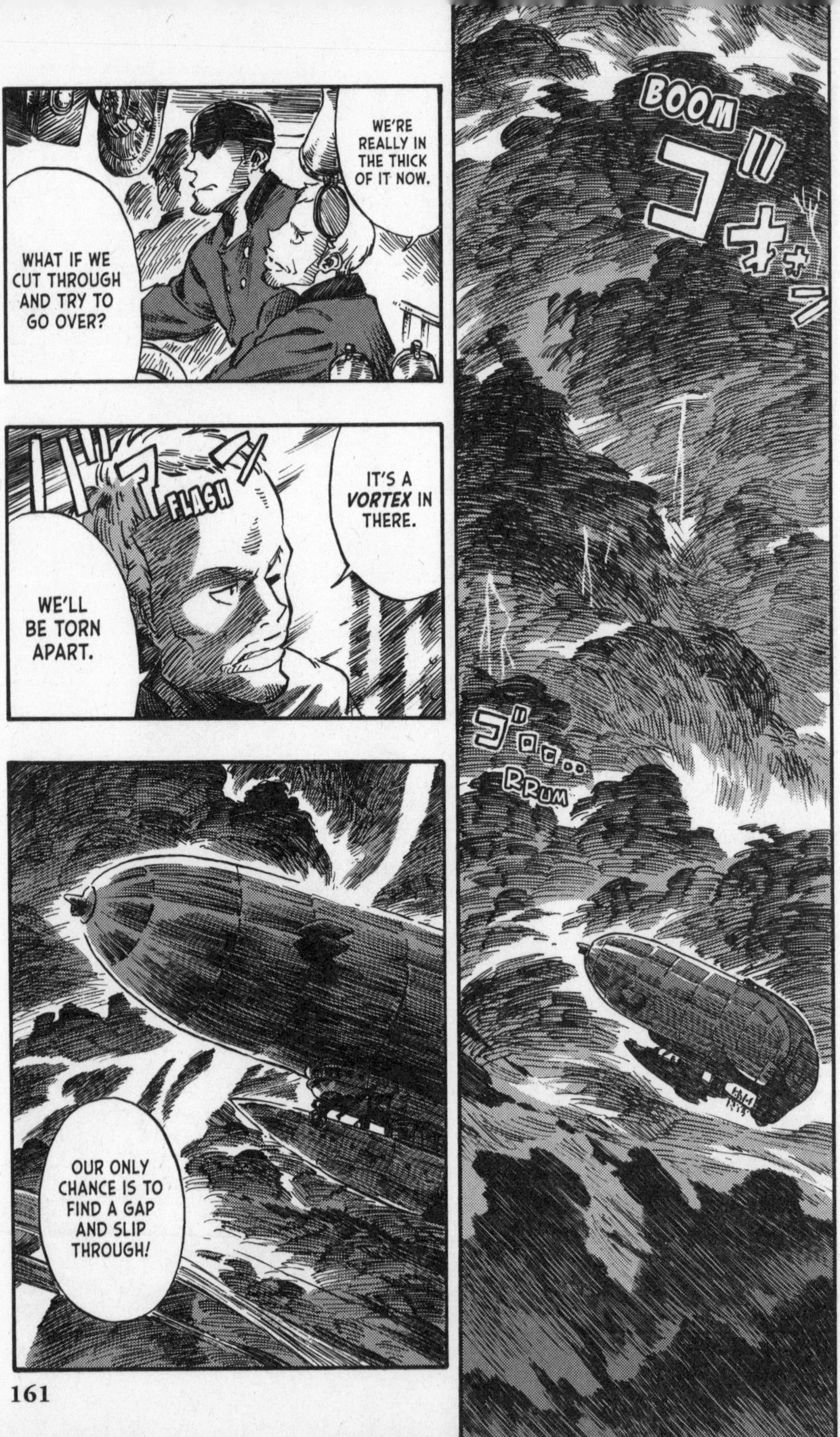
BOOM
ゴォォン
ゴロロ...
RRUM
WE'RE REALLY IN THE THICK OF IT NOW.
WHAT IF WE CUT THROUGH AND TRY TO GO OVER?
FLASH
IT'S A *VORTEX* IN THERE.
WE'LL BE TORN APART.
OUR ONLY CHANCE IS TO FIND A GAP AND SLIP THROUGH!

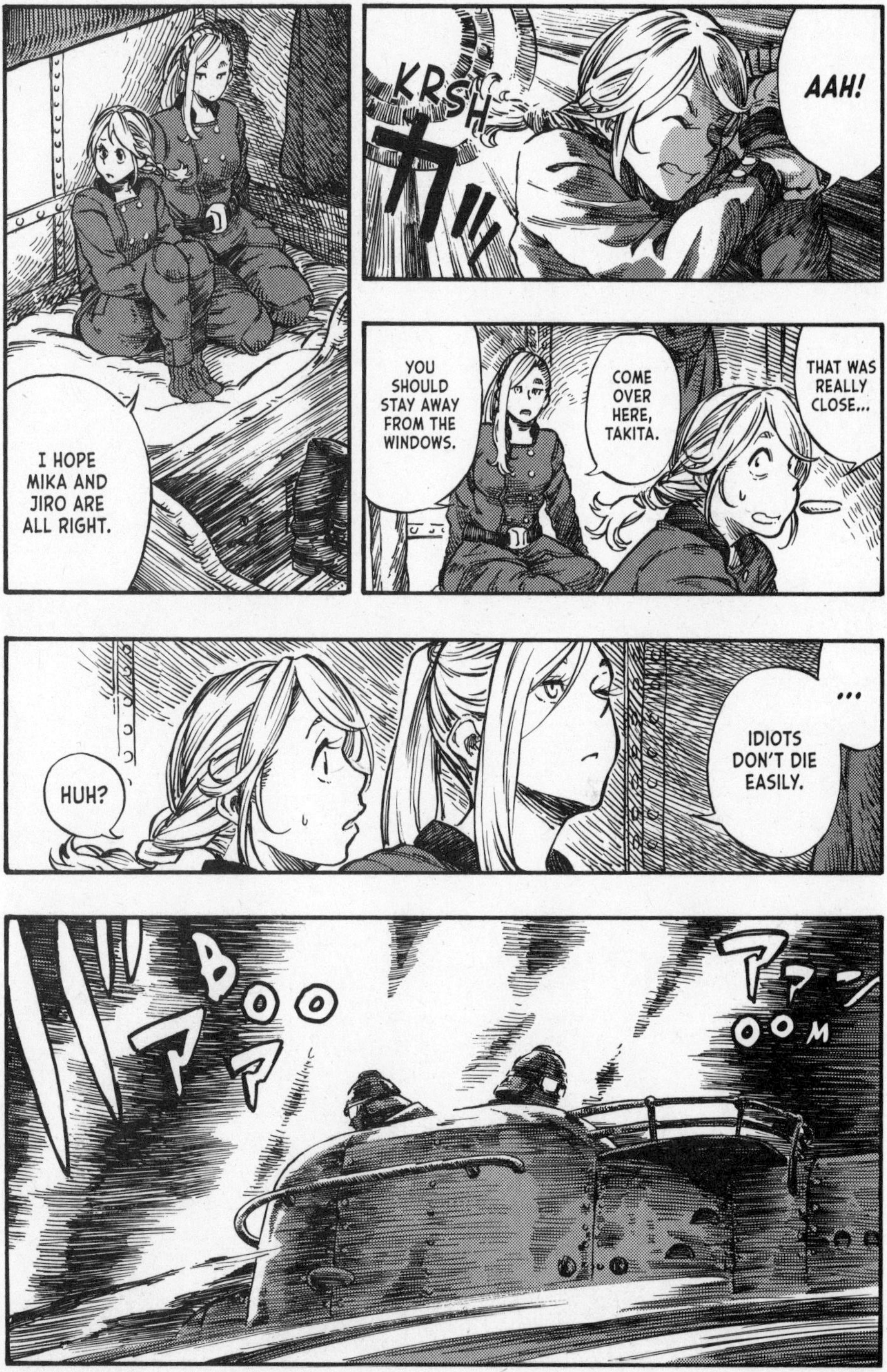

AAH!
KRSH
カッ
THAT WAS REALLY CLOSE...
COME OVER HERE, TAKITA.
YOU SHOULD STAY AWAY FROM THE WINDOWS.
I HOPE MIKA AND JIRO ARE ALL RIGHT.
...
IDIOTS DON'T DIE EASILY.
HUH?
OOM
BOO

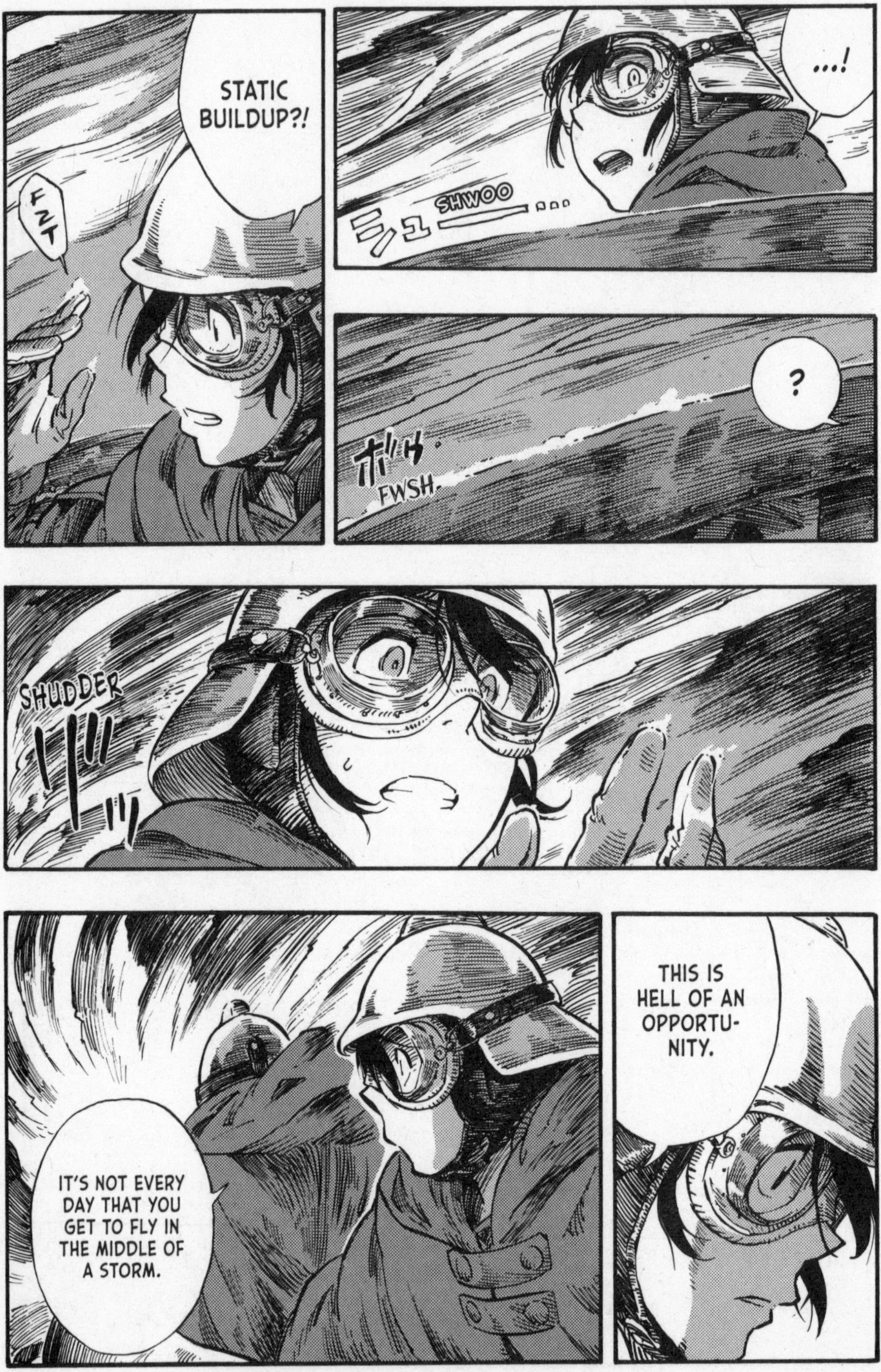
...!
SHWOO
?
FWSH
STATIC BUILDUP?!
FZT
SHUDDER
THIS IS HELL OF AN OPPORTU-NITY.
IT'S NOT EVERY DAY THAT YOU GET TO FLY IN THE MIDDLE OF A STORM.

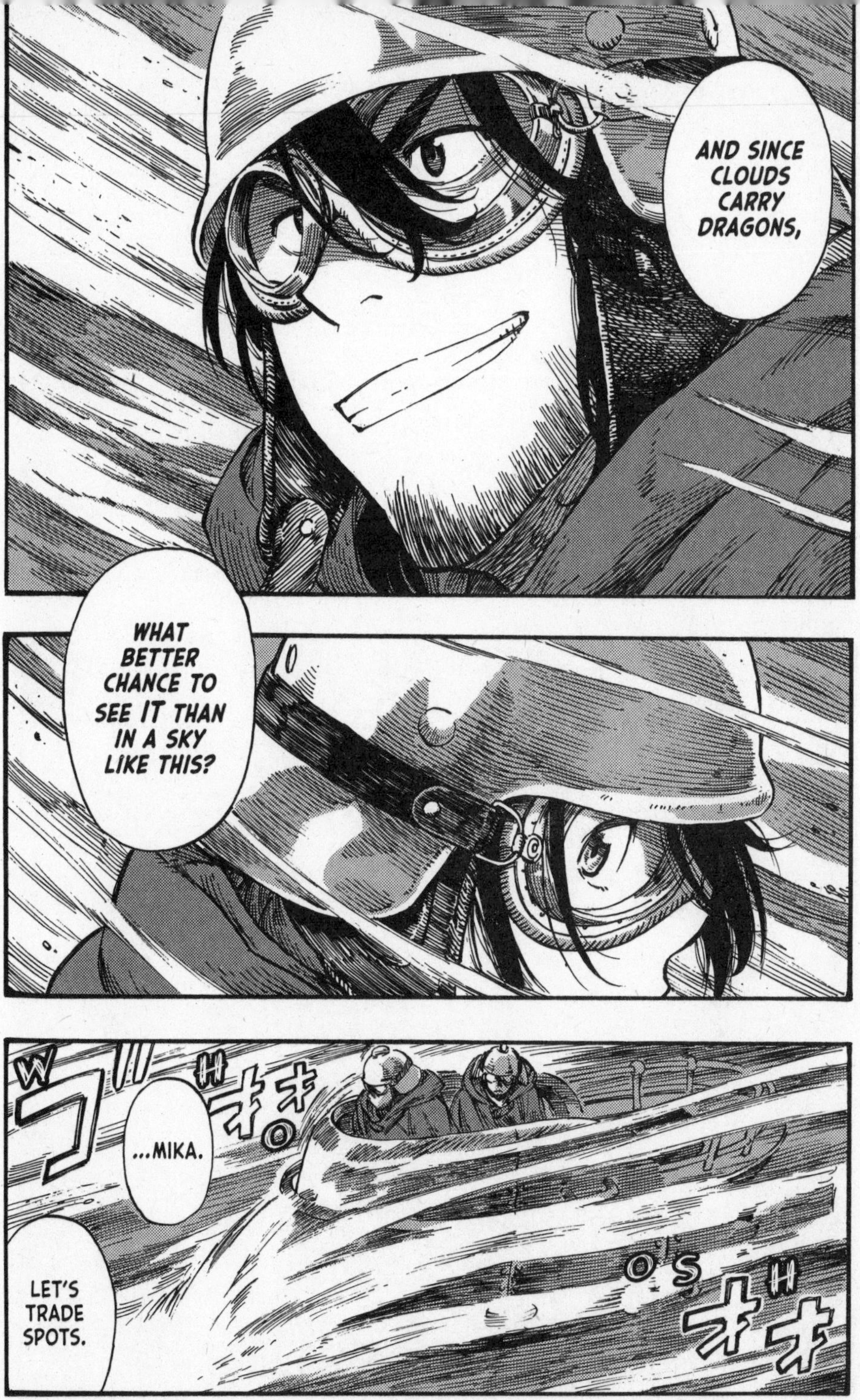
AND SINCE CLOUDS CARRY DRAGONS,
WHAT BETTER CHANCE TO SEE IT THAN IN A SKY LIKE THIS?
WHOOSH
...MIKA.
LET'S TRADE SPOTS.

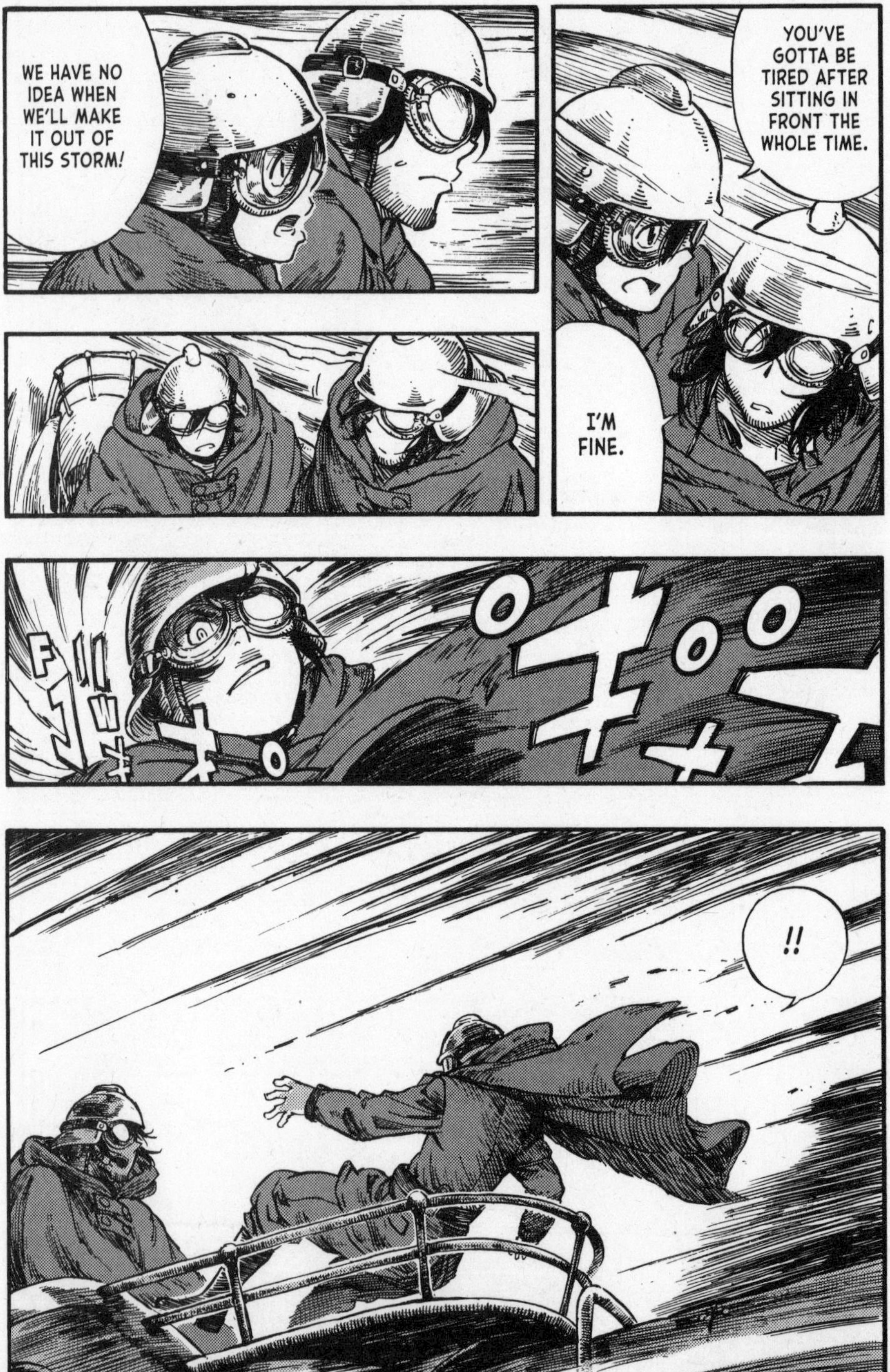
YOU'VE GOTTA BE TIRED AFTER SITTING IN FRONT THE WHOLE TIME.
I'M FINE.
WE HAVE NO IDEA WHEN WE'LL MAKE IT OUT OF THIS STORM!
!!

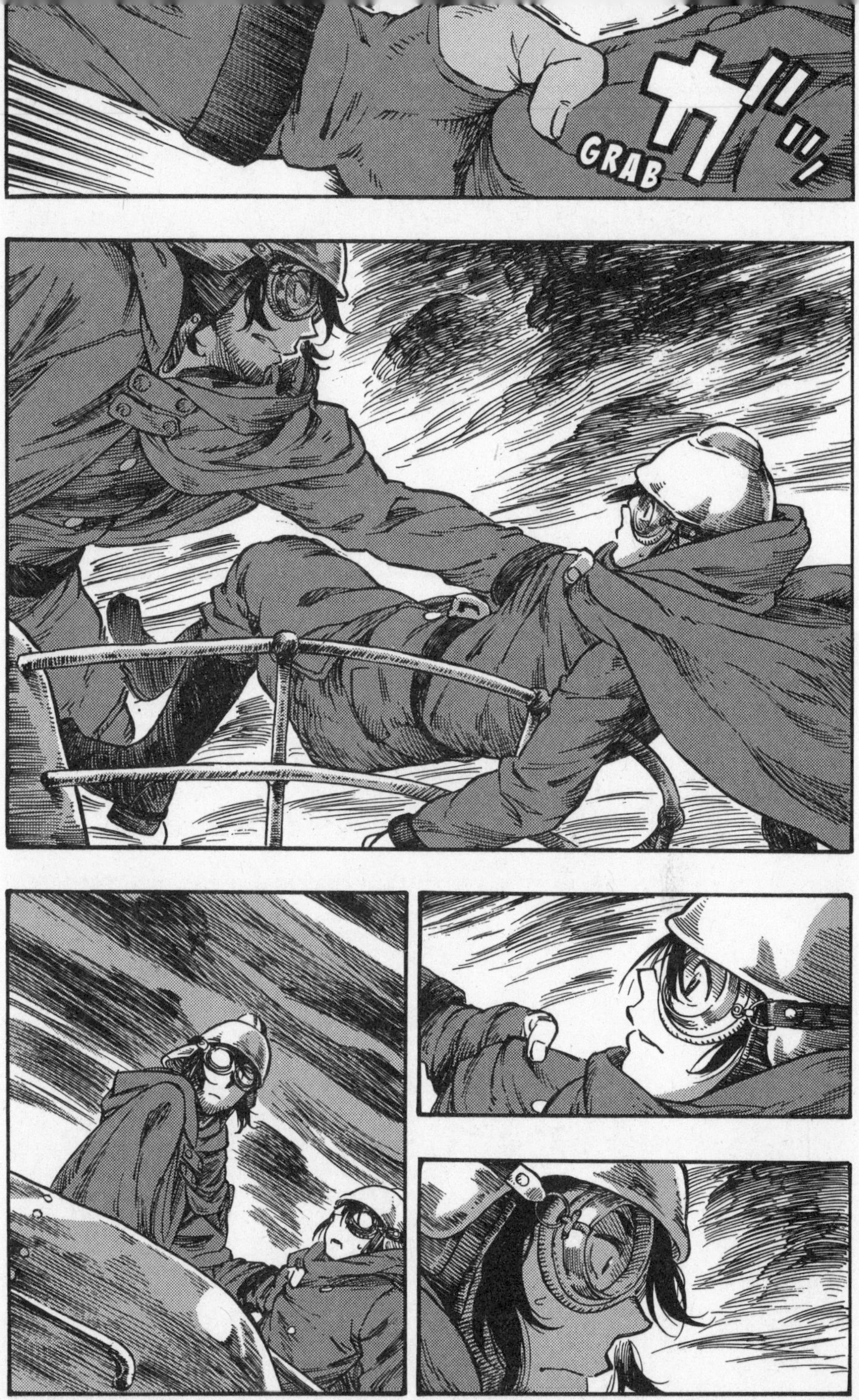
ガッ
GRAB

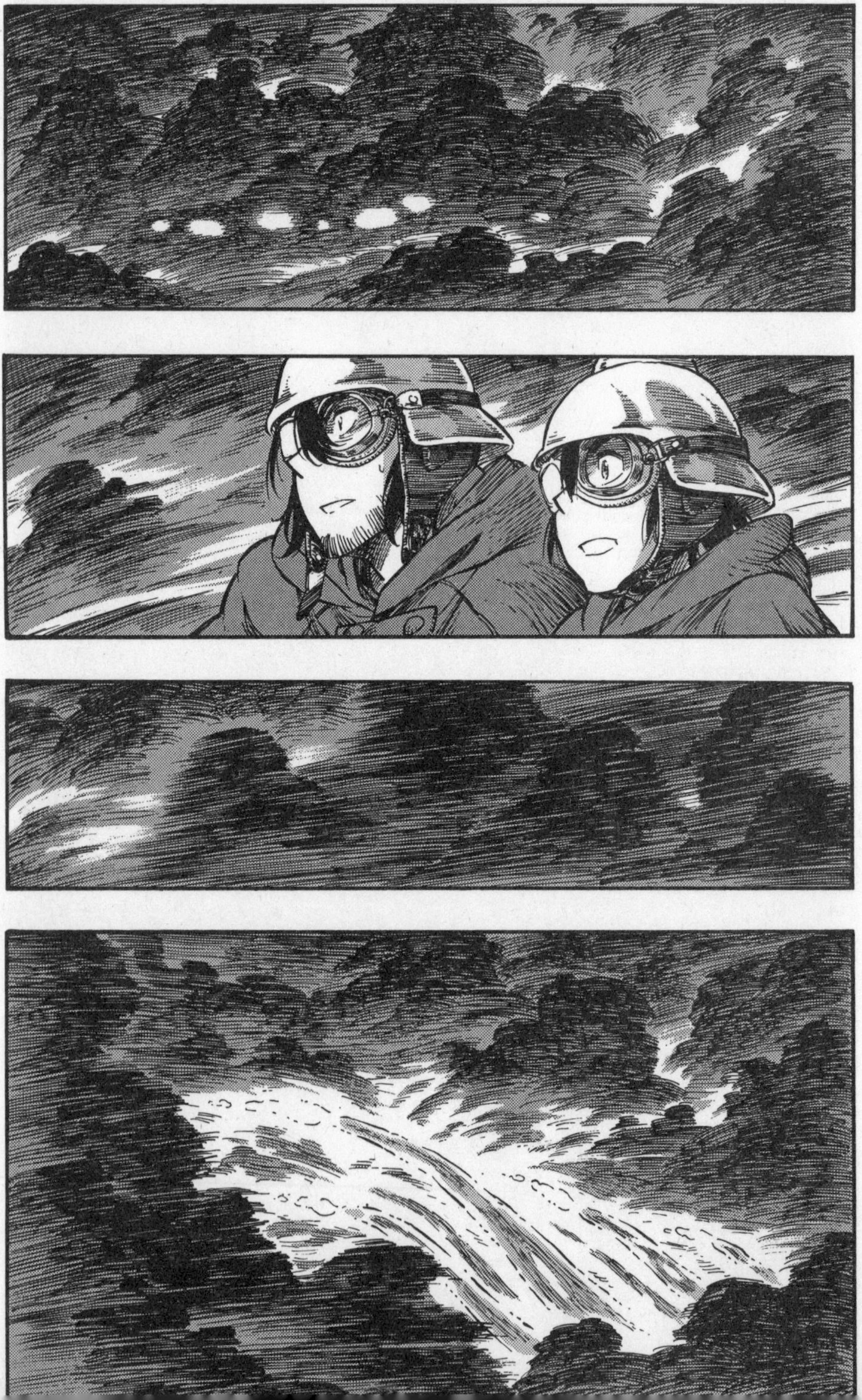

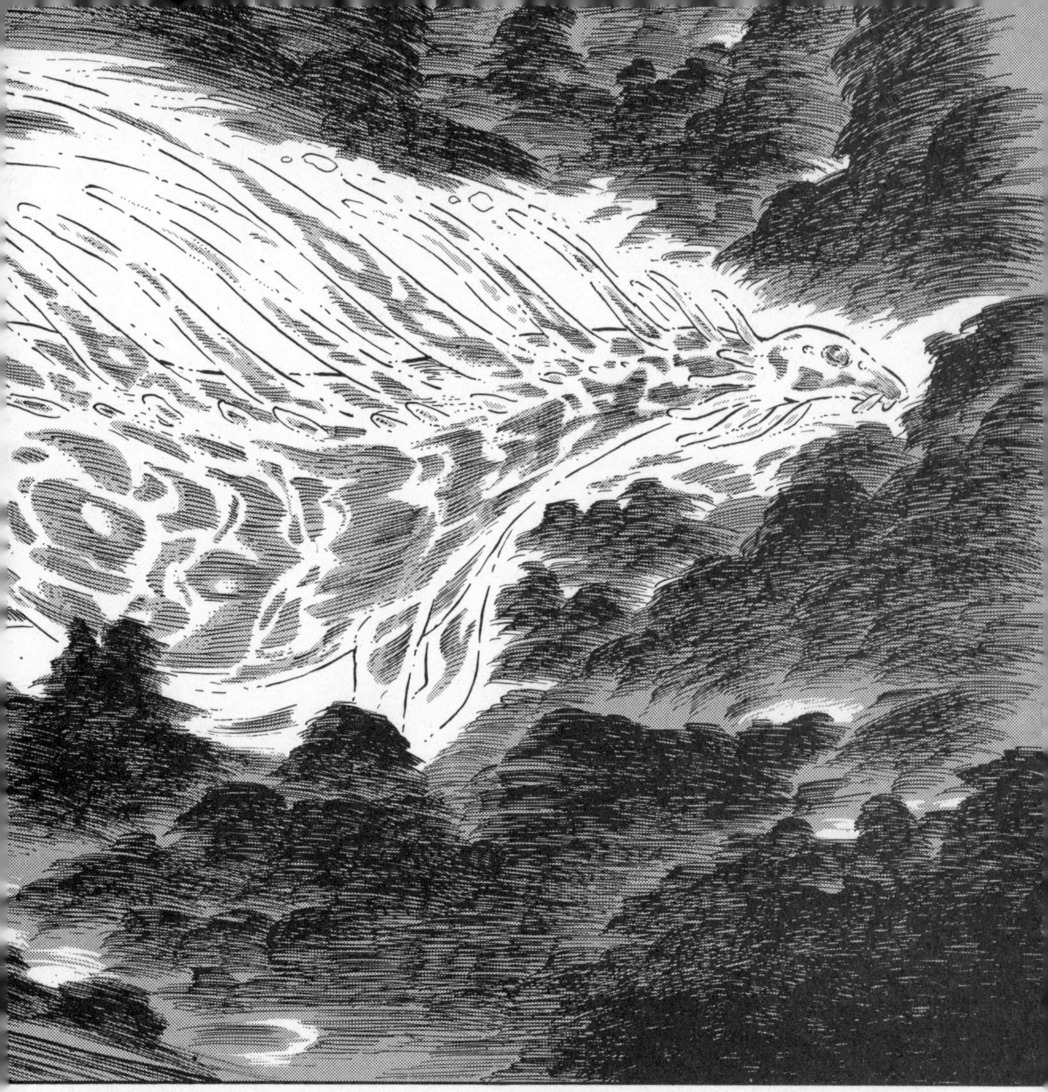
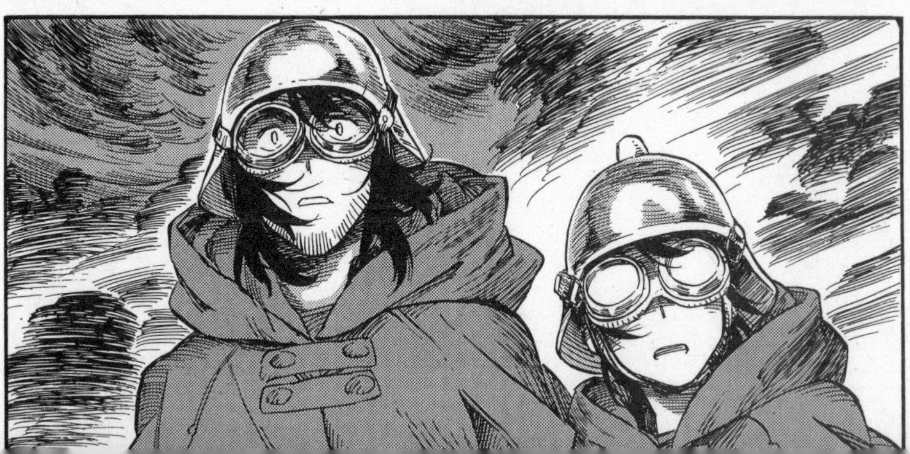

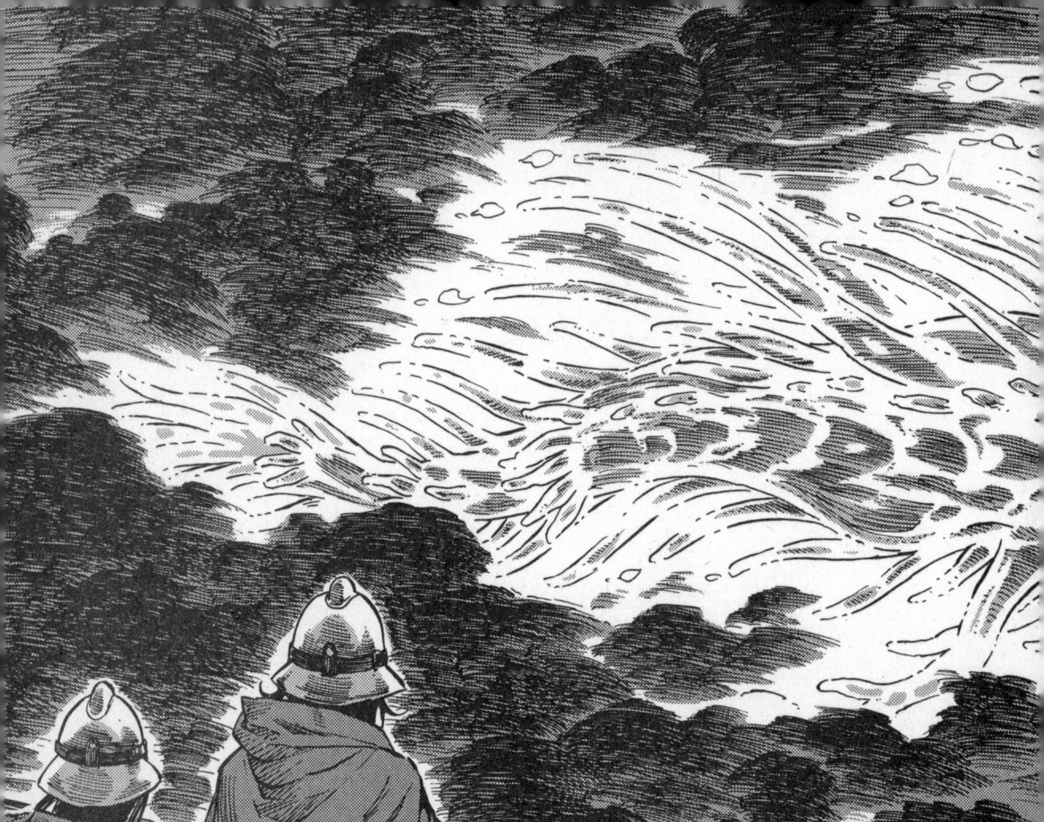
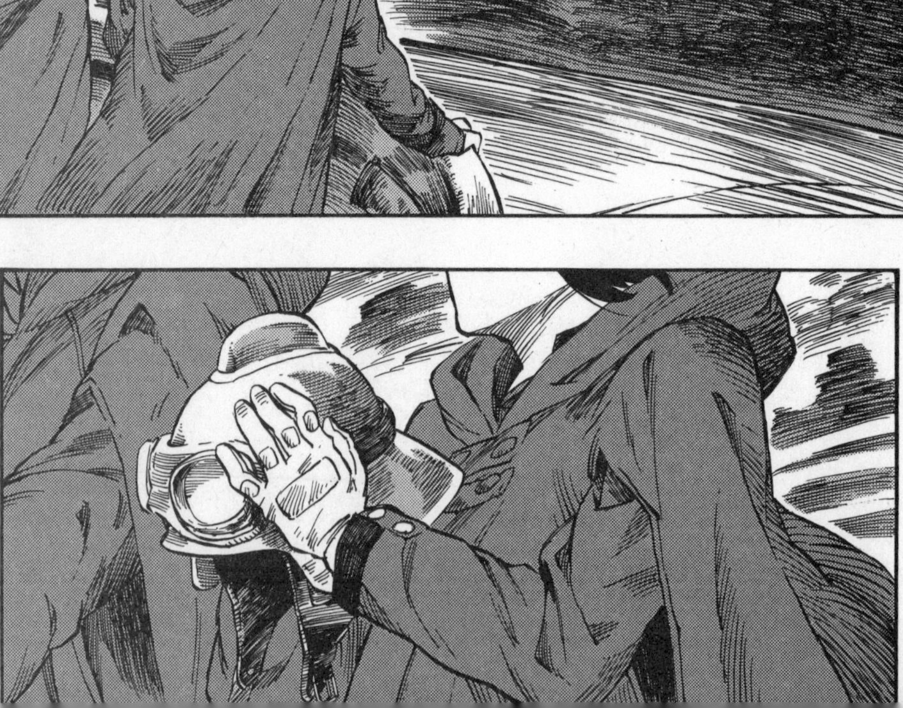

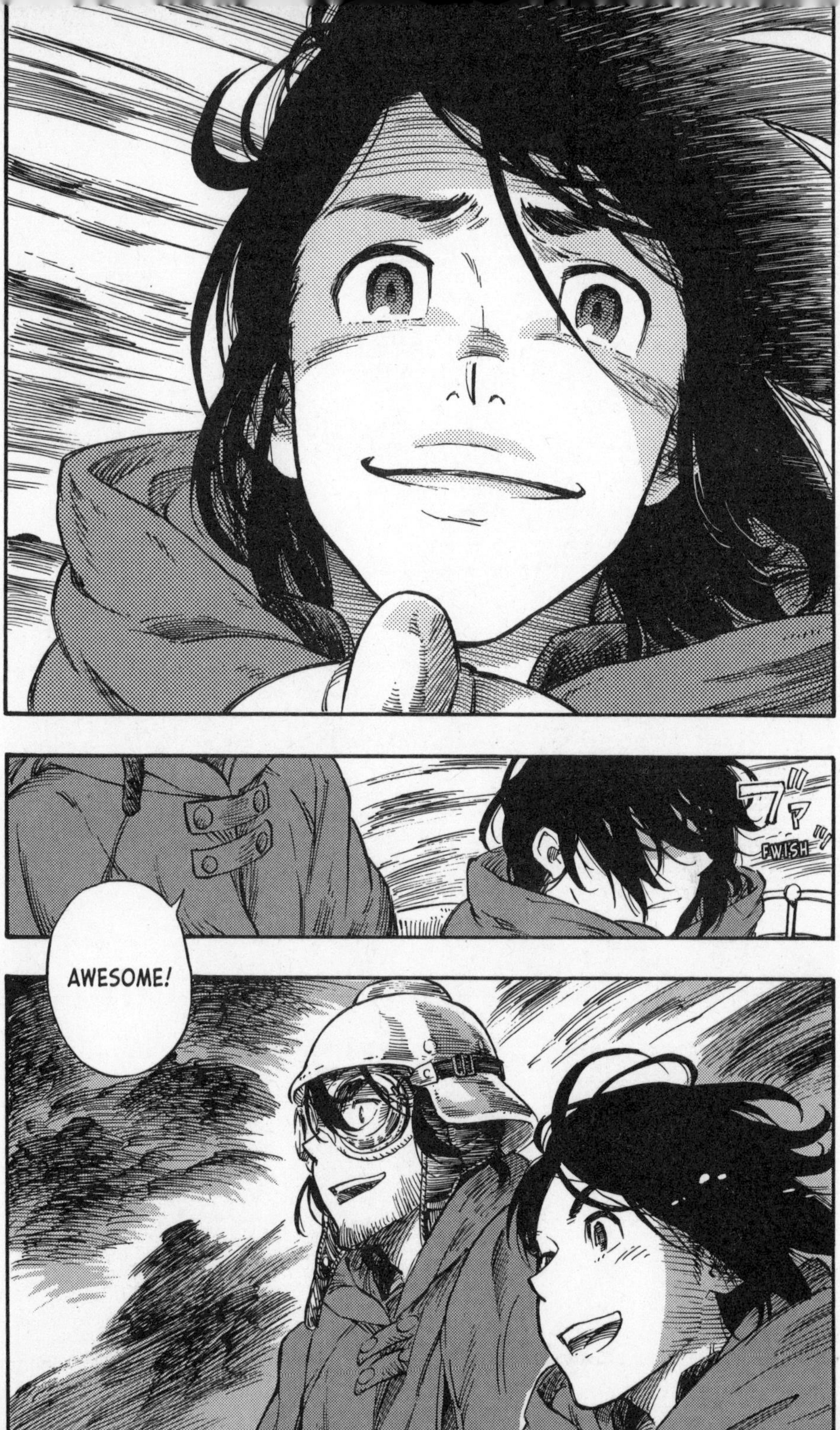
ヴァッ
FWISH
AWESOME!

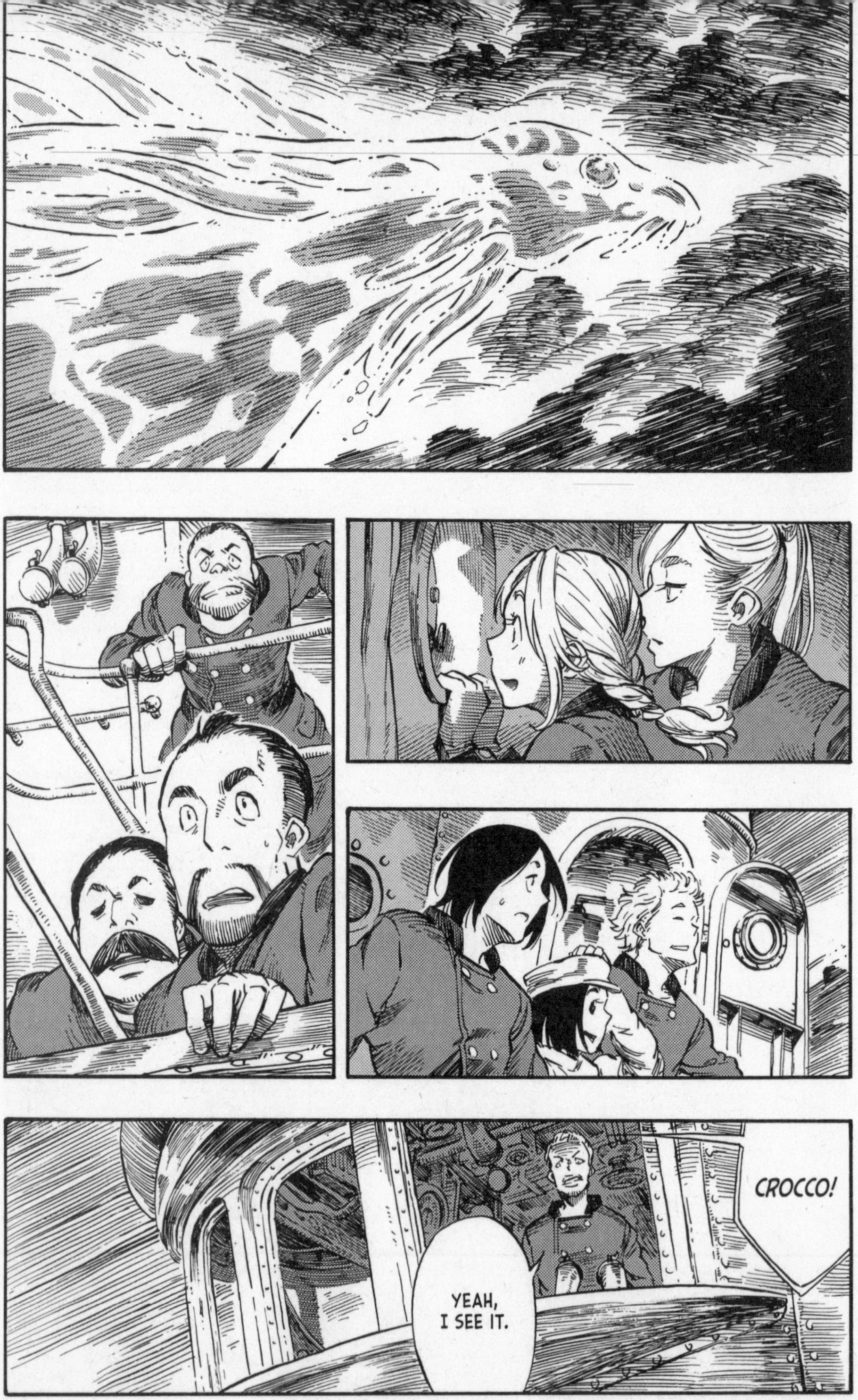
CROCCO!
YEAH, I SEE IT.

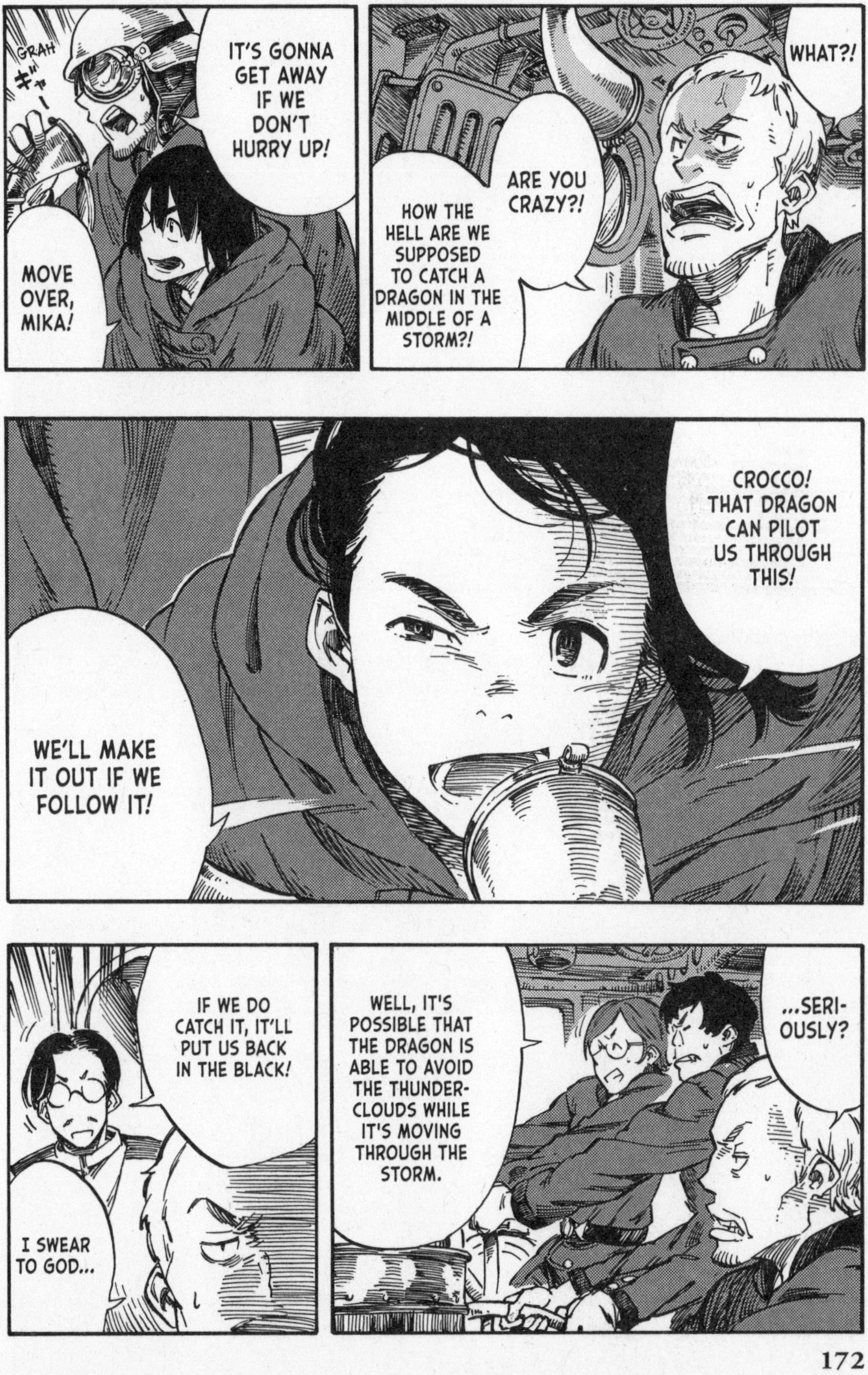
WHAT?!
ARE YOU CRAZY?!
HOW THE HELL ARE WE SUPPOSED TO CATCH A DRAGON IN THE MIDDLE OF A STORM?!
GRAH
ギャー
IT'S GONNA GET AWAY IF WE DON'T HURRY UP!
MOVE OVER, MIKA!
CROCCO! THAT DRAGON CAN PILOT US THROUGH THIS!
WE'LL MAKE IT OUT IF WE FOLLOW IT!
...SERI-OUSLY?
WELL, IT'S POSSIBLE THAT THE DRAGON IS ABLE TO AVOID THE THUNDER-CLOUDS WHILE IT'S MOVING THROUGH THE STORM.
IF WE DO CATCH IT, IT'LL PUT US BACK IN THE BLACK!
I SWEAR TO GOD...

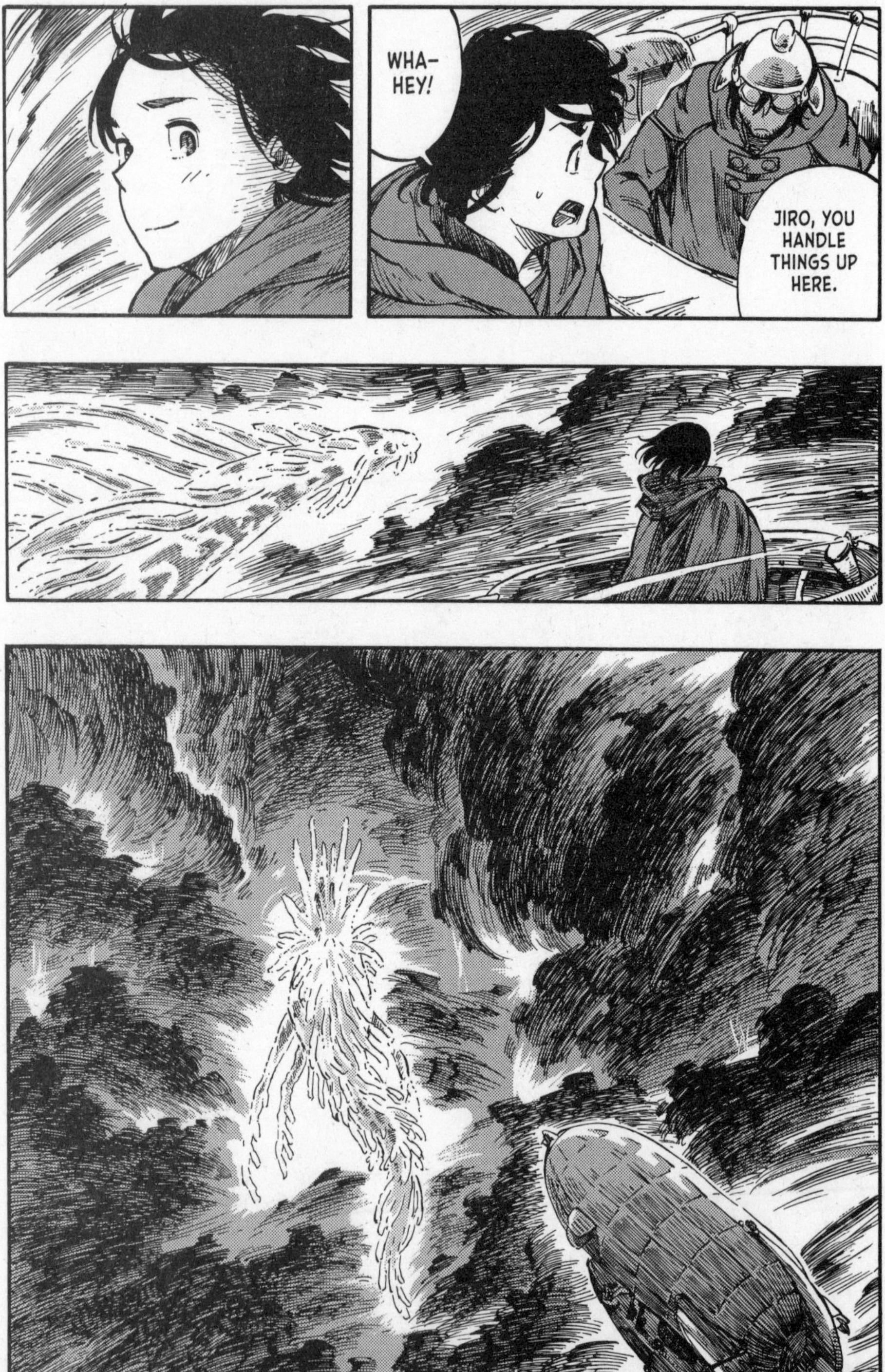
JIRO, YOU HANDLE THINGS UP HERE.
WHA-HEY!

Smoked Dragon Salo on Rye Bread

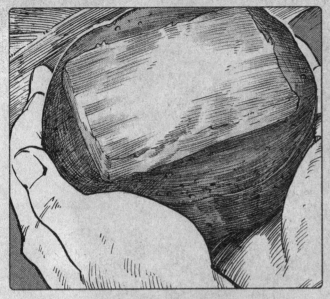

Ingredients (serves one, about 10 g)

✦ 1kg dragon fatback

✦ 50g salt

✦ 20g pepper

✦ Herbs and spices to taste

✦ 2 slices rye bread

✦ Smoking wood (the crew used oak)

01
Slice the fatback into 4-8 pieces and rub with salt, pepper, and herbs.

02
Fit the pieces tightly in a container (such as a pot or jar) making sure there are no spaces and place a weighted drop lid over the meat.

03
Leave to sit at room temperature for 3-4 days. A large amount of water will start to seep from the fat, but do not discard it.

04
After 3-4 days, discard the excess water, wrap each piece of fatback with paper and leave in a cool, well-ventilated place to dry for a day.

05
Smoke the salted fat for 2 hours at roughly 30 degrees.

06
Slice it up, put on rye bread, and enjoy.

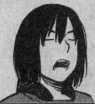

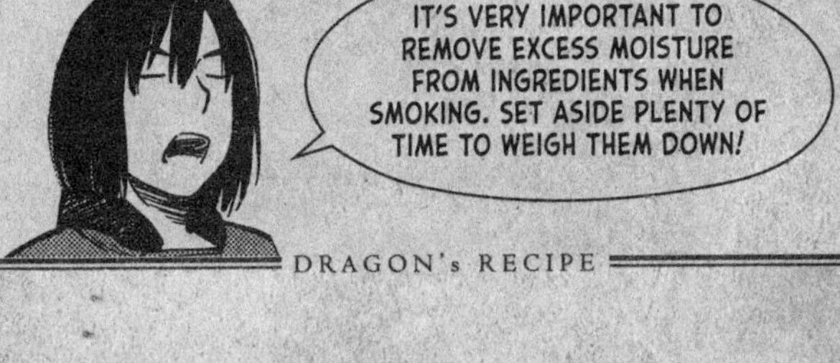

IT'S VERY IMPORTANT TO REMOVE EXCESS MOISTURE FROM INGREDIENTS WHEN SMOKING. SET ASIDE PLENTY OF TIME TO WEIGH THEM DOWN!

DRAGON's RECIPE

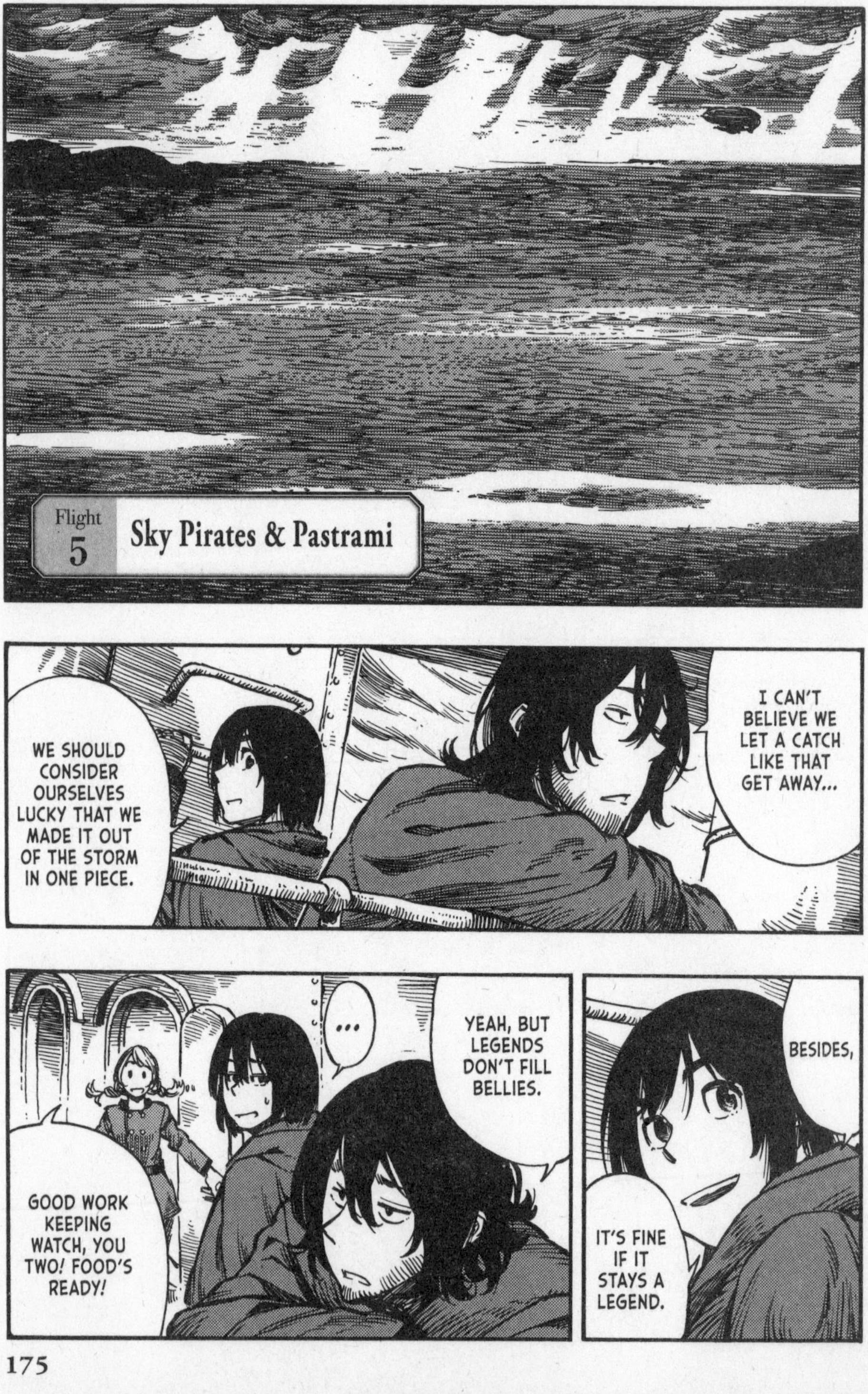
Flight 5
Sky Pirates & Pastrami
I CAN'T BELIEVE WE LET A CATCH LIKE THAT GET AWAY...
WE SHOULD CONSIDER OURSELVES LUCKY THAT WE MADE IT OUT OF THE STORM IN ONE PIECE.
BESIDES,
IT'S FINE IF IT STAYS A LEGEND.
YEAH, BUT LEGENDS DON'T FILL BELLIES.
...
GOOD WORK KEEPING WATCH, YOU TWO! FOOD'S READY!

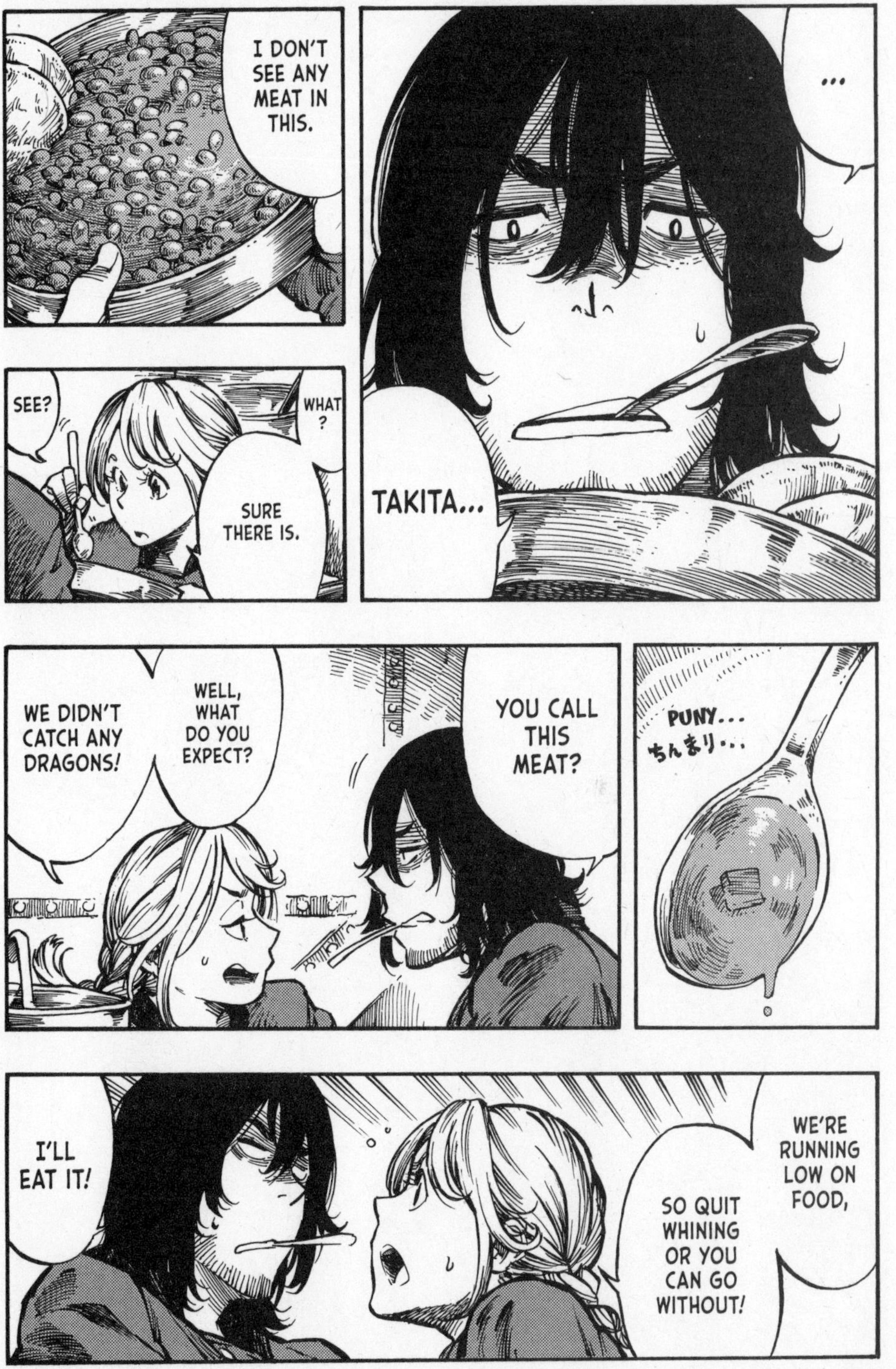
...
TAKITA...
I DON'T SEE ANY MEAT IN THIS.
WHAT?
SURE THERE IS.
SEE?
PUNY...
ちんまり...
YOU CALL THIS MEAT?
WELL, WHAT DO YOU EXPECT?
WE DIDN'T CATCH ANY DRAGONS!
WE'RE RUNNING LOW ON FOOD,
SO QUIT WHINING OR YOU CAN GO WITHOUT!
I'LL EAT IT!

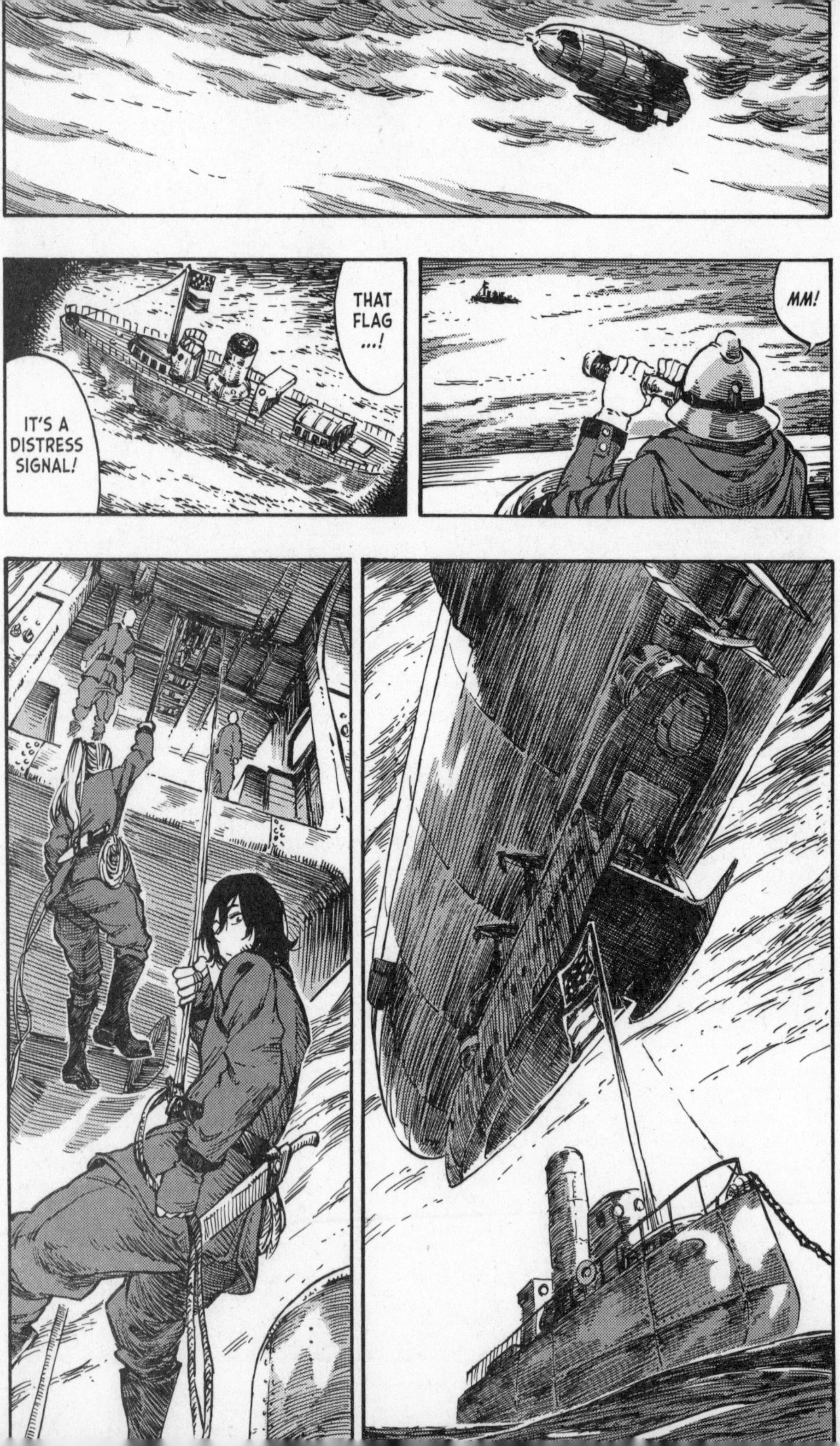
MM!
THAT FLAG ...!
IT'S A DISTRESS SIGNAL!

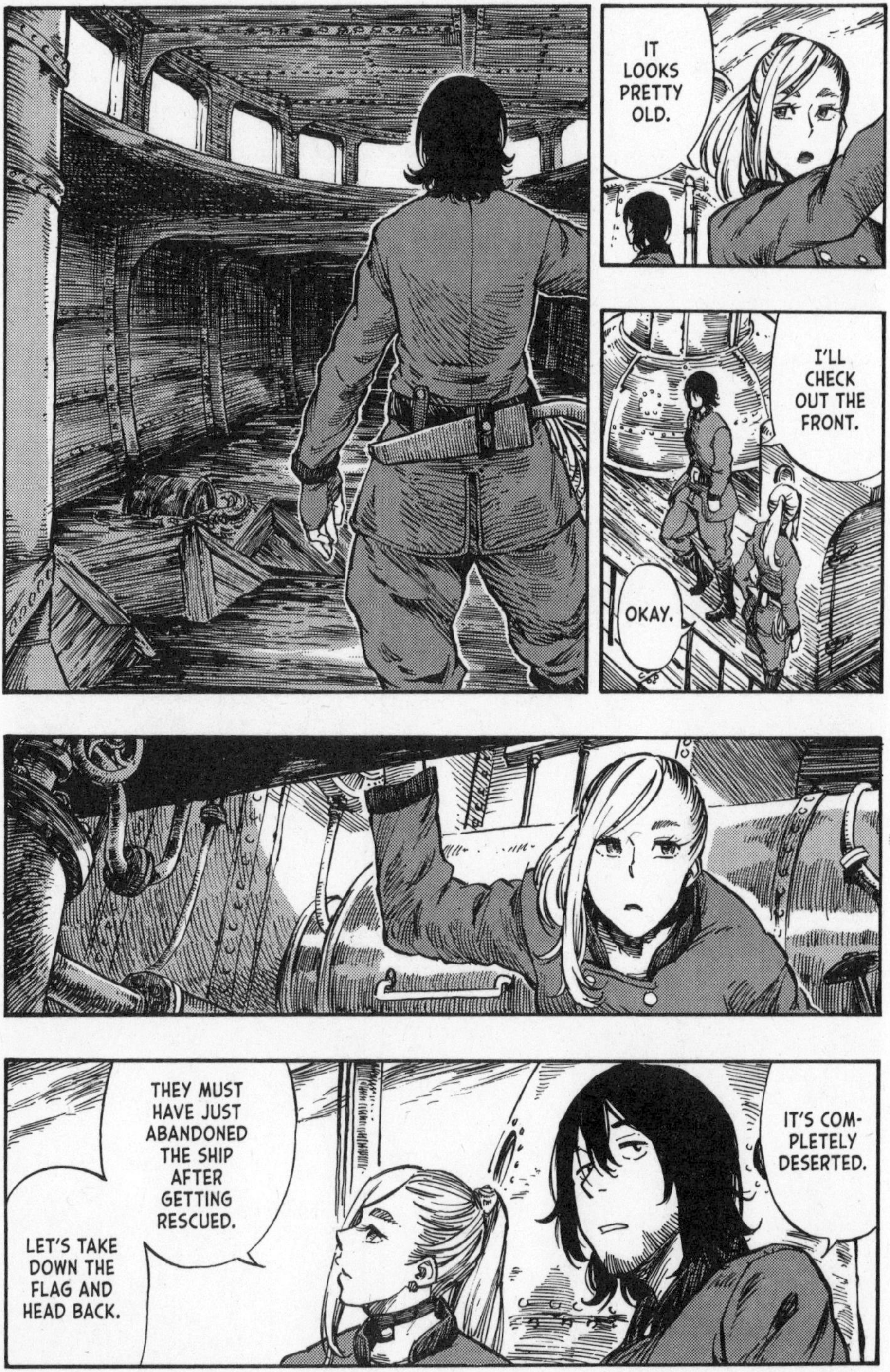
IT LOOKS PRETTY OLD.
I'LL CHECK OUT THE FRONT.
OKAY.
IT'S COM-PLETELY DESERTED.
THEY MUST HAVE JUST ABANDONED THE SHIP AFTER GETTING RESCUED.
LET'S TAKE DOWN THE FLAG AND HEAD BACK.

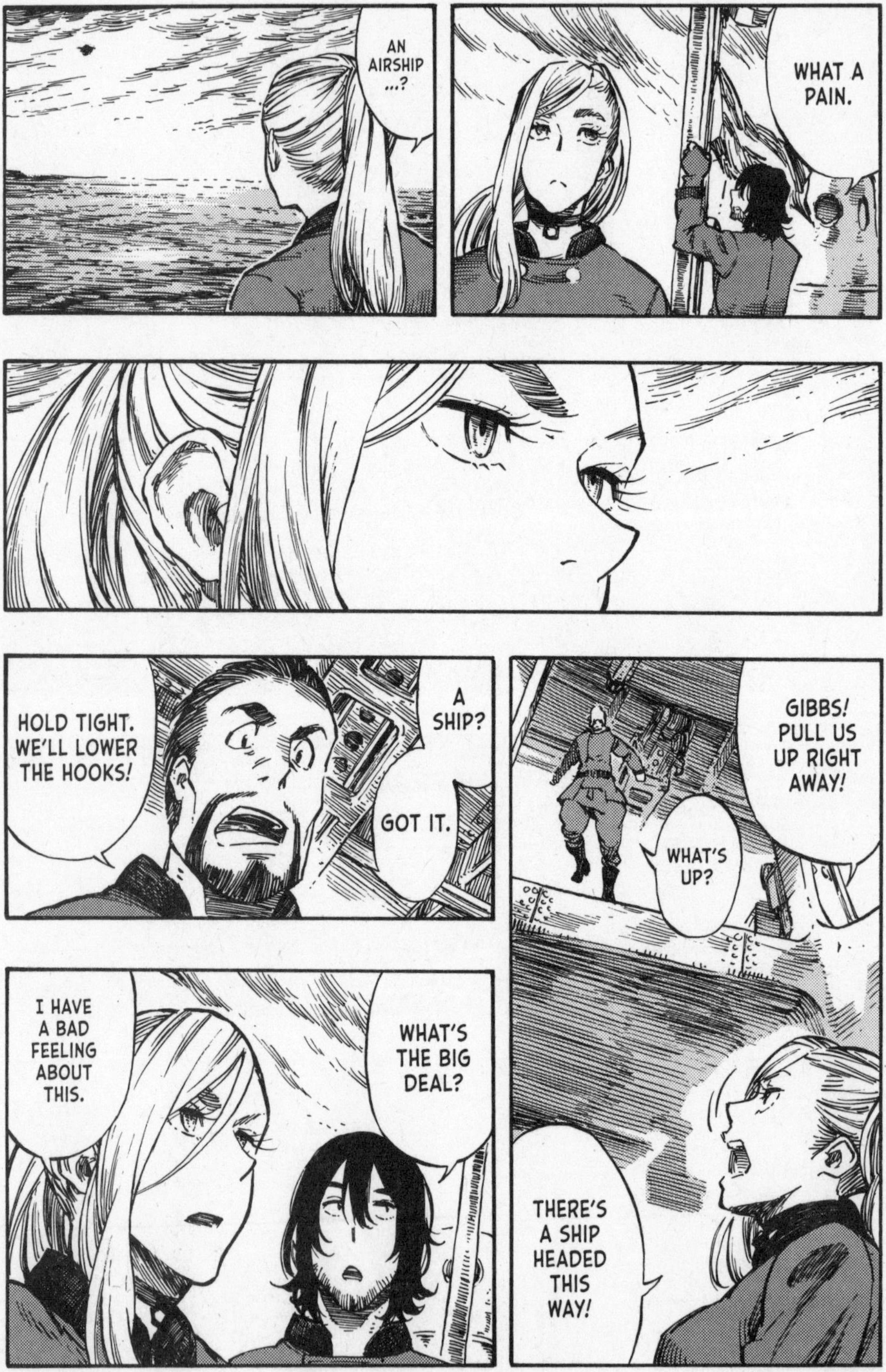
WHAT A PAIN.
AN AIRSHIP ...?
GIBBS! PULL US UP RIGHT AWAY!
WHAT'S UP?
THERE'S A SHIP HEADED THIS WAY!
A SHIP?
GOT IT.
HOLD TIGHT. WE'LL LOWER THE HOOKS!
WHAT'S THE BIG DEAL?
I HAVE A BAD FEELING ABOUT THIS.

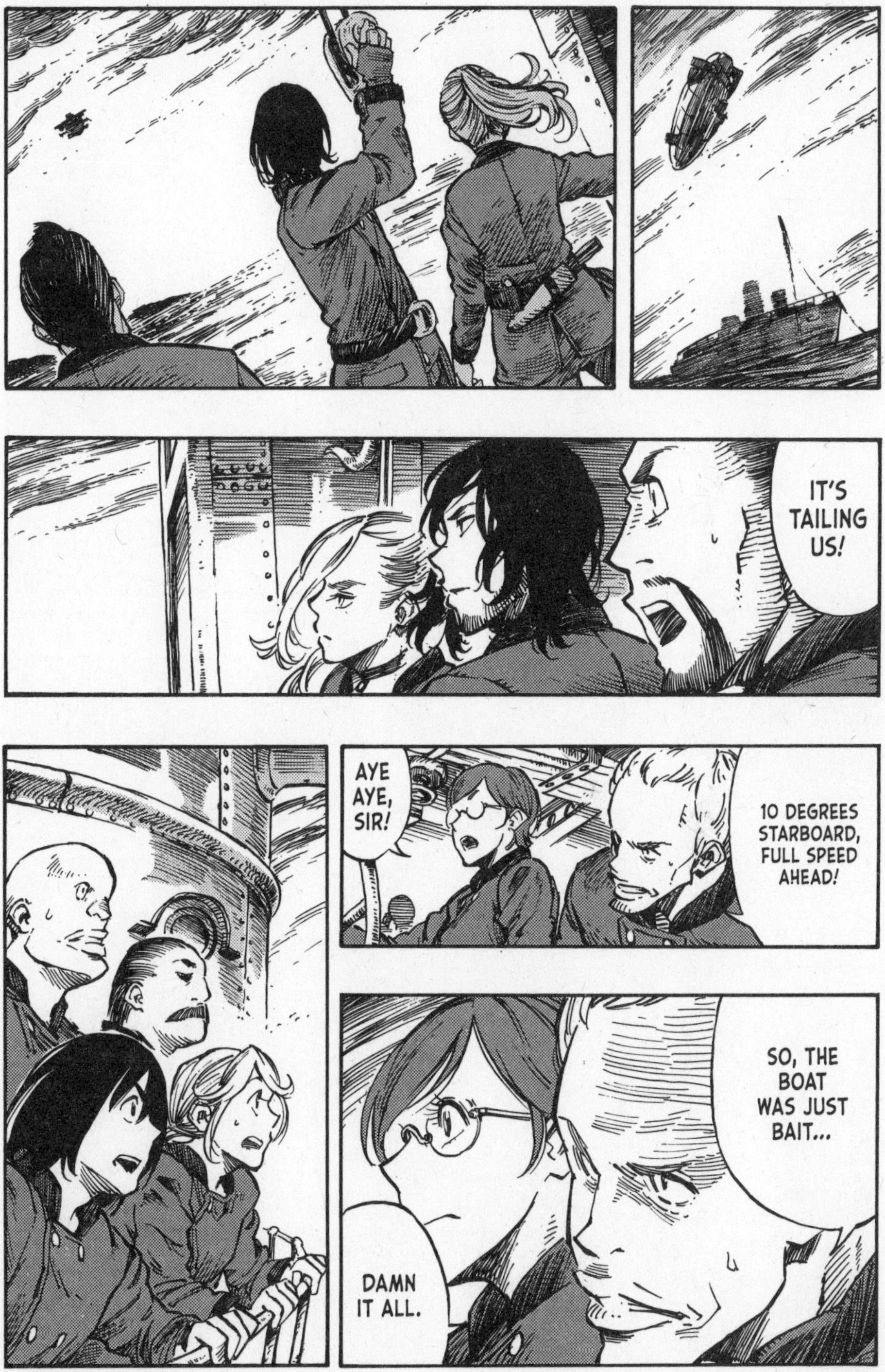
IT'S TAILING US!
10 DEGREES STARBOARD, FULL SPEED AHEAD!
AYE AYE, SIR!
SO, THE BOAT WAS JUST BAIT...
DAMN IT ALL.

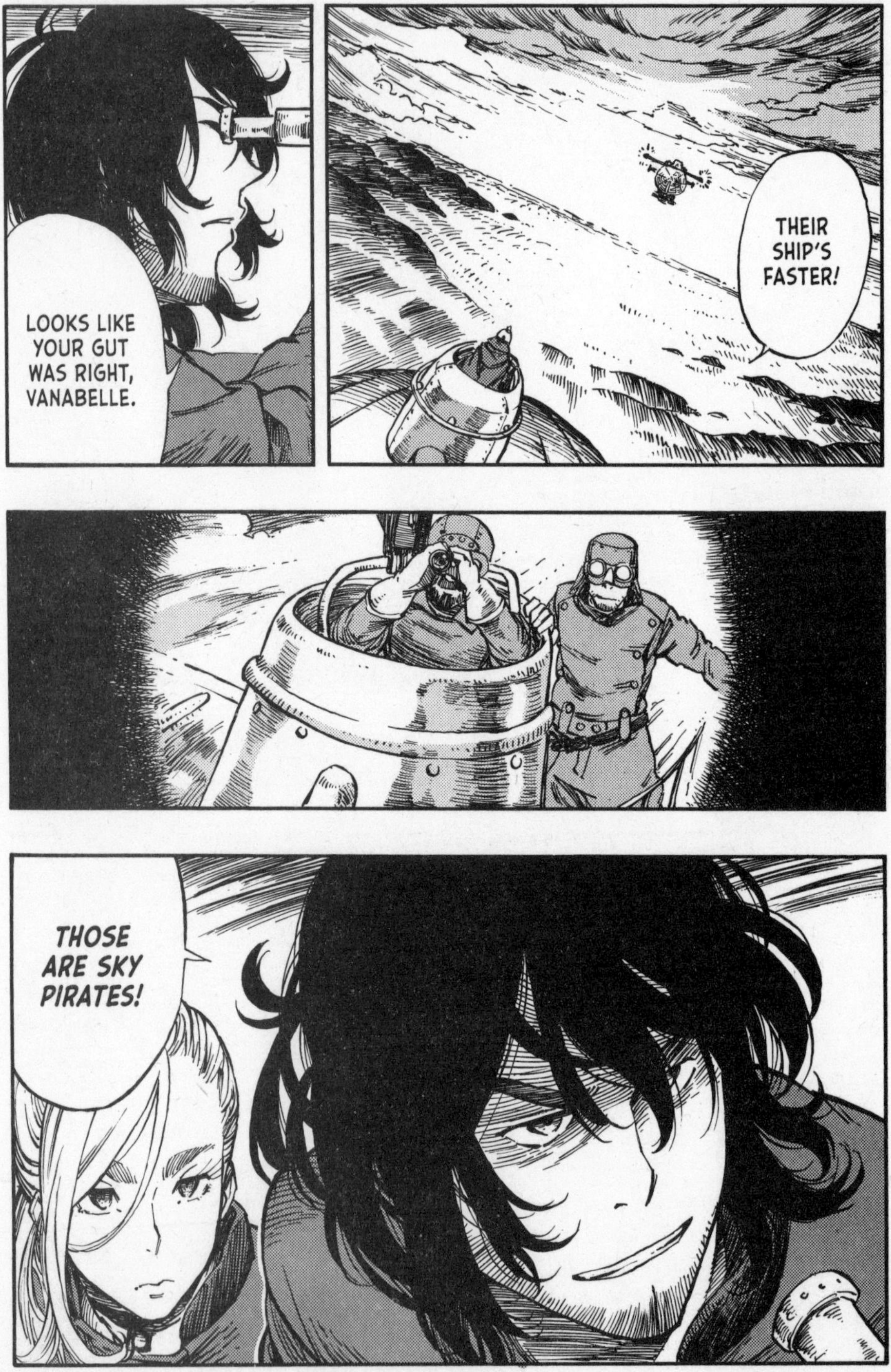
THEIR SHIP'S FASTER!
LOOKS LIKE YOUR GUT WAS RIGHT, VANABELLE.
THOSE ARE SKY PIRATES!

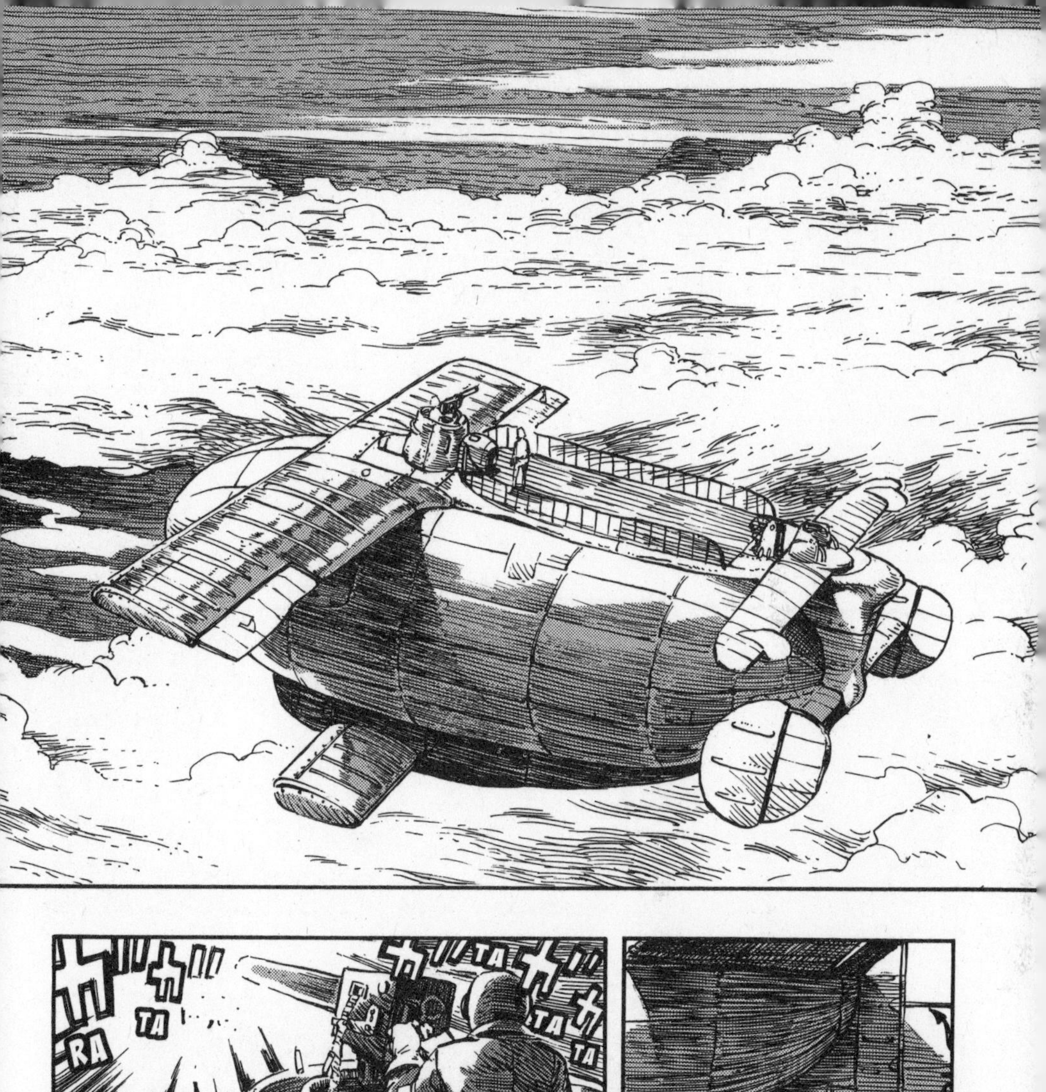

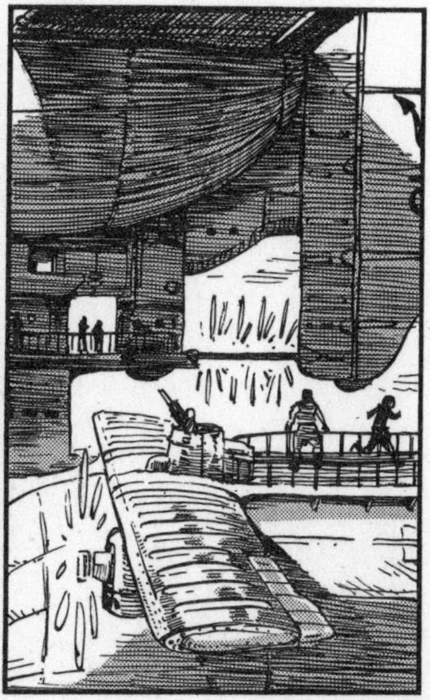

TA
TA
TA
TA
TA
RA

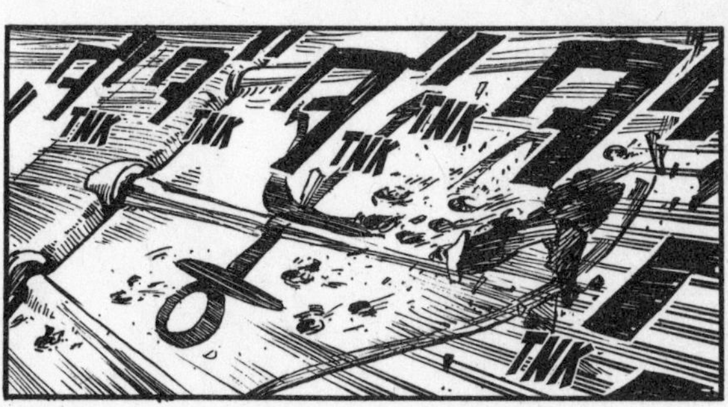
TNK
TNK
TNK
TNK
TNK

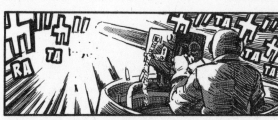

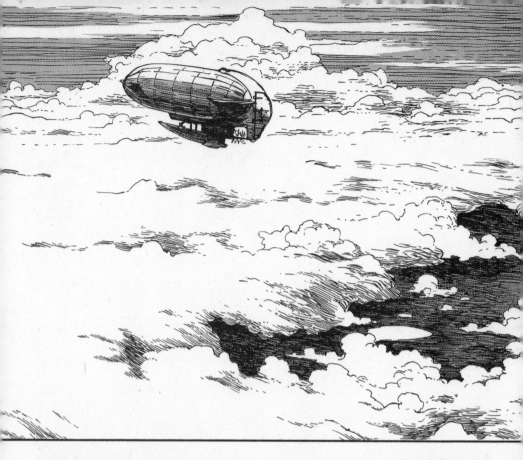

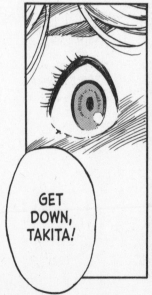

GET
DOWN,
TAKITA!

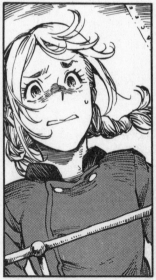

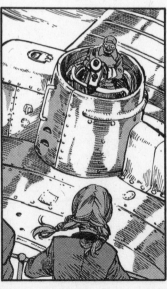

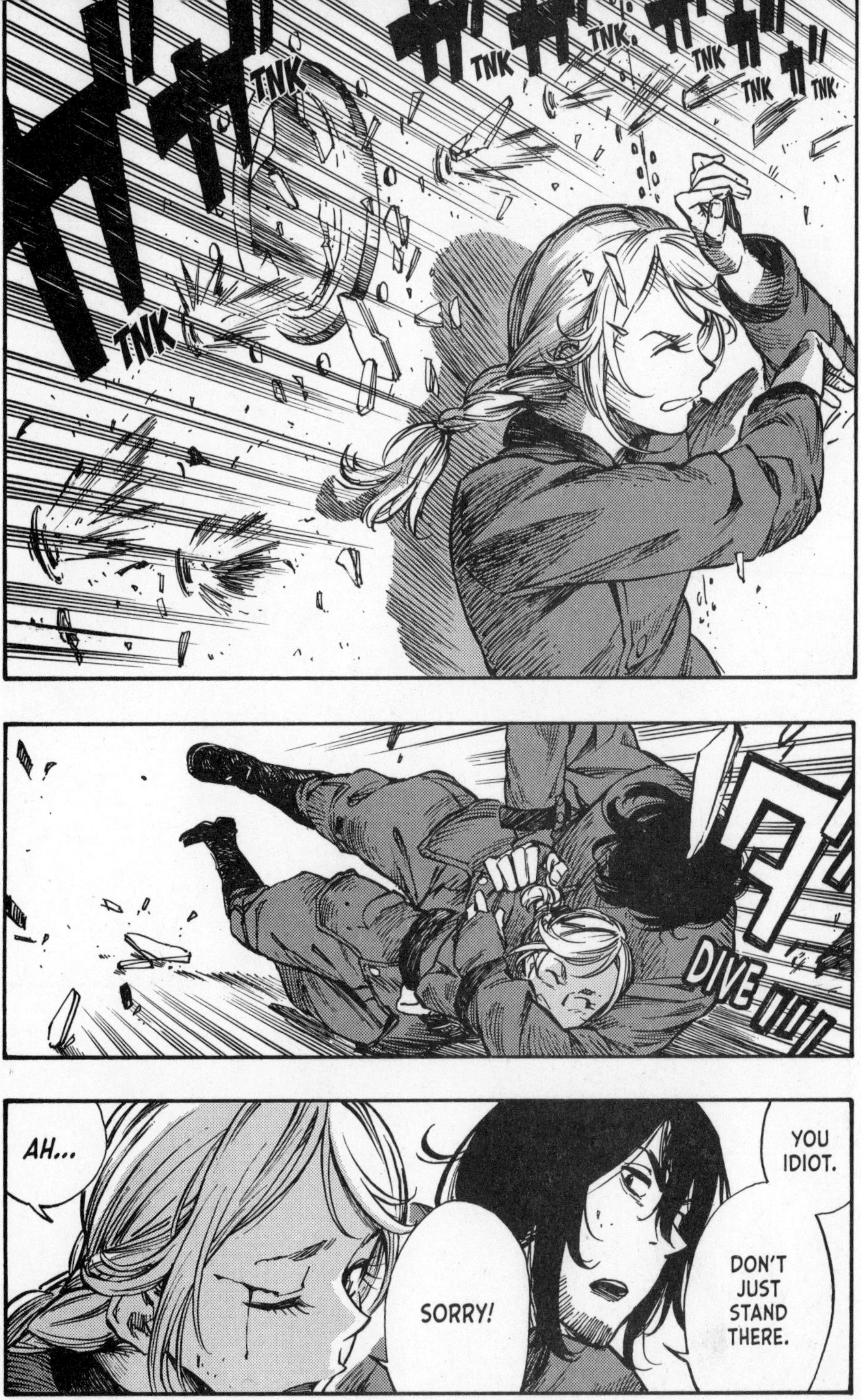
TNK
TNK
TNK
TNK
TNK
TNK
TNK
DIVE
YOU IDIOT.
DON'T JUST STAND THERE.
SORRY!
AH...

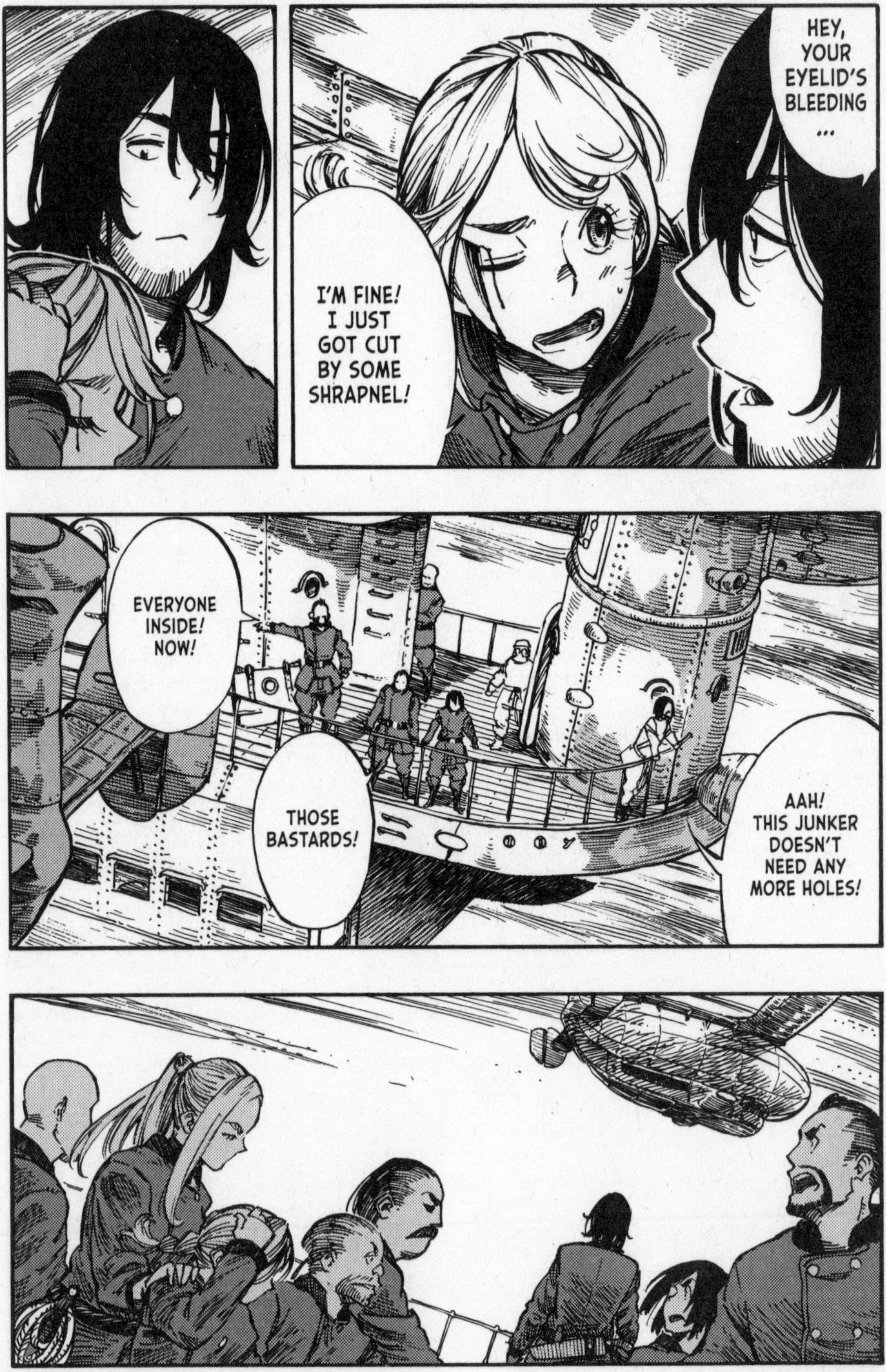
HEY, YOUR EYELID'S BLEEDING ...
I'M FINE! I JUST GOT CUT BY SOME SHRAPNEL!
AAH! THIS JUNKER DOESN'T NEED ANY MORE HOLES!
THOSE BASTARDS!
EVERYONE INSIDE! NOW!

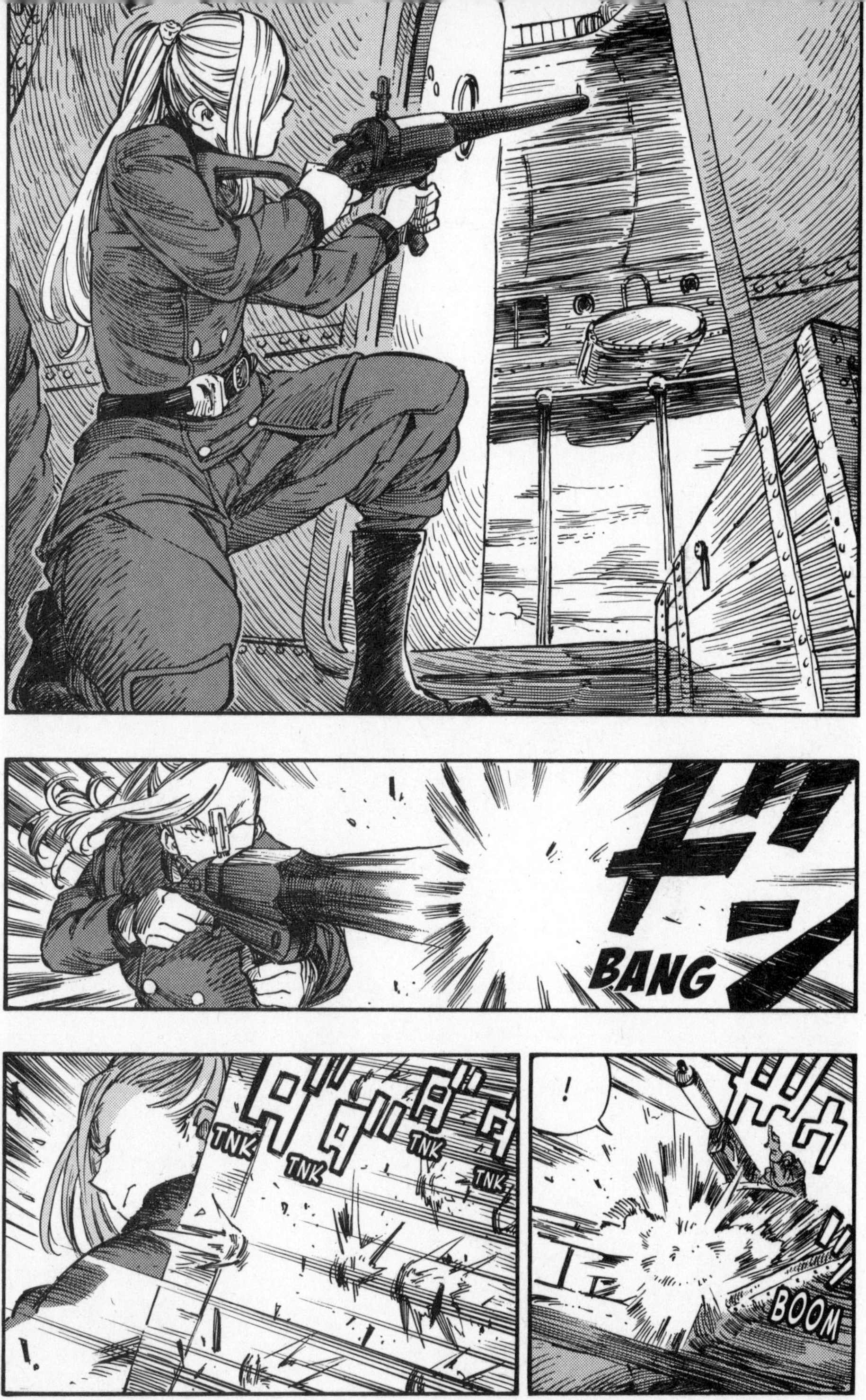
BANG
!
BOOM
TNK
TNK
TNK
TNK

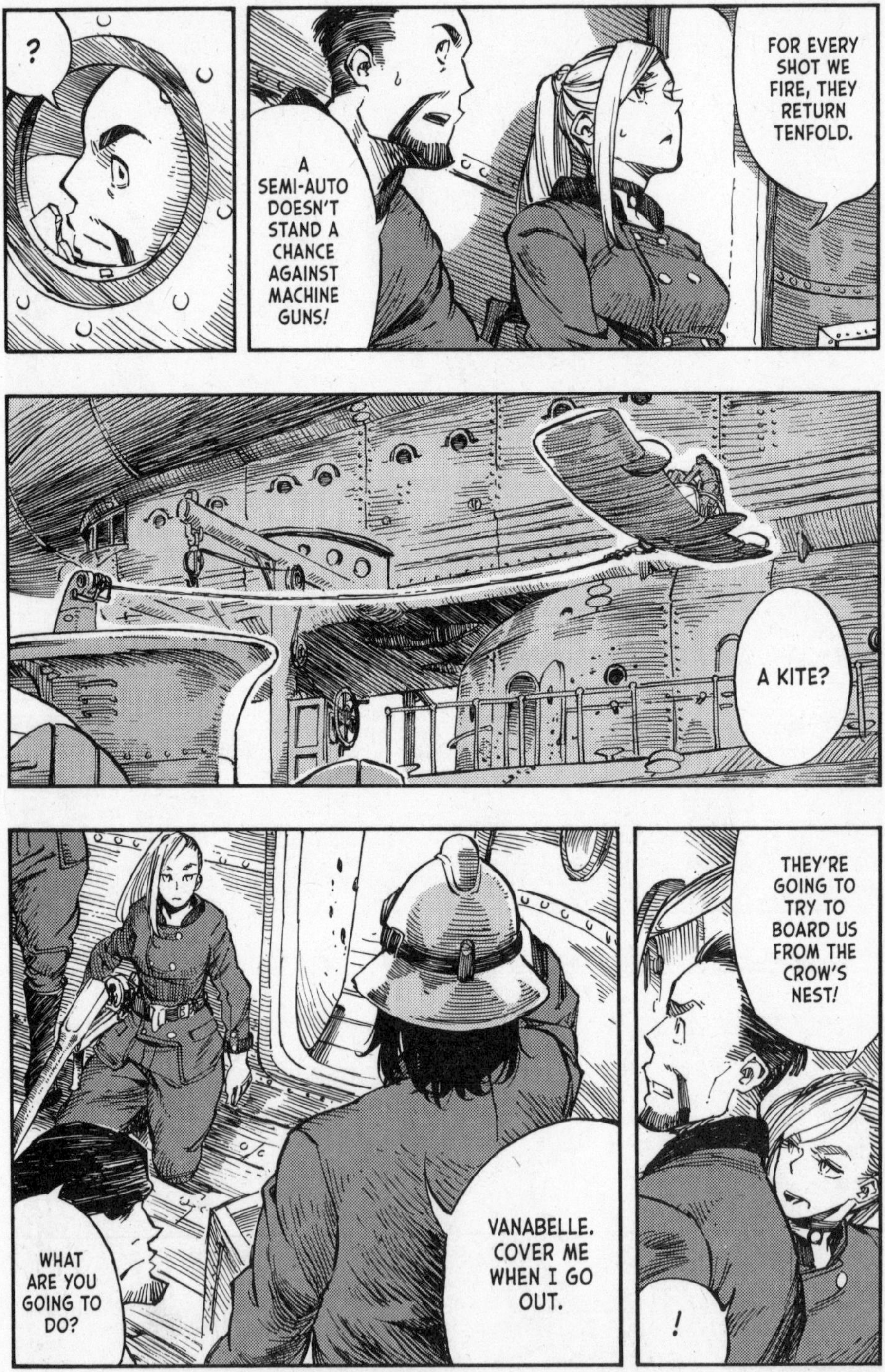
FOR EVERY SHOT WE FIRE, THEY RETURN TENFOLD.
A SEMI-AUTO DOESN'T STAND A CHANCE AGAINST MACHINE GUNS!
?
A KITE?
THEY'RE GOING TO TRY TO BOARD US FROM THE CROW'S NEST!
!
VANABELLE. COVER ME WHEN I GO OUT.
WHAT ARE YOU GOING TO DO?

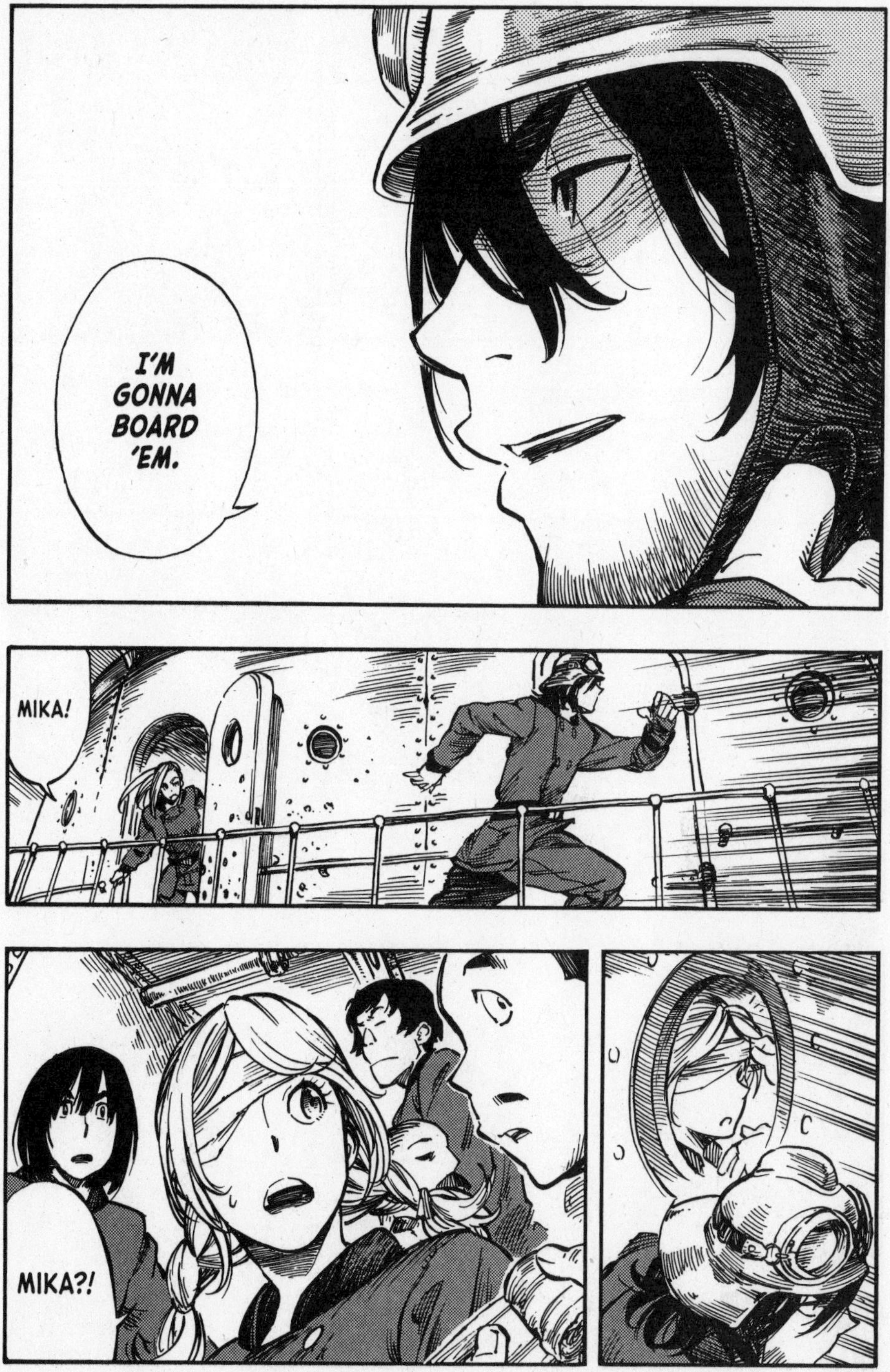
I'M GONNA BOARD 'EM.
MIKA!
MIKA?!

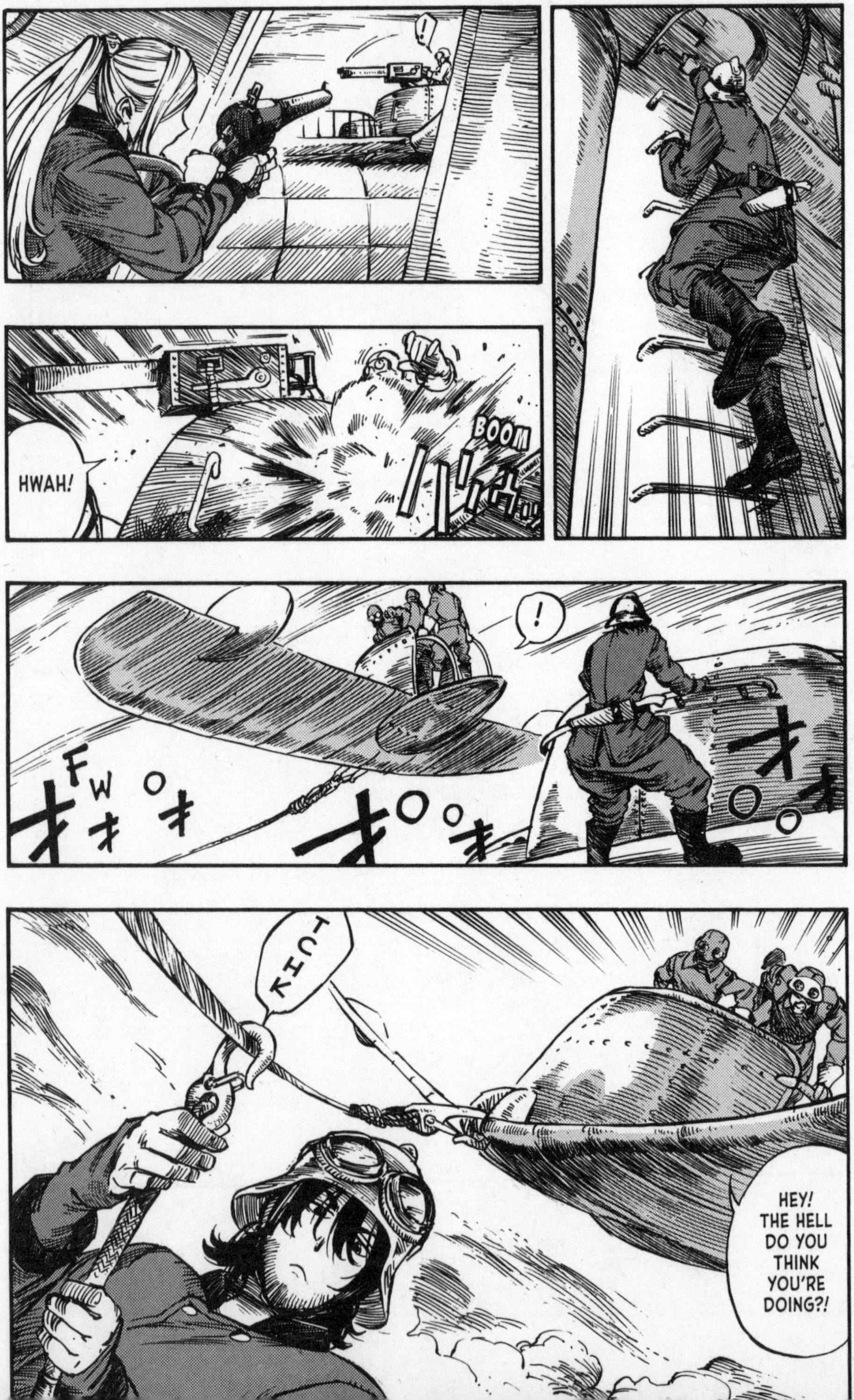
!
HWAH!
BOOM
!
FWOOO
TCHK
HEY! THE HELL DO YOU THINK YOU'RE DOING?!

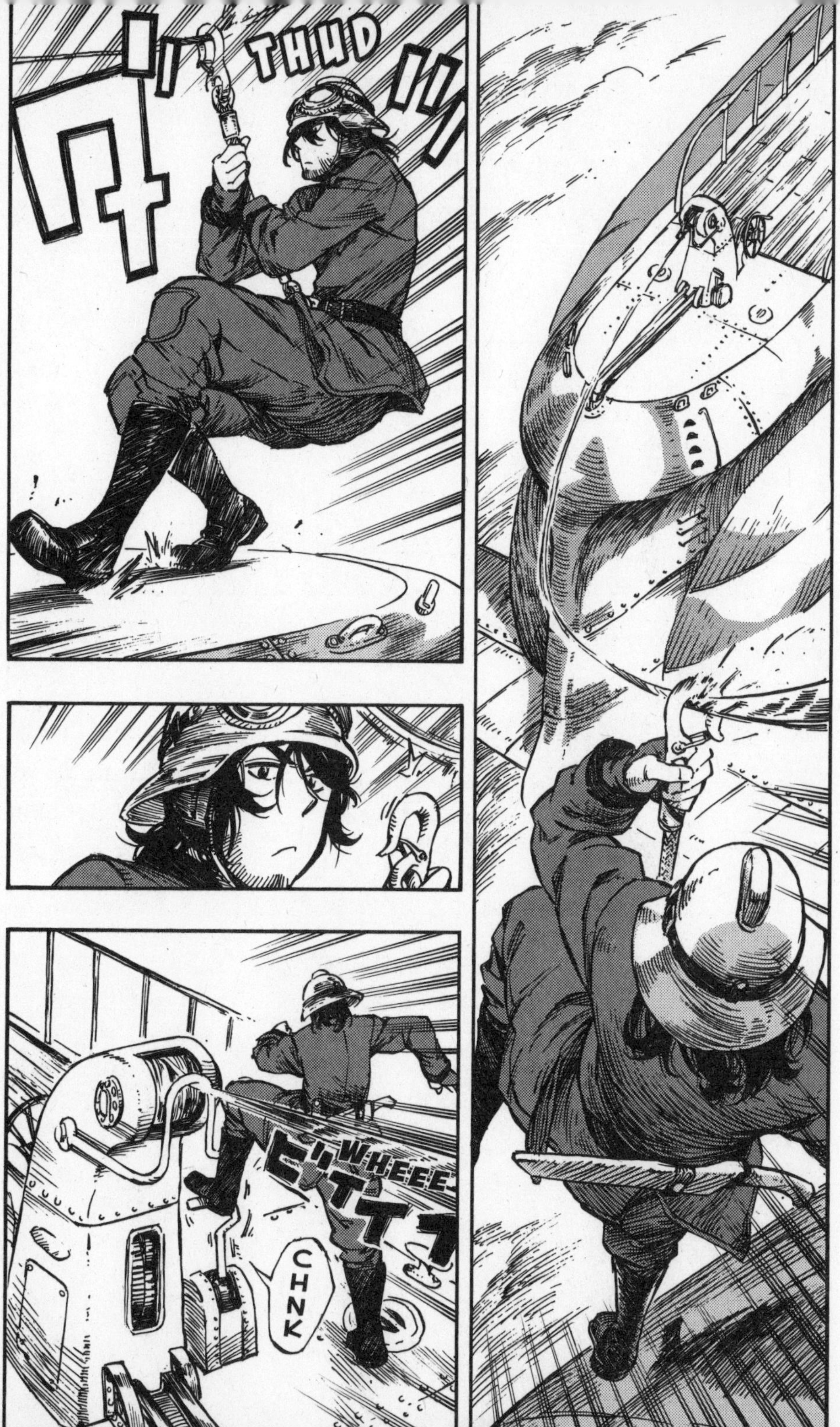
THUD
WHEEE
CHNK

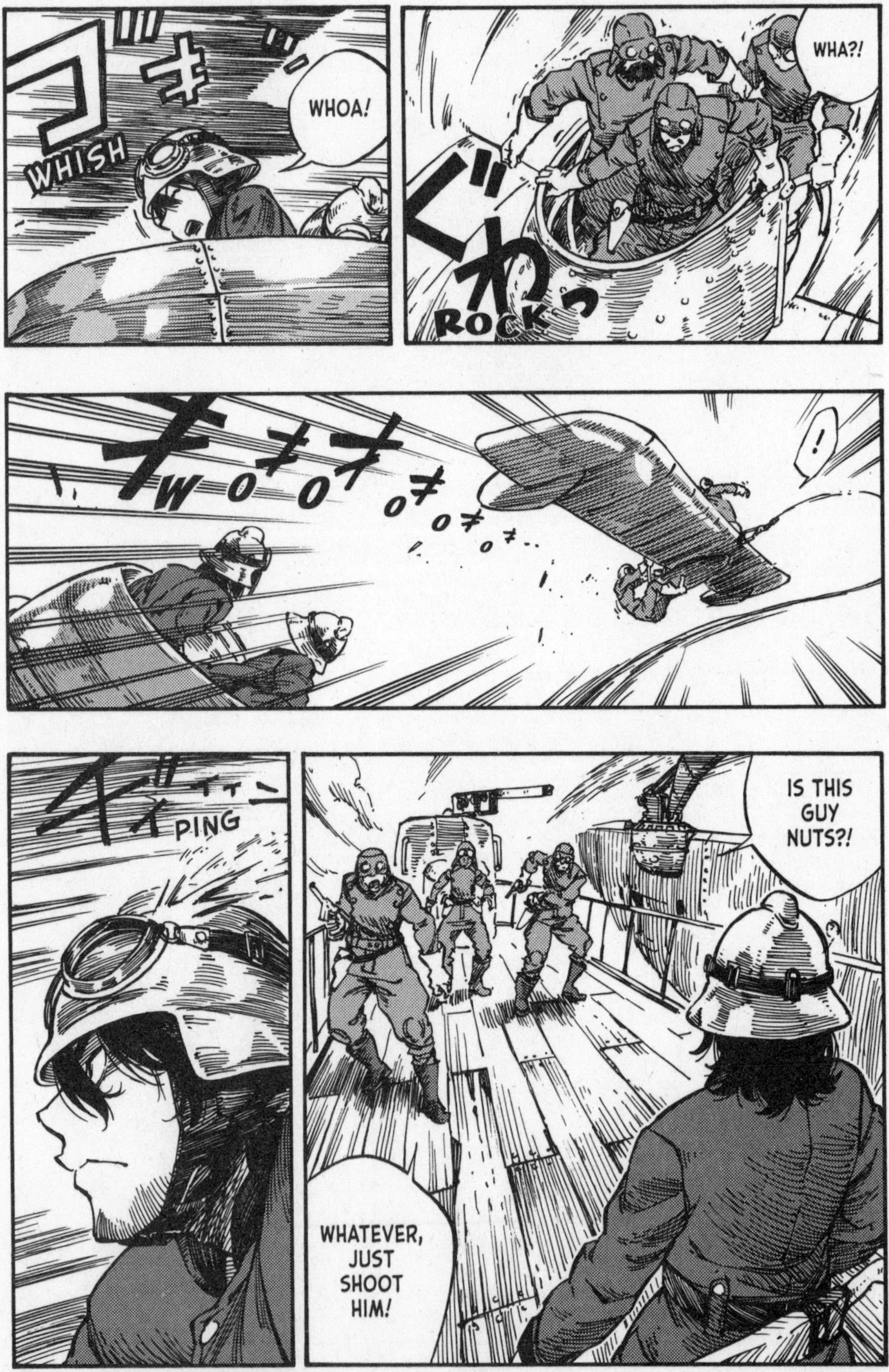
WHA?!
ぐわっ
ROCK
WHOA!
WHISH
!
WOOO
IS THIS GUY NUTS?!
WHATEVER, JUST SHOOT HIM!
PING

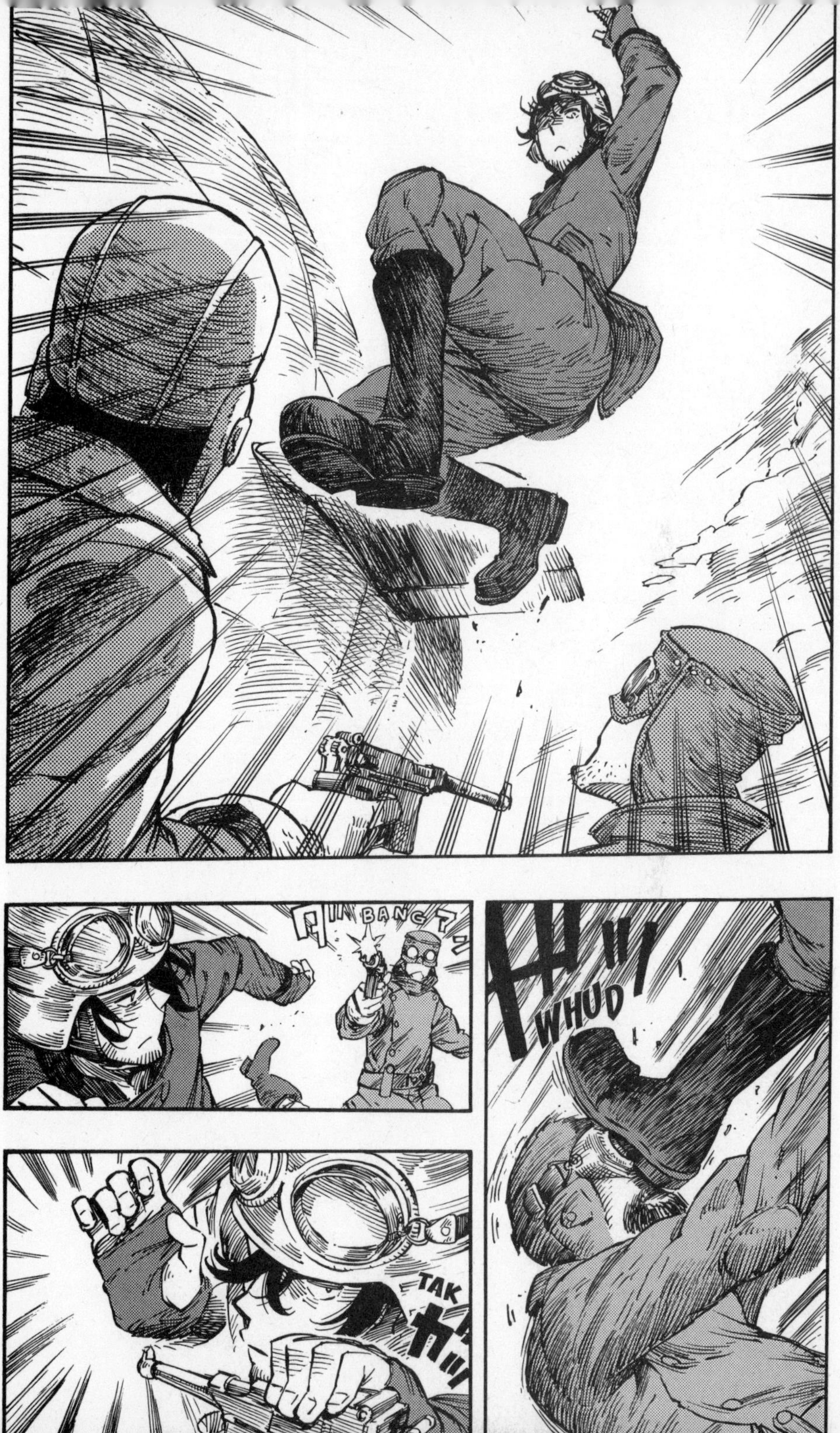
WHUD
BANG
TAK

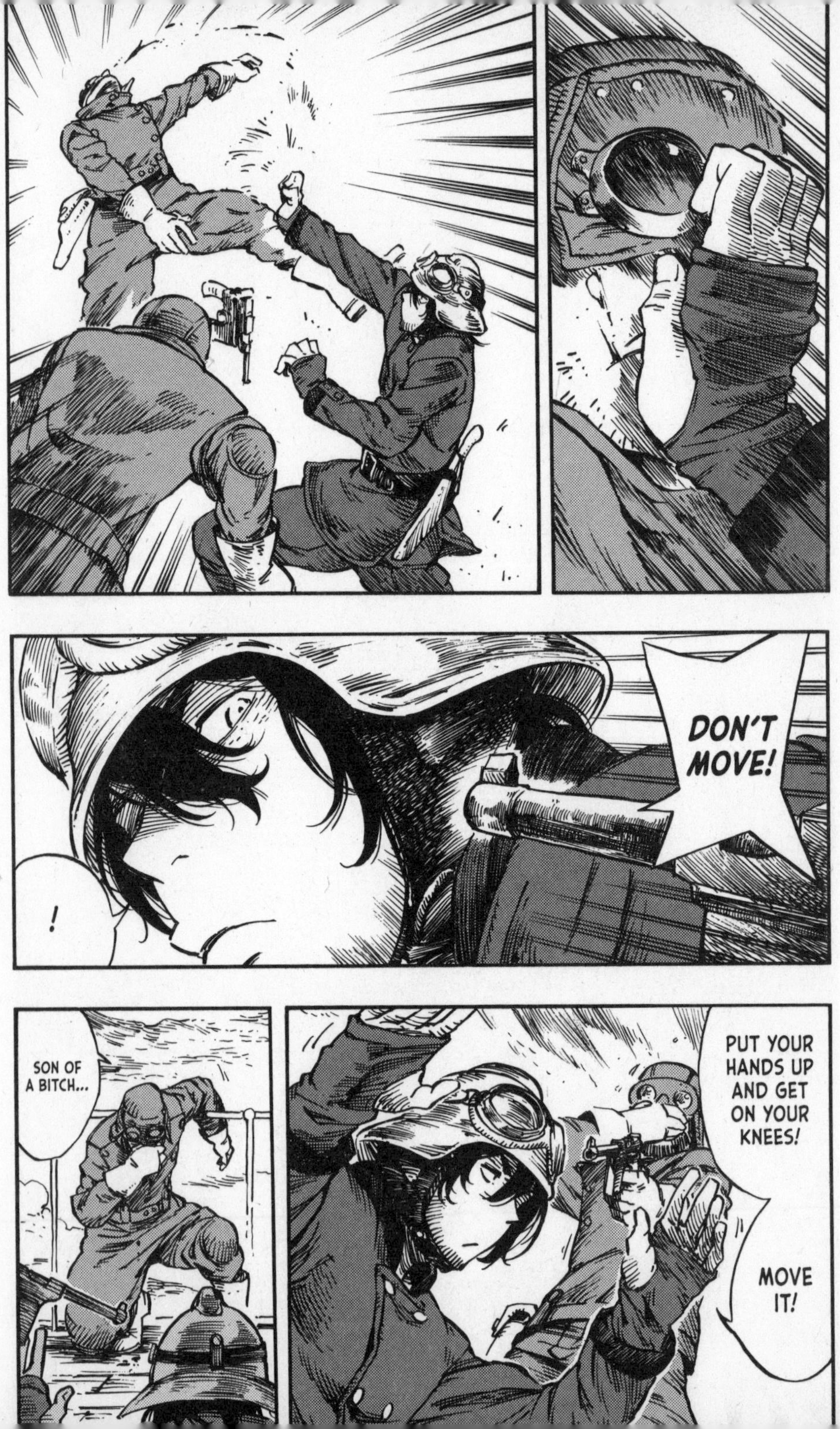
DON'T MOVE!
!
PUT YOUR HANDS UP AND GET ON YOUR KNEES!
MOVE IT!
SON OF A BITCH...

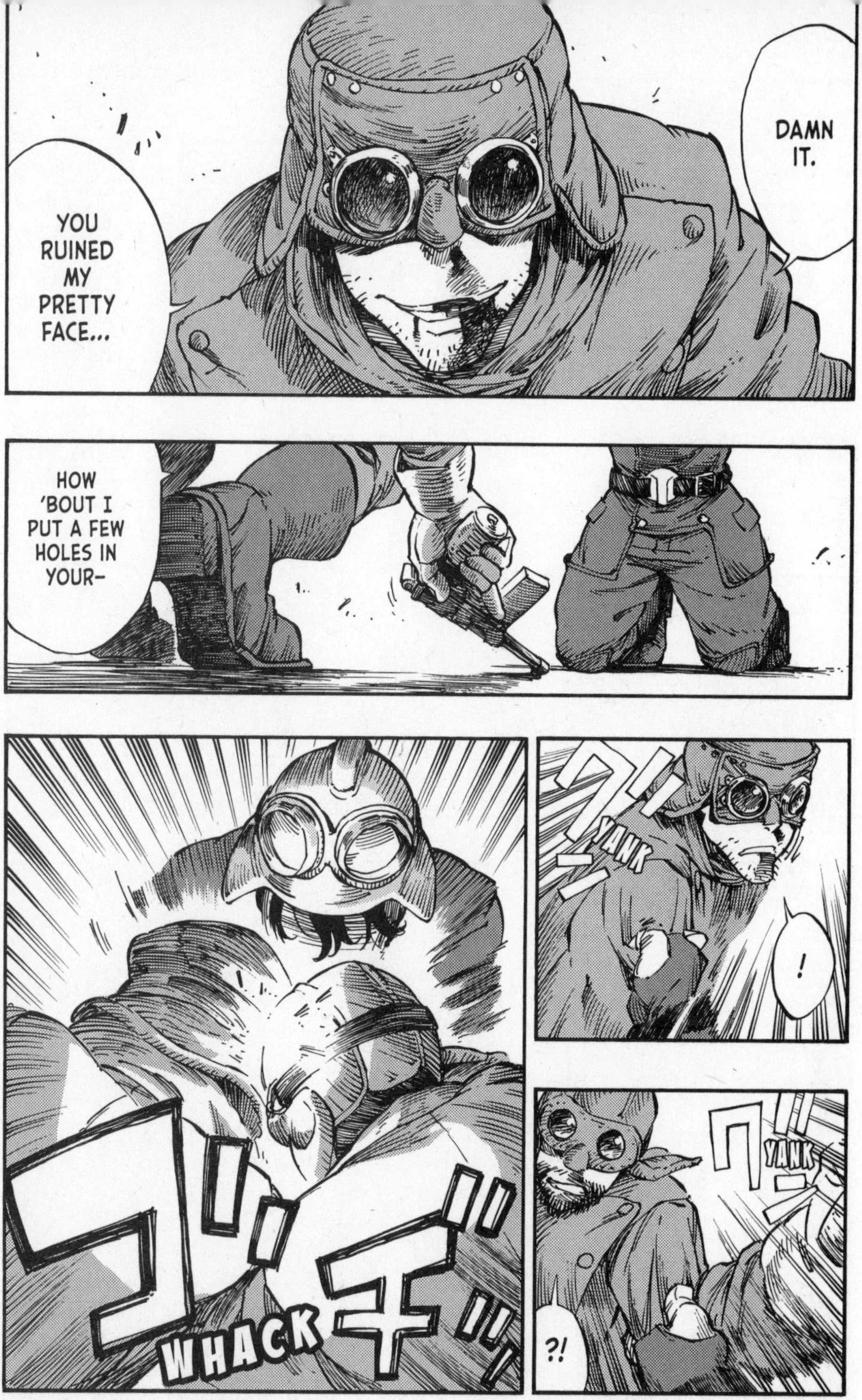
DAMN IT.
YOU RUINED MY PRETTY FACE...
HOW 'BOUT I PUT A FEW HOLES IN YOUR–
YANK
!
YANK
?!
WHACK

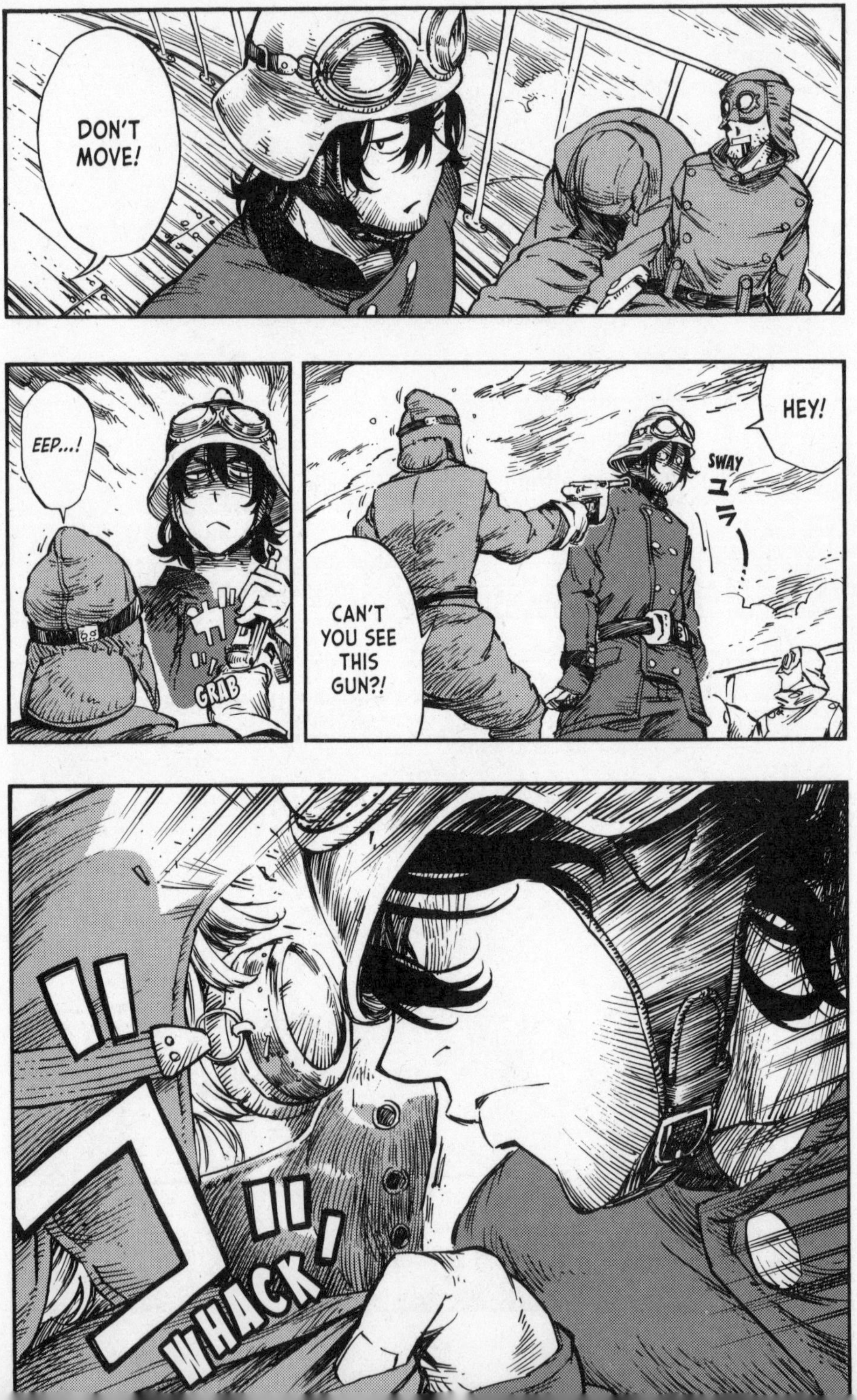
DON'T MOVE!
HEY!
SWAY
ユラ
CAN'T YOU SEE THIS GUN?!
EEP...!
GRAB
WHACK

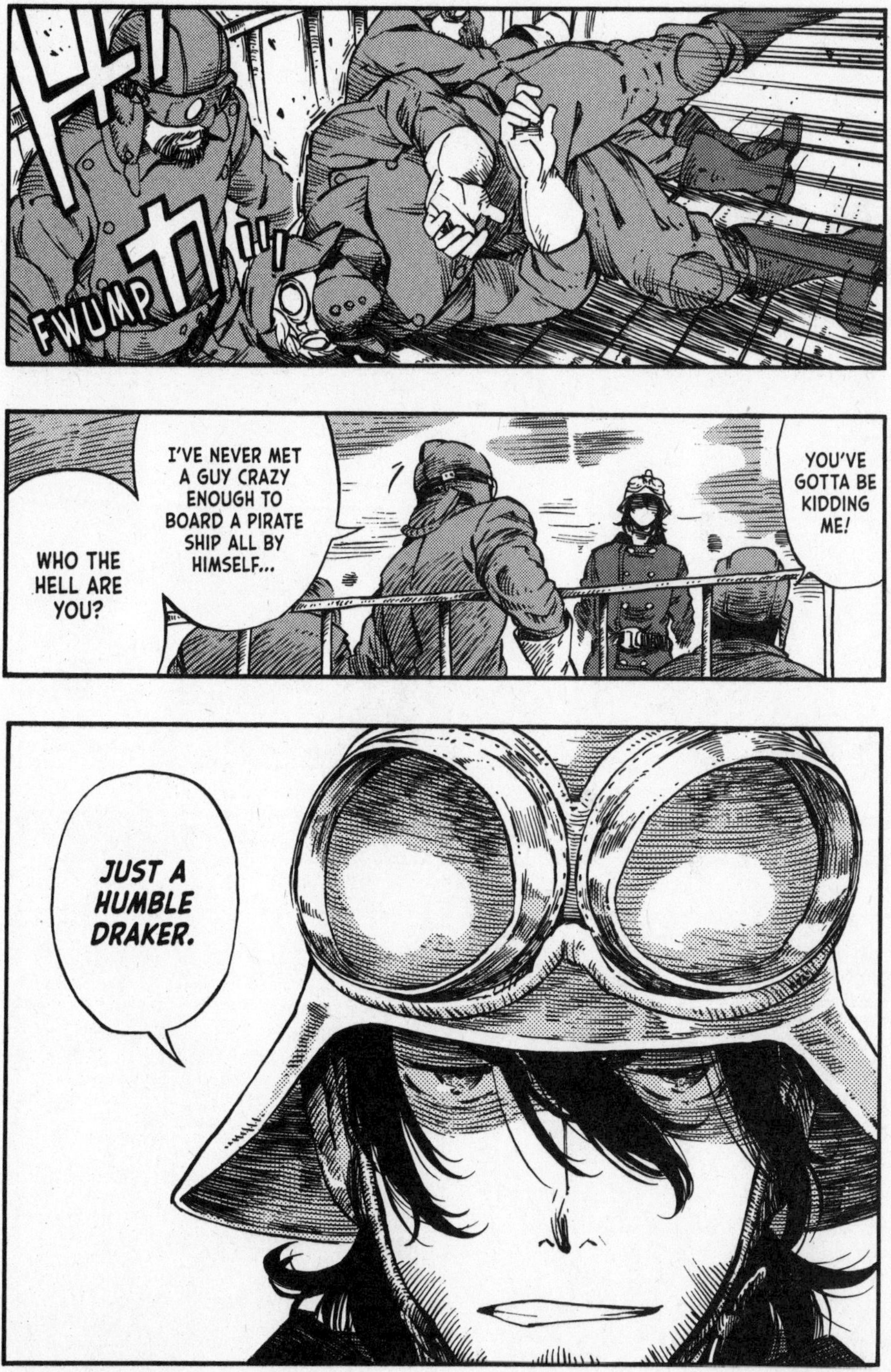
FWUMP
YOU'VE GOTTA BE KIDDING ME!
I'VE NEVER MET A GUY CRAZY ENOUGH TO BOARD A PIRATE SHIP ALL BY HIMSELF...
WHO THE HELL ARE YOU?
JUST A HUMBLE DRAKER.

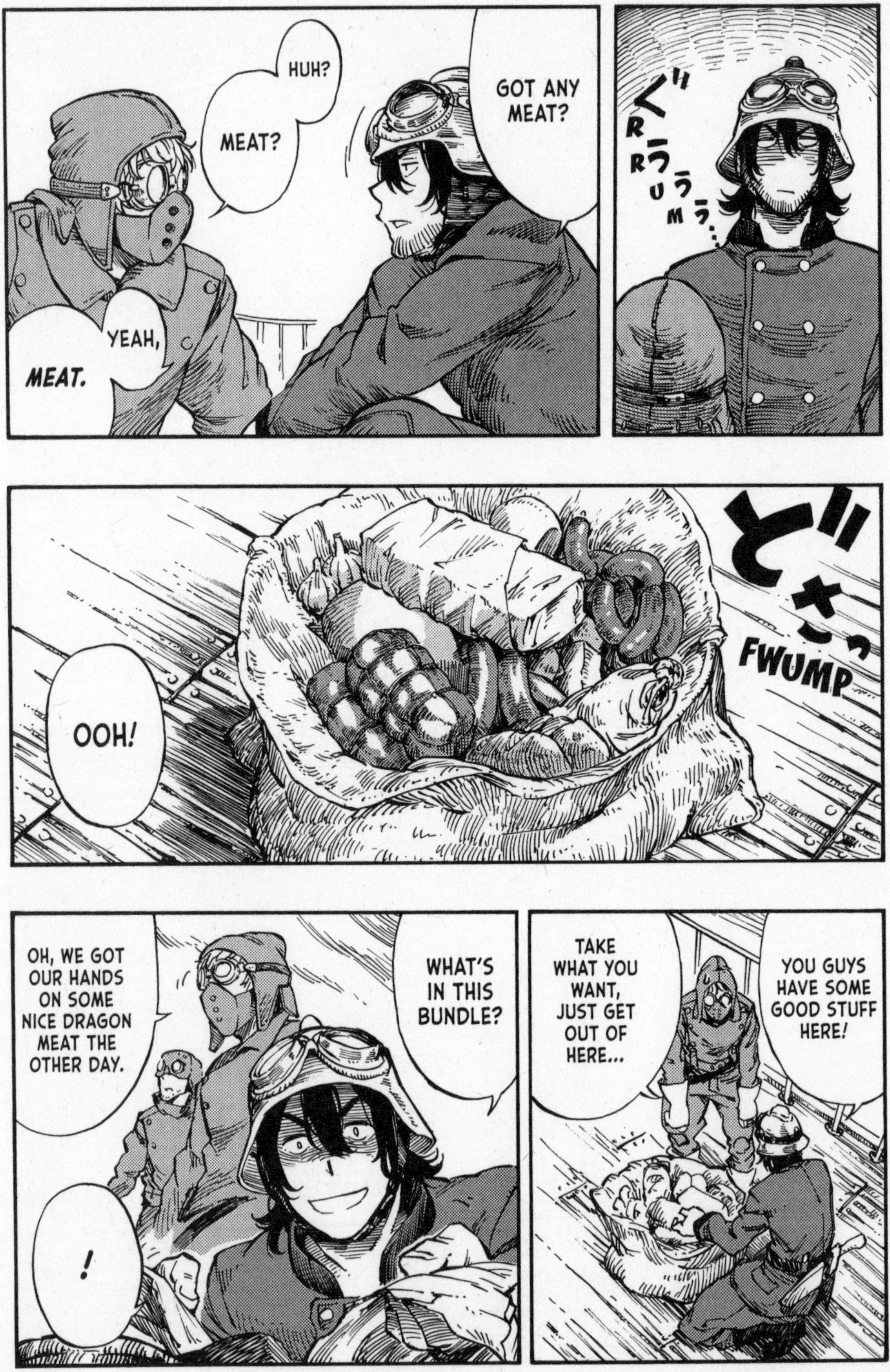
RRUM
GOT ANY MEAT?
HUH?
MEAT?
YEAH, MEAT.
どさっ
FWUMP
OOH!
YOU GUYS HAVE SOME GOOD STUFF HERE!
TAKE WHAT YOU WANT, JUST GET OUT OF HERE...
WHAT'S IN THIS BUNDLE?
OH, WE GOT OUR HANDS ON SOME NICE DRAGON MEAT THE OTHER DAY.
!

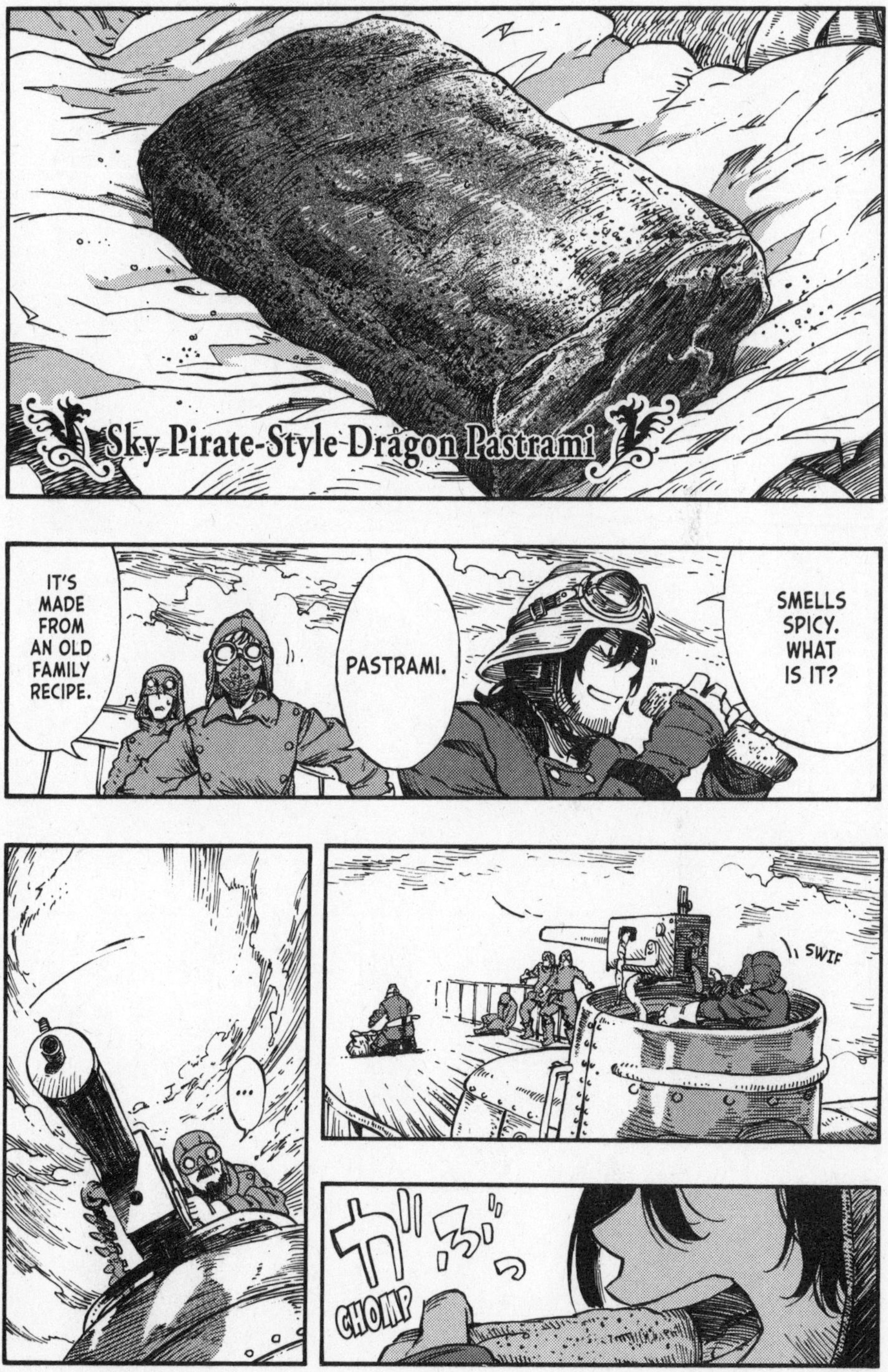
Sky Pirate-Style Dragon Pastrami
SMELLS SPICY. WHAT IS IT?
PASTRAMI.
IT'S MADE FROM AN OLD FAMILY RECIPE.
SWIF
ガぶっ
CHOMP
...

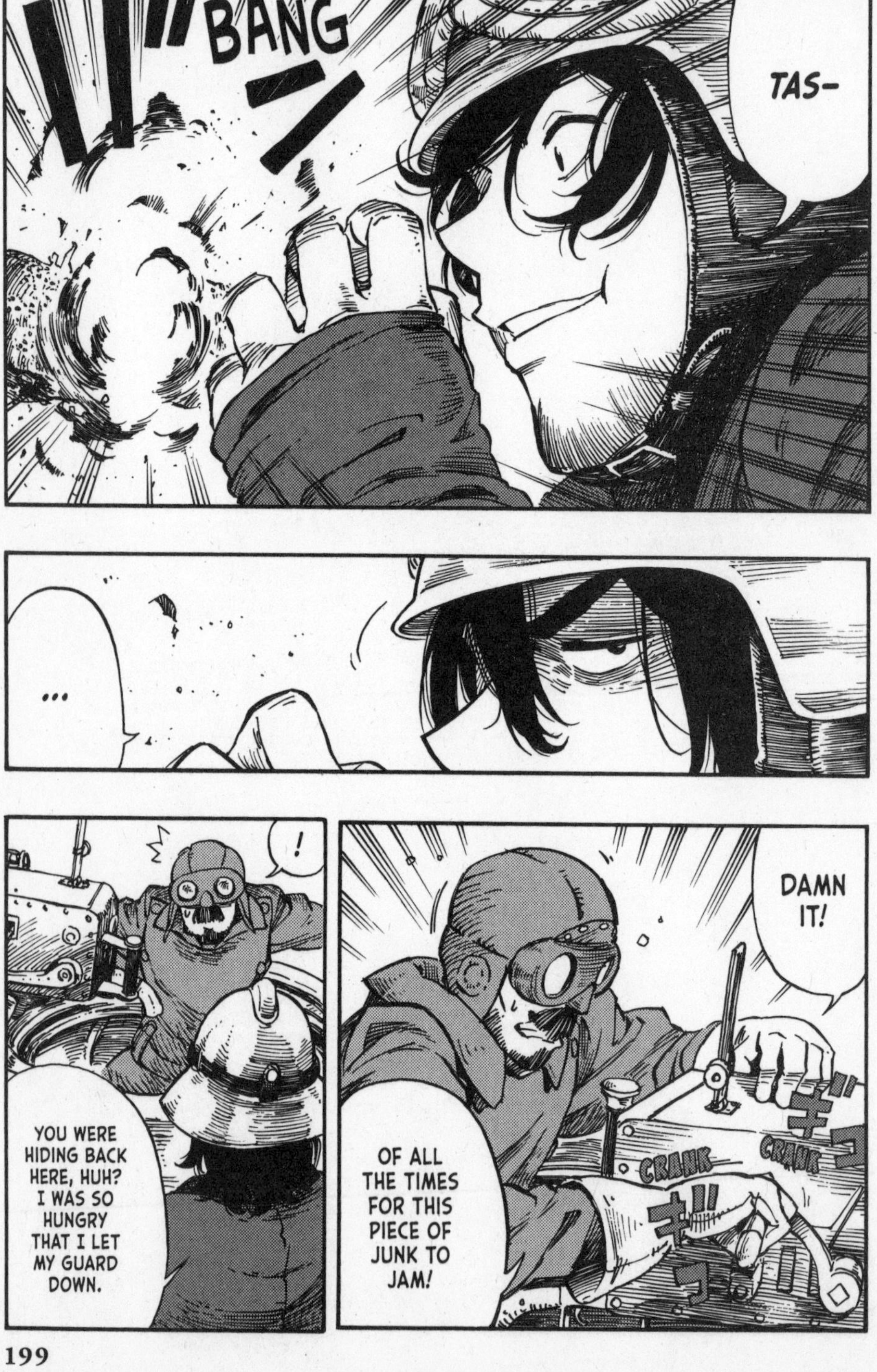
TAS-
BANG
...
DAMN IT!
OF ALL THE TIMES FOR THIS PIECE OF JUNK TO JAM!
CRANK
CRANK
!
YOU WERE HIDING BACK HERE, HUH? I WAS SO HUNGRY THAT I LET MY GUARD DOWN.

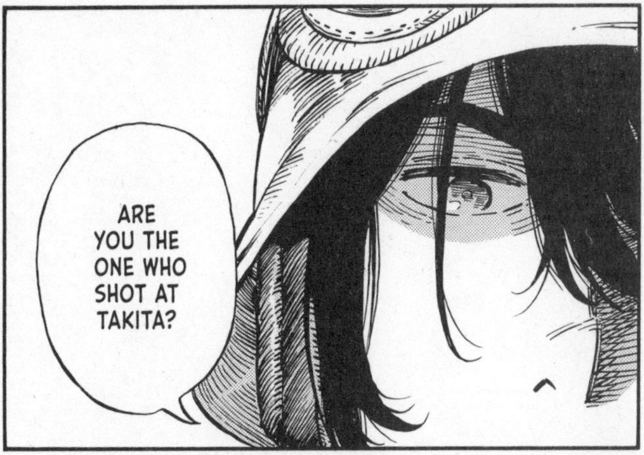
ARE YOU THE ONE WHO SHOT AT TAKITA?
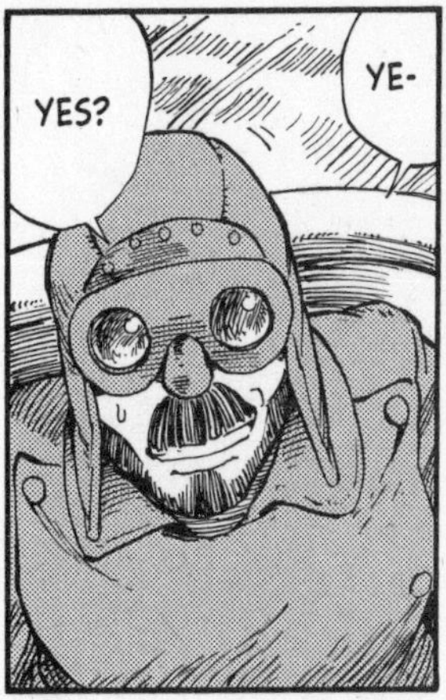
YE-
YES?
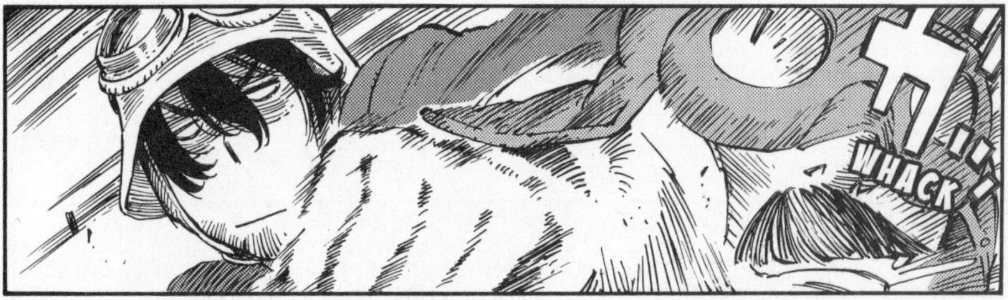
WHACK
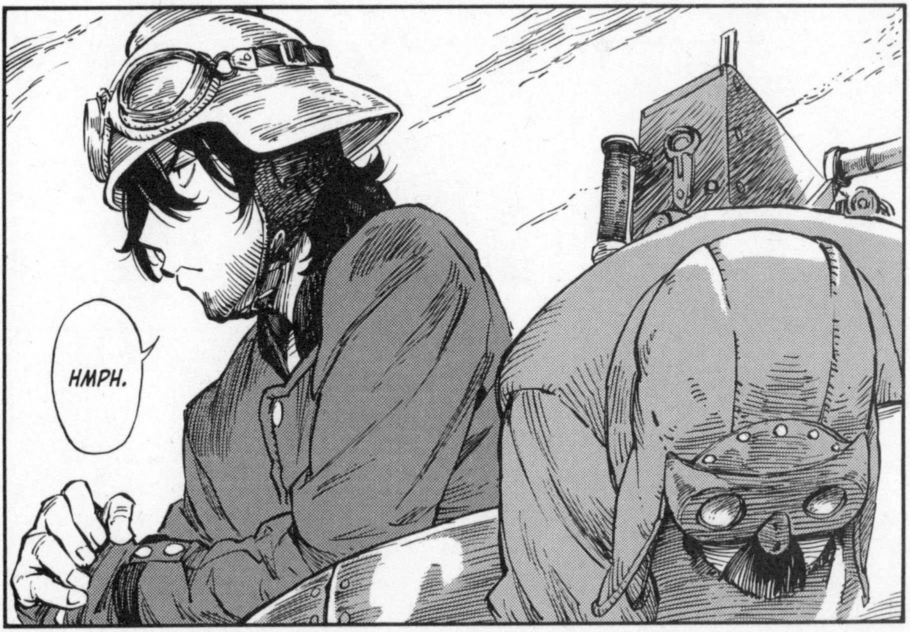
HMPH.

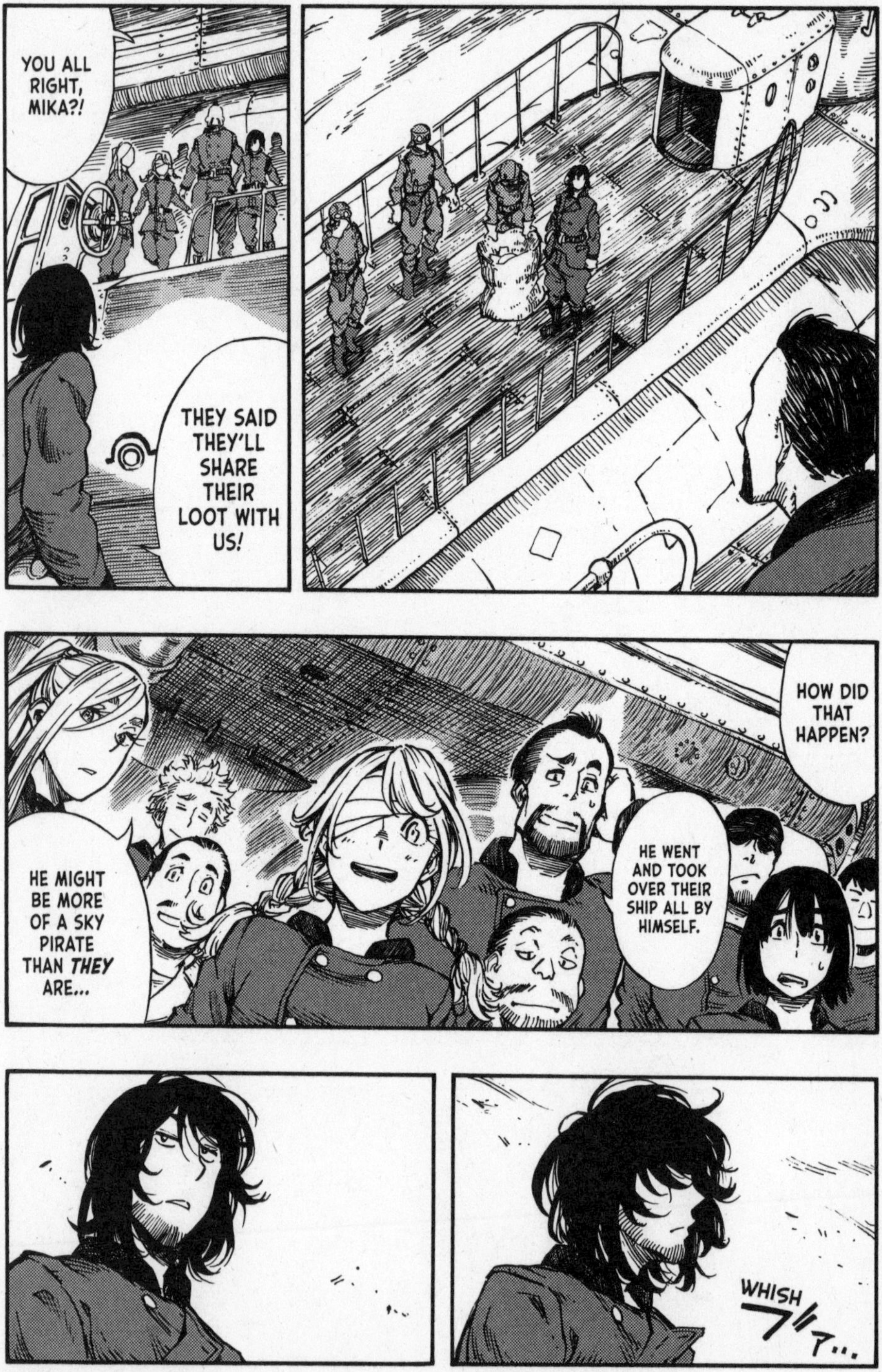

YOU ALL RIGHT, MIKA?!
THEY SAID THEY'LL SHARE THEIR LOOT WITH US!
HOW DID THAT HAPPEN?
HE WENT AND TOOK OVER THEIR SHIP ALL BY HIMSELF.
HE MIGHT BE MORE OF A SKY PIRATE THAN *THEY* ARE...
WHISH

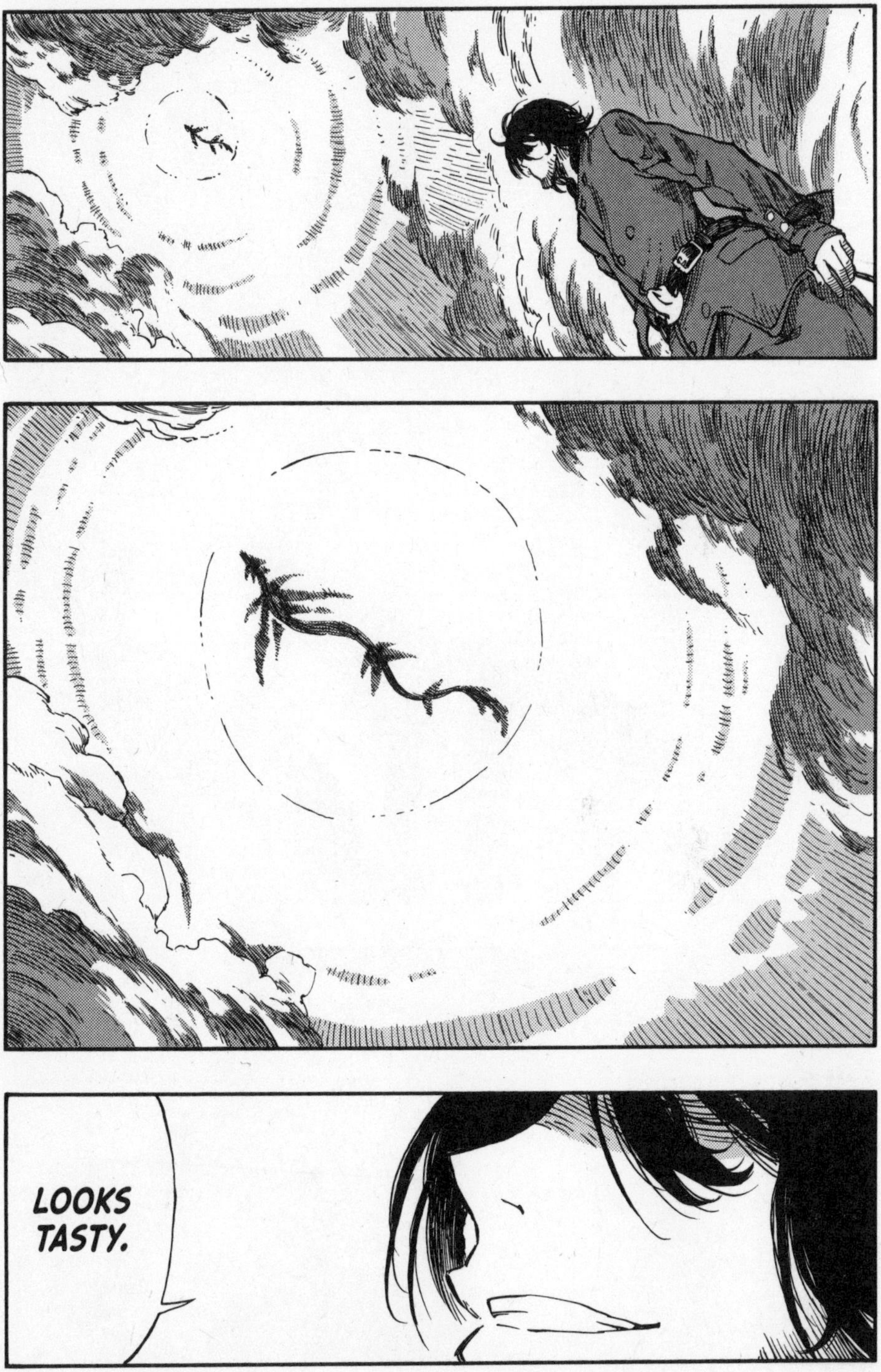
LOOKS TASTY.

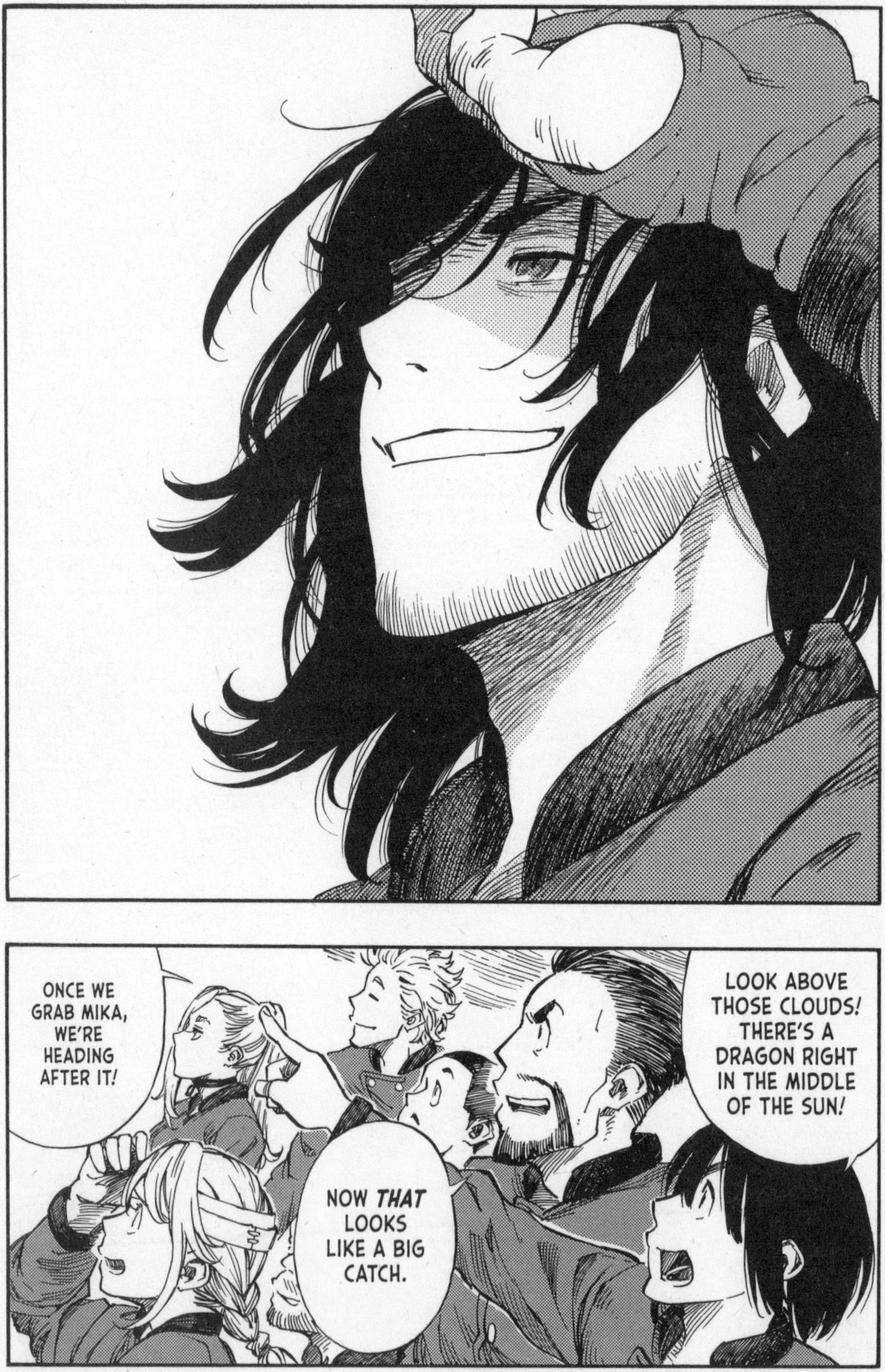
LOOK ABOVE THOSE CLOUDS! THERE'S A DRAGON RIGHT IN THE MIDDLE OF THE SUN!
NOW *THAT* LOOKS LIKE A BIG CATCH.
ONCE WE GRAB MIKA, WE'RE HEADING AFTER IT!

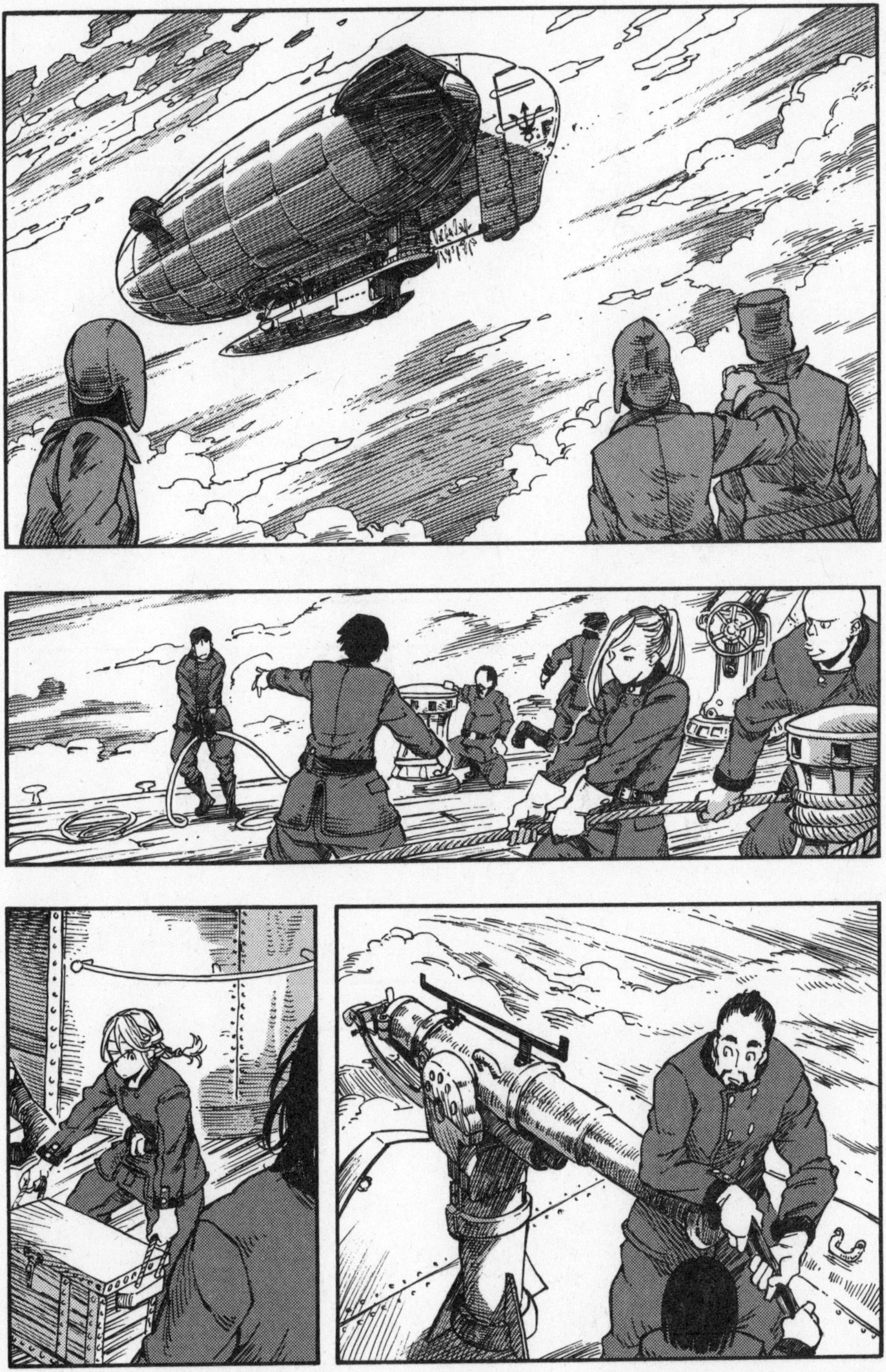

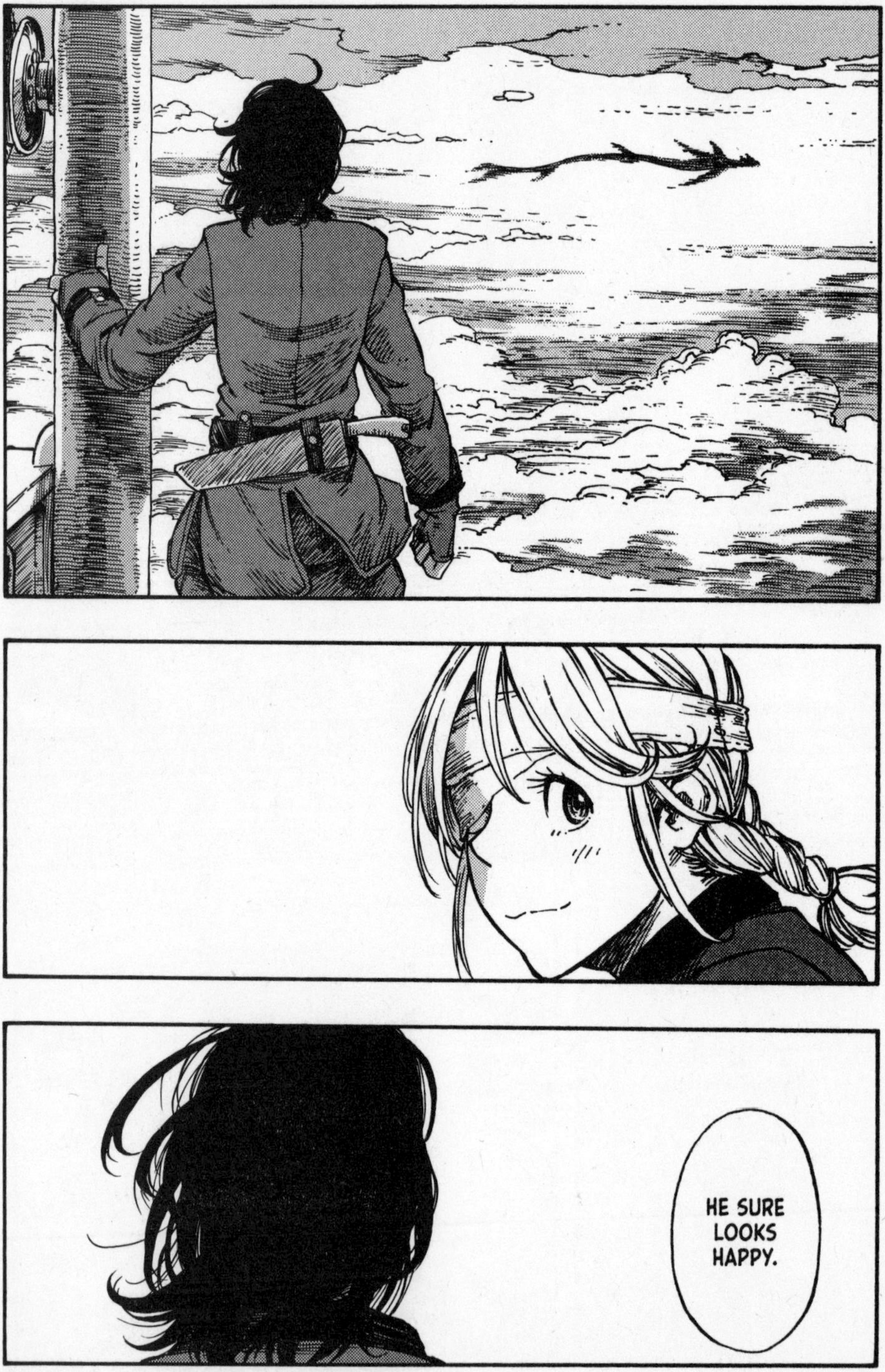
HE SURE
LOOKS
HAPPY.

Sky Pirate-Style Dragon Pastrami

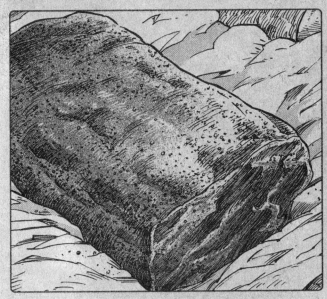

Ingredients (makes one batch)

✦ 1 kg dragon red meat

✦ Black pepper to taste

✦ Allspice to taste

★ Brine:

  1 liter water, 150 g salt

  70 g sugar, a pinch of black pepper,

  a pinch of sage, a pinch of thyme,

  a pinch of garlic

  Other seasonings of choice to taste

  1 tbsp brandy

✦ Smoking wood

01
To make the brine, bring water to a boil and stir in all ingredients listed underneath, except the brandy. Simmer for 20 minutes. Remove the brine from heat and strain through a fine mesh strainer, then allow to cool to room temperature. Once cool, add the brandy.

02
Submerge the meat in the finished brine and pickle for 5-7 days.

03
Rinse the pickled meat under running water for 2-6 hours to remove excess salt.

04
Hang in a well-ventilated, dark place and allow the meat to dry.

05
Smoke the meat using your wood of choice for roughly 2 hours.

06
Sprinkle the smoked meat with crushed black pepper and allspice and it's done.

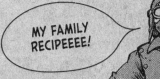

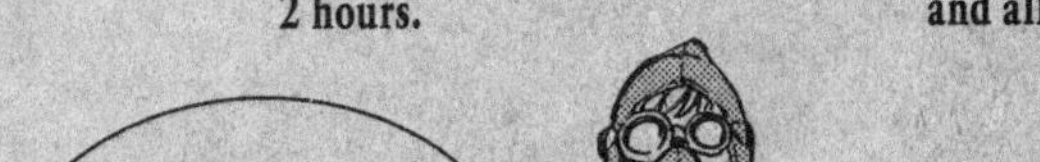

MY FAMILY RECIPEEEE!

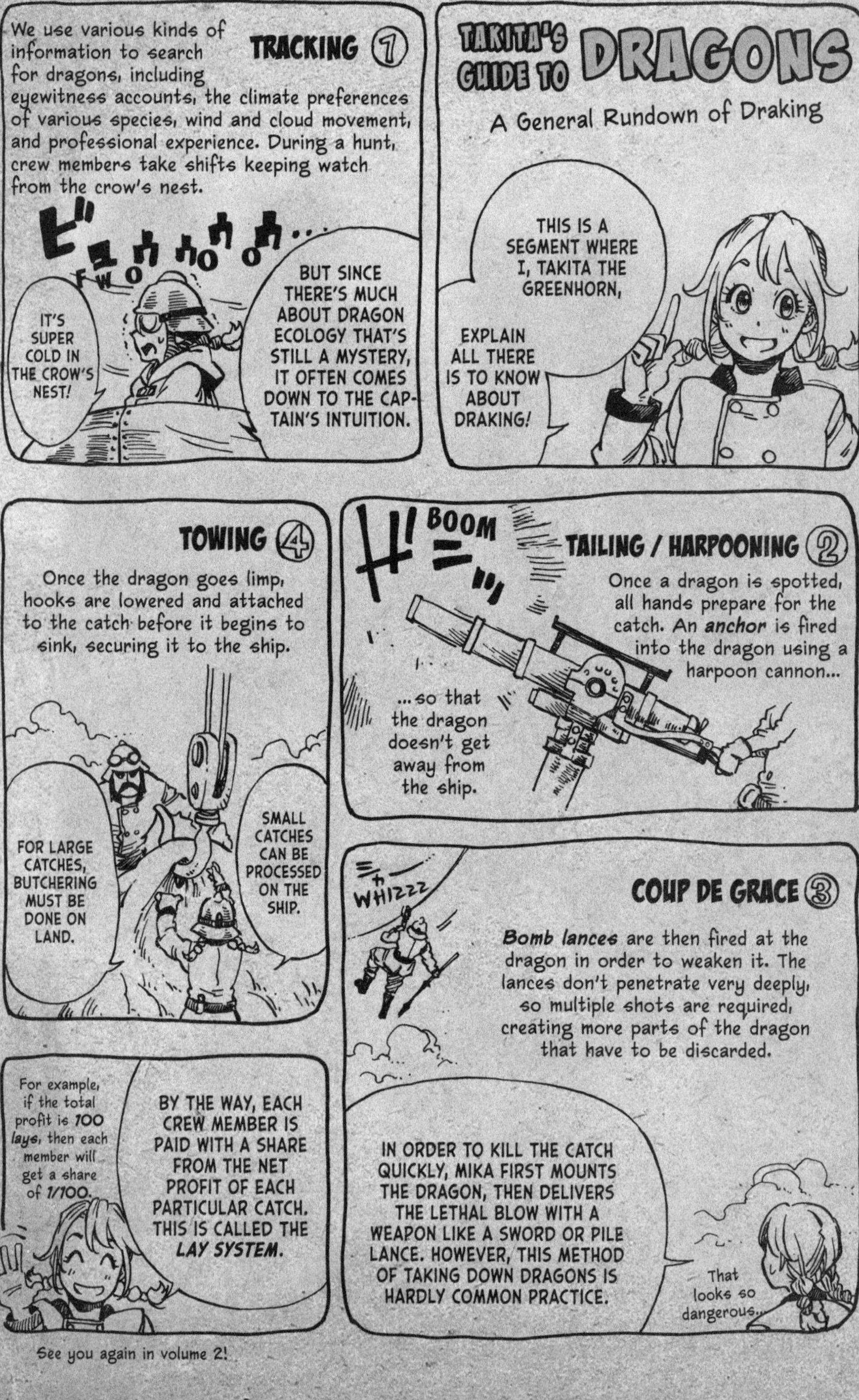

TAKITA'S GUIDE TO DRAGONS
A General Rundown of Draking
THIS IS A SEGMENT WHERE I, TAKITA THE GREENHORN,
EXPLAIN ALL THERE IS TO KNOW ABOUT DRAKING!
TRACKING ①
We use various kinds of information to search for dragons, including eyewitness accounts, the climate preferences of various species, wind and cloud movement, and professional experience. During a hunt, crew members take shifts keeping watch from the crow's nest.
FWOOO...
BUT SINCE THERE'S MUCH ABOUT DRAGON ECOLOGY THAT'S STILL A MYSTERY, IT OFTEN COMES DOWN TO THE CAPTAIN'S INTUITION.
IT'S SUPER COLD IN THE CROW'S NEST!
TAILING / HARPOONING ②
Once a dragon is spotted, all hands prepare for the catch. An *anchor* is fired into the dragon using a harpoon cannon...
BOOM
...so that the dragon doesn't get away from the ship.
COUP DE GRACE ③
Bomb lances are then fired at the dragon in order to weaken it. The lances don't penetrate very deeply, so multiple shots are required, creating more parts of the dragon that have to be discarded.
WHIZZZ
IN ORDER TO KILL THE CATCH QUICKLY, MIKA FIRST MOUNTS THE DRAGON, THEN DELIVERS THE LETHAL BLOW WITH A WEAPON LIKE A SWORD OR PILE LANCE. HOWEVER, THIS METHOD OF TAKING DOWN DRAGONS IS HARDLY COMMON PRACTICE.
That looks so dangerous...
TOWING ④
Once the dragon goes limp, hooks are lowered and attached to the catch before it begins to sink, securing it to the ship.
SMALL CATCHES CAN BE PROCESSED ON THE SHIP.
FOR LARGE CATCHES, BUTCHERING MUST BE DONE ON LAND.
BY THE WAY, EACH CREW MEMBER IS PAID WITH A SHARE FROM THE NET PROFIT OF EACH PARTICULAR CATCH. THIS IS CALLED THE *LAY SYSTEM*.
For example, if the total profit is 100 *lays*, then each member will get a share of 1/100.
See you again in volume 2!

Magus of the Library

Mitsu Izumi

Magus of the Library © Mitsu Izumi/Kodansha Ltd.

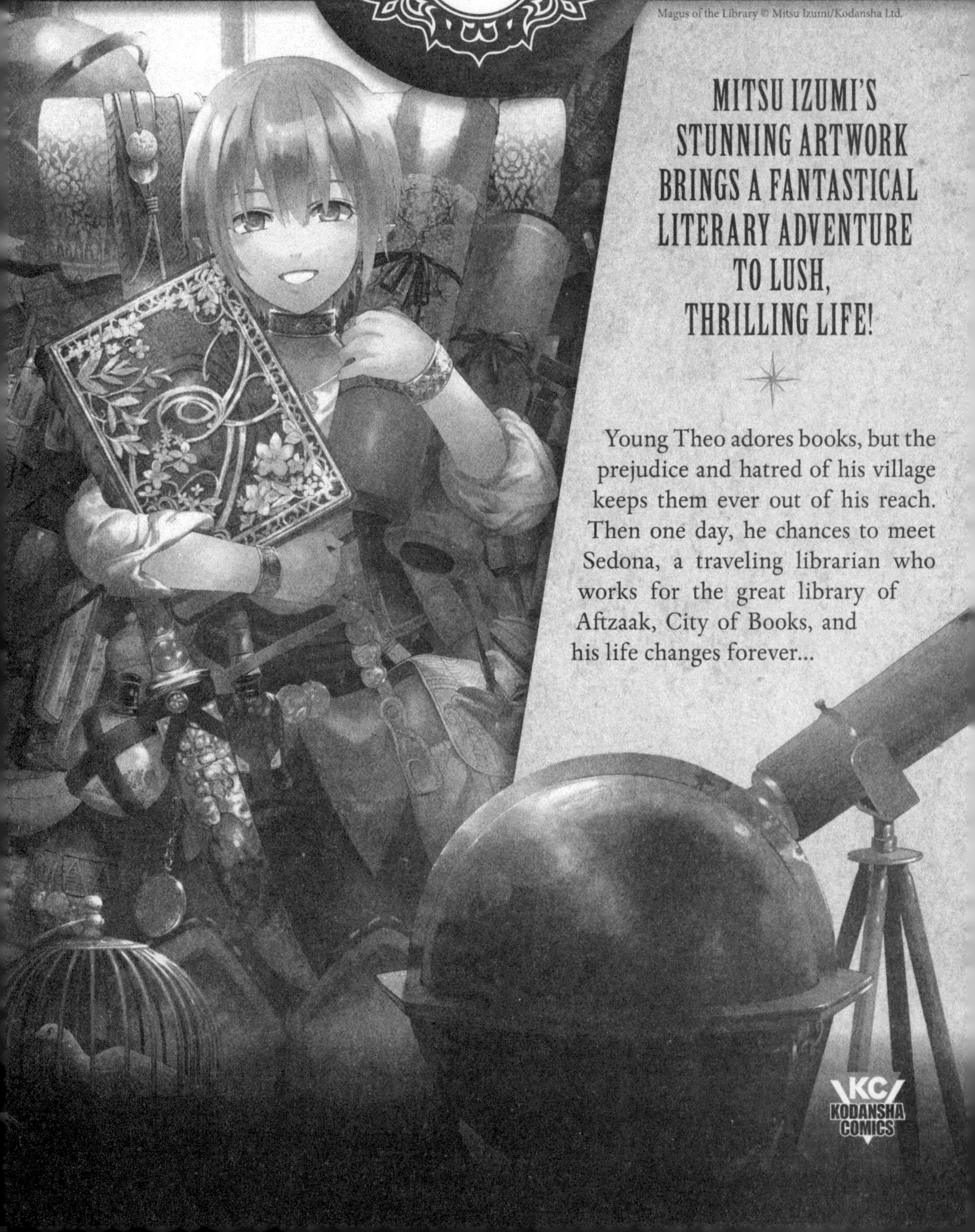

MITSU IZUMI'S STUNNING ARTWORK BRINGS A FANTASTICAL LITERARY ADVENTURE TO LUSH, THRILLING LIFE!

Young Theo adores books, but the prejudice and hatred of his village keeps them ever out of his reach. Then one day, he chances to meet Sedona, a traveling librarian who works for the great library of Aftzaak, City of Books, and his life changes forever...

KC
KODANSHA
COMICS

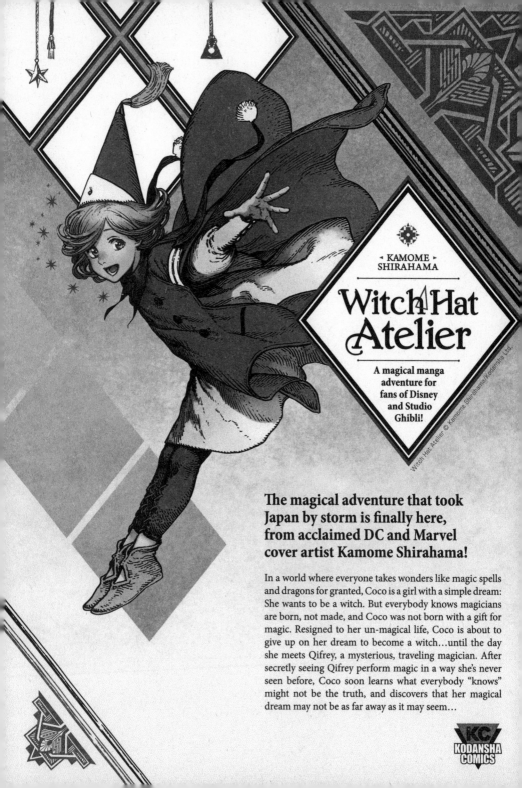

◄ KAMOME ►
SHIRAHAMA

Witch Hat Atelier

A magical manga adventure for fans of Disney and Studio Ghibli!

Witch Hat Atelier © Kamome Shirahama/Kodansha Ltd.

The magical adventure that took Japan by storm is finally here, from acclaimed DC and Marvel cover artist Kamome Shirahama!

In a world where everyone takes wonders like magic spells and dragons for granted, Coco is a girl with a simple dream: She wants to be a witch. But everybody knows magicians are born, not made, and Coco was not born with a gift for magic. Resigned to her un-magical life, Coco is about to give up on her dream to become a witch...until the day she meets Qifrey, a mysterious, traveling magician. After secretly seeing Qifrey perform magic in a way she's never seen before, Coco soon learns what everybody "knows" might not be the truth, and discovers that her magical dream may not be as far away as it may seem...

KC
KODANSHA
COMICS

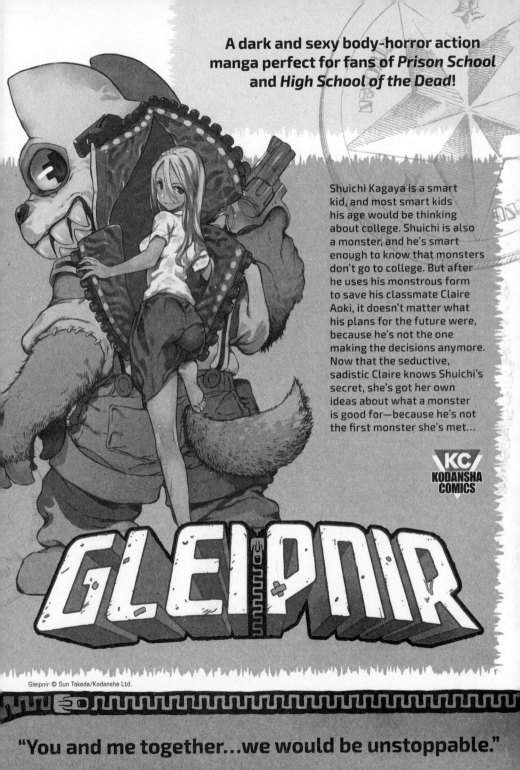

A dark and sexy body-horror action manga perfect for fans of *Prison School* and *High School of the Dead*!

Shuichi Kagaya is a smart kid, and most smart kids his age would be thinking about college. Shuichi is also a monster, and he's smart enough to know that monsters don't go to college. But after he uses his monstrous form to save his classmate Claire Aoki, it doesn't matter what his plans for the future were, because he's not the one making the decisions anymore. Now that the seductive, sadistic Claire knows Shuichi's secret, she's got her own ideas about what a monster is good for—because he's not the first monster she's met...

KC
KODANSHA COMICS

GLEIPNIR

Gleipnir © Sun Takeda/Kodansha Ltd.

"You and me together...we would be unstoppable."

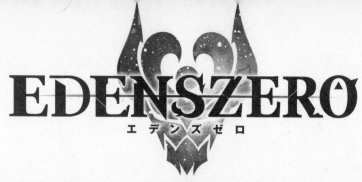

EDENS ZERO
エデンズゼロ

HIRO MASHIMA IS BACK! JOIN THE CREATOR OF *FAIRY TAIL*
AS HE TAKES TO THE STARS FOR ANOTHER THRILLING SAGA!

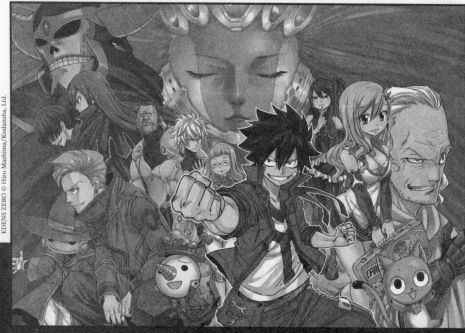

EDENS ZERO © Hiro Mashima/Kodansha, Ltd.

A high-flying space adventure! All the steadfast friendship
and wild fighting you've been waiting for...IN SPACE!

At Granbell Kingdom, an abandoned amusement park, Shiki has lived his entire
life among machines. But one day, Rebecca and her cat companion Happy appear
at the park's front gates. Little do these newcomers know that this is the first
human contact Granbell has had in a hundred years! As Shiki stumbles his way
into making new friends, his former neighbors stir at an opportunity for a robo-
rebellion... And when his old homeland becomes too dangerous, Shiki must join
Rebecca and Happy on their spaceship and escape into the boundless cosmos.

KC KODANSHA COMICS

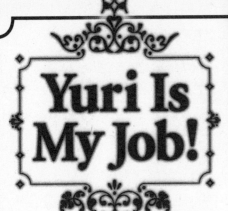

Yuri Is My Job!

miman

Yuri is My Job! © Miman/Ichijinsha Inc.

JOIN US FOR AFTERNOON TEA WITH EQUAL PARTS YURI, ROM-COM, AND DRAMA!

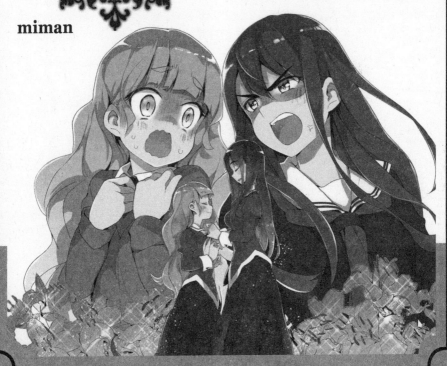

Hime is a picture-perfect high school princess, so when she accidentally injures a café manager named Mai, she's willing to cover some shifts to keep her façade intact. To Hime's surprise, the café is themed after a private school where the all-female staff always puts on their best act for their loyal customers. However, under the guidance of the most graceful girl there, Hime can't help but blush and blunder! Beneath all the frills and laughter, Hime feels tension brewing as she finds out more about her new job and her budding feelings...

KC KODANSHA COMICS

"A quirky, fun comedy series... If you're a yuri fan, or perhaps interested in getting into it but not sure where to start, this book is worth picking up."
— Anime UK News

THE MAGICAL GIRL CLASSIC THAT BROUGHT A
GENERATION OF READERS TO MANGA, NOW BACK IN A
DEFINITIVE, HARDCOVER COLLECTOR'S EDITION!

CARDCAPTOR SAKURA
COLLECTOR'S EDITION

CLAMP

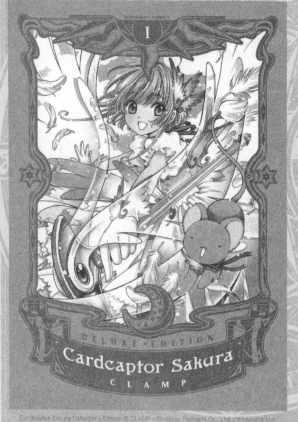

Ten-year-old Sakura Kinomoto lives a pretty normal life with her older brother, Tōya, and widowed father, Fujitaka—until the day she discovers a strange book in her father's library, and her life takes a magical turn...

- A deluxe large-format hardcover edition of CLAMP's shojo manga classic
- All-new foil-stamped cover art on each volume
- Comes with exclusive collectible art card

Cardcaptor Sakura Collector's Edition © CLAMP · Shigatsu Tsuitachi Co., Ltd. / Kodansha Ltd.

KC
KODANSHA
COMICS

Drifting Dragons 1 is a work of fiction. Names, places, and incidents are the products of the autho or are used fictitiously. Any resemblance to actual e persons, living or dead, is entirely coincid

A Kodansha Comics Trade Paperback Original
Drifting Dragons copyright © 2016 Taku Kuwabara
English translation copyright © 2019 Taku Kuwabara

All rights reserved.

Published in the United States by Kodansha Comics, an imprint of
Kodansha USA Publishing, LLC, New York.

Publication rights for this English edition arranged through
Kodansha Ltd., Tokyo.

First published in Japan in 2016 by Kodansha Ltd., Tokyo
as *Kuutei Doragonzu*, volume 1.

ISBN 978-1-63236-890-4

Printed in the United States of America.

www.kodanshacomics.com

9 8 7 6 5 4 3 2 1
Translation: Adam Hirsch
Lettering: Thea Willis
Editing: Paul Starr
Kodansha Comics edition cover design by Phil Balsman

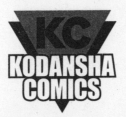

Publisher: Kiichiro Sugawara
Managing editor: Maya Rosewood
Vice president of marketing & publicity: Naho Yamada

Director of publishing services: Ben Applegate
Associate director of operations: Stephen Pakula
Publishing services managing editor: Noelle Webster
Assistant production manager: Emi Lotto